DOL

Language, Society
and Identity

THE LANGUAGE LIBRARY
EDITED BY DAVID CRYSTAL

Language, Society and Identity

JOHN EDWARDS

Basil Blackwell
in association with
André Deutsch

Copyright © John Edwards 1985

First published 1985
Reprinted 1988, 1989

Basil Blackwell Ltd
108 Cowley Road, Oxford OX4 1JF, UK

Basil Blackwell Inc.
432 Park Avenue South, Suite 1503
New York, NY 10016, USA

in association with André Deutsch Limited
105 Great Russell Street, London WC1B 3LJ, England

British Library Cataloguing in Publication Data
Edwards, John, *1947 Dec 3-*
  Language, society and identity.—(The Language
  library)
  1. Sociolinguistics
  I. Title
  401'.9 P40
  ISBN 0–631–14232–0
  ISBN 0–631–14233–9 Pbk

Library of Congress Cataloging in Publication Data
Edwards, John R.
  Language, society and identity.
  (The Language library)
  Bibliography: p.
  Includes index.
  1. Sociolinguistics. 2. Ethnicity. 3. Nationalism.
  I. Title. II. Series.
  P40.E37 1985   401'.9   85-3872
  ISBN 0–631–14232–0
  ISBN 0–631–14233–9 (pbk.)

Typeset by System 4 Associates, Gerrards Cross, Buckinghamshire
Printed in Great Britain by
Billing & Sons Ltd, Worcester

To
Colin, Emily and Katherine

Other Books by John Edwards

Language and Disadvantage

The Social Psychology of Reading

The Irish Language:
An Annotated Bibliography of Sociolinguistic Publications, 1772–1982

Linguistic Minorities, Policies and Pluralism

Contents

Preface

This book is about the relationship between language and identity as it occurs in the social context. While much has been written on and around this topic, it is generally of a unidisciplinary nature and adequate interconnections have not been made. Further, whatever the disciplinary perspective, there has been a serious lack of attention to the confirmation of academic investigation in the real world. This is particularly important given the nature of the language–identity link. Understanding and analysis require the assessment of material from a variety of approaches – historical, sociological, educational, psychological – and all must be seen within the context of the real-life record. Thus, an important objective in this work was one of synthesis.

I have also been concerned to present as disinterested an account as possible. Readers can easily ascertain for themselves the degree to which language and identity have been treated in highly value-laden ways, and I have become convinced, from my reading of the literature, that a more even-handed discussion is long overdue. I had this sense reinforced when, in the final stages of writing, I attended a large European linguistics meeting. I was gratified to find a large number of papers dealing with such topics as language-maintenance, ethno-linguistic identity, multiculturalism, the role of education in identity preservation, and so on. I was also struck, however, by how many adopted a particular value position and discussed it as if it were the only one possible to enlightened persons or the only one with morality on its side. Words like 'should' and 'ought' cropped up a little too frequently in what were supposedly academic treatments of serious issues. There was a great deal of what one writer has referred to as 'tepid humanism', wishful thinking, empty rhetoric and general lamenting over social injustice leading to the shrinkage, suppression or erosion of minority languages – but there was very little dispassionate assessment or description. My view is simply that, even if one is wholeheartedly and unashamedly committed to a particular ideological position on, say, language and pluralism, the only way to avoid endless and vacuous debate is to confront the issues as they exist, not as one would wish them to exist.

Themes like ethnic identity, nationalism and language-maintenance obviously possess strong emotional associations, but they can and should (particularly in the academic literature) be presented, discussed and evaluated in more neutral tones. I am not claiming, of course, that my own work is value-free – that would be impossible – but I hope that the reader will at least find here a more balanced account than is often the case. Nothing is value-free; some things are less value-laden than others, however.

I have provided a large number of references in this book, many of them to works reflecting ideas with which I do not agree. Perhaps this can be taken as a safeguard against the narrow predominance of any given line of argument. Certainly, my own thrust here leads fairly clearly to some quite definite conclusions but I would not want to suggest that these are the only ones possible. Obviously, however, my own thinking has led me to what *I* consider the most reasonable position; I hope I have provided enough material for the reader to judge for himself or herself.

Although the book does possess a strong thematic line, it is also my hope that it can serve as an introduction to the topic for students of language, psychology, sociology and other courses. Again, the extensive referencing should be a help here, supplemented perhaps by the appendix. I have inspected a large number of books during the writing of this one and, while many are useful for students, it is my belief that none presents the topic in the broad, cross-disciplinary perspective adopted here.

Because this book represents the culmination of several years' work there is a degree of overlap, in some sections, with some of my earlier writings; this has been inevitable, given my attempt here to draw together strands of the language–identity thesis previously presented in more highly specific contexts. In most cases, the earlier material has been substantially reworked.

I should like to acknowledge the specific assistance of Dominic Abrams, David Crystal and Alastair Walker, and many others with whom I have exchanged views over the years. I am also grateful for the critical probing of audiences in Great Britain, Canada, Ireland, West Germany and Belgium to whom I have presented various segments of the argument. Finally, I must thank the University of Bristol, its Psychology Department, and its library for general hospitality and for specific assistance and the provision of facilities during the course of the sabbatical year within which this book was written.

John Edwards

1
Some Basic Concepts

INTRODUCTION

Questions of language and identity are extremely complex. The essence of the terms themselves is open to discussion and, consequently, consideration of their relationship is fraught with difficulties. This is not to say that treatments of the theme are few; indeed, the relationship has been dealt with in a number of disciplines. This in fact is part of the difficulty – there has been much isolated discussion, and some reinventing of the wheel too. Naturally, different perspectives present things in different lights, often for quite understandable reasons, but this can mean a less than complete overall picture. So, one finds that historians, sociologists, psychologists, linguists, educators and others have all attended to the language–identity link in some form or other, usually without much consideration of potentially relevant work in neighbouring disciplines.

An example of this can be found in the way in which *ethnicity* or ethnic-group identity has been treated. As Connor (1978) has pointed out, the term itself has proved a problematic one; but, however it is defined, there would seem to be a connection between it and the concept of *nationalism*.[1] Yet one sees very little mention of nationalism in treatments of ethnicity, especially within social science, and, conversely, those dealing centrally with nationalism often ignore ethnicity. One may or may not want to agree with Connor that 'A nation is a self-aware ethnic group.' (p. 388), but it is difficult to disagree with his rather inelegant statement that 'The student of nationalism and the student of ethnicity seldom cross-fertilize' (p. 387).

Even though Mead (1934/1959) stressed the importance of language 50 years ago, sociologists have largely ignored it in their work. It is also true that studies of political, economic and social history have seldom attended to linguistic matters (see e.g. Schlossman, 1983a). Seton-Watson (1977), in an excellent study of nationalism, has pointed out how undesirable this is, and how the neglect vitiates the discussion of historical processes – especially, of course, those relating to his own field. More recently, he has reiterated the point: 'The history of language is not just a subject for philologists, but forms a very important part of social history, and one which seems to me to be relatively neglected by most historians' (Seton-Watson, 1981, p. 2). There are signs that this neglect is lessening, however. Seton-Watson's own work shows this and, outside the realm of nationalism *per se*, other social historians have begun to integrate language into the story. A good example here is Brown's (1981) recent social history of Ireland from 1922, in which Irish language and literature are part of the general thread.

Another apparently obvious link in which ethnicity figures, but which has not been adequately explored, is that between group identity and bilingual education. I shall be looking in some detail at bilingual education in chapter 5; for present purposes, we can simply note that some varieties of this educational approach are supported precisely because they are seen to be important for ethnic identity retention. It seems rather strange, therefore, that Fishman (1977a) has recently called for the investigation of the ethnicity–bilingual education link, an exercise seen to be 'rewarding'. Surely the analysis of such a link is vital, not only for its own sake but also for the light it might shed upon each of the constituents (see Edwards, 1981a, 1983a). There have been many *assumptions* about relationships between bilingual education and identity retention, but these have not been adequately tested nor even, in many cases, stated. Related to this has been a lack of due regard for the social context in which educational programmes operate. Fishman (1977a, p. 45) thus noted that 'The only aspect of bilingual education that has been even less researched than student attitudes and interests is that of parental attitudes and interests.' Again, I shall turn to these matters later. Here we need only observe, with some amazement perhaps, that programmes intended to bolster identity have not considered the existing parameters of that very phenomenon.

A more general difficulty, one which extends beyond the educational scene to include many aspects of linguistic identity, is the highly charged and often polemical writing which passes for disinterested social analysis. Identity *is* of course a subject of much emotional power and it has been dealt with in a personal and subjective way for a very long time; within modern times, at least since the writings of the linguistic nationalists of the early nineteenth century. Indeed, there is nothing wrong with treatises of an advocatory nature. The difficulty arises when such writing is disguised in the appropriate scientific language of the day. In short, it can be a difficult and tedious exercise to try and tease out a more or less dispassionate assessment of language, identity and their concomitants from less objective outbreaks of special pleading.

The task, therefore, is to attempt an investigation of language and group identity which draws together relevant threads from a diversity of sources, avoids as much as possible the traps and snares of intrusive value judgement and, therefore, provides a useful synthesis of descriptive information. This, in the main, is necessarily a pre-theoretical effort, although some introductory theoretical conclusions may perhaps be advanced.[2] At the least, however, it should be possible to present some testable hypotheses, hypotheses which will be based upon a broader and firmer foundation than is usually provided. As well, this study of language and identity might incorporate and make more illuminating some of the existing empirical and theoretical studies, by giving them a richer and more realistic context. There is, in other words, a possible fusion of 'macro' and 'micro' perspectives which, if at all successful, can only be of benefit to both.

This broadly conceived analysis is, it must be admitted, a daunting exercise and, some might be inclined to say, a foolhardy one. It necessitates, for example, thought and selection in a variety of topics – many of them fully-fledged in their own right – outside one's own particular field of focus. I shall not be surprised, therefore, if this book evokes critical reaction from those into whose areas of expertise I trespass. This is a risk I think is well worth taking, since an integrative consideration of the topic is, I am convinced, much needed. I can only hope that there are few particularly egregious errors. It should also be pointed out, unnecessarily perhaps, that this can be looked upon very much as an introductory effort at synthesis. Much of whatever value the work possesses resides in summarising and ground-clearing and this, I hope, will serve some heuristic purposes.

SOCIOLINGUISTICS AND IDENTITY

It can be seen straight away that there exist a multitude of markers of group identity (age, sex, social class, geography, religion, etc.) of which language is but one. While I hope that the particular relevance of language will become evident in the chapters to follow, it is important not to lose sight of its non-unique status as a marker, nor to succumb to the sort of tunnel vision which often affects workers considering broad matters from narrow perspectives.

It is clear, however, that the link between language and identity is a reasonable one to study and, as we shall see, many have considered that the possession of a given language is well-nigh essential to the maintenance of group identity. In a broader sense, language has increasingly been investigated as an integral part of human social life, within areas of linguistics, sociology and psychology. It seems remarkable, perhaps, that language could ever *not* have been so regarded, but an examination of main trends of research in the fields just noted reveals that, until quite recently, the social aspects of language (i.e. those matters lying outside the bounds of *linguistics*) have not been given due attention. Within social psychology, for example, Giles (1979a) notes the rather conspicuous absence of language studies.[3] Similarly, what now appear to be obvious over-lapping interests between linguistics and sociology were underdeveloped for many years. Thus, Giglioli (1973) points out that language has been neglected within sociology and that linguistics, for its part, has ignored the social context within which language occurs.

The emergence of *sociolinguistics* reflects a desire to reform this situation and to acknowledge a renewed interest in context. It seems to me that, implicit in this, is a concern for group and individual identity, i.e. sociolinguistics (the sociology of language or the social psychology of language: see below) is *essentially about identity*, its formation, presentation and maintenance. This being so, it is important to consider very briefly the growth and development of this hybrid discipline.

In 1953, Hertzler wrote a paper entitled *Toward a sociology of language* in which he advocated that more attention be paid to the interaction of language and social situation. In 1965 he published a book on the topic and, in 1966, Bright edited the proceedings of a sociolinguistics conference held in California. Since the early 1960s then, developments have accelerated rapidly.

There has been some debate over whether *sociolinguistics* or *the sociology of language* is the best title for the approach or, indeed, if the two terms represent different emphases altogether. Fishman (1971a) has noted that, generally, the latter term implies a broader field of interest, the emphasis being upon social behaviour as can be elucidated through the study of language. Sociolinguistics, on the other hand, tends to stress the linguistic variation presented in different contexts. Perhaps the terms are best viewed as reflecting two sides of the one coin. However, the distinction just noted is not necessarily endorsed by all who use the terms, and some (like Fishman) have alternated in their usage, while carrying on with the same sort of work. Fishman (1971a, p. 8) points out that, after all 'Both are concerned with the interpenetration between societally patterned variation in language usage and variation in other societally patterned behavior, whether viewed in intra-communal or inter-communal perspective.' Fishman also makes another possible distinction. Sociolinguistics may have within it the seeds of its own demise, since it represents what many feel to be a necessary broadening of the larger field of linguistics. Once it is accepted that there can be no meaningful linguistics without attention to context, then sociolinguistics may be absorbed. This 'self-liquidation', as Fishman calls it, obviously does not apply to a field termed *the sociology of language*, which may be seen as a new, enduring and autonomous sub-topic of sociology. As A. Edwards (1976, p. 9) notes, the sociology of language is a relatively loose conception 'falling easily into the growing company of sociologies of this and that'.

Fishman suggests, in fact, that the sociology of language logically encloses the narrower field of sociolinguistics. This follows from the fact that his 'fundamental bias [is] to view society as being broader than language and, therefore, as providing the context in which all language behavior must ultimately be viewed. It seems to me that the concept "sociology of language" more fully implies this bias than does the term "sociolinguistics", which implies quite the opposite bias' (1968, p. 6).

So, the two terms may be different in emphasis and in degree of autonomy, and with regard to the relative importance placed upon language and context. As well, the terms are used loosely and sometimes interchangeably. In any event, there is a mingling of context and language, and it is possible to see that *both* terms might be more or less accurately used within the same investigation. One might, for example, use social situational information to comment upon linguistic forms produced or linguistic usage might be studied in order to better understand the context. As Herman (1961) has noted, context can influence linguistic choice, and linguistic choice can serve as an index to perceptions of situation.

The intertwining of these terms in real-life contexts is particularly apposite in studies of linguistic identity. Language revival efforts, for example, are often interpreted as being in the service of a renewed or resuscitated social identity. Yet, it is also true that altered perceptions of group identity – based upon many social factors – may lead to desires for language shift. It is, in fact, an interesting exercise in studies of linguistic nationalism to try to disentangle such chicken-and-egg relationships. Even at this early stage, however, it can be appreciated that such an exercise *may* be rather pointless. A 'packet' of tightly related factors, linguistic and other, often proves singularly resistant to attempts at such disentanglement. Nonetheless, bearing Fishman's quotation in mind, we might want to opt, for present purposes, for a scenario in which the overall social context is perforce larger than any of its constituent parts, language included. This simple observation has some interesting implications which I shall attempt to deal with later. It also rather implies that the sociology of language is a more accurate description, when considering the language–identity link, than is sociolinguistics. Yet the simple difficulty of deriving an adjectival term from the former will account for the continued use of the latter.

ETHNIC IDENTITY

Connor (1978) has discussed, in a useful article, the great confusion surrounding the concept of ethnicity:

With nationalism pre-empted, authorities have had difficulty agreeing on a term to describe the loyalty of segments of a state's population to their particular nation. Ethnicity, primordialism, pluralism, tribalism, regionalism, communalism, and parochialism are among the most commonly encountered. This varied vocabulary further impedes an understanding of nationalism by creating the impression that each is describing a separate phenomenon. (p. 386)

Not only does this comment illustrate something of the terminological confusion in the area,[4] it also indicates the close relationship between ethnicity and nationalism. Nationalism has, in fact, been seen as an extension of ethnicity or, as Baron (1947) put it, organised ethnocultural solidarity. Francis (1947, 1976) has referred to ethnicity as nationalism which is not completely self-aware and Weber (1968), on the same theme, noted that the presence of ethnic solidarity does not in itself constitute a sense of 'nation'. This presents the possibility of what Connor discusses as 'pre-national' groups or 'potential nations', and leads him to endorse Barker's (1927) view that a nation is essentially a self-aware ethnic group. Thus, 'while an ethnic group *may*...be other-defined, the nation *must* be self-defined' (Connor, 1978, p. 388).[5]

But, what are the necessary and sufficient conditions for ethnic or pre-national groups, and how important is the question of self- versus other-definition? At a very simple level, ethnicity can be thought of as a 'sense of group identity deriving from real or perceived common bonds such as language, race or religion' (Edwards, 1977a, p. 254). But, although true, this definition is very general and invites more questions than it answers. What, for example, are the most important common bonds? Are some more central than others? Are some essential? And why exactly is the phrase 'real or perceived' necessary? If we turn to the extensive literature on ethnic identity, attempting to resolve these matters, we find that we have opened Pandora's box. Isajiw (1980) examined 65 studies of ethnicity, and found that 52 of them gave *no* explicit definition of ethnicity, accepting, by default as it were, the sort of general view cited above. Isajiw also considered theoretical treatments of the subject, assessing 27 definitions. A fairly broad range of opinion thus was evaluated and, although there was a great deal of variation, several themes recurred. It is an examination of these that promises to lead to a comprehensive definition of identity.

First, there is the often-expressed equation of *ethnic* group with *minority* group, or with a social subgroup. This is found more often among those treating ethnicity in a North American, immigrant-group context. Theodorson and Theodorson (1969) define an ethnic group as a subgroup within a larger society, as does Gordon (1964). Yet even the most casual observer can see that *all* people are members of some ethnic group or other; in fact *ethnos* is a Greek word for nation, where this signifies a common-descent group. Intrinsically, therefore, there is no need to associate *ethnic* with *minority*. However, and especially perhaps in immigrant societies, the politics of power ensure that, as Royce (1982, p. 3) says 'dominant groups rarely define themselves as ethnics.' My point here is simply that the ethnic–minority link is not a necessary one, but rather one reflecting power and status relationships.

The situation is clarified somewhat if we move from the immigrant context to one in which *indigenous* groups are involved. Isajiw (1980) notes that European sociological definitions of ethnicity, for example, do not make the ethnic group–subgroup association. On the one hand, terms like 'nation' or 'nationality' are used because of the homogeneity of societies existing as states. [6] On the other hand, 'national minority' is often used to refer to groups within heterogeneous societies – and this, as Isajiw rightly notes, does tend to avoid the connotations of *sub*-groups which the term 'ethnic minority' sometimes possesses.

In any event, a combination of European, American and other experiences does usefully demonstrate the logical fallacy of thinking of ethnicity as a minority phenomenon. While dominant groups in mixed societies may not usually consider themselves in ethnic terms, they clearly *can* be conceived of in this way. Indeed, ethnic communities can not only be majority ones within a given society, they may also cross political boundaries, as contemporary and historical pan-ethnic groupings indicate. All of this Isajiw takes as evidence for an *abstract–specific* distinction in definitions of ethnic identity, in which the geographical context of ethnicity determines, at least in part, its constitution

– thus, the relevance of majority–minority considerations. It seems to me, however, that the distinction is not so much between abstract and specific approaches to ethnicity as between different specific ones. As we have seen, definitions of ethnicity which assume or do not assume minority status differ along contextual lines rather than varying in degrees of abstractness or specificity. The important first point in the argument, then, is just that ethnic identity should not be taken to imply, necessarily, minority-group identity.

A second factor in the discussion is the importance of emphasising group *boundaries* or group *content*. Barth (1969) is perhaps the most influential of contemporary scholars who have stressed that the essential focal point is the boundary between groups. His reasoning is that the cultures which boundaries enclose may change – indeed, we should stress that they *do* change, since all groups are dynamic – but the continuation of boundaries themselves is more longstanding. This emphasis has the attraction of illuminating group maintenance across generations; for example, third- and fourth-generation immigrants in the United States are generally quite unlike their first-generation forebears yet, to the extent to which they recognise links here (and differences from other groups), the concept and utility of group boundary has significance. In some ways, too, Barth's emphasis came as a relief from earlier approaches which focused on group cultural content since, as Royce (1982) points out, these often proved little more than lists of alleged ethnic traits.

Nevertheless, I think we can agree with Royce that the received notion in some quarters, after Barth, that boundaries were 'in' and content was 'out' is not completely justified. The fact that group culture may have been less than adequately dealt with is not, *per se*, a good reason for neglecting it altogether. Both perspectives are important. I shall be suggesting later some ways of looking at group cultural markers which might bring together both content and boundary approaches. An examination of traits which disappear (or become less visible) versus those which show more longevity, for example, would not only clarify content change over time, but would also elucidate the ways in which boundaries are maintained in the face of changing circumstances. As a more specific instance, we might consider that the decline of an original group language may represent a change in cultural content – the loss of that language as a regular communicative instrument, and the adoption of another. But, to the extent to which language remains as a valued symbolic feature of group life, it may yet contribute to the maintenance of boundaries.

A third major feature of ethnic identity has to do with *objective* versus *subjective* definitions (cf. Royce's *material–ideological* dichotomy). As Isajiw (1980) has noted, this distinction reflects that between structural and phenomenological approaches, especially within sociology. On the one hand, we can consider definitions of ethnicity which include objective characteristics (linguistic, racial, geographical, religious, ancestral, etc.). From such a perspective, ethnicity is 'given', an inheritance which is an immutable historical fact. Such an 'involuntary' approach to group membership can be further understood as emphasising common ties of socialisation. It thus allows us to conceptually differentiate between ethnic groups and other forms of association, like clubs and societies, membership of which is not involuntary and does not depend upon common socialisation patterns (although it may do, of course, if the organisations persist over generations). To this point, then, we might tentatively view ethnicity as an involuntary state in which members share common socialisation practices or culture.

However, this objective approach has some serious difficulties. Indeed, Isajiw (1980) notes that only one definition in his sample made explicit reference to the purely objective approach: Breton and Pinard (1960) asserted that ethnic group membership is not a matter of choice, but rather an accident of birth. It is true that they also mention emotional and symbolic relationships among group members but these, no less than more visible entities like language and ancestry, are seen to be basically related to socialisation. The main difficulty here is that the objective or involuntary approach – useful as it first appears as a quick means of categorisation – does not adequately explain the persistence of ethnicity across generation, within rapidly changing social contexts.[7] The obvious example here is the North American immigrant experience. As noted above, continuity of group boundaries may outlive that of specific cultural content; a sense of 'groupness' may persist long after visible or tangible links with earlier generations have disappeared. On what basis is this maintained?

It is at this point that the 'subjective' perspective is useful. An example is provided by Shibutani and Kwan (1965) who note that 'an ethnic group consists of people who conceive of themselves as being of a kind . . . united by emotional bonds'; although they may share a common heritage, 'far more important, however, is their belief that they are of common descent' (pp. 40–1). Or, consider Weber (1968): 'We shall call "ethnic groups" those human groups that entertain a subjective belief in their common descent . . . it does not matter whether or not an objective blood relationship exists. Ethnic member-ship . . . differs from the kinship group precisely by being a *presumed* identity' (p. 389; my italics). Ethnicity, then, is seen above all as a matter of belief.

We find in Isajiw's (1980) survey that attributes cited include such things as 'sense of peoplehood' and shared values. Further, where the studies surveyed gave *no* definition of ethnicity, the implicit definition often seemed to be something as loose as 'any group of people who identify themselves or are in any way identified as Italians, Germans, Indians, Ukrainians, etc.' (p. 14). Yet it is very important to understand, as Isajiw notes (and as is implied in the subjective approaches cited above), that the subjectivity here is not completely arbitrary but is, like the more material or objective perspective, based upon ancestry. There must be *some* real linkage, however much change groups and individuals have undergone, between past and present. It is in this sense, perhaps that the terms 'objective' and 'subjective' are best seen as reflections on the perceived immutability or mutability of ethnic group markers (see Fishman, 1977b).

It seems clear that some combination of objective and subjective perspec-tives is necessary in understanding ethnic identification. If this appears at first to require a paradoxical mingling of mutable and immutable elements, recall the distinction between group content and group boundaries. Cultural content is, of course, mutable – ethnic groups are dynamic entities, particularly when they exist as minorities within heterogeneous and developing (or highly developed) societies – but boundaries are less so. Indeed, when boundaries disappear, when even the most subjectively or symbolically sustained group markers vanish, then the ethnic group itself has ceased as a viable concept. This usually takes a very long time, and those who are now members of a large homogeneous group, e.g. English speakers in England, will have to delve deep into history to rediscover boundaries.

The final factor I want to discuss here comprises questions of ethnicity as myth, and what Gans has referred to as 'symbolic ethnicity' (1979; see also chapter 4). Steinberg (1981) has considered the current American interest in ethnicity – the 'new ethnicity', as some have termed it – as representing the dying gasp of ethnic vitality. For Steinberg, economic and social-class approaches are now far more explanatory in understanding groups and group behaviour than is ethnic-group membership. The 'myth', then, is that ethnicity *per se* is a continuingly useful concept. Steinberg notes that ethnicity is willingly set aside for socioeconomic advance: 'ethnic groups...have been all too willing to trample over ethnic boundaries...in the pursuit of economic and social advantage' (1981, p. 256). The myth of ethnicity resides in the attempt to artificially sustain it beyond limits of usefulness and meaningfulness. Steinberg's final sentence adverts to the mistaken belief that a continued association with symbols of the past can realistically protect group members from contemporary discontents. Patterson (1977), too, has reacted against the rhetoric of current ethnicity. It is, for him, a chauvinistic impulse, a retrogressive longing for boundaries now very much out of place and, indeed, destructive (see also Vallee, 1981, on 'ethnicity as anachronism' and Porter, 1975, on 'ethnicity as atavism'). The major feature of revivalist ethnicity is, for Patterson, the adherence to 'empty symbols'.

I shall have more to say about ethnic revival, its progress and proponents, and value judgements of pluralism; here I simply want to consider the notion of ethnic symbols. Both Steinberg and Patterson see these as essentially meaningless, or empty and unworthy longings for a past that is unrecapturable. If, however, we can conceive of ethnicity, e.g. among American immigrants, as a real and continuing force, and one which is genuinely felt, then perhaps the idea of symbols is important. I have already alluded to the continuation of boundaries among some groups in which cultural content has altered dramatically over generations, and it is perhaps to these groups that we should look in order to see the power of ethnic symbols.

Here, Gans (1979) has clarified the situation. He notes, first of all, that there has been *no* ethnic revival in the United States, and that assimilation and acculturation have continued. Nevertheless, there *has* been a 'new kind of ethnic involvement...which emphasizes concern with identity' (p. 1). This apparent paradox is resolved, Gans claims, when one understands that this new involvement is a minimal one, does not require traditional ethnic culture or institutions, but does give importance to symbols. Like many critics of the 'new ethnicity', Gans acknowledges that this symbolic ethnicity is 'an ethnicity of the last resort' (p. 1) but, unlike them, does not feel that this is perforce a negative quality nor one doomed to imminent demise; it is something which might persist for a long time. Presumably this reflects the fact that when ethnicity has altered to symbolic status only, it is no longer any sort of barrier to social advance and, as such, can be maintained indefinitely without cost. The ethnic revival, in Gans's terms, is a misnomer; what is actually occurring is symbolic ethnicity which, because of upward mobility, is a visible quantity. Some of the forms that symbolic ethnicity can take include religious *rites de passage* and holidays, 'ethnic' foods, and ethnic characters in the mass media. This last is particularly interesting because, as Gans aptly points out, although 'films and television programs with ethnic characters are on the increase', these characters do not engage in very 'ethnic' behaviour and 'may only have ethnic names'; thus, 'they are not very different from the ethnic audiences who watch them' (p. 10).

Bearing these four factors in mind, we may now attempt a definition of ethnic identity. Such a definition must take into account: (a) the fact that ethnic identity need not be a minority phenomenon; (b) the continuation of perceived group boundaries, across generations which are likely to show significant changes in the cultural 'stuff' of their lives; (c) that objective, material trait descriptions do not fully encompass the phenomenon; and (d) the power of so-called 'symbolic' ethnicity, which can be too easily discounted.

On the basis of his analyses, Isajiw (1980) concluded that 'ethnicity refers to an involuntary group of people who share the same culture or to descendants of such people who identify themselves and/or are identified by others as belonging to the same involuntary group' (p. 24). As a minimal statement, Isajiw's is unexceptionable; it certainly accords with the features discussed here. On the other hand, it defines by excluding non-essential or non-contributory aspects. I suggest, therefore, that the following might be of slightly greater value:

Ethnic identity is allegiance to a group – large or small, socially dominant or subordinate – with which one has ancestral links. There is no necessity for a continuation, over generations, of the same socialisation or cultural patterns, but some sense of a group boundary must persist. This can be sustained by shared objective characteristics (language, religion, etc.), or by more subjective contributions to a sense of 'groupness', or by some combination of both. Symbolic or subjective attachments must relate, at however distant a remove, to an observably real past.

NATURALISM

I have already discussed some general views which suggest a connection between ethnicity and nationalism, e.g. nationalism as self-aware ethnicity, ethnicity as a state of 'pre-nationalism', nationalism as 'organised ethnocultural

solidarity', etc. There is obviously a link between the two concepts, and many
of the notes (above) on criteria for ethnic identity apply, at a broader level,
to national identity. For this reason I can perhaps be briefer here than I would
have to be otherwise. Nonetheless, nationalism is a large and complicated topic,
has received a great deal of attention from many quarters, and must be given
at least a cursory treatment here.

Royce (1982) points out that, although nationalism and ethnicity share much
in common, most importantly the sense of 'groupness' or 'peoplehood', they
are not identical. The obvious difference, however, is not one of principle but
of scale. Nationalism is an extension of ethnicity in that it adds to the belief
in shared characteristics a desire for political autonomy, the feeling that the
'only legitimate type of government is national self-government' (Kedourie,
1961, p. 9).[8]

Nationalism is often seen as a modern phenomenon. Kohn (1961) has traced
in great detail the progress of the concept, and it is clear that early uses of
the term *nation* do not accord with contemporary views. It is a fairly recent
perspective which associates *nation* with common sympathies, sentiments, aims
and will, a perspective which dates to the beginning of the last century.
Kedourie (1961), for example, describes nationalism as a doctrine invented
in Europe at that time. It makes three major assumptions: (a) that there is
a natural division of humanity into nations; (b) that these nations have identifiable characteristics; and (c) that (as noted above) their only legitimate form
of government is self-government. The linguistic criterion is the most important
here in marking one nation from another: 'A group speaking the same language
is known as a nation, and a nation ought to constitute a state' (Kedourie, 1961,
p. 68). In linking language centrally to nationalism, Kedourie claims that there
are no substantive distinctions between linguistic and (say) racial nationalism,
that there is simply *a* conception of nationalism which may embrace various
features (language, race, religion, etc.). This may have, incidentally, the effect
of heightening the importance of language for ethnicity too, if we accept that
nationalism is 'organised' ethnicity. On the other hand, perhaps the increase
in scale from ethnicity to nationalism, and the concomitant requirement for
large organising principles, may raise language from *a* marker to *the* marker.
In any event, Kedourie's *own* view is that nationalism is a pernicious doctrine,
particularly with regard to its emphasis upon linguistic unity; possession of
the same language should *not* entitle people to governmental autonomy. More
generally, political matters should not be based upon cultural criteria.

Smith (1971) has criticised Kedourie's analysis of nationalism, largely on
the grounds that it emphasises negative aspects and language. There are
instances in which language is not so important for nationalistic sentiment as
are other markers; Smith claims that, in Africa, national identity is rarely
associated with language *per se* since this could lead to 'balkanisation' and that,
in countries like Greece, Burma and Pakistan, religion has been the pre-eminent
'self-definer'. Thus, 'in general, the linguistic criterion has been of sociological
importance only in Europe and the Middle East (to some extent)' (pp. 18–19).

Smith essentially endorses Kedourie's basic description of nationalism (see the three assumptions above), but rejects his emphasis on language. In fact, Smith claims that Kedourie's error is to outline the naked doctrine of nationalism, then add the linguistic criterion (which is applicable only in some instances and based, Smith tells us, on the 'German romantic version'), and then, finally, to amalgamate these two features. It is on this basis that Kedourie's criticism of the overall concept is misguided.

Smith expands upon Kedourie's basic assumptions underlying nationalism when he outlines what he calls the 'core nationalist doctrine'. It holds that humanity is divided naturally into nations having particular characteristics. Freedom and self-realisation depend upon identification with the nation, the source of political power, and loyalty to the nation-state overrides all other allegiances. There is, thus, a need for nations and states to coincide, and the strengthening of this natural nation-state is the *sine qua non* for freedom and peace for all.

Smith thus provides an easy conceptual link between ethnicity and nationalism. He notes, for example, that the core doctrine does not define the characteristics of perceived nationhood; supporting theories are required for this. Surely this is exactly the point at which we can insert, as it were, the previously defined concept of ethnicity. Nationalism can indeed be seen as ethnicity writ large, ethnicity with a desire for self-government (total or partial) added. Just as ethnicity does not inevitably require language (or any other specific feature) as a component, neither does nationalism.

We should give some brief further consideration to the notion that nationalism is a recent phenomenon. I have already noted Kohn's (1961) point that the idea of a *nation* being erected upon common sympathies and aims is a modern one. Before the nineteenth century, in feudal, dynastic and essentially socially immobile societies, the idea of a common consciousness can hardly be said to have characterised even those groups sharing certain sociocultural traits. Thus, Rustow (1968), for example, connects modernisation with nationalistic feeling. But what elements of modernisation led to national consciousness or 'corporate will'? Two important factors were the French Revolution, with its ideals of a popular sovereignty, and the growth of romanticism (especially in Germany: see below). Kohn (1967) thus details the beginnings of the ideas of nationalism and nation-state in a book entitled *Prelude to nation-states: The French and German experience 1789–1815*; earlier, he had made the often-quoted statement that 'before the [French] Revolution there had been states and governments, after it there emerged nations and peoples' (1961, p. 573).

Yet these very elements of 'modernisation' refute the idea that nationalism was a concept which somehow sprung, fully formed and independent, from the social philosopher's mind or a radically altered social context. Both the French Revolution and the romantic reaction to rationalism sit firmly embedded in historical context. In this sense, Kedourie's description of nationalism as an 'invented' doctrine may have misleading connotations;

indeed, his own subsequent discussion of revolution, reaction and romanticism underlines the unfortunate nature of his choice of the word. Smith's (1971) analysis of a gradual evolution from a 'pre-modern age' to a 'post-revolutionary' one is surely more accurate. Here, Orridge (1981) makes the useful observation that nationalism, like other political phenomena, is an emergent process; its roots go deep. Thus, the 'first and most influential kind of nationalism has been that of the nation-states of Western Europe...the prototypes of modern nationalism' (p. 42). It is of course possible to say that units like England, France and Denmark were never completely nation-states, but that they developed into larger homogeneous entities: 'at their core lay a sizeable population with a degree of initial cultural similarity that increased as time went on' (p. 42).

Further to this matter, we might agree with Barker (1927). He accepts that national self-consciousness dates from the nineteenth century and, in this sense, the nation is a modern invention. But, 'nations were already there; they had indeed been there for centuries' (p. 173). The apparent paradox here is perhaps resolved if we acknowledge that pre-nineteenth century 'nations' were waiting, as it were, for the spark of consciousness which brought them alive. Groups possessing ethnic solidarity but lacking the final feature – the desire for some degree of autonomy – may be thought of as *pre-national* groups or *potential* nations (Connor, 1978). Barker goes on to say that 'a nation must be an idea as well as a fact before it can become a dynamic force' (p. 173). However, perhaps on balance it would be clearer to think of potential nations (i.e. ethnic groups) *becoming* nations rather than to speak of the nation as a group first lacking, and then acquiring, this vital consciousness, i.e. while we should accept that nations do not materialise suddenly (and, in that sense, are hardly 'inventions') they are not, strictly speaking, *nations* before the 'idea' has occurred; the transition is thus from ethnic group to nation, and is made possible by the self-conscious desire for autonomy. The 'idea' here relates primarily to the imagined possibilities of autonomy. As regards this, Connor's (1978) comment upon Barker's idea is a bit misleading. He claims that Barker's meaning is that 'a nation is a self-aware ethnic group...while an ethnic group *may*, therefore, be other-defined, the nation *must* be self-defined' (p. 388). But, *both* ethnic group *and* nation are self-defined; the difference between them resides in the nation's possession of the additional 'idea', the conscious wish for self-control. It is in *this* sense that both Gellner (1964), when he speaks of nationalism inventing nations, and Anderson (1983), when he defines the nation as an *imagined* political community, are correct.

I cannot delve further here into the historical forces bearing upon nationalism; many useful treatments may be found (e.g. Kohn, 1961, 1967; Seton-Watson, 1977; Smith, 1971, 1979b). Suffice it to say that it was in the rhetoric surrounding 1789 that nationalism, national loyalty, the notion of the 'fatherland' and, above all, the belief in unity and autonomy first found forceful expression. It was in the German romanticism that the notion of a *volk* and the almost mystical connection between nation and language were expounded

so fervently in modern times. In 1807, Fichte stressed as absolutely crucial
the linguistic criterion of nationhood (in his famous *Addresses to the German
nation*, 1922/1968). Indeed, Fichte not only emphasised the importance of his
own language, he actively deprecated that of others, thus foreshadowing much
of the negative rhetoric of nationalism. For example, he pointed out that 'the
German speaks a language which has been alive ever since it first issued from
the force of nature, whereas the other Teutonic races speak a language which
has movement on the surface only but is dead at the root (1968, pp. 58–59).
From a linguistic standpoint this sentiment is absurd, yet it illustrates the essentially irrational (or, to be less pejorative, non-rational) power and appeal of
linguistic nationalism.

It is from these roots that our modern understanding of nationalism has
sprung. Connor (1978) points out that the very term *nationalism* seems first
to have appeared around the end of the eighteenth century. Although it did
not find a permanent place in dictionaries until almost a hundred years later
– and the term *nationality* apparently received *its* contemporary launching from
Lord Acton in 1862 (1907) – these were the beginnings. From then on, many
important commentators discussed national consciousness and the 'corporate
will' of a people, Disraeli, John Stuart Mill and Renan among them (see Royce,
1982; Smith, 1971).[9] I shall have more to say about assessments of nationalism
in the next chapter.

The final points to be made here have to do with recurring problems of
definition and confusion. Nationalism, to reiterate, can be understood as ethnic
sentiment expanded to include desires for at least some degree of self-
government, for group boundaries to coincide with those of governmental units,
and for the preservation, strengthening and dignity of the group. It is in the
relationship between nation and state that confusion often occurs. *Nation*, after
all, is commonly used in referring to countries, political units which may or
may not be ethnically homogeneous, which are more properly termed *states*.
States are easily defined. Nations, on the other hand, are more elusive; we
have seen here that nationalism, like ethnicity, has both objective and subjective
aspects. While we can attempt to list characteristics of nations, no particular
tangible traits are essential to the definition. A psychological bond, a sense
of community residing in affective ties, these are the common and necessary
conditions for nationalistic sentiment. Thus, as Seton-Watson (1977) notes,
no scientific definition of the notion can be devised. Self-awareness and self-
consciousness are the marks of nationalism, and objective features like religion
and language 'are significant to the notion only to the degree to which they
contribute to this notion or sense of the group's self-identity and uniqueness'
(Connor, 1978, p. 389). It will thus be understood that nations can alter or
lose characteristics without losing the necessary self-consciousness. Tangible
features are, of course, necessary as rallying-points, and they are needed to
give the all-important national consciousness a visible form, but none is essential
per se (see e.g. Smith's arguments against identifying nations with language
groups, 1971).

The state, then, is a political and territorial unit; the nation involves more subjective elements, being essentially an 'imagined' community in Anderson's sense (1983). Connor (1978) suggests that the earliest uses of the term *nationalism* did not confuse nation and state; but, latterly, nationalism has been used to indicate loyalty not to the nation, properly conceived, but to the state. Indeed, we commonly refer to the 'nations of the world' and the 'United Nations', even though these uses are clearly incorrect.

Loyalties can interact and overlap, of course. Loyalty to nation can coincide, indeed, with state loyalty, but only when the unit in question is a *nation-state*, a political entity comprising a homogeneous national group. Turning again to Connor (1978), we see that the true nation-state is a rare bird. Surveying the 132 states existing in 1971, he found that only 12 (9.1 per cent) were nation-states. Another 50 (37.9 per cent) contained a major ethnic group comprising more than three-quarters of the total population. Of the remaining 70 states, 31 (23.5 per cent) had a majority ethnic group accounting for between half and three-quarters of the population, while in 39 more (29.5 per cent) the largest single ethnic community formed less than half of the total population. So, while in many countries there is a large, often numerically dominant, ethnic group, there are few indeed for whom we could assume that national and state loyalties coincide. Elsewhere (in a review of Patterson, 1977), Connor discusses continuing confusion. Patterson correctly notes that Great Britain, the United States and Canada are not nation-states, but claims that Ireland, France and most other European states *are*. A case might be made for Ireland, but France and other continental countries are clearly not nation-states, containing as they do many groups. Connor (1980) mentions, by way of illustration, that France contains groups of Alsatians, Basques, Bretons, Corsicans, etc. Even Royce (1982), in her useful work on ethnic identity, seems to confuse nation and state, and to muddy the relationship between ethnicity and nationalism. Thus, 'one does not have to give up allegiances based on primary ties such as ethnic group membership in order to function within a unit such as a nation, which operates on the basis of civil ties' (p. 107). Of course, 'civil ties' are not absent in nations, but Royce seems to refer here to what should more properly be called a state.

In summary, nationalism can indeed be thought of, in Baron's terms (1947), as 'organised ethnocultural solidarity', so long as we recognise that the organising has to do with a desire for self-control. The definition of ethnicity, then, can be expanded in this way to become one of nationalism. It is important to realise that both notions rest upon a *sense* of community which can have many different tangible manifestations, none of which is indispensable for the continuation of the sense itself. The visible 'content' of both ethnicity and nationalism is eminently mutable; what is immutable is the feeling of groupness. When *this* disappears then boundaries disappear. Any analysis of nationalism which concentrates solely upon objective characteristics misses the essential point. On the other hand, it must be remembered that the subjective fidelity which is so important is not itself arbitrary; a sense of solidarity must ultimately depend upon 'real' communalities, however diluted or altered over time. The continuing power of ethnicity and nationalism resides exactly in that intangible bond which, by definition, can survive the loss of visible markers of group distinctiveness.

LANGUAGE AND DIALECT

If we are to consider the relationship of language and identity, we should clarify our conceptions of language itself. This may seem an obvious and unnecessary excursion, yet, since there have been almost as many definitions of language as writers on the topic, some brief attention is necessary. As well, I want to introduce here a note on two broad types of language function which are not immediately self-evident. Similarly, we should ensure that we understand what is meant by dialect.

Language

In 1921, Sapir noted that 'language is a purely human and non-instinctive method of communicating ideas, emotions, and desires by means of a system of voluntarily produced symbols' (p. 7). Morris (1946) described language as composed of arbitrary symbols possessing an agreed-upon significance within a community. Furthermore, these symbols are independent of immediate context, and are connected in rule-governed ways. First, then, language is a *system* – this implies regularity and rules of order. Second, the system is *arbitrary* inasmuch as the particular units employed have meaning only because of users' agreement and convention. Third, language is used for communicative purposes by a group of people who constitute the speech or language community.

Implicit here is the idea that languages differ from one another in terms of just how they assign meaning to sounds and symbols. Not wishing to deal at all with the question of *how* different speech communities evolved, or the origin of language(s), I will only make the obvious statement that there exist numerous language communities in the world, whose patterns of communication are not mutually intelligible (although many, of course, are related in language 'families', e.g. Indo-European, Semitic, Finno-Ugric).[10]

It is of some interest that, in the face of the obvious pragmatic advantages of a reduction in the number of distinct languages, thousands of varieties continue to flourish. Some have seen the reason for this as the human desire to stake particular linguistic claims to the world, to create unique perspectives on reality and to protect group distinctiveness. Thus, Steiner (1975) speaks of separate languages enabling groups to keep secret the 'inherited, singular springs of their identity' (p. 232). Language can be seen as a vehicle for concealment, secrecy and fiction. This idea is not Steiner's alone, of course. Popper has suggested that what is most characteristic of human language is the possibility of story-telling, and Wittgenstein in the *Tractatus* refers to language disguising thought (see Edwards, 1979a). Further, Jespersen (1946) reminds us of Talleyrand's famous observation that language exists to hide one's thoughts, and also relates Kierkegaard's extension of this, that language is used by some to hide their lack of thought! The idea of language as concealment may seem contrary to that of language as communication, but the communication is a within-group phenomenon and the concealment an attempt, through language, to maintain inviolate the group's own grasp of the world. The historical equation, *traduttore–traditore*, suggests a disinclination to see 'hoarded dreams, patents of life...taken across the frontier' (Steiner, 1975, p. 233).

This speculation may be overstatement, but it seems clear enough that there has been, and continues to be, a strong resistance to the abandoning of a particular language, even for the practical attractions of a lingua franca (see chapter 2), and a desire at most for an instrumental bilingualism in which the original variety is retained (often, however, within ever-decreasing domains). This suggests that there can be a distinction, within a language, between what I have called *communicative* and *symbolic* functions (Edwards, 1977a, 1984a).

The basic distinction here is between language in its ordinarily understood sense as a tool of communication, and language as an emblem of groupness, as a symbol, a rallying-point. We have already seen that language can be important in ethnic and nationalist sentiment because of its powerful and visible symbolism, quite apart from the revived communicative aspect which is often desired within minority groups. However, we need not look at self-conscious group movements to apprehend that power of language which extends beyond the communicative function. For any speech community in which the language of use is also the ancestral language, the intangible symbolic relevance is tied up with the instrumental function. Steiner (1975) has pointed out, for example, that communication inevitably involves translation and interpretation; this is true for communication *within* a language, as well as for the obvious translation needed across languages. Steiner simply means that the symbolic value of language, the historical and cultural associations which it accumulates and the 'natural semantics of remembrance' (p. 470) all add to the basic message a rich underpinning of shared connotations. It is in this way that we translate when we communicate, and this ability to read between the lines, as it were, depends upon a cultural continuity in which language is embedded, and which is not open to all. Only those who grow up within the community can, perhaps, participate fully in this expanded communicative interaction. Steiner notes, indeed, that 'we possess civilization because we have learnt to translate out of time' (p. 31).

The complicated interweaving of language and culture which depends upon a fusion of pragmatic linguistic skills and the more intangible associations carried by language is not always immediately apparent to native speakers within a majority-speech community. The ordinary English-speaker in Great Britain, for example, uses the language in all regular domains; as well, it is the language of the past in which tradition and culture are expressed. However, the two aspects of language *are* separable – the communicative from the symbolic – and it is possible for the latter to retain importance in the absence of the former. This is most clearly seen when we examine language use and attitudes among minority groups undergoing (or having undergone) language shift within majority, other-language-speaking populations or, indeed, among any group where a shift has occurred in the fairly recent past.[11] Ireland is an example here. A 1975 research study (Committee on Irish Language Attitudes Research) sampled some 3,000 respondents, when investigating Irish language use, ability and attitudes. Only about three per cent of the overall population now use the language in any regular way, there is little interest in Irish restoration, and many are pessimistic about the maintenance of the little Irish still used. Yet, there *does* remain a value for Irish in the symbolic sense, and it can be argued that Irish continues to occupy some place in the constitution of current Irish identity (see Edwards, 1984b; and chapter 3).

The continuing symbolic role of language can also be observed among immigrant groups in the United States. Eastman (1984) discusses the notion of an 'associated' language – one which group members no longer use, or even know, but which continues to be part of their heritage (see also Eastman & Reese, 1981; Edwards, 1984c).[12] When language operates only as a symbol, it may be argued that it is no longer really language. Certainly, the symbolic function of language which co-exists with the communicative (as discussed by Steiner) is not quite the same thing as the more purely symbolic entity which is divorced from the communicative (e.g. Irish for most Irish people, Polish for most fourth-generation Polish-Americans, etc.). Still, it should be remembered that language, unlike other purely emblematic markers, is itself a complex system, capable (at least theoretically) of being resuscitated to instrumental status. I shall return to these matters again. Here, I simply note that the two functions of language, as outlined above, are separable – even if they are usually joined – and that ignorance of the distinction between them can lead to lack of clarity and, indeed, misdirection of effort among linguistic nationalists.

A common distinction drawn between language and dialect is that dialects are mutually intelligible varieties of one language (see next section), while languages are mutually unintelligible. It is obvious that speakers of French, for example, cannot understand German; the two languages are different. However, is it the case that one language can be seen, in some sense or other, as better, more logical or more expressive than another? This question has proved a controversial one, although it is perhaps a more reasonable one to ask, in the minds of many, if the languages being compared are not relatively close to each other (e.g. French and German) but are, rather, somewhat farther apart (e.g. French and Yup'ik). Is one somehow more primitive or less developed than the other? The idea has appealed to many in the past and has contemporary adherents too (see Edwards, 1983b; Honey, 1983). However, on purely linguistic grounds, it is quite clear that no language can be described as better or worse than another. Given that language is an arbitrary system in which communication rests upon agreement among members of the speech community, it follows that the only 'logic' of language is to be found in its grammar (i.e. a logic of convention). What is grammatical in French (e.g. the use of two elements to express verbal negation) is not in English (where only one is used), but this surely says nothing about the relative quality of the two systems. And, even if we compare the language of a technologically advanced society with that of an 'undeveloped' one, we find the same different, but not deficient, relationship. Gleitman and Gleitman (1970) have noted that there are no 'primitive' languages, and Lenneberg (1967, p. 364) puts it this way: 'Could it be that some languages require "less mature cognition" than others, perhaps because they are still more primitive? In recent years this notion has been thoroughly discredited by virtually all students of language.'

Languages are best seen as different systems reflecting different varieties of the human condition. Although they may be unequal in complexity at given points, this does not imply that some have, overall, greater expressive power. Environments differ and, therefore, the things that must be detailed in language differ. The shop-worn example of Eskimos using many different words to refer to various types of what English speakers simply term *snow* does not reflect a capability constitutionally denied to non-Eskimos. It *does* reflect the fact that different environments evoke, in habitual ways, different linguistic behaviour. However, to continue with the example, English-speakers could learn to differentiate among types of snow if they were transplanted to an Arctic setting and, indeed, English-speaking skiers concerned with snow conditions have demonstrated this in more realistic contexts.[13] The general point here is that a language can be seen as 'better' than another only with regard to certain specified intellectual tasks, tasks which are not themselves comparable across environments (see also Langacker, 1972; Trudgill, 1974a).

Further to this, we can note that ideas of languages *decaying* are not well-founded. Languages change, certainly – adapting to new conditions and requirements – but they do not do so in terms of linguistic purity. Thus, 'at any stage, a language is fully adequate to its purpose...the idea of a "pure" language is illusory' (Langacker, 1972, p. 100). To remake the point, this does not mean that all languages contain the same capabilities; different social, geographical and other conditions determine what elements will be needed and, therefore, developed. All are, however, potentially functionally equivalent. Hymes (1974) has noted that languages differ in many aspects of complexity – lexical, grammatical, phonological – and that bilingual speakers will often prefer one language to another for specific purposes. But, the question of overall language 'goodness' is spurious, unless we were willing to define, compare and judge the goodness of situations, contexts and milieus.[14]

Dialect

A dialect is a variety of a language which differs from other varieties in terms of vocabulary, grammar and pronunciation (accent). Dialects are often distinguished from languages on the basis that, unlike the latter, they are mutually intelligible, e.g. Yorkshire dialect and Cockney dialect are varieties of English and (perhaps with some difficulty) speakers of one can understand the other. However, the nature of dialects is not without problems, and Petyt (1980) provides a useful discussion. He notes that if we consider dialects as different forms of the same language, how fine-grained do we admit these differences to be? It is certainly the case that, within an accepted dialect, there can be found a number of sub-varieties. Trudgill (1974a) thus points out that, within Norfolk dialect, one can speak of East Norfolk and South Norfolk. Continuing subdivisions would ultimately lead us to *idiolect*, or the speech of one person. It is simply a matter of convention that we usually stop the analysis at some group level, having decided beforehand, perhaps, how much detail we require. Petyt (1980, p. 12) states: 'Sometimes we speak of "Yorkshire dialect", thus implying that the features shared by all Yorkshire speakers in contrast to outsiders are important...at other times we speak of "Dentdale dialect" with the "essential" features being much more detailed.'

The notion of mutual intelligibility as a criterion of dialect (as opposed to language) falters on two points. First, there are *degrees* of intelligibility, such that some dialect speakers may understand each other very well, while others may have considerable difficulty. Second, the existence of dialect continua means that 'adjacent' forms may be mutually understood, but non-adjacent ones may not. Trudgill (1974a) reminds us that the idea of a clear and sharp linguistic discontinuity between dialect speakers is invalid. Consider four dialects, A, B, C and D. As Petyt (1980, p. 14) says: 'if A can just understand C, but cannot really be said to understand D, does the language division come between C and D? But C and D may understand each other quite well.'

These difficulties lead Petyt to the conclusion that criteria supplementary to the intelligibility notion must be provided. He suggests two. The first has to do with the existence of a written language: if groups who differ in speech patterns share a common written form, they may be said to speak different *dialects*. The second involves political allegiances. Cantonese and Mandarin speakers, despite a lack of mutual intelligibility, are both considered to have dialects of Chinese, not only because they use the same written form but also because they are both members of the Chinese state. Norwegian and Danish speakers, although they can understand one another well, are seen to speak different languages because of different sociopolitical allegiances. A further example here is provided by Wolff (1959), who describes how the concept of intelligibility itself may be subject to social pressure. Among the Urhobo dialects of south-western Nigeria, mutual intelligibility was generally considered quite high, until speakers of Isoko began to claim that their 'language' was different from the rest, a claim coinciding with their demands for increased political autonomy. Another group, speakers of the Okpe dialect which is almost identical to Isoko, were not making such nationalistic claims and continued to perceive mutual intelligibility (see also Heine, 1979). (See Maurud,

1976, for related findings on reciprocal comprehension among Danes, Norwegians and Swedes.)

As with languages, dialects cannot be seen, linguistically, in terms of better or worse. However, while there may be relatively few people who would want to argue that French is better than English, the idea that Oxford English is better than Cockney remains of wider appeal. Dialect has long been used, of course, to denote a substandard deviation from some prestigious variety or standard form. Dictionary definitions have supported this view; e.g. the *Oxford English Dictionary* has considered a dialect as 'one of the subordinate forms or varieties of a language arising from local peculiarities'. In a sense this is correct, but it is incorrect to assume that the subordinate status of some dialects has any inherent linguistic basis (see e.g. Trudgill, 1975a). Neither should it be thought, as some have done (e.g. Wyld, 1934), that some varieties simply *sound* better than others or are more aesthetically pleasing. Studies by Giles and his colleagues have shown that listeners unfamiliar with language varieties (of French in one study, and of Greek in another), asked to judge them in terms of pleasantness, were unable to single out the more standard forms as more aesthetic (Giles *et al.*, 1974, 1979). In each case the standard dialects of these two languages were, within their own speech communities, routinely accorded higher aesthetic and prestige status. The studies demonstrate that, shorn of their usual associations (familiar to speakers *within* the communities), non-standard dialects were not perceived as less pleasant than others.

If we rule out inherent linguistic and aesthetic qualities, on what basis can dialects be judged superior or inferior? It must surely be on the basis of the social prestige and power of their speakers. I used the term *non-standard* above, and this non-pejorative label should be taken to mean that some dialects have not received the social imprimatur given to others. This is *not* to say that such varieties are *sub*standard in any substantive way. In many societies particular dialects rise to the top, as it were, with the fortunes of their speakers. The process is one of historical movement and accident. Thus, Standard English may be considered the dialect most often used by educated members of society; it is the form employed in official pronouncements, public records, writing and (often) the broadcast media. But, there is nothing of a linguistic or aesthetic nature which confers special status upon the standard. It is solely because of its widespread social acceptance that it has become *primus inter pares*. Thus, is is understandable that not all languages possess standard dialects, and in some a case can be made for several standards, each of which may hold sway in a given context or region.

We should also note that there exists more than a simple dichotomy between standard and non-standard dialect; there are often status hierarchies, e.g. Trudgill (1975a) has suggested that in Great Britain, urban non-standard forms are generally viewed as more unpleasant than rural ones. The explanation again resides in the real or perceived social characteristics of speakers. And, finally, the obvious point should be made that the language–dialect distinction is, in addition to the complexities noted above, also subject to change over time.

The Romance languages were once dialects of Latin which, under the influence of time and geography, came to achieve language status.

The fact that there is no linguistic or aesthetic basis for the superiority or inferiority of dialects – standard or non-standard – makes it easier to understand how important *any* variety can be as part of individual or group identity. Still, it is quite clear that some dialects attract negative evaluations, and can be seen as *socially* deficient; even so, they are maintained, and speakers can have pride in them. Group solidarity can be expressed through low-prestige varieties (see e.g. Ryan, 1979). As well, dialects lacking in social status often evoke *high* ratings on dimensions relating to interpersonal warmth and integrity (Edwards, 1982a). Further information in this area will be presented in chapter 6.

SUMMARY

In this opening chapter I have presented some basic ideas and brief descriptions. I have, for example, attempted to clarify ethnicity, nationalism, and the relationship between them. For each of these powerful elements of group identity, the most important ingredients are the subjective sense of groupness and the continuation of group boundaries. Indeed, these two are related; given that specific aspects of group culture are always subject to change, it seems obvious that a continuing identity must depend upon elements which transcend any purely objective markers. This is not to say, of course, that visible markers are dispensable, but rather that the presence of any particular marker is not essential. Thus, although we can say that language can be an extremely important feature of identity, we cannot endorse the view that a given language is essential for identity maintenance. We shall see, however, that many *have* considered language an essential pillar – this point of view, of course, is part of the justification for discussing the language–identity link in this book. The *perception* of identity in its relationship to certain objective markers, particularly language, and analyses of the history and future of group identity are the social and psychological elements which give the subject its compelling interest. Renan (1882/1947, p. 892) touched upon this in observing: 'l'essence d'une nation est que tous les individus aient beaucoup de choses en commun, et aussi que tous aient oublié bien des choses.' Selective historical awareness, as we shall observe later, is a potent weapon in the arsenal of group consciousness.

My introductory remarks on language and dialect were also intended to clear the ground. All varieties, prestigious or not, have the capability to carry identity. Even when language has receded to a purely symbolic role it can still have an important place. The relationship between group identity and language is always interesting and often powerful and, in the remainder of this book, I shall try to demonstrate some of the complexities of the relationship.

2
Language and Nationalism

INTRODUCTION

We have seen how the relationship between language and nationalism is often a strong one and, in the eyes of many, essential. Indeed, nationalism from its modern inception was inextricably bound up with language; language was seen as 'an outward sign of a group's peculiar identity and a significant means of ensuring its continuation' (Kedourie, 1961, p. 71). The linking of language with identity and with nation is in large part a product of the German romanticism of the late eighteenth and early nineteenth centuries and, for any student of language and identity, this period is an instructive chapter in the history of the topic.

THE RISE OF LINGUISTIC NATIONALISM

In 1772, Johann Gottfried Herder (1744–1803) published his first major philosophical work, *Ueber den Ursprung der Sprache*, which had been the prize essay at the Berlin Academy of Sciences two years earlier. Of great linguistic and philological interest, this essay also proved to be of seminal importance in the history of linguistic nationalism. Herder argued against both the divine origin of language and its origin in human invention. He stressed, rather, that man was innately endowed with the capacity for reason and speech. The diversity of languages was seen to be rooted in the variety of social environments and thus, over time, a group comes to share a common language. Further, these speech communities only survive as discrete entities as long as they preserve their language as a collective inheritance. A nation's self-respect hinges upon its ability and willingness to defend itself, but its very existence is inconceivable without its own language (see Barnard, 1965, 1969).

For present purposes, then, Herder's writings are important because he proceeds from a discussion of language origins to a philosophy of linguistic nationalism, in which ancestral language and national continuity are intertwined. The 'new humanism' which Herder reflected and sustained was an important part of the romantic reaction to the rationalism of the Enlightenment and the classical themes in art and literature. Much of this feeling in Germany was summarised in anti-French sentiment – like many subsequent nationalist movements, the German romantic variety found it easier to maintain a coherent position when there existed a reviled 'out-group'; it is also a continuing truism that it is easier to define what your group is *not* than what it is.[1] The French were culturally dominant in eighteenth-century Europe and specifically adopted a neo-classic stance.[2] The German consciousness certainly rejected the general French cultural superiority; as for neo-classicism, there was a feeling that, if it were to be at all meaningful, it should be a *German* neo-classicism. Fichte, in particular (see below), felt that a suitable comparison was between the Greeks and the Germans – the former were the torch-bearers of classical antiquity and the latter were the obvious inheritors in any post-classical Europe. Thus, the French version was considered to be 'spurious neo-classicism' (Kedourie, 1961, p. 60).

None of this anti-French sentiment is necessarily implied in Herder's famous statement: 'Has a nation anything more precious than the language of its fathers?' (cited in Berlin, 1976, p. 165). Nor is it evident in the following, from Herder's prize essay: 'What a treasure language is when kinship groups grow into tribes and nations. Even the smallest of nations...cherishes in and through its language the history, the poetry and songs about the great deeds of its forefathers. The language is its collective treasure (Barnard, 1969, p. 165).

Indeed, Berlin's study of Herder led him to conclude that the philosopher was nationalistic, but not chauvinistic or superior. Herder did not claim that 'ours is best', but simply that 'ours is ours'. He felt that 'to brag of one's country is the stupidest form of boastfulness' (p. 157) and that 'aggressive nationalism...is detestable' (p. 157). In short, Berlin feels that Herder did not fall prey to either the excesses of nationalism generally, or to Gallophobia in particular.

However, although Herder was less strident than some of his followers, he was also able to write a poem containing the lines:

> And you German alone, returning from abroad,
> Wouldst greet your mother in French?
> O spew it out, before your door
> Spew out the ugly slime of the Seine
> Speak German, O you German![3]

It seems clear enough that although Herder is often portrayed as the more or less neutral first proponent of the language-nation link, he was, like his disciples, prone to the chauvinism and anti-French feelings which represent the dark side of nationalism.

Another important character of the time was Wilhelm von Humboldt (1767–1835), anthropologist, philologist and brother of the explorer-scientist Alexander von Humboldt. Like Herder, von Humboldt believed in a strong interconnection between language and the development of 'intellectual peculiarity'; both are seen to 'emerge simultaneously and in reciprocal coincidence' (von Humboldt, 1971, p. 20). His foreshadowing of Whorfian relativism is made clear in his insistence that language is the 'spiritual exhalation' of the nation; thus, 'its language is its spirit and its spirit is its language' (Cowan, 1963, p. 277) and 'language is the formative organ of thought' (p. 287). Like both Herder and Fichte (see below), von Humboldt felt that nothing was more important for national culture and continuity than possession of the ancestral tongue.

It is Fichte, however, who is most responsible for translating Herder's ideas into a broader sociopolitical position. Johann Gottlieb Fichte (1762–1814), in his *Addresses to the German nation* (1807; also see chapter 1), praised the German language and deprecated others. This was in fact the outcome of his social theorising about language and culture which is, as Kedourie (1961) has pointed out, an interesting and ingenious extrapolation from Herder's contention that loss of language entailed loss of identity. Fichte's basic argument is quite simple. Of all the 'Teutonic' peoples (roughly, Europeans, including the French), only the Germans remained in their original location and retained and developed the original language. Fichte dismissed the first difference as unimportant. But, the language shift of others was the central pillar in his argument. He pointed out that it was not German *per se* that was superior to, say, French; rather, it was superior because it was the original, and French was inferior because it represented an adoption of foreign elements (i.e. Latin). Given that the original German was superior to the bastardised French (and other 'neo-Latin' languages), it followed that the German *nation* was superior. Again, there is more than a little Whorfianism in Fichte's claim that the important feature was not 'the previous ancestry of those who continued to speak an original language; on the contrary, the importance lies solely in the fact that this language continues to be spoken, *for men are formed by language far more than language is formed by men*' (Fichte, 1968, p. 48; my italics). He felt that the adoption of foreign elements seriously weakened a nation's speech and – as the quotation already reproduced in the first chapter shows – given enough time, essentially killed the language. As we might expect, purely linguistic evidence for this assumption is not forthcoming, and although Fichte can point to *differences* between German and other languages it is not the case that these are also deficiencies. For Fichte, however, the infiltration of Latin influence produced a 'lack of seriousness about social relations, the idea of self-abandonment, and the idea of heartless laxity' (p. 57).

Given the German notion of the superiority of the Greeks to the Romans, the sense of being the natural inheritors of the Greek legacy, and the pernicious Latin influence upon other European languages, it is understandable that Fichte felt that no valid comparisons could be made between German and neo-Latin languages: 'If the intrinsic value of the German language is to be discussed, at the very least, a language of equal rank, a language equally primitive, as, for example, Greek, must enter the lists' (p. 59).

It was quite clear to Fichte that, because of historical circumstances, German was superior to other languages and, because of the power of language itself, the German nation too was superior. Perhaps the final point in the argument is that the German who learns Latin will also acquire a grasp of the neo-Latin derivatives. He will be able, in fact, to learn Latin *better* than will others and, Fichte claims, will then understand the neo-Latin varieties more intimately than will speakers of these forms themselves!

Hence the German. . .can always be superior to the foreigner and understand him fully, even better than the foreigner understands himself. . .On the other hand, the foreigner can never understand the true German without a thorough and extremely laborious study of the German language, and there is no doubt that he will leave what is genuinely German untranslated. (p. 60)

Perhaps the only redeeming feature in all this is that Fichte and his German compatriots were not alone in extolling their own language and culture and downgrading those of others. I have already noted (see footnote 2) that French had strong sentiments attached to *it*, and not just by French persons themselves. It was the European language of culture and other varieties were viewed as unsophisticated vernaculars. There also existed the feeling that foreigners were constitutionally incapable of appreciating French, e.g. Maurras felt that no Jew could ever apprehend the beauty of Racine's line, 'dans l'orient désert quel devint mon ennui' (see Kedourie, 1961, p. 72). Shafer (1955) has noted that the French philosopher, Limoge, felt that the true spirit of the nation could only be expressed in the mother tongue, and was only accessible to French speakers.

It would be quite incorrect, then, to assume that the linguistic nationalism of the time was purely a German production. It is, however, fair to say that the German influence was the greatest and was the most systematically presented, beginning with Herder (see McEachran, 1939). Certainly it was enthusiastically received elsewhere, e.g. in Eastern Europe (Magocsi, 1982), and the ideas of the German nationalists have been important throughout the world since, wherever languages have been defended (Fishman, 1972; Vossler, 1932).

Smith (1971) summarises it as follows: 'The notion that nations are really language groups, and therefore that nationalism is a linguistic movement, derives from Herder's influence' (p. 182). It should be remembered here, of course, that we have already rejected the idea of an *essential* link between language and nationalism. In this section, I have been concerned simply to demonstrate something of the origins of this linkage, which has proved so powerful and attractive to nationalist movements ever since. Smith has made the useful point that emphasis upon language *follows* the growth of nationalistic fervour; it does not create it. Thus, for nationalists:

linguistic studies, like historical, become an often unselfconscious means of justifying their prior nationalist conviction – to themselves as well as others. . .nationalist movements, therefore, even in Europe, are not linguistic movements – any more than they are historical or ethnic or religious or territorial movements. All these attempts to 'reduce' nationalism to some kind of more readily intelligible variable end up by defeating themselves on empirical grounds – or become tautologies. (1971, pp. 149–50)

We might quibble with Smith's inclusion of 'ethnic' in the list above, but his basic point – that nationalism reflects, at root, a complex sense of groupness which defines attempts at solely objective labelling – is a reasonable one. Language *is* important, and it is the task of this book to study this importance, but possession and/or promotion of an ancestral group language is not a necessary condition of either ethnic or nationalist sentiment.

LINGUISTIC PURITY: ACADEMIES AND DICTIONARIES

Some of the ideas of linguistic nationalists reveal naive, not to say absurd, conceptions of language. Nonetheless, the power of language as a factor in nationalism is indisputable. Similarly, the notion of keeping one's language 'pure' and free from foreign taint reveals a profound misunderstanding of the dynamics of all natural languages. Yet, again, this idea has proved very attractive to some and, as it reflects strongly held views – often those of powerful agencies – its influence is not without interest and historical impact.[4] The link between linguistic nationalism and language purity and preservation is, unsurprisingly, a strong one; thus, 'protagonists of national languages tend to involve themselves with questions of linguistic purity' (Quirk, 1982, p. 59). However, if we accept that (in the modern era at least) linguistic nationalism dates from about 1800, then it is clear that the desire for language purity predates it by several hundred years. We should not be surprised at this, for the wish to purify a language and protect it from outside incursions (and, in this way, to attempt to preserve, codify and standardise an important aspect of group identity) clearly need not depend upon a more generally articulated sense of nationalism. It is perhaps possible, on the other hand, to see the work of language academies providing a useful base for nationalists to build upon; *after* the beginnings of modern nationalism, certainly, linguistic prescriptivism and national consciousness became closely entwined.

Nahir (1977) tells us that the beginning of 'institutionalised' purism came with the establishment of the Accademia della Crusca in Florence in 1582.[5] It was, however, the Académie Française (founded 1635) which set the pattern for many subsequent bodies. In the beginning, the academy addressed quite a small number of people, many of whom saw other languages as at least equal to French for cultured discourse. Its major aim was to reinforce its conceptions of clarity, simplicity and good taste, to encourage all that was 'noble, polished and reasonable' (Hall, 1974, p. 177; see also Bourhis, 1982; J. Gordon, 1978). The 40 'immortals' of the Academy were given their job initially by Richelieu 'to exert absolute power...over literature and language' (p. 180), although Hall also notes that only two men trained in philology or lexicography have ever been members. Most academicians have been drawn from the church, nobility or military. Still, these are the bodies which, historically at least, would have been considered the inheritors of the best French and the obvious arbiters of good linguistic taste. And, since the notion of language purity is a fiction anyway, there is no requirement on linguistic grounds for 'experts'. However, dictionary-making *does* require some skill, and so it comes as no surprise to learn that the academy's first effort here (1694) was 'manifestly an inferior job', as expected from 'a group of dilettantes' (Hall, 1974, p. 180). It is only surprising that so little effort was directed towards recruiting linguists, especially within more recent times, if only to produce a more defensible 'image'. One apparent concession to image seems to be the election, in 1980, of the first woman member.

In modern times, the Académie Française has become best known for its attempts to keep French free of foreign borrowings – particularly English ones – and, relatedly, to create where necessary French terms for the products and processes of science and technology. It has thus acquired a modernising function to supplement the original purifying objective. The special aim of keeping out English influence, the 'attacks on *anglomania* and the tendency to *angliciser*' (Fishman, 1971, p. 10) were, as might be expected, features beginning in the nineteenth century. This thrust has continued; recently, for example, an 'anti-Franglais' law has been promulgated (Quirk, 1982).

Dalby (1983) reports on a language-teaching exhibition held in Paris under official auspices. Only very recently has the French government shown much tolerance for linguistic variation within the francophone domain and, although a Breton group at the exhibition criticised continued French intransigence, Dalby acknowledges a general loosening-up of official attitudes. What is interesting, for present purposes, was the more subtle aim of the exhibition, namely to garner the support of 'small' languages in confronting English influence. As Dalby puts it: 'The dawn of tolerance towards other languages is not unrelated to the search for allies in the fight against world domination by English.' Dalby suggests that the French do not like to think that their language has lost international impact, and are concerned to combat English 'hegemony'. Exhibition organisers stated that 'apart from the Anglo-Saxons, we are all minorities' and a French minister of state feared that French was in danger of dying, 'having been penetrated from within'. As in older times, much energy is mis-spent fighting against English borrowings while the massive traffic the other way, the influence of French upon English, is conveniently ignored. The minister's fears are naive: even if French were dying (an unlikely prospect), it would not be because of foreign borrowings. However, the exhibition generally shows that linguistic prescriptivism and the desire to fend off powerful language neighbours are not ideas of the past alone. This type of 'sociolinguistic thunder', to use Quirk's apt term, is still very much with us.

It is also interesting to note the influence of academy-style thinking on the establishment of L'Office de la Langue Française in Quebec. This body has been particularly concerned with combatting English influence and, in some ways, this aim seems more relevant in Quebec than it does in France; after all, the Québécois are six million surrounded by a North American, English-speaking population 40 times larger. The office has produced lists of 'acceptable' terms for a variety of trades and professions heavily influenced by English terminology. However, as in all such exercises, there are sometimes rather ludicrous results. A very recent publication, for example, aims to instruct French Canadians not only in correct telephone terms but also in 'proper' telephonese (*Vocabulaire de la téléphonie*, Martin & Pelletier, 1983). At the end of a conversation, a person who has been thanked for providing information should *not* say *bienvenue*, for this 'est un anglicisme et est donc incorrect' (p. 18). Similarly, for a caller, 'il est incorrect de s'annoncer par *Monsieur*, *Madame*, *Mademoiselle*, de même que par la formule *Mon nom est*, qui est un calque de l'anglais' (p. 16).

Similar in intent to the French academy, and much influenced by it, was the Real Academia Española, founded in 1713 by the Bourbon king Philip V. Its royal motto, 'Limpia, fija y da esplendor', emphasises once more the desire to clarify, purify and glorify the language. The Spanish academy produced a dictionary in 1730 and a grammar in 1771; the latter built upon earlier work by Antonio de Nebrija, described by Milán (1983) as the first Spanish language planner, which was presented to Queen Isabella in 1492. Much of the importance of the academy consists of the way in which it spread its influence to the Spanish New World, spawning other, associated academies in Colombia (1871), Mexico and Ecuador (1875), El Salvador (1880), Venezuela (1881), Chile (1886), Peru (1887) and Guatemala (1888). Later, in the twentieth century, further bodies were established in Bolivia, Costa Rica, Cuba, Dominican Republic, Honduras, Panama, Paraguay and Puerto Rico (Guitarte & Torres-Quintero, 1974). Today, there exists a formal association of Spanish academies. Its brief is to work for the unity of Spanish and to enshrine historically based standards. It is important to realise that these are not the sentiments of language 'dilettantes' (see Hall above), but rather reflect the views of Spanish linguists. This, as Quirk (1982) points out, demonstrates an interesting difference in national aspirations between such professionals and their counterparts in the English-speaking world, where national academies have not been generally supported (see below).

Academies charged with maintaining linguistic standards do not exist only among the Romance languages. Altoma (1974) discusses the work of three Arabic academies (in Syria, Iraq and Egypt); Jordan and Ethiopia also have language bodies. A Swedish academy was founded in 1786 by Gustav III, a Hungarian academy in 1830 and we have already noted the existence of a German (Berlin) body. Nahir (1977) discusses the Committee for the Hebrew Language (1890) which became, in 1953, the Hebrew Language Academy. Anderson (1983) has described the work of the Russian academy; like the Spanish, it was modelled after the Académie Française and produced both a dictionary (1789–94) and a grammar (1802). Even in countries having no formal academy, similar prescriptive bodies exist, e.g. in Africa, where the academic task of language purification must often be preceded by one of language *selection*. Thus Kenyatta, acting as a one-man Kenyan academy, proclaimed on 4 July 1974 that henceforth Swahili would be the national language. There is now in Kenya a National Cultural Council, which may come to act as an academy with regard to Swahili and, in neighbouring Tanzania, the National Swahili Council and the affiliated Institute for Swahili Research already act in this capacity (see Eastman, 1983).

Conspicuous by its absence here is any English-language academy. Quirk (1982) has noted a longstanding Anglo-Saxon aversion to 'linguistic engineering' of any kind and, indeed, a 'superior scorn' in attitudes to academies and their purposes. Their goals are 'fundamentally alien' to English speakers' conceptions of language. Commenting on the work of the associated Spanish academies, Quirk feels that their intention to maintain the unity of the language would be unexceptionable in an English context (although not likely to be copied); however, the related aim of maintaining linguistic tradition 'would be totally unacceptable if not incomprehensible' (p. 68). It is not that there have been no proponents of an English academy spirit – Quirk cites the views and work of Verstegan in 1605, Defoe and the eighteenth-century bishop, Robert Lowth. Indeed, late in the seventeenth century, the Royal Society appointed a committee to improve English, particularly with regard to scientific terminology. Later, Swift advocated the establishment of an English academy, in a letter to the Lord Treasurer in 1712. Swift's proposal was for 'correcting, improving and ascertaining [i.e. "fixing"] the English tongue' (see Vallins, 1954, who also notes others concerned with language reform). Of all these, perhaps Lowth was the most influential. In his *Short introduction to English grammar* (1762/1967), he proposed rules based essentially on his own linguistic assumptions and eccentricities. Yet, the formal academy advocated widely in the eighteenth century did not come about.

Instead, in both Great Britain and the United States, the production of dictionaries by individuals took the place of the committee approach to officially sanctioned prescriptivism. From the middle of the seventeenth century, English lexicographers knew of the work of the French and Italian academies. Samuel Johnson, who published his dictionary in 1755 – often seen as the English equivalent of the efforts of European academies (see McDavid, 1970) – specifically acknowledged them. Johnson himself had somewhat conflicting views about the function of his work. In his *Plan of a dictionary* (1747), he supported the 'purity' function and, in the preface to the dictionary proper, he hoped that a work based upon the undefiled English of prominent authors might stabilise the language and check its degeneration. At the same time, Johnson opposed an academy, which seemed to him contrary to the 'spirit of English liberty', rejected linguistic 'embalming' and implied that academies could not, in any case, prevent linguistic change (Heath, 1977). Johnson, as intriguing a figure as the eighteenth century produced, seems to echo the Anglo-Saxon ambivalence: on the one hand, the idea of a select body imposing their will was distasteful; on the other, the need for some guidelines in an era when spelling and usage were fluid was clear.[6] Hence the one-man approach.

Indeed, this approach also characterised the production of the next great English dictionary, the one which is currently the standard – the *Oxford English Dictionary*. Work began on the 12-volume OED in 1857 and was only completed in 1928 (with a thirteenth, supplementary volume appearing in 1933). The moving force here was James Murray, and an appreciation of his immense labours, often undertaken in very unfavourable surroundings (his 'scriptorium' was an iron hut in the garden, so cold and damp that he began work in the early morning with his feet inside a box), can be found in his grand-daughter's delightful biography (Murray, 1977). By coincidence, it is, as I write these lines, exactly one hundred years ago to the day (1 February 1884) that the first volume (*A to Ant*) of Murray's dictionary appeared. Like Johnson before him, Murray knew that dictionaries could only restrain change, not halt it: 'The pen must at length comply with the tongue; illiterate writers will...rise into renown, who, not knowing the original import of words, will use them with colloquial licentiousness, confound distinction, and forget propriety.'

The lack of an English academy meant that, unlike France or Spain, England could not extend the same degree of lexicographical influence to her colonies in the new world. Part of this was no doubt due to that Anglo-Saxon reticence to prescribe officially; as well, however, the colonists themselves took English with them, they went largely out of self-interest and were not, in the main, motivated by the political or religious zeal for proselytism which animated French and Spanish settlers. Missionaries there were, of course, but they had not the close association with officialdom of their Latin counterparts. This is not to say that linguistic imperialism was lacking among English officials, however. Perhaps the classic statement here is Thomas Macaulay's 'Minute on Education' of 1835, referring to languages in India (see Cutts, 1953). Macaulay became involved in a debate over the medium of educational instruction, and was the president of a committee looking into the matter. When its papers came to him, in his other capacity as a member of the Governor-General's executive council, he wrote his famous minute. He was not against Indian vernaculars *per se* but:

The claims of our own language it is hardly necessary to recapitulate. It stands pre-eminent even among the languages of the West...It may safely be said that the literature now extant in that language is of greater value than all the literature which three hundred years ago was extant in all the languages of the world together...The question now before us is simply whether, when it is in our power to teach this language, we shall teach languages in which, by universal confession, there are no books on any subject which deserve to be compared with our own. (Sharp, 1920, p. 110; see also Durkacz, 1983; Nurullah & Naik, 1951; Quirk, 1962)

As Anderson (1983) has pointed out, Macaulay's intent was to produce 'a class of persons, Indian in blood and colour, but English in taste, in opinion, in morals and in intellect' (p. 86). The growth of Anglo-Indian culture shows that, to a great extent, this effort was successful. Macaulay's minute itself was completely endorsed by Bentinck, the Governor-General.

In other parts of the world, where English settlers did not come into contact with such highly developed society, linguistic zeal was almost non-existent. In North America, New Zealand, Australia and South Africa, indigenous peoples were not co-opted into the establishment as they were in India.

When the United States became independent in 1776, it naturally inherited the British linguistic tradition. In considering a language policy, it had no academy to consult directly and, as Heath (1977) points out, the Spanish and French models lacked appeal because of their association with 'crowned heads and royal courts'. While the American founding fathers, no doubt on the basis of the pluralistic American experience, often pointed to the advantages of multilingualism, they were nevertheless certain of the continuing dominance of English. This *de facto* status made official recognition unnecessary; an academy was not seen to be essential and English was not officially enshrined in government policy. The security of the language meant that settlements of non-English speakers were not seen as threats and, indeed, other languages were supported. For example, Benjamin Rush favoured the establishment of a German college, although his underlying rationale was an interesting one, and one which we shall meet again – he felt that it would make Germans appreciate the importance and utility of *English*, and might in fact be the only democratic way of spreading English competence among them (Heath, 1977).

There were, of course, those who favoured some type of academy, the most prominent here being John Adams. Influenced by a trip to Europe, Adams recommended an academy to the Continental Congress. Like Samuel Johnson before him, Adams felt that such a body could check the 'natural tendency' languages had to 'degenerate'. Adams also believed that, since England had no academy, there was an opportunity here for the United States to put *its* official stamp on English purity and preservation. But Adams, often suspected of monarchist sympathies, had no success in moving Congress. There were also societies whose interests included language, among them the American Philosophical Society (founded by Franklin in 1743), the American Academy of Arts and Sciences (established 1780) and a New York philological association founded in 1788. The most relevant organisation was the American Academy of Language and Belles Lettres, a body which existed only for a short time during the 1820s. Like the Académie Française, it was directly interested in standardisation and purity, and had an elitist membership lacking in linguistic expertise. The founders knew well the objections to a national language academy but proceeded in spite of them. An example of their determination and sense of rightness in the face of adversity can be seen in their statement that 'happily for us, our forefathers came chiefly from that part of England where their language was most correctly spoken' (Heath, 1977, p. 30). The members had no more success than had Adams in getting government backing, however. The Academy's publications were characterised by 'hyperbole and empty rhetoric' and demonstrated an unresolved tension between a desire to promote an American literary model and reliance upon the English of England.

In the United States, as in England, such standardisation as occurred was essentially the result of one man's work, the American Johnson being, of course, Noah Webster. Webster too felt that standardisation was important, but he had a practical view of linguistic change and thought that no dictionary could establish final norms. Webster was, above all, concerned for the linguistic independence of the United States and this culminated in his *American dictionary of the English language*, published in 1827 (see Hulbert, 1968). Earlier, in his *Dissertations on the English language* (1789), Webster had urged spelling changes; these would underline the difference between American and British English. Webster's view here (one we have seen before) was that 'a national language is a bond of national union' (Quirk, 1982, p. 65). This language belonged to the people and was their responsibility; Webster wanted Americans to stop using foreign borrowings, particularly from French. But, strangely perhaps for one concerned with a 'people's language', he also saw part of his task as the removal of 'improprieties and vulgarisms...and...those odious distinctions of provincial dialects' (Webster, 1783, p. 7). Webster further felt that Great Britain and the United States would become more and more linguistically separate, and that different languages would result in time. He was not at all opposed to this for it reinforced his nationalistic feelings, and he was no doubt glad to be able to observe that, already, the American people spoke the purest English. [7]

In modern times, prescriptivism in the English-speaking world has not been popular, particularly with linguists. While linguists in many countries have both approved and supported the goals of academies and other similar bodies, their English colleagues have not generally done so (see Ferguson, 1983). However, concern for English has not vanished. As Quirk (1982) notes, there have been many – often viewed by linguists as 'amateur do-gooding missionaries' (p. 99) – prepared to defend the language. The letters pages of newspapers are full of anguished outcries over barbarisms and bastardisations. Influential journals and newspapers carry regular columns on language (e.g. William Safire in the *New York Times*). Books appear with great frequency on the degeneration of English and how to halt it (Douglas, 1982; Kenner, 1982).

Two examples of book-length treatments of English are those of Newman (1974, 1976) – one of them entitled *Strictly speaking: Will America be the death of English?*. Among newspaper commentaries, the choice is vast. I have before me, for example, several pieces in which writers complain of murder: Honor Tracy writes about the BBC Pronunciation Unit in *The murderers of English* (*The Daily Telegraph*, 10 April 1977); Archibald Petty asks, 'Who is murdering whom?' (*The Sunday Times*, 22 January 1978) in reply to a leader of 1 January 1978 which noted that 'murdering the English language is a very popular crime all over the world'. Others are concerned with 'careless, ill-educated, smart-alec gabble' (Godfrey Talbot in *The Daily Telegraph*, 3 January 1984); with less defiled varieties ('Ireland, where the English spoken is vivid, colourful and individual and, I am assured by an erudite friend, basically Shakespearean': W. McCoubrey, *The Daily Telegraph*, 17 December 1983);

or with the usefulness of retaining 'good' accents (a report by Sally Emerson entitled 'Professor Higgins lives on', *The Sunday Times*, 3 March 1978).

Language decline has also been the subject of parliamentary debates in the English-speaking world (e.g. in November 1979 and again in January 1981 in the House of Lords). And, especially in Great Britain, the use of the broadcast media to maintain linguistic standards has been a topic since the 1930s although, as Quirk (1982) says of the BBC, this has typically been a secondary responsibility, after the obvious need to ensure comprehension (see also Bell, 1983).

Now, all of this 'amateur' interest in language protection can easily be derided. Indeed, some of it is clearly based upon prejudice and ignorance. There continues to be 'anxiety (hysteria, some would say) about literacy and linguistic standards on both sides of the Atlantic'; this is not, as we have seen, a new phenomenon by any means and earlier verions have not yet 'deprived us of a rich, sinewy, vibrant English today' (Quirk, 1982, p. 23). Some of the criticism, however, is more reasoned, particularly that which deals with deliberate or ignorant misuse of existing words, propaganda, jargon and unnecessary neologism. Here we find literary critics – not linguists, perhaps, but not rank amateurs either – adding their voices to the debate. One thinks immediately, I suppose, of Orwell (1961) but there are many other thoughtful treatments of linguistic corruption (e.g. Cottle, 1975; Johnson, 1977; Robinson, 1973; Steiner, 1967, 1972, 1978).

I only wish to note here that running through all these efforts is a concern for language, however poorly expressed or ill-conceived, behind which lies the desire to protect an important component of group identity. In their rush away from prescriptivism, linguists may have abdicated a useful role as arbiters, and have left much of the field open to those less well-informed. In an essay reviewing a book by Bolinger (1980), who is one of the few linguists willing to participate in debates about the 'public life' of language, Quirk (1982) is critical of those professionals who have not entered the fray. Bolinger rightly rejects the crank element, but also understands the public's desire for standards. There is clearly a great need for more illumination of that persistent no-man's-land between academic linguistics and public language.

LINGUE FRANCHE: NATURAL AND ARTIFICIAL

Given a strong connection between language and identity, and the nationalistic desire to sustain particular languages as unique windows on reality, the matter of *lingue franche* (pl. of *lingua franca*) is worth some brief attention.[8] It is true, of course, that the use of a 'large' language, across group boundaries, has immediate appeal on purely communicative grounds, and those for whom such a lingua franca is not the mother tongue do not inevitably desert their original variety. However, it is apparent that lingue franche may, over time, also assume that symbolic significance which is so important in the language–identity link.

This is so for naturally occurring varieties like Latin and Greek, but also for so-called 'artificial' languages like Zamenhof's *Esperanto* and Jespersen's *Novial*. Furthermore, the development of pidgins into creoles demonstrates that initially constricted forms can become 'natural' ones.

Greek and Latin have both been important lingue franche. Bodmer (1943) tells us that by the fourth century BC the Greek *Koiné* (an accepted standard) had spread over the Near and Middle East. The Romans, more ardent imperialists, ensured that Latin became widespread across North Africa, and from Iberia to the Danube. Only in Great Britain and Germany did the vernacular languages resist displacement. And, even after the emergence of the neo-Latin, Romance languages (so despised by Fichte), Latin remained important as the medium of scholarship and religion. Only with the rise of what Bodmer calls 'Protestant mercantilism' did Latin weaken. It survived longest (until about the beginning of the eighteenth century) in German universities – in 1687, Thomasius was expelled from Leipzig for lecturing in German rather than Latin. But eventually, of course, Latin did disappear as a lingua franca. After Bacon's *Novum Organum* and Newton's *Principia*, no important English philosophical or scientific work appeared in Latin. It is interesting to note that when construction of artificial languages began in earnest, towards the end of the nineteenth century (the *idea* of such languages, of course, goes back considerably further), one proposal was based upon Latin – Peano's *Latino sine flexione*.

Following the disappearance of Latin, European vernaculars came into the fore, providing new contenders for lingua franca status. French, as we have already noted, became extremely important and, by the eighteenth century, acted as a lingua franca in the West generally, and in the developing French empire. Italian was also an important lingua franca, especially in the eastern Mediterranean from the sixteenth century. Following the Islamic conquests, Arabic too became a major medium. Today, there are many who would claim that English, or American at any rate, is a lingua franca whose domain is more widespread than that of any of its predecessors.[9]

Other varieties of naturally occurring lingue franche take the form of pidgins and creoles. A pidgin language is a simplified mixture of a European and a small, indigenous language which arises through contact between conquerors/ merchants/settlers and a native population. Lexicon and grammar are restricted to a skeleton form, the minimum necessary for simple dealings. A pidgin is the native language of no-one. While such a variety has little claim upon the psychological identity of those who use it, it can become *creolised*, a creole being a pidgin which has become a native language, learned as a mother-tongue. As one would expect, creoles develop away from that simplicity and reduction which engendered them, and towards full language status. It is interesting to note that, at this point, they too may be pidginised. Thus, the national (creole) language of Sierra Leone is Krio, and it is now used, in combination with other languages, to form pidgins.

Artificial, constructed languages make up a third category of lingue franche.

It might be thought that varieties like Esperanto, Volapük, Occidental and Novial have, like pidgins, little relationship to group or individual identity. After all, their construction is motivated chiefly by a desire to provide a simple, easily learned auxiliary tool for communication. Yet it is clear that the inventors of these forms often had more in mind than this, and the production of original literature in Esperanto, for example, shows that these languages are not theoretically incapable of symbolic nuance. Steiner may point to the absence of cultural and historical background which condemns artificial languages to no 'natural semantics of remembrance' (1975, p. 470) but they could, perhaps, come to possess this quality, as do creoles for example.

Lieberman (1979), in his examination of Esperanto, is right in his general observation that sociolinguistics has neglected artificial languages.[10] There are 'facts, texts and living subjects readily available for objective study' but the area has been 'ignored or prejudged by scholars' (p. 100). There is much of interest here, indeed, not only to sociolinguists but to psychologists (e.g. to study the motivations of the language inventor and the language learners), historians (e.g. to investigate the contexts within which artificial languages are constructed, flourish and die) and others. It is true that the British psychologist Flugel wrote about Esperanto and its creator, Zamenhof, but his work is in a psychoanalytic framework and hardly qualifies as a social scientific exercise (Flugel, 1925). Forster (1982) provides a more objective account, at least with regard to sociolinguistic matters. Lieberman himself attempts some ground-clearing, and perhaps the most important point made, for present purposes, is that Zamenhof wanted Esperanto to be much more than merely a communicative tool. He disliked chauvinistic nationalism and, while respecting cultural diversity, was intent on contributing to a larger human unity. This may brand Zamenhof as a romantic but, compared to others we have seen, this is romanticism which transcends national bounds. As well, Zamenhof was quite capable of pragmatic observation: 'If the nationalism of the strong is ignoble, the nationalism of the weak is imprudent' (Lieberman, 1979, p. 96). The title of Lieberman's article, Esperanto and trans-national identity, neatly captures Zamenhof's hopes, and demonstrates that discussion of the language–identity link is not devoid of meaning just because the language involved is a construction (see also the references in Tonkin, 1977). Flugel observed that Esperanto was, for its adherents, an emotionally charged symbol, and this is surely reminiscent of nationalistic attachment to natural languages.

It is not necessary here to dwell upon the linguistic details of modern artificial languages. It should be noted, though, that the idea of artificial (or constructed) languages is not new. Jespersen (1928) reminds us of the interest of Descartes, Comenius, Leibniz and Schuchardt. The modern impulse towards constructed forms has essentially proceeded from a rejection of Latin (too difficult) and of powerful international languages like French and English (tinged with 'imperial prestige'). The major attempts have been Volapük (produced by Schleyer in 1880), Esperanto (the most successful, created by Zamenhof in 1887), Latino sine Flexione (or Interlingua, produced by Peano in 1903), Ido

(Linguo Internaciona di la Delegitaro, created by de Beaufront, 1907), Occidental (invented by de Wahl, 1922) and Novial (Jespersen, 1928). Useful descriptions of the development of these languages may be found in Jacob (1947; see also Jespersen, 1928). All of the makers of these varieties hoped to see their own construction become an international lingua franca, a universal auxiliary language, perhaps even a world language. Indeed, there have been native speakers (of Esperanto, at least). Perhaps the thinking behind artificial languages is not so much wrong as out of step with history. Haugen (1972) has noted that world political trends have, in the past, moved us from tribes to nation-states and that accompanying this has come a linguistic 'pruning and grafting', such that we now have a relatively small number of standard languages. Thus, 'when the time is ripe, we will move beyond the nation, into world government, and with it we will find our way to a world language' (p. 264). Nationalists and others, of course, would tell us not to hold our breath.

ASSESSMENTS OF NATIONALISM

Nationalism, with or without a linguistic component, is based essentially upon that same sense of groupness which informs ethnicity. Particular objective criteria are important but none is essential to the formation and continuation of nationalistic consciousness. This means that nationalism is largely a non-rational phenomenon; indeed, some have seen it as frankly irrational. Benn, for example, noted that the symbolism of 'blood and soil' nationalism removes it from the field of serious study: 'enormously important as it is for the historian and sociologist, it would be absurd to treat it as if it invited serious rational criticism' (1967, p. 445). This, however, is confusing on several counts. First, while we may admit that a topic depends more on emotion than intellect, this alone does not remove it from intellectual study. Second, if the bases of nationalism *are* taken to be largely affective, it does not follow that all elements of the nationalist 'superstructure' are. Third, Benn implies that historical and sociological analysis does not constitute rational criticism. However, Benn's point reflects a common view, that nationalism is illogical and can thus be excluded from serious academic attention. When we realise that, for some at least, the illogicality is also seen as pernicious, then it is easy to understand how nationalism has often had a very bad press indeed.

The first modern, well-argued criticism of nationalism was that of Lord Acton in 1862. He claimed that liberty and prosperity became victims of the quest for self-determination, which ultimately leads to material and moral ruin. This argument, which has clear contemporary descendants, is based upon the potential danger that nationalism, as a group phenomenon, poses for individual freedom. Many felt that, having escaped the shackles of feudalism and oppressive aristocracy, it was ironic and disappointing that men should almost immediately wish to lock themselves again within the confines of a group mentality (or that they should be led into this by others). John Stuart Mill showed, in 1861, an awareness of the powerful appeal of national self-consciousness and its bonding function (see Snyder, 1964). He advocated nationalism: 'it is, in general, a necessary condition of free institutions that the boundaries of government should coincide in the main with those of nationality' (cited in Smith, 1971, p. 9, who classes Mill as pro-nationalistic; see also Mill, 1861/1968). But earlier, in 1849, Mill had referred to the negative aspects of nationalism; he saw it as anti-social and barbarously indifferent to all those who we would now term the 'out-group' (see Quirk, 1982). We can thus add to Acton's concern, that nationalism erodes personal liberty, Mill's idea that in-group solidarity may go hand-in-hand with prejudice towards others.

A third nineteenth-century commentator on nationalism was Renan (1882/1947). Smith classes him, too, as favourably disposed towards the idea, though he acknowledges some of Renan's 'qualifications' (Smith, 1971). In fact, a close reading of Renan's famous *Qu'est-ce qu'une nation?* reveals a balanced view of nationalism which deserves some attention. Renan agreed that specific characteristics – he discusses language, religion, common interests, geography and race (clearly rejecting, incidentally, the idea of 'pure' races) – do not capture the essence of nationalism. Above all, 'une nation est une âme, un principe spirituel...la possession en commun d'un riche legs de souvenirs...le désir de vivre ensemble' (p. 903). Language is certainly not essential: 'Il y a dans l'homme quelque chose de supérieur a la langue; c'est la volonté' (p. 899). As well, mere similarity of interests does not make a nation: 'un *Zollverein* n'est pas une patrie' (p. 902). Further, as the quotation reproduced at the end of chapter 1 shows, Renan felt that that will which constitutes nationhood is based not only upon a sense of sharing, but also upon a capacity to *forget* certain things from the past.

Renan also felt that nations need not live forever – a view not generally reflected in the static conceptions of most nationalists – and predicted that a European confederation would probably eventually replace contemporary collectivities. His point was simply that nations were, for the moment, both good and necessary. From their different perspectives, an overall humanity could emerge. *This*, for Renan, was the highest aim, and the ultimate contribution of nations: 'ce grand concert de l'humanité' (p. 905). This, after all, was a condition foreshadowed by the great figures of the Renaissance, who were *world* citizens. 'Avant la culture française, la culture allemande, la culture italienne, il y a la culture humaine' (p. 900). In fact, Renan noted that if individuals possessed the characteristics of nations, they would be rather unpleasant, vainglorious, jealous, egotistical and troublesome. But, among nations, 'toutes ces dissonances de détail disparaissent dans l'ensemble' (p. 905). This again suggests a global view not typically associated with most nationalists, and it also makes clear the negative features which so often accompany 'la volonté'.

The best recent extension of these nineteenth-century cautionary notes on nationalism is found in Kedourie (1961). He clearly endorses the view of

Lord Acton in particular: nationalism substitutes one set of shackles for another. In seeking redress for past injury and injustice, more is created and 'no balance is ever struck in the grisly account of cruelty and violence' (p. 139). The modern history of Europe, according to Kedourie, has shown clearly the disastrous possibilities of nationalism; 'it has created new conflicts, exacerbated tensions, and brought catastrophe to numberless people innocent of all politics' (p. 138). It is because nationalism seeks to reinterpret history and hopes to improve present conditions for its supporters that it is inward-looking and contemptuous of things as they are. This 'ultimately becomes a rejection of life, and a love of death' (p. 87) – here, Kedourie cites the philosophy of the German romantic tradition which, indeed, can be seen as a sort of stagnant wistfulness for the unattainable.

But, it is precisely this association of nationalism with German romanticism for which Smith (1971) has criticised Kedourie. As I outlined in the first chapter, Smith believes that the true nationalist doctrine need not embrace the views of the romantics; Kedourie has thus misrepresented the case by castigating the former for the sins of the latter. We should not forget, Smith notes, the 'advantages and blessings' of nationalism, which has inspired all sorts of cultural activities, historical research, and so on.[11] Nationalism has, admittedly, possessed negative features in some instances, but it is unfair to consider only these. Besides, the claims of nationalists themselves are often over-blown and easy to condemn; thus, 'Kedourie takes the assertions of nationalists seriously, perhaps too seriously, and in doing so obscures the real message behind the florid appeals' (Smith, 1971, p. 14).

We might, however, want to ask Smith about this 'real message', and we might want some guidance about the exact degree of seriousness we should accord to nationalists' 'florid appeals'. I think, generally, that Smith's argument is not a strong one. It is of course true that there are positive aspects of nationalism, but these seem almost inevitably to accompany negative ones. While it is theoretically possible for nationalism to operate without a disdain for the claims of others, there is not much evidence for this in practice. Kedourie does not specifically reject nationalism's potential for good, and he may have overstated the negative side, but his attention to what Quirk (1982) has called 'the darker side of nationalism' (p. 70) seems, unfortunately, to be justified.[12]

Smith is not alone in his criticism of the Acton–Kedourie line. Fishman (1977b) has seen it as a road-block which plagues modern treatments of nationalism and ethnicity, which should not be seen as the 'despoiler of civility and modernity' (p. 43). Fishman essentially takes Smith's viewpoint, that nationalism and ethnicity are not inherently negative phenomena: 'It is unfortunate to confuse the exploitation of ethnicity with the phenomenon of ethnicity *per se*' (p. 43). However, a distinction between exploited and (presumably) unexploited ethnicity really does not work. The self-consciousness which characterises both nationalism and ethnicity is, if it is not to become moribund and non-existent, an essentially active and assertive ingredient. Thus, 'exploitation' (not, perhaps, the *mot juste* here) is an inevitable component of nationalism itself. [13]

Another major contemporary perspective on nationalism is the Marxist. Nationalism has been the great anomaly for Marxism, which has seen it as bourgeois romanticism and has not adequately explained its continuation. The Marxist–Leninist view is not opposed, of course, to the struggles that often animate nationalism, but such struggles are subordinate (or should be) to those waged on class lines. This means that nationalism within capitalist societies is good, because it loosens the hold of the bourgeoisie; but, within socialist states, continuing nationalism should be unncessary and, indeed, would be viewed as reactionary undermining of socialist unity. Further complicating the matter is the possibility of bourgeois nationalism, a movement which promotes national culture as yet another means of oppressing the workers. The weapon against this is proletarian *inter*nationalism, as the famous slogan in the Communist Manifesto indicates (see also Lenin, 1951).

It is true, as Smith (1971) points out, that Marx and Engels themselves did not formulate a theory of nationalism – leaving extensive attention to their followers – and that, where they did discuss the mater, they were inconsistent; however, they *were* concerned with the uses of nationalism by the working class in capitalist society. Marx rejected the idea that nations were based upon intellectual or emotional abstractions; rather, they emerged when material disparities became evident. Marxist support for German unification, for example, was based simply on the benefits it would provide for workers. A similar interest motivated considerations of the 'Irish Question' as a factor in an English revolutionary movement (Marx & Engels, 1978).

The Marxist rejection of that nationalism which is a tool of the bourgeoisie was given greater force, in an international perspective, by what Anderson (1983) has described as 'official nationalism' – a power which recalls Zamenhof's observation that the nationalism of the strong is ignoble. Anderson points out that the existing powers, faced with the emerging nationalist ethos of the last century, saw that it could become a feature of their own imperial activities; examples here are the 'Russification' programmes of the Tsars and the nationalistic anglicisation pursued by the British in India and elsewhere (see Macaulay's minute above). There is a circularity here, in that the powerful are fired by the fervour of nationalism and this, in time, produces anticolonial nationalisms in the controlled territories. Anderson notes that 'official' nationalism is really a bastardisation, by dynastic and aristocratic forces, of the original ideological thrust of the concept, in order to sustain monopolistic interests. Furthermore, the subject peoples 'nationalised' in this way were hardly allowed to become *maîtres chez eux*, and were never wholly a part of the ever-extending family. This did not only apply to the 'coloured races'. Australian family members, for example, 'did not serve in Dublin or Manchester, and not even in Ottawa or Capetown. Only "English English" did, i.e. members of a half-concealed English nation' (Anderson, 1983, p. 89).

The Marxist line also presents nationalism as anachronistic, at worst a 'survival of barbarism' (Fishman, 1977b), when it conflicts with socialist class principles. It is also possible, however, to see nationalism (and ethnicity) as anachronistic within a capitalist framework. Toynbee (1956), with characteristic bluntness, referred to the 'spirit of archaism' which underpinned the 'nationalistic craze for distinctiveness and cultural self-sufficiency' (p. 508). Many of his specific comments here had to do with the desire to revive 'dead' languages, but Toynbee was more generally concerned with the backward-looking feature of nationalism which produced this desire. This feature is seen not only as naively romantic, but also as one retarding progress, in its treatment of everything modern as crass. An interesting modern example of this is found in the Irish revival movement of the late nineteenth and early twentieth centuries. This was led, in large part, by Douglas Hyde who, in 1892, gave a now-famous address on the necessity of de-anglicising Ireland – often considered to be the direct spur to the establishment of the major Irish revival organisation, the Gaelic League (see Hyde, 1894). It is now clear that Hyde simply equated anglicisation with modernisation (see Kiberd, 1980; Lee, 1973), and this had the perverse effect of transforming the revival movement from a dynamic to a static entity. Brown (1981) thus suggests that the revival became (if it was not always, latently at least) a conservative force. Kedourie's observations (above) would suggest, further, that stasis or conservatism is commonplace in nationalist movements generally. O'Faolain (1951) makes a similar point, specifically referring to Ireland: 'This is the central evil of nationalism: that, sooner or later, it ossifies the mind' (p. 48); and, further in the same essay, he observes that 'the ultimate evil of nationalism (and most other *isms*) is this threat to the creative individual by the tyranny arising from the idolisation of an abstraction' (p. 53).

The threat to progress posed by nationalism has recently been discussed by Patterson (1977); his title, *Ethnic chauvinism: The reactionary impulse*, reflects well the basic theme. It is true, as Connor (1978) has pointed out, that Patterson's work is 'more exhortatory than academic' (p. 356) and is thus similar in tone to that of the ethnic romantics which he dismisses. Still, Patterson does make some useful points. He notes, for example, the distressing lack of historical perspective in most treatments of ethnicity and nationalism; he reminds us that ethnicity is essentially an ideology, a faith; he draws attention to the negative and distasteful aspects of nationalistic fervour. Patterson is particularly exercised over the 'ethnic revival' in the United States (see chapter 4) for in the New World setting there were perhaps the best prospects for the development of universalist ideas. Patterson discusses some of the reasons for the revival; these include the example given to White 'ethnics' by the Black civil rights movement, and the 'romantic discontent' of older intellectuals allied with the affluent but disaffected young. He recognises these forces, of course, but is angry about the way the sentiment has been expressed in the literature. Here, Patterson claims, there are two main varieties. On the one hand there is a body of work that is frankly pro-ethnic, romantic and anti-modern. An example here is the writing of Novak (1971), who is considered by Patterson to mount a sophisticated attack on modernity. Other, lesser works within this framework are seen as nothing more than 'vulgar, chauvinistic polemics' (p. 152). On the other hand, there are more insidious supporters of ethnicity who cloak their bias in the guise of social scientific objectivity; here, Greeley (1974) is seen as typical. Ultimately, Patterson acknowledges that the rejection of modernity which seems to be an important part of the 'reactionary impulse' is a possible option. But he notes that, in practice, most people (and most ethnics) want the solace of the past *without* sacrificing the rewards of progress. This is unworkable, Patterson claims, because those participating in industrialised, technological society have simply altered too much; they cannot go home again, even if this were a worthy objective (see chapter 4). Patterson reserves his greatest scorn here for those irresponsible leaders and writers who fan the flame of ethnicity, creating confusion and discontent. There is little doubt that Patterson overstates his case, imputing evil motives to ethnic leaders. This is not only unlikely, it is simply an unnecessary burden on the argument (see Edwards, 1981a, 1982b). However, we shall encounter some of Patterson's basic concerns again.

More dispassionate criticism of ethnicity, on the grounds that it is regressive and promotes particularism, can be found in the work of Porter (1972/1980, 1975; see also Vallee, 1981). He is concerned that claims made in respect of *groups* can lead to mistreatment of individuals. Thus, 'it seems to me that making descent groups of such importance because they are the carriers of culture borders on racism with all the confused and emotional reactions that that term brings' (1972/1980, p. 330). Now that ethnicity has become a 'good thing' the standard liberal position has become seen (and condemned) as assimilationist. According to Greeley (a prominent spokesman for the 'new ethnicity' in the United States; see above) and other apologists for pluralism, this liberalism is now considered to be flawed by an overly rational and secular element which ignores the continuingly powerful attachments of ethnicity. Porter, on reflection, states:

Considering as alternatives the ethnic stratification that results from ethnic diversity and the greater possibilities for equality that result from the reduction of ethnicity as a salient feature of modern society, I have chosen an assimilationist position, and between the atavistic responses that can arise from descent group identification and the more liberal view that descent group membership is irrelevant to human interaction, I have chosen the latter. (1972/1980, p. 335)

In a second treatment of the theme, Porter (1975) pays attention to the rhetoric of ethnicity in the wake of the Canadian multicultural policy (see chapter 4). But, he notes that 'it is my intention to raise some serious doubts about this revival of ethnicity, not only for Canada, but for other advanced societies and perhaps developing ones as well' (p. 288). Porter begins by restating his fear that ethnicity is regressive, promotes and sustains ethnic stratification, is historically naive, and ultimately acts against the best interests of individuals. Again, his viewpoint is worth stating at some length: 'Along with the arguments supportive of the revival of ethnicity can be found also the view that cultures have a right to live and individuals and societies have an obligation to see that they survive, although surely history is as much the graveyard of cultures as it is of aristocracies' (p. 299).

Porter seems to refer here to processes of historical inevitability which pluralists may be unaware of or, more likely perhaps, choose to ignore. He is critical of the extreme relativism which affects and animates pluralists, which may lead them into difficulties. 'Not all cultures have equal claims on our moral support' (p. 300) because some may include values and practices that are generally unacceptable. This is a delicate position, of course, but Porter claims we have a right to judge cultures, not from the standpoint that ours is perfect, but because social evolution has shown some aspects of human life to be more 'morally supportable' than others (see also Musgrove, 1982; and chapter 4). Porter further claims that the call for sustained ethnicity derives largely from the fear of desertion by ordinary group members; here, he touches upon interesting possibilities of quite different viewpoints among ethnic leaders, or nationalists, and their 'followers' (see chapter 6). Finally, Porter condemns ethnicity because it emphasises 'cultures of the past' which are less and less relevant for modern life. This emphasis is static or regressive, and desires for a return to ethnic roots fly in the face of historical evolution.

The idea that ethnicity is a backward-looking view, that nationalism is ultimately a withdrawal from reality, has been attacked, e.g. Smith (1971) states that, far from being atavistic, 'nationalism is a vision of the future' (p. 22) and is 'both traditionalist and modernist' (p. 256). How can this be? Nationalism looks back, true, but only to gather the necessary material to reconstitute identity. 'Nationalism may be described as the myth of the historical renovation' in the process of which 'a pristine state of true collective individuality' (p. 22) is rediscovered, nurtured and used to forge an identity needed for the present and future. Fishman (1972) puts the matter similarly: 'Nationalism is not so much backward-oriented...as much as it seeks to derive unifying and energizing power from widely held images of the past in order to overcome a quite modern kind of fragmentation and loss of identity' (p. 9).

It seems to me, however, that these views only reinforce the criticisms of those who see in nationalism a regressive phenomenon. For one thing, surely the drive to the past – which often needs reinterpreting to serve well – reveals an inability to come to grips with present realities and, more specifically, the social evolution which connects past to present. Relatedly, there is no reason to suppose that elements of the past can be usefully pulled to the present, bypassing, erasing or reconstituting evolutionary processes, to serve as replacements for the products of those forces. The fact that nationalism can be produced by fears of present 'fragmentation' in the face of modern pressures and by yearnings for some more 'pristine' collectivity, indicates that it is a sincerely felt response to human insecurities. But surely both current considerations and historical precedent would suggest that it is a force which attempts to counter the inevitable.

A more sinister interpretation is that nationalism seeking to repair or forestall social fragmentation is also an exercise in power, that the formal consolidation of groupness in this way leads inevitably to a striving *over* others. This process is abetted by historical manipulation and selectiveness, indifference to reality, and a strong inclination to racist propaganda. The nationalist, in Orwell's view, believes that his group is the strongest and most deserving and 'is able to stick to his belief even when the facts are overwhelmingly against him. Nationalism is power-hunger tempered by self-deception' (1961, p. 283). Nationalist thought is characterised by obsession (e.g. with language), instability and the belief that the past can be altered. Of course, Orwell was prompted to write by the existence of some of the most distasteful modern manifestations of nationalism, but his claim would be that his argument applies in principle to all nationalisms. For example, he detected strong tinges of racism in Celtic nationalism (see also Mac Lochlainn, 1976, 1977): 'The Celt is supposed to be spiritually superior to the Saxon – simple, more creative, less vulgar, less snobbish, etc. – but the usual power-hunger is there under the surface' (Orwell, 1961, p. 294). Now, Orwell can hardly be considered an academic scholar of nationalism, and Edwards (1968) has called his writings here 'brilliantly wrong-headed', particularly where he attempts a distinction between patriotism and nationalism. Orwell thought that the former was good, representing a devoted, defensive stance, while the latter was characterised as offensive, power-hungry and bad. It goes without saying that Orwell considered himself a patriot, not a nationalist. Still, Orwell's powers of social comment cannot be easily dismissed, and Edwards himself is not without admiration for his overall treatment of the topic.

What conclusions can we draw from all the material presented in this section, especially if we agree that the essence of nationalism itself is intangible? Furthermore, some might agree with Orwell that 'all nationalist controversy is at the debating-society level. It is always entirely inconclusive' (p. 293). To begin with, it will be apparent from the shape of my argument so far, and from the writers whose views I have stressed, that I believe there is strong evidence for the negative impact of nationalism. Nationalist identity shares with other varieties of groupness the following potential perils: a promotion and maintenance of 'us-and-them' boundaries, a de-emphasis of *individual* rights and interests, and a hardening of group interest into perceived superiority and racism. Nationalist identity also comprises romanticised yearnings for a past which, suitably interpreted and restructured, is seen as a bulwark against present inequalities or indignities. It can change quickly from a radical ideology to a reactionary one. It can be static or regressive in the face of unpalatable aspects of modernity.

On the other hand there is no doubt that – partly *because* of some of these features – nationalism has proved a powerful force in the world, and has endured well beyond the lifespan that many would have predicted. It is indisputably produced important cultural manifestations. It has been a positive force, particularly in the lives of those who have felt threatened by larger or more influential neighbours.

While it is possible to reject nationalism as a force in which bad outweighs good, this is neither completely accurate nor, more importantly, does it deal best with a continuingly powerful phenomenon. Social scientists have much interesting work to do in studying the dimensions and degrees of attachments people have for ethnic and national groups. It will be useful to recall here that psychology has already made clear that individuals' group memberships can be many and overlapping, and that not all of one's behavioural repertoire need reflect a particular membership. It should also be remembered that the features of nationalism noted above (particularly, perhaps, the negative ones) may remain latent for most group members most of the time. A simple affirmation of one's ethnic identity need go no further than providing a personal point of reference. Translation into action is what may create problems, and this translation may, for many group members, never occur. There is, for example, often a considerable gulf between the views and behaviour of ordinary group members and those of their 'spokesmen' (see chapter 6). Perhaps, in this sense, Fishman's notion of 'exploited' ethnicity has some force (see above).

National and ethnic identity may be anachronistic and it may lead to difficulties for group members and others, but it *is*. Perhaps, as Porter and others feel, our ethnicity should be jettisoned and we should become state citizens only. But it is a phenomenon of continuing interest – especially among minority groups in perceived danger – that ethnicity remains salient, or that some consider that attempting to make it salient is a worthwhile exercise. Recall here, too, that ethnic identity does not inevitably mean minority identity; we are all 'ethnics'. Nationalism, Seton-Watson (1982) tells us, is intrinsically neither good nor bad, and national identity is at least 'passively treasured by nearly all citizens of modern societies, even if they do not know it' (p. 13). Its appeal, which continues to exist precisely because of its ability to remain latent and because it need not be tied to any given objective marker, may be a negative force when roused. But, things last for reasons.

I want to end here, however, on a cautionary note which I shall return to later. Positive assessments of nationalism are sometimes made by those who cloak advocacy in social scientific jargon. We must continue, of course, to pay attention to group concerns wherever they are expressed, and here we are right to be especially alert to *minority*-group matters. But, as O'Brien (1973) notes: 'We ought not, after all, to idealize minorities, or to forget that today's under-dog may be tomorrow's power-crazed bully' (p. 50). Group spokesmen may be atypical and individual rights may lose ground to demands for group power. O'Brien sees an emphasis on *group* identity and rights to be understandable but often regrettable. His solution is to stress *human* rights. Obvious rationales for this approach can be found when, in supporting group positions, we discover ourselves supporting a complete social framework, many of the elements of which are reprehensible, e.g. O'Brien mentions Hindu castes, the Islamic treatment of women, female circumcision, etc. Support for group rights may thus constitute a continued *denial* of rights to certain group members.

Of course, some would argue that we have no right to judge other cultures at all and that cultural relativism is the *sine qua non* of objective research. However, there are some aspects of some cultures that we would be hard pressed to support. We might also argue that human social evolution has shown some features to be much less defensible than others. Cultural relativism is a moral stance which is now enshrined in much of social science. As an antidote to ethnocentrism and arrogance it has had a useful influence – particularly, perhaps, in linguistic matters. But, there are difficulties with cultural relativism and the concept is currently undergoing reconsideration (see chapter 4).

SUMMARY

It is clear that, whatever one may feel about ethnicity and nationalism and whatever criticisms may be made of them, they remain vital forces in group identity. Seton-Watson (1982) reminds us that we are *all* members of national collectivities, even though 'dominant groups rarely define themselves as ethnics' (Royce, 1982, p. 3). We deal here, then, with a universal feature of human life, which is emphasised more in some contexts than in others. Minority-group members, whose identity appears at risk, are thus much more likely to stress their groupness than are majority-group members, many of whom will find nationalism and its agitations foreign and distasteful. Still, majority-group status need not be permanent, and those once secure may undergo a revitalised nationalism if they lose it (e.g. immigrants to the United States, dominated indigenous groups in Europe).

Nationalism, for all its essential irrationality – and probably because of it – remains potent. Viewed distastefully by liberals, it has shown a continuing power to recruit intellectual support. Scorned by Marxists as outdated sentimentality, nationalism has forced from them a grudging admiration. Both liberalism and Marxism are 'rationalist creeds' which, naturally enough, have difficulty coming to terms with 'what can only count as irrational attachments' (Ryan, 1984). But Ryan also notes that Gellner (1983), in a recent discussion of nationalism, has been concerned 'to get liberals to stop being affronted' by what they perceive as the 'moral and intellectual scandal' of the phenomenon. This, then, is the point from which we can move on – nationalism, for better or for worse, is a force that simply must be reckoned with.

3

Language Maintenance and Language Shift

INTRODUCTION

So far in the argument I have noted that ethnic or national identity is a powerful, sometimes non-rational group attachment, that language is often considered to be its central pillar, and that official and semi-official agencies and institutions have historically supported group language purity. I have also tried to point out that, although all aspects of the language–identity link become particularly conspicuous when minority groups are involved, this does not mean that the link itself does not apply to majority, dominant groups too. It is simply the case that matters of language and identity become most visible when social obstacles appear. Consequently, it is with group contact that linguistic identity issues become most pressing.

Drake (1984) has observed, in connection with language maintenance and shift in the United States, that 'the best predictor of future social behaviour is past social behaviour, all other things being equal' (p. 146). He was particularly critical of the assumption that bilingual education programmes were significantly altering long-standing patterns of immigrant assimilation, but his note has broader relevance (see also Fishman, 1966, 1980c). Assessments of any linguistic scene will profit, to say the least, from historical awareness, and analyses of what people *have* done are likely to be useful not only in determining what they will probably continue to do, but also in ascertaining what their desires and needs are in linguistic (and other) matters. Naturally, 'all other things' are *not* always equal, but this itself hardly argues against due attention being given to historical trends. If we wish to understand the dynamics of the language–identity link as it exists in the lives of ordinary speakers (as opposed to the moral–imperative links proposed by linguistic nationalists and group 'spokesmen', interesting though these are in their own right), we must consider the real-life record. Two modern examples of the usefulness of this approach, which I shall be looking at in some detail, are Ireland (and the course of Irish) and the United States (with its patterns of immigrant adaptation). Each has important lessons for the student of language and identity, and I

48   *Language Maintenance and Language Shift*

have already drawn attention to the value of the historical record in each (Edwards, 1982a, 1983e, 1984b; Giles & Edwards, 1983).

True lessons here depend, of course, upon at least some degree of group volition. If alteration of language patterns occurs only at gunpoint, useful generalisations will obviously be fewer than if language shift was voluntary. The interesting point here is that, in conditions of linguistic coercion, there still usually exist elements of group volition; and, in cases in which it seems that groups have shifted voluntarily, there are often elements of coercion. The useful questions, therefore, are those which focus upon *types* and *implications* of volition and coercion in language maintenance and shift. What explains the very rapid shift from Irish to English in Ireland? Why did Norman French not continue to dominate English in England? Why have minority languages in the United States 'shrivelled in the air of freedom' while stubbornly holding on in more severe contexts elsewhere?[1] In all these situations of linguistic mobility we see at least some elements of volition and, therefore, some illumination of the language–identity link.

LANGUAGE SHIFT, DECLINE AND DEATH: GENERAL NOTES

I have already made the point that group identity is not indissolubly linked to any given marker, including language. Rather, since identity essentially rests upon the continuation of boundaries which, in turn, depend upon a maintained sense of groupness, the erosion of an original language – at least in its ordinary, communicative aspects – does not inevitably mean the erosion of identity itself. Italian-Americans may still feel themselves different from others in the larger society, even though Italian may be only a symbolic cultural entity, or an 'associated' language (Eastman, 1984; see chapter 1). Two points of interest remain, however. First, communicative language shift entails obvious *changes* in the cultural content of group identity. Second – and perhaps more relevant and important – the widely held assumption of the centrality of language for identity means that further probing is required, i.e. while disinterested analysis may suggest that a particular language is *not* vital for identity continuation, we should not be deluded into thinking that such analysis ends the matter.[2] With regard to our general topic, there can be few areas that have the emotional poignancy of language decline and death.

How do languages die? One view, once popular, held that they were organic and that they had, therefore, a 'natural' lifespan. An early expression of this idea is found is Thomas Jones' *The British language in its lustre* (1688): 'To Languages as well as Dominions. . .there is an appointed time; they have had their infancy, foundations and beginning, their growth and increase in purity and perfection; as also in spreading, and propagation: their state of consistency; and their old age, declinings and decays' (cited in Morgan, 1983, pp. 44–5). Further, Jespersen (1922, p. 65) cites the views of the great linguist, Franz Bopp (1791–1867): 'Languages are to be considered organic natural bodies, which are formed according to fixed laws, develop as possessing an inner principle of life, and gradually die out because they do not understand themselves any longer!' This, notes Jespersen (whose exclamation mark it is, by the way) is highly figurative language, not to be taken at face value. Aitchison (1981) – who also reproduces the Bopp quotation, although omitting Jespersen's mark of incredulity – tells us that, nowadays, it is no longer believed that 'languages behave like beans or chrysanthemums, living out their allotted life, and fading away in due course' (p. 208). Yet it is easy to see why the organic metaphor has appealed. Languages themselves obviously obey no organic imperatives, but their speakers do. Languages do not live or die at all. Languages do not possess 'an inner principle of life', nor do they have intrinsic qualities which bear upon any sort of linguistic survival of the fittest. Yet they clearly *do* have an 'allotted life' which is granted, not by the laws of nature, but by human society and culture. The fortunes of language are bound up with those of its users, and if languages decline or 'die' it is simply because the circumstances of their speakers have altered. The most common scenario here is that involving language contact and conflict: one language supplants another.

In a very recent article, Kloss (1984) notes three main types of language death: (a) language death *without* language shift (i.e. the speech community dies out); (b) language death because of language shift (the speech community does not exist within a 'compact speech area', or the language succumbs to 'the intrinsic hostility of the technology-based infrastructure of modern civilization' [p. 65]); and (c) *nominal* language death through a metamorphosis (e.g. a language is downgraded to dialect status when the speech community stops writing it and begins to use another, closely related variety or the language undergoes 'partition' – Kloss gives the example of 'Upper Sorbian' and 'Lower Sorbian' ousting the more general Sorbian).

It is clear that Kloss' first and third categories are less interesting, in connection with group identity at least, than his second. If an entire community dies out while speaking its original language, then the language–identity link has remained undisturbed to the end. Similarly, Kloss' notion of 'nominal' death need not involve any direct interruption of the linkage, although it is possible that this sort of decline may, in time, lead to a more complete process of language shift.

It is language death as a result of language shift which is the most relevant here. Dispersal of speakers and/or the lack of a linguistic heartland are features almost always addressed by those concerned to stem decline or to revive moribund varieties. The shrinking *Gaeltacht* (Irish-speaking area) in Ireland is a good case in point here. Language revivalists have recognised for a long time that the vitality of the region where the remaining Irish native speakers live is of the greatest importance for overall language maintenance. However, history shows that little was actually *done* to preserve and sustain the Gaeltacht (see also below) and, in any event, the treatment of shrinking minority-language heartlands is problematical. If nothing is done, they continue to contract under pressure from strong outside influence; if things *are* done, e.g. if special economic aid is provided, then there is the danger of creating enclaves which are seen to be artificial, precisely because they have been specially relieved of certain pressures, by insiders and outsiders alike. Even assuming, however, that a viable heartland exists, there are further difficulties. A strong Gaeltacht would still be a rural concentration within a society in which urban, industrial forces predominate. Greene (1981) notes the great problems of languages confronted by modern, urbanised societies. Irish simply does not possess a concentrated, urban speech community; nor, indeed, do any of the other Celtic languages (see also Betts, 1976). We could add, further, that the possession of an *urbanised* heartland need not itself be a sign that all is well for a minority language. Williams (1984) discusses the Basque heartland, parts of which are industrially strong but weakened by the *in*-migration of Spanish speakers seeking employment.

What of Kloss' observation about language death caused by 'the intrinsic hostility of the technology-based infrastructure of modern civilization'? This inelegant phrasing does not really capture the issue. Why is there 'hostility', and why is it 'intrinsic'? We have already noted that many linguistic nationalists fear modernisation. Part of this apprehension stems from the association between the forces of modernity and dominant languages; but, it is also interesting to consider that a dislike of modern, technologically sophisticated life may itself be a spur to some sort of return to 'roots' in which an original group language may figure almost incidentally. The 'intrinsic hostility' of technological society is based simply upon the economic power and dominance possessed by speakers of that society's language. In fact, while there is often hostility on the part of the threatened speech community, there is often very *little* on the part of the dominant group – dominance and affluence lead more often to ignorance and neglect than to outright hostility. Power breeds its own myopia. Furthermore, we cannot even use the word 'hostility', when looking at the minority group, without some qualification. Language contact leading to language shift often involves hostility, to be sure, but there are interesting admixtures of admiration, envy and pragmatism. The shift from Irish to English in the last century, for example, can only fully be explained with reference to active desires to shift (see below). Language shift often reflects pragmatic desires for social mobility and an improved standard of living, and these are ignored by revivalists at their peril. 'In many cases we observe that language activists find themselves in pretty much the same situation as the earnest ecologist who asks the people of some area of natural beauty not to permit development there, and is met with the reply: "You can't eat the view"' (Greene, 1981, p. 5).

There is no doubt, overall, that the most obvious and usual cause of language decline and death is an inadequate concentration of speakers faced with economically powerful and technically sophisticated neighbours. The most familiar process by which death occurs is lack of transmission of an original language from parents to children. This was clearly the case in Ireland a century and more ago; thus, de Fréine (1977, 1978) speaks of a self-generated collective movement to abandon Irish. Today, *within the Gaeltacht itself*, most parents have decided to bring up their children in English (Fennell, 1981). Denison (1977) documents a similar case concerning German and Friulian in the face of Italian in Sauris, a small, northern Italian village. Harris (in Saville-Troike, 1982; see also Harris, 1982) has described the fortunes of Yiddish and Ladino (Judaeo-Spanish) *vis-à-vis* Hebrew. Yiddish traditionally served as a lingua franca for Ashkenazic Jews; Ladino did so for Sephardic. But when the status of Hebrew was heightened through becoming the language of Israel, Yiddish and Ladino became somewhat redundant. More than 75 per cent of Harris' Ladino subjects in New York and Israel were unable to give valid reasons for passing on the language; not one grandchild could speak the language. It is interesting to note here that the Ladino speakers themselves continued to have a strong attachment to the language; this seems a general phenomenon in contexts in which languages are no longer transmitted, i.e. the reasons behind non-transmission are not related to some personal repudiation of the language but rather to pragmatic assessments of the likely utility of competing varieties. Trudgill (1983) provides another example, that of Albanians in Greece. Arvanitika (an Albanian dialect) is a dying speech, current attitudes to it are unfavourable, and it is not being taught to children. Yet, most of Trudgill's respondents (97 per cent) felt pride in their Arvanite traditions (while also feeling themselves Greek). It is quite possible, then, for favourable cultural attitudes to coincide with language shift based upon practical considerations. This is further exemplified in the attitudes of immigrant group members in the United States; Fishman (1964) reports that as original varieties become more and more restricted in use, attitudes towards them actually become more favourable. Finally, to return to the Irish scene, the Committee on Irish Language Attitudes Research (1975) found that strong sentimental attachments to Irish were not accompanied by language *use*, nor by desire to actively promote it, nor yet by optimism concerning its future, among the population at large.[3]

Languages may die: are they murdered, or do they commit suicide? Writers have discussed linguistic demise in these very emotional terms and, as one would expect, varying conclusions have been reached, e.g. many have felt that Irish was murdered by English (see Pearse 1912/1976). Corkery (1968) held generally that languages do not die 'natural deaths' but are killed by those wishing to destroy the nation. This view has been endorsed more recently by Khleif (1978, 1980) in his studies of Welsh. Others have held, if not the suicide view, a perspective somewhat more complex than the linguistic murder approach. Binchy (1945) felt that a 'persecution' theory was unable to explain the dramatic decline of Irish. Brooks (1907) thought the English culpable, but also noted that 'it is impossible to stamp out a language which the people are determined to keep alive' (p. 22). Thus, Irish *did* commit suicide. This is also the view of the Irish writer Flann O'Brien (Myles na gCopaleen) who – unmistakably pro-Irish himself – resented and rejected the revivalist cause and its rhetoric of linguistic oppression: 'The present extremity of the Irish language is due mainly to the fact that the Gaels deliberately flung that instrument of beauty and precision from them' (noted by Ó Conaire, 1973, p. 125; see also Kiberd, 1981). O'Rahilly (1932/1972), the Irish dialectologist and phonetician, took a similarly harsh view of linguistic demise generally: 'When a language surrenders itself to foreign idiom, and when all its speakers become bilingual, the penalty is death' (p. 121).

The whole issue of 'murder or suicide' is muddied, of course, by ideological leanings, i.e. those supporting the encouragement, restoration or revival of a threatened language are likely to hold the murder view; this can have the effect of simplifying things into an 'us-and-them' format in which oppressors and oppressed are easily separable and in which, furthermore, the presence of a 'victim' makes quite clear which side has the moral advantage. On the other hand, the suicide perspective seems to be more espoused by those attempting a disinterested assessment of linguistic decline.

The factors in the decline of languages are many and varied, and I shall be turning to them in some detail below. 'No single cause' explains language loss according to Gregor (1980); a 'chain of events' is involved (Denison, 1977); the 'search for a single cause which inevitably leads to language death is futile' (Dorian, 1979, p. 69). Aitchison (1981) suggests that *both* murder and suicide occur – murder when dissimilar languages are in contact and where a high-prestige variety extends across domains, and suicide when *similar* languages come into contact but where, again, one possesses higher status; the suicide here involves the ever-increasing borrowing from the prestigious form. However, it seems that both forms of decline ultimately involve suicide, in the sense that, at some point, a new variety is adopted. This is the view of Denison (1977) who notes that the *direct* cause of language death is lack of transmission to children. This occurs because a community 'sometimes "decides", for reasons of functional economy, to suppress a part of itself' (p. 21).

It is possible, however, that a community does not see the process as one of self-suppression, but rather of simple alteration. In this way, we might resolve the murder–suicide matter (if these terms must be used at all) by considering the social pressures under which suicide occurs. In personal suicide, stress is involved; people do not kill themselves on a whim. Usually, the pressures are varied, although there sometimes exists a 'significant other' who in some sense has caused the suicide. In linguistic suicide, on the other hand, there is *always* a significant other (language) which creates the pressures leading to language shift and decline; there is always a murderer. But, just as a person may cause another's suicide without being a murderer in law, so a language can bring about another's demise without directly and actively planning to do so. Very rarely, in fact, is linguistic demise so carefully planned that we can invoke the label of murder. Equally, however, we should realise that linguistic suicide is – unlike its personal counterpart – virtually always associated with an easily identifiable competing form. Discussions of language decline and death would do well to avoid terms like 'murder' and 'suicide' altogether, and to emphasise the complexities of social situations in which these phenomena occur.

THE IRISH LANGUAGE

As a case study, Irish has much to recommend it.[4] The language has a long history, in which many of the chapters have already been written. Once a widespread vernacular capable of assimilating other varieties, Irish is now a more confined speech. The decline of the language, and the nineteenth-century revival movement, illustrate the fascinating interweaving of language with other important facets of social life, including education, politics and religion. The relationship of Irish to nationalism, its influence upon the literary revival and its associations with prominent historical personalities all illuminate the language–identity link.

History

Until the Norman invasions in the twelfth century, Irish was secure. Indeed, it had been so for several centuries, displacing earlier varieties and establishing itself as a literary medium. In the so-called 'Golden Age' of the sixth to ninth centuries, Ireland was the only Western European country whose vernacular was seen to be suitable for education and literature. By the eighth century, Irish had largely replaced Latin as a religious medium and was cultivated by the monastic orders. Before the coming of the Normans, most other Celtic colonists, Picts, Anglo-Saxons, Norse and Danish were Gaelicised (Adams, 1970; Cahill, 1935a, 1935b). With the advent of French and English speakers, however, the process of change began, although it was not a rapid one. Only in the towns within the Pale (the eastern coastal area, including Dublin) did French and English really establish themselves, and the Pale itself tended to shrink. There was considerable Gaelicising of these new inhabitants, too, who became *Hibernis ipsis Hiberniores*. In 1366 the Statutes of Kilkenny were passed to try to keep English settlers from adopting Irish ways; the legislation reflects the apprehension over the power of Gaelicisation. The 36 statutes (written, incidentally, in Norman French – a telling indication of linguistic realities) were not effective. By 1600, English existed only within a diminished Pale and in one or two rural enclaves.

When the house of Plantagenet gave way to that of Tudor, however, the fortunes of Irish really began to change. Henry VIII issued many proclamations discouraging Irish, e.g. in 1536 a note to the people of Galway included the following: 'Every inhabitaunt within the saide towne indevor theym selfe to speke Englyshe, and to use theym selffe after the Englyshe facion; and specyally that you, and every of you, do put forth your child to scole, to lerne to speke Englyshe' (Corcoran, 1916, p. 41; see also Corcoran, 1928). More important were the plantation schemes intended to replace Irish with English settlers. These began in the mid-sixteenth century, and reached their zenith under Cromwell. Elizabeth encouraged the use of Irish for proselytism (a theme to be revived in the nineteenth century), providing type and press for an Irish Bible. She was also the force behind the establishment of Trinity College, Dublin (1591), founded for the same religious reason. There is no doubt that measures like these, involving Irish, were intended to (among other things) expedite its demise; we shall see their like again. O'Neill and his Spanish allies were defeated by Lord Mountjoy at Kinsale in 1601, and this was followed in 1607 by the 'flight of the Earls' – the exile of many Irish chiefs. After and because of this came the acts of plantation in Ulster which have had such long-standing consequences (see Beckett, 1981). All of this amounted to the passing of the Gaelic order and although Irish was still the majority language at the end of the Tudor period, its future was now in doubt.

English began making steady advances; between 1600 and 1800, it became the language of regular use for about half the population – the more powerful half. Irish speakers were, more and more, the poor, and their language received no official recognition. In the early nineteenth century, other problems beset Irish. Wall (1969, p. 81) notes that 'every school child in Ireland will tell you that Daniel O'Connell, the Catholic clergy and the National Schools together killed the Irish language.' While oversimplification, it is true that each element here *was* important. O'Connell spoke Irish but, in his own famous phrase, was 'sufficiently utilitarian not to regret its gradual abandonment'. The Catholic Church had turned to English, particularly since the British founding of Maynooth College in 1795, and since Irish continued to be used by Protestant proselytising societies. The general view seemed to be that it was better to save souls than Irish and, as priests were often managers of primary schools, the language was often actively discouraged there (O'Donnell, 1903). The National School system itself, established in 1831, excluded Irish; it was called the 'murder machine' by Pearse. Also, the Famine occurred within the first half of the nineteenth century. Its ravages and the emigration which it prompted had their greatest effect in rural, Irish-speaking areas.

All of this favoured English. By the mid-nineteenth century, the number of Irish monolinguals was already very small and, in the context, bilingualism was usually a way-station on the road to English only. However, those factors noted above – singly or in combination – are insufficient to explain the *rapidity* of the language shift which occurred. We must also take into account the willingness of the population; thus, de Fréine (1977) notes that 'most of the reasons adduced for the suppression of the Irish language are not so much reasons as consequences of the decision to give up the language' (p. 84). Other writers (e.g. Binchy, 1945) have stated similar views. To fall back upon clichés like 'seven hundred years of oppression' or 'the stifling of the will of a nation' is to succumb to a black-and-white theory of history.

From the mid-nineteenth century on, the most relevant matters have to do with attempts to maintain, encourage and revive Irish. These were generally made by upper-middle-class individuals and organisations and, for many of them, Irish was an acquired competence rather than a maternal one. The most important language body was the Gaelic League (*Conradh na Gaeilge*), founded in 1893; it was prompted in large part by Hyde's famous address to the Irish National Literary Society on the necessity for de-anglicising the country. The League's objective was essentially to maintain Irish but it is generally, and not unfairly, seen as wishing to do more – to revive Irish as the ordinary language (although Hyde himself did not think this very likely; see Hyde, 1886). Overall, the Irish revival movement was part of a larger European trend, particularly within the Celtic areas, in which romantic, nationalistic efforts were made to transform the 'Celtic twilight' into the 'Celtic Renaissance'.

The Gaelic League declined in importance (though it is still extant) with the establishment of the Irish Free State in 1921.[5] It had had considerable success in introducing Irish in schools and university and had commanded a widespread (if somewhat evanescent) public support. It had not, however, resuscitated Irish among English speakers at large, nor did it make any lasting impact upon the maintenance and development of the Gaeltacht (see below). It *did* play an important role in the revolutionary movement and many of its members became political leaders in the Free State. It was thus felt, as Macnamara (1971) points out, that language restoration, as part of the larger national movement, could be reasonably transferred to governmental responsibility. Corkery commented that 'for the first time since 1169, the Irish language has a state behind it' (1968, p. 128). It is, in fact, quite debatable whether or not statehood has helped Irish very much over the last 60 years.

With the founding of the Free State, Irish was enshrined as the national and first official language. But, by this time, the number of Irish speakers was very small; the mass of the population had long since switched to English. Census figures for 1926 indicate 18 per cent could speak Irish and, of course, Irish monoglots were scarce indeed – 1901 figures recorded only 21,000 of them (about 0.6 per cent of the population). Despite these figures, Irish obviously had a special hold on the founders of the new state (see Solomonïck's notion of a 'people's language', 1984). It was closely tied to nationalism and, as Akenson (1975) suggests, possessed a value quite beyond purely educational, intellectual and, indeed, pragmatic concerns. Akenson (p. 36) reproduces de Valera's famous opinion that 'Ireland with its language and without freedom is preferable to Ireland with freedom and without its language.' In this sentiment, de Valera (and others like him) were essentially continuing the highly romanticised tradition so carefully accented by the Gaelic League. At the same time, it was good political sense to endorse Irish since doing so established a visibly non-British line.

Under these circumstances, the government passed the burden of Irish restoration to the schools. Although Akenson and others refuse to accept the simplistic notion that the National School system was a prime factor in the decline of Irish, the idea presented an immediate and much-discussed possibility: given that the British schools had killed the language, let the Irish schools revive it. Even if the first half of the statement were true, the second does not necessarily follow but, nevertheless, the Irish language was seen largely within the educational context.

Education

From the beginning, Irish was to be a compulsory subject. In addition, infants' classes were to be conducted entirely through Irish, even though this was an unknown language for the great majority. These measures arose from recommendations of the Irish National Teachers' Organization conference of 1921 largely, it would seem, on the advice of Timothy Corcoran, then Professor of Education at University College, Dublin. Clearly anti-English, Corcoran was the *éminence grise* of the INTO conference, and continued to promote a naive but fanatical linguistic nationalism. He outlined a scheme for the revival of Irish which was totally unsupported by any evidence (1923a) and he felt that almost all girls who had been educated in Irish themselves would be 'natural teachers' (1923b). His view of the English language was that it transmitted English thought, which itself reflected 'narrow insularity, repellent materialism and chronic indifference to what is of real worth in life' (1923c, p. 272). Consequently, acknowledging the need for English (grudgingly, no doubt), Corcoran recommended the use of Catholic European literature, translated into English (see also Malone, 1935). In 1925 Corcoran made the astonishing statement that 'the popular schools can give and can restore our native language. They can do it even without positive aid from the home' (p. 387). Corcoran repeatedly stressed the role of the school in Irish restoration, noting in 1939 that the policy was 'ratified and reinforced by the emphatic, if quiet, mind of the whole mass of the Irish people' (p. 285; see also Corcoran, 1934). The two words between the commas must have been distasteful to Corcoran, but even he can hardly have failed to notice the lack of general activity in support of Irish. Corcoran was not alone, of course, in these sorts of sentiments, but his position at the University gave him some prominence when language and education were under discussion.

The finding of suitable teachers of Irish was difficult from the beginning, and necessitated the establishment of preparatory colleges, a system which lasted until the 1960s. Teachers were (and continue to be) uneasy with aspects of Irish at school (O'Connell, 1968). In particular, they objected to the use of the language as a teaching medium in cases in which this might not be 'profitably done'. This is not to say that the INTO wanted compulsory Irish removed from the curriculum, but teachers did resent the implicit decision of the Government to revive Irish through schools alone. At the very least, teachers felt that they should have greater flexibility in the teaching of the language (INTO, 1942, 1947). Recent comments by teachers indicate continuing unease. Comber (1960, p. 27) noted that 'the teacher loses heart flogging a dead horse while the experts debate whether another whip might not revive him.' Harrison bluntly stated that 'Irish, except as an arcane minority rite, is on its way out. Don't blame the teachers for its demise' (1976, p. 35). And McSweeney, outgoing president of the INTO, noted (in Murphy, 1981) that Irish must be taken outside the school and that the burden of revival should not be entirely placed upon teachers and children (the latter termed 'digits in the Irish revival statistics' by Akenson, 1975).

The all-Irish infants' class has now been abolished, and increasing recognition is given to the idea that the use of Irish as a medium of instruction for other subjects is not invariably productive. Irish remains compulsory in secondary education and, until quite recently (1973), a pass in it was necessary to obtain the Leaving Certificate.[6] At the university level, Irish courses and degrees through Irish are, of course, offered.

Still, the bulk of the restoration effort (and most of the interest for present purposes) has occurred at the primary-school level, for obvious reasons. This has created enduring problems since the system has not been self-supporting. The teacher-training colleges no longer instruct their students mainly through Irish; consequently, those who are to be teachers of Irish are not themselves especially competent. All of this has led to what a recent newspaper report called the 'crisis in Irish' (Murphy, 1981). Standards are allegedly low, in both teaching quality and student proficiency. Pupils who have studied Irish for a dozen years cannot speak it. Teachers are critical of both oral competence and grammatical skill, and there are discontinuities of emphasis between primary and secondary levels. One notes quite traditional complaints about second-language teaching and learning, but it must be remembered that there is a special piquancy here – Irish is a second language to most children, but it is a rather special one, at least in the eyes of many. This makes the failure of the schools a bitter one, even though a thin wash of Irish competence *has* been applied to almost everyone. This failure may indeed be bitter, but it is hardly surprising; as we shall see below, there is very little to be found in other spheres of current Irish life which supports the schools' efforts.

Finally, it can be noted that the Government produced a White Paper on educational development in 1980 which deals, among other things, with Irish (see under Ireland in References). The restoration aim is reaffirmed, although it is now recognised that schools alone cannot achieve this. Methods and teacher competence are singled out for attention, and emphasis is given to regular objective evaluation of standards. Also stressed (and not before time) is continuity between first and second levels of schooling. Remarks are also made about the need for Gaeltacht support (see next section) and for broadcast-media attention. Generally, the emphasis is now to be upon spoken Irish. The White Paper may be seen, at least in part, as a response to the report of the Committee on Irish Language Attitudes Research (1975; see below).

The Gaeltacht

The Gaeltacht must be given some special attention here. As we have seen, all Ireland was once a Gaeltacht, but now the Irish-speaking areas are almost entirely concentrated on the western seaboard. The total Gaeltacht population is now about 70,000 but the number of regular Irish *speakers* is smaller (Ó Danachair, 1969, estimated it to be 50,000 – under two per cent of the total Irish population; Fennell, 1981, puts it at 30,000).

Gaeltacht Irish speakers have always occupied a central position in discussions about the language since, small though they may be, they constitute the remaining concentrations of Irish. Gaeltacht areas have typically been rural and poor, and subject to out-migration. Relief measures, e.g. the establishment of industry, have often meant English-speaking in-migration (of ideas, if not always of people). In short, the Gaeltacht has always been a problem for the language movement, inasmuch as it has created an association between Irish and 'penury, drudgery and backwardness' (Ó Danachair, 1969, p. 120). The paradox is this: the Gaeltacht is vital to the language but, because of its socioeconomic situation, is constantly encroached upon by English-language influences. If nothing is done, it will continue to shrink; if things *are* done, an artificial enclave may be created. Further, special measures may actually expedite English influence. In such a situation, can a language survive in anything like its usual unselfconscious state? Ó Sé (1966) put it as follows: since the Gaeltacht is not urbanised, emigration continues; if it *were* urbanised, what would stop it becoming anglicised, like the rest of the country?

The Gaeltacht has been at the heart of agonised discussion since the Gaelic League focused attention on it in the 1890s (see e.g. Bergin, 1911; Byrne, 1938; Gaelic League, 1937; Lyons, 1971). However, the League's attention was in large part lip-service only (Brown, 1981; Kiberd, 1979). Although the very existence of Irish can be seen to hinge upon the Gaeltacht, it has typically been romanticised (life there was rich and 'poetic', according to Byrne, 1938), visited occasionally but never properly understood by the Dublin-based language movement. The Gaeltacht continues to languish. As Macnamara (1971, p. 85) pointed out, the 'material advantages that the Gaeltacht people have seen in Irish have not outweighed those that they could see in English.' This is true, and it implies that if anything might possibly have been done to support the Gaeltacht it was unlikely to have grown out of prevailing Irish nationalist sentiment.

In 1972 the government set up a body, *Comhairle na Gaeilge*, to advise on Irish-language matters and it recommended that all Gaeltacht development be under a central agency. Such an agency, *Údarás na Gaeltachta*, was established in 1979 but, so far, it has had to wrestle with inherited problems and its impact cannot yet be assessed. Perhaps the most important event in recent years was the founding of *Raidío na Gaeltachta* in 1972 – described by one writer, perhaps too severely, as a 'modest' success (Ó Gadhra, 1978). A recent research report does, however, note that the influence of the service is weak compared to that of English-language television (Ní Ghallchóir, 1981).

It is a truism that language attitudes and use are the most important factors for the Gaeltacht and for Irish, and the most recent assessment here is that of Fennell (1980, 1981). He feels that the attempt to save the Gaeltacht –

such as it has been – has failed, and now only a 'crumbling archipelago' remains. Fennell blames much of the failure on the language movement, which saw in the Gaeltacht a sort of 'never-never land', and on the inadequacy of official measures. Fennell also notes, however, that the people themselves seem not to be as devoted to Irish as many might have wished, and he rather neglects the powerful influence of the people's own linguistic choices. Now, Fennell claims, most parents in the Gaeltacht have decided to rear their children in English – a decision reminiscent of the countrywide process 150 years ago. Fennell's claim is supported in a recent report by Harris (1984), which reveals that 45 per cent of pupils in officially designated Gaeltacht areas now come from English-language homes.

Irish in official life

Support for Irish continues at the state level. Most official documents are printed bilingually and the government has made specific moves towards the restoration effort (apart from the educational thrust). In 1958, for example, the Commission on the Restoration of the Irish Language was established to advise on steps to hasten the revival. In their report (1963), the Commissioners noted the national goodwill towards the language and discussed how this might 'spark off' national advance; many recommendations were made. In 1965, the government responded with a White Paper setting out its policy *vis-à-vis* these recommendations. This report is prefaced by the observation that the 'national aim is to restore the Irish language as a general medium of communication' (p. 4), and calls for the widespread passive support of Irish to be translated into something more active. Progress reports were published in 1966 and 1969 detailing grants for Irish books, for the Gaeltacht, and for language organisations (see under Ireland in References). Yet, there seems little transformation apparent in the lives of ordinary Irish people. It would be easy to say that commissions and white papers provide an immediate and facile way of giving lip service to a cause – easy to say and true, at least in part. But the government is caught in a difficult position. It cannot, realistically, go all out for Irish and advocate wholesale switching to it but neither can it renounce the language movement altogether (although some have said that this would be the more honest course, in the light of history and the contemporary scene).

In 1975, the Government established *Bord na Gaeilge*, which is charged with the general promotion of Irish. Progress here has been slow, many have been critical of the Board, and it has suffered from a certain amount of internal disruption. It has attempted to put Irish before the people via advertisements and it provides language advice and information, courses at all levels, and translation services. In 1982 it created a book distribution centre. However, by the end of its first statutory term, in 1980, the Board had not succeeded (according to Ó Gadhra, 1981) in creating a great deal of public awareness of its role.

In daily Irish life there are places for the language but almost all are either ceremonial or trivial, or exist only in tandem with English. Bus scrolls, street signs, advertisements, labels on the bottom of souvenirs which say 'Made in Japan' in Irish – these are the commonest places for Irish. Until very recently (1974), entrance to the Civil Service required a knowledge of Irish; this was, however, almost entirely nominal, although its abandonment was strongly opposed by the Gaelic League. Indeed, the report of the Committee on Irish Language Attitudes Research (1975) noted that even in sections of the Civil Service officially designated as Irish-speaking, the majority 'rarely if ever *spoke* Irish... during work hours' (p. 196). Nominal language qualifications are also required (or have been) for the Police, the Army and for the practice of law.

There are state requirements for Irish on television and radio. Macnamara (1971) reports that during a monitored week in 1969, about eight per cent of television time and four per cent of radio time were given to Irish. In 1974 Conor Cruise O'Brien, then Minister for Posts and Telegraphs, mentioned a proposed reform for broadcasting policy on Irish, to take the form of an amendment to part of the Broadcasting Act dealing with national cultural development. O'Brien wanted the matter re-examined with a view to a more realistic appraisal of the position of Irish, and to clear the way for the use of non-Irish material on the proposed second television channel (now established). The Gaelic League was very critical of O'Brien's proposal, considering that it might de-emphasise the centrality of the Irish language to national culture. A public meeting on the dangers of increasing assimilation by British mass culture was sponsored and, in 1978, the League published a lecture by an American professor of communications, Herbert Schiller, in which the power of foreign-media influence was outlined. Schiller, in a claim reminiscent of earlier and cruder antiforeign sentiment, stated that the banning or jamming of foreign media was defensible (see also Ó Caollaí, 1976).

Research

The revival of Irish as a regularly spoken language has not succeeded. It is true that 790,000 people reported themselves as Irish speakers in the 1971 census; this is 28.3 per cent of the total population, the highest figure for almost a century. Indeed, the reported Irish speakers in 1861 only formed 24.5 per cent of the total. However, that quarter were Irish speakers in a sense not applicable to the present quarter. There has been a steady decline in speakers of Irish as a maternal language and, with school Irish compulsory since 1922, a great increase in more cursory competence. Today, outside the Gaeltacht, perhaps four per cent of the Irish people use the language with any regularity.

With all the rhetoric surrounding Irish, comparatively little has ever been done to investigate matters of attitude, ability and usage, although there are increasing numbers of reports available on school achievement in Irish. Some were no doubt fearful that the results of such studies would prove unpalatable or embarrassing. Certainly, when Macnamara published his survey of bilingualism and primary education in 1966, there was a furore. His main point, that time devoted to Irish caused lowered English standards, has proved a provoking one for students of bilingualism in general. In Ireland the effect was considerable, for it was only two years previously that Brennan had said that 'if research were to show an undoubted drop in standards of English it would be regrettable; but it would have to be tolerated for the greater good: the production of integrated *Irish* personalities' (1964, p. 271). I have already mentioned the Irish teachers' survey which called for more curricular flexibility with regard to the language (INTO, 1942, 1947). This report prompted silence from the Minister of Education at first, followed by anger and criticism from the Government and Gaelic League (O'Connell, 1968). In 1974, Streib reported on what he termed 'patterned evasion' – a process by which conflicts between language ideals and actual language behaviour were reduced. It would seem as if patterned evasion, in one form or another, has been characteristic of the Irish language scene for a long time.

In 1971, Macnamara reproduced the findings of an attitude survey which indicated that, although 83 per cent felt that Irish could not be restored as the vernacular, there still existed considerable goodwill towards the language and efforts on its behalf, especially at school (see also Ernest Dichter Institute, 1968). This general goodwill still apparently exists (see below), yet Ó Catháin (1973) reported hostility towards Irish as well. The seeming paradox can be resolved if we take into account the difference between volition and coercion in language matters. Many, for example, were upset over compulsory Irish for Civil Service appointments and over the pass in Irish needed to obtain the secondary-school leaving certificate.

Attitudes towards Irish are also clearer if one recalls the communicative and symbolic aspects of language (see chapter 1). The Irish case shows clearly that these are separable. The report of the Committee on Irish Language Attitudes Research (1975; see also Edwards, 1977a, b) indicated that most people valued the language as a 'symbol of national or ethnic identity, or as a symbol of cultural distinctiveness'. A national sample of about 2,500, as well as a special Gaeltacht sample of 500, supplied information on Irish attitudes, ability and use. Apart from support for the language as a symbol, there was found also pessimism about its future, support for governmental moves on its behalf, and a general lack of interest in restoration-promotion groups. With regard to ability the results showed, as expected, a decrease in conversational competence (which native speakers possess) and an increase in basic reading and writing skills (which have been emphasised in school Irish). This, interestingly enough, shows the *importance* of school instruction in situations in which larger social support is lacking. For language usage, the findings mirrored more subjective evaluations – Irish was little used. Even where it would be most expected (e.g. in Civil Service units officially Irish-speaking, among teachers, and even in the Gaeltacht), usage was minimal (a recent update on the Committee's report is found in Ó Riagáin & Ó Gliasáin, 1984).

Overall, research, such as it is, tends to show that Irish restoration is not likely. By the time the state was established, most people had been

English-speaking for some generations and vague, abstract or cultural/
traditional appeals for widespread change have not succeeded. Unless one is
a fanatical revivalist, this is hardly to be wondered at; as in other matters,
people are linguistically pragmatic. A more cynical view was expressed by
Ussher when he noted that 'the Irish of course like their Irish, but they like
it *dead*' (1949, p. 107). At the same time, one should not conclude that the
Irish people have completely turned their backs on the language, or that the
restoration effort has been a total failure. Indeed, of all the Celtic revival
attempts, that for Irish has been, in some ways, the most successful. Nevertheless, it has been severely criticised. The only movement to proceed from a
national-government base, it has been a 'terrible failure' in the eyes of some
(e.g. Ellis & Mac A'Ghobhainn, 1971). Yet, as Macnamara aptly notes: 'It
seems unlikely, indeed, that the native government could ever have secured
a substantial material advantage for Irish at any level of society without methods
so dictatorial that Irish democracy would have been destroyed. And in the final
analysis, neither Irish politicians nor the Irish people wanted that' (1971, p. 86).

The Irish as a group seem not to have lost their national identity, but to
have enshrined it in English. Of course, there has been much debate over the
specific language–identity link. Many held the view that Irish is essential for
identity (e.g. Brennan, 1969; Cahill, 1935b; O'Hickey, 1898). But Ryan (1905)
disputed this, and Brown noted that language is not an 'essential constituent
of a distinctive nationality' (1912, p. 503; see also Dillon, 1958; and Kavanagh,
1948, on the 'humbug' revival). Others have emphasised points which now
seem decidedly dated, e.g. the popular view that Catholicism was part and
parcel of Irish (e.g. Cashel, 1917; Malone, 1935; O'Reilly, 1898) and the idea
that keeping Irish was a defence against crass English materialism and irreli-
gious thought. Still others, including Hyde himself (1886), felt that the vocal
organs of Irish people were especially suited to the Irish language (see also
Fullerton, 1912).

Conclusions and implications

In general, the decline of Irish is popularly put down to English occupation.
This is, of course, the overriding reason; if English had not arrived in Ireland,
it could hardly have displaced Irish. But this alone is simplistic. Why did Irish
first successfully counter English, and then lose ground? Why did things not
follow the course of, say, Norman French and English in England?

The facts relate, above all, to the increasing prestige of English and its
speakers which, from about 1800, proved a powerful attraction. The view that
the National Schools, the Catholic Church and O'Connell were the killers of
the language is an oversimplification too, but they are important factors, seen
against a background of a language increasingly associated with rurality, poverty
and an unsophisticated peasantry. Thus, de Fréine states that:

the worst excesses were not imposed from outside. The whole paraphernalia of tally
sticks, wooden gags, humiliation and mockery – often enforced by encouraging children

to spy on their brothers and sisters, or on the children of neighbouring townlands – were not the product of any law or official regulation, but of a social self-generated movement of collective behaviour among the people themselves. Most of the reasons adduced for the suppression of the Irish language are not so much reasons as consequences of the decision to give up the language. (1977, pp. 83–4)

This he feels is of special importance with regard to the role and function of the National School system. De Fréine has expanded his thesis in *The great silence* (1978). The title of the book does not refer to the loss of Irish itself, but to the fact that historians have virtually ignored the decline in their treatments of Irish social history. The author dilates at some length on the reasons for this, which he essentially ascribes to national psychological inhibitions. Whatever can be made of de Fréine's psychologising (and it *is* an interesting approach to the massive language shift), one fact does emerge which is corroborated elsewhere. The mass of the Irish people were more or less active contributors to the spread of English, for pragmatic reasons brought into being by long-standing historical forces.

If one accepts that the Irish themselves expedited the language shift, then it is easier to understand why so few investigations have been made in the sociolinguistics of Irish–English relations. The results might force recognition of unpalatable facts, facts which revivalists and, indeed, the State itself have been unwilling to acknowledge – at least publicly (see Breatnach, 1956). We can also understand why those critical of aspects of Irish revival or teaching have very often been unwilling to make public their feelings; and why, when they *have* done so, they have aroused such hostility. In short, the Irish scene has been a powerful exemplar of the highly charged, emotional topic of language and nationalism.

A very recent example here is given by Murphy (1981) in her discussion of teachers' views of Irish at school. A teacher, critical of teaching Irish to disadvantaged pupils, 'did not want his name used, as was the case with many teachers criticising the situation in relation to Irish. It is still a very sensitive area.' In the atmosphere which has prevailed, it has proved difficult to induce people to express their feelings about Irish and, when they do, the results are often interpreted very widely indeed – generally in ways supporting previously held positions. Thus, when the Committee on Irish Language Attitudes Research produced its report (1975), both the Gaelic League (ardently pro-Irish) and the Language Freedom Movement (*not* ardently pro-Irish) welcomed it as vindicating their positions.

What generalities can we extract from the Irish language situation? There are, of course, a great many points here which will be recognised as applicable to situations elsewhere, but I will mention what are perhaps the most important. First, the Irish scene enables documentation in some detail of the progress of a language over time. For about 400 years Irish remained strong in the face of linguistic competition, Gaelicised the new settlers, and forced the passage of laws intended to bolster English. This changed with new political and social conditions, but it took more than 200 years for English to gain a firm hold.

And then, in the last century, we note that a large-scale shift occurred because of a complex of circumstances which cannot be easily attributed to something as simple as oppression. It is surely clear, then, that language shift reflects sociopolitical change and this, given the historical perspective, absolutely dwarfs efforts made on behalf of language alone. This is not to say that language cannot serve a rallying purpose in nationalist political movements, but it only does so when it retains some realistic degree of communicative function. This was not the case for Irish by the time the revivalists appeared.

The second, related point is that language revival efforts can be seen as artificial when they operate in the face of historical realities. This is true in two senses. They are artificial, first of all, in that they are divorced from the forces of day-to-day life for the masses. It is simply not possible to bring about widespread language shift when the appeal is made on the basis of abstractions like culture, heritage or tradition. These are not, of course, trivial or ignoble aspects of life, but they are not conscious priorities for most people. In Ireland we see that those who might have been expected to respond best to revival rhetoric – the Irish-speaking Gaeltacht residents – did not do so in any united way (Fennell, 1981). Second, revivalism is often artificial in the type of language form it attempts to resuscitate. From a desire to standardise, to upgrade and to give fair play to various dialects, an academic variety may be produced which is some way removed from the maternal patterns of any native speaker. Certainly, the speech of many Gaelic Leaguers fell curiously on the ears of Gaeltacht inhabitants (see also Toynbee, 1956).

A third feature of the Irish situation which is generally applicable is the importance of a living heartland for a language, a place where the language is regularly used across a broad range of domains. If this has shrunk to such an extent that it is seen to require special support, then what I have described as the 'paradox of the Gaeltacht' occurs. If nothing is done, there is every likelihood of continued erosion. If things *are* done, then a danger exists of creating a fishbowl in which language (and other) matters are treated with the same self-conscious attention which characterises the half-an-hour-a week German class. It is my view that, although there is nothing wrong with this attention *per se*, it hardly contributes to that unselfconscious use of language which we associate with normal personal interaction. Furthermore, the process of out-migration which is associated with isolated heartlands says much about the desires and priorities of residents, which often interfere with the hopes of revivalists.

Fourthly, it seems clear that the Irish experience indicates that the link between original language and identity is not essential. There exists, today, a strong Irish identity which does not involve Irish, in a communicative sense, for the vast majority. At the same time, the language continues to serve a symbolic function for many. The revivalist error was to single out communicative language as the most important marker of identity, ignoring the evidence of history and daily life. Some would argue, I know, that existing Irish identity is less than it might be, because of the loss of the language, but this is a condescending and historically naive line to take.

Further important points have to do with the role of education in language efforts, to which I shall be turning again, and the communicative–symbolic distinction, discussed above and in chapter 1. Generally, the Irish scene demonstrates that attempts to halt the decline of shrinking minority languages are not likely to be successful. This is because the shrinking itself reflects larger trends which cannot be significantly affected by linguistic action alone. Language support can be a dubious quantity and may do harm if linguistic moves damage group solidarity by leading people to believe that broad social change is going to occur.

THE OTHER CELTIC LANGUAGES

I have discussed the Irish case in some detail; the other five Celtic languages, as well, have interesting lessons for the student of language and identity. In each situation, we see an indigenous minority under pressure from powerful neighbours – French or English – and a continuing linguistic decline.

Manx and Cornish, the weakest of the six, are now no longer the maternal languages of anyone. The last native Manx speaker died quite recently, but the nineteenth-century decline common to all Celtic languages makes this fact nothing more than a minor anomaly. The 1871 census showed that more than a quarter of the total population (about 50,000) described themselves as Manx-speaking. However, as Greene (1981) notes, this quarter was largely made up of elderly people living in remote areas. Manx itself had no official status other than its ceremonial use in the Tynwald. By 1901, Manx speakers constituted only eight per cent of the population, although the Celtic revival had by then touched the island – a Gaelic League (*Yn Cheshaght Ghailckagh*) was founded in 1899. However, the rapid decline continued unabated: from 4,500 speakers in 1901, to 500 in 1931, to only one native speaker in 1962 (Ned Maddrell, who died in 1974). Gregor (1980) states that, of the 56,000 in the island in 1971, 300 could speak Manx to some degree but that all of these had English as the mother-tongue. A harsh judgement was passed on Manx by O'Rahilly, in his classic book on Irish dialect (1932):

From the beginning of its career as a written language English influence played havoc with its syntax, and it could be said without exaggeration that some of the Manx that has been printed is merely English disguised in a Manx vocabulary. Manx hardly deserved to live. When a language surrenders itself to foreign idiom, and when all its speakers become bilingual, the penalty is death. (p. 121)

There are three important points to be extracted from O'Rahilly's observations. First, he refers specifically to English syntactical influence. Second, he mentions language surrendering to outside influence. Third, he points to the dangers of bilingualism as a way-station on the road to the demise of the original language. The last two are matters I shall take up again – can we reasonably talk of language shift as 'surrender', and its bilingualism an inherently unstable

66	*Language Maintenance and Language Shift*

condition? The first point, though, represents an area with which I shall not deal, since it treats specifically *linguistic* aspects of language shift; it is obviously, however, an important subject. [7]

Cornish, the other Celtic language which no longer has native speakers – Gregor (1980) estimates about 200 Cornish-as-a-second-language speakers in 1971, out of a total population of 380,000 – passed from the scene before Manx (a useful overview is given by Evans, 1969). Dolly Pentreath of Mousehole, often considered the last native Cornish speaker, died in 1777. Certainly, by the end of the eighteenth century, regularly spoken Cornish had ceased to be; the last *monoglots* had gone a hundred years before.

Before the Reformation, Cornish was still in wide use but afterwards English came in 'like a flood'. Increased mobility and the introduction of an English prayer-book and bible hastened the decline. By the beginning of the seventeenth century few Cornishmen were monolingual, and their bilingualism was fated to be an unstable and temporary condition. The religious factor seems particularly important here, and we can contrast the Cornish and Welsh situations: the Reformation produced religious literature *in* Welsh but not in Cornish. A link was forged between Protestantism and Welsh which did much to protect that language; Cornish continued to be associated with Catholicism. Thus, Hughes-Parry (cited in Betts, 1976, p. 121) noted that:

it was the status enjoyed by Welsh and its regular use as the official language of worship in the Established Church (and later among the Dissenting congregations) which has marked it off from its sister Celtic languages in Great Britain and Ireland. It appears to be the principal reason why Welsh held its ground so successfully in contrast to the much swifter decay of languages like Irish, Gaelic or Cornish. [8]

The Celtic revival came to Cornwall too: *Cowethas Kelto-Kernuak* (Celtic-Cornish Society) was founded in 1901 to restore the language and encourage Cornish cultural activities. Fifty years later, a political organisation was established, called *Mebyon Kernow* (Sons of Cornwall), which aimed to promote and sustain culture and to press for self-determination in domestic affairs. While several Cornish MPs associated themselves with some of this body's ideas, and while *Mebyon Kernow* members have served in county government, the group had no success when it presented its candidate for the British parliament in the 1970 elections (see Ellis, 1974).

Many would agree with Evans (1969, p. 306) that, sadly perhaps, the value of Cornish lies in its completion: 'Within what may be called the late historical period...a language went through all the painful processes of birth, life and death. And we are able to observe, although not clearly at all times, the stages of this story from start to finish.' However, Evans' final observation – 'subjected people who do not reassert themselves cannot preserve their language indefinitely, and...for good or ill a language and a people die together' (p. 306) – is more questionable. It is not clear, for example, that national reassertion is a guarantee of linguistic revival (e.g. the Irish case). Neither is it true that language and people die together; it is, in fact, the thrust of this book that identity survives language loss. Identity can alter radically of course (see chapter 1), but it is not inexorably bound up with language.

It is probably true, as Durkacz (1983) notes, that brutal repression of Celtic languages by British central authority was mainly a feature of the sixteenth and seventeenth centuries, but Breton has had a more prolonged and systematic ill-treatment at the hand of government (see generally Reece, 1979). The Bretons are unique inasmuch as they *returned* to continental Europe from the British Isles. This Celtic people moved from Devon and Cornwall to Armorica (Brittany) and also, incidentally, to Galicia in Spain, fleeing from Saxon and Irish aggression, from the fifth century (Chadwick, 1970; see also Falc'hun, 1977). Contact between Cornwall and Brittany was sustained, to their mutual benefit, but the status of the latter began to come under strong French pressure from the late fifteenth century. In 1532 Brittany became an autonomous unit within the French kingdom, but this ended with the revolutionary French Assembly of 1789. From that time on, Brittany and Breton were kept firmly under the French heel.

A Breton association (*Kevredigez Vreiz*) was banned by the government in 1858. More recently, because of the collaborationist activities of *some* Bretons during the Second World War (Germany had promised an independent Breton state if Brittany remained non-partisan), there were reprisals by the French *maquis*. This led, in turn, to the formation of a Breton military force which fought with the Germans; this caused, according to Ellis (1974, p. 171):

a massive persecution of all Bretons with any 'nationalist' tendencies during the period 1944–8. Well over a hundred were executed and thousands imprisoned in special camps while sentences of banishment, confiscation of property, civic degradation...were imposed on many more...The Breton language was prohibited by law...France was using the pretext of an attempted collaboration by a few extremists, prior to 1939, to smash the Breton nation.

There is some indication that today the 600,000 speakers of Breton may have more to hope from the French, although French motives, in providing some relief to cultural manifestations including language, are at least partly derived from desires to defuse and co-opt the Bretons. Dalby (1983) notes, for example, continuing protest by Bretons who observe in new French tolerance for small languages a less than completely altruistic wish for allies in the fight against 'world domination' by English. As well, those who might initially be reassured by the number of Breton speakers should bear in mind that a hundred years ago there were four times as many (Ellis, 1974; see also Dressler & Wodak-Leodolter, 1977; Lewis, 1980).

Timm (1980) has admirably summarised the present state of Breton. First, it occupies no central domain from which French is absent. She notes that even in the *cercles celtiques* – Breton cultural festivals – the language is used much less frequently than is French. Song and dance are stressed, but only a few cultivate the language. I have found a similar pattern in Scottish culture in Nova Scotia. Cultural activities were widely supported, but language was not emphasised. This enables, of course, non-speakers to participate in traditional events and is not a bad thing in itself, although decried by the more severe linguistic nationalists. It was particularly interesting to discover that the meetings and activities of the principal Gaelic society in Nova Scotia were conducted entirely in English (Edwards, 1982c). More generally – but still in a New World context – one notes the many ethnic festivals and 'days' celebrated throughout the United States and Canada, most of which make very little (if any) use of the original group language.

Breton is more regularly used than French only in agricultural work and in cafés. The rural setting of course represents a context which can at once remain strong and condemn a language with connotations of 'penury, drudgery and backwardness' (as Ó Danachair said of the Irish scene: 1969, p. 120). A difference exists here, Timm notes, between the sexes. More Breton is used in the fields by men, not only because there are simply more of them there, but also because Breton women have been rejecting the language precisely since it symbolises for them a rurality and backwardness from which they wish to move. This also accounts for the use of Breton in cafés, essentially male preserves, and the dominance of French in bars which cater for both sexes. Relatedly, cafés tend to be poorly furnished, while bars are altogether more sophisticated settings.[9]

Timm also reports that Breton is not being passed from parents to children, and is thus more and more a speech of the elderly, particularly, of course, the rural elderly. 'It seems at the moment that the fate of Breton as a family language is in the hands of urban *neo-bretonnants* who are reported teaching it to their children' (Timm, 1980, p. 39). Again, there are parallels here with other language situations, in which urban, middle-class individuals learn a language being abandoned by its native speakers. Such people have been referred to as 'secondary bilinguals', to distinguish them from 'primary' native speakers. The motivations, life styles and linguistic significance of these two groups are clearly very different.

This relates to another point made by Timm: language-promotion efforts do not touch the vast majority of *bretonnants*. While it is now unusual to find anyone openly expressing aversion to Breton, it seems that the greatest linguistic interest takes the form of 'une molle adhésion de principe' (Hélias, 1975, p. 535). This captures exactly the stance of most Irish people too, as we have seen; Irish is a valued cultural possession but it is not something which must be personally acquired.

Timm also points out that increasing industrialisation (she calls it 'serious', which is nicely chosen) is bringing large numbers of foreign workers – principally Portuguese and Algerian – into Brittany. Some already know French, and the rest will certainly learn it rather than Breton. There are similarities here with Wales and Euzkadi (the Basque country). Movement *into* a heartland can be just as destructive of linguistic continuity as can migration from it.[10]

Scots Gaelic, now spoken mainly in the Hebrides, is also in difficulty. Greene (1981) notes an *increase* from 80,000 to 90,000 speakers between the 1961 and

1971 censuses, but the new speakers are urban dwellers, outside the Highlands and Islands stronghold (see also above; Edwards, in press b; Price, 1984a, 1984b; Wood, 1979). Greene points to the lack of an urban centre for the language; even Stornoway, on Lewis, is not a Gaelic-speaking town.

Scots Gaelic began to lose ground in southern and central Scotland with the coming of English merchants and soldiers. During the eighteenth century, English was promoted in schools in Scottish-speaking areas although, after the suppression of Jacobitism, somewhat more linguistic tolerance was evident. Indeed, once English forces were dominant, Gaelic was actually encouraged, but for the familiar reason of facilitating assimilation. Bilingualism was again to be an unstable phenomenon.

McKinnon noted (1974) that the contemporary Gaelic-speaking areas are bilingual and that education in the language does not carry through to secondary-school level where 'even Gaelic is taught to Gaelic-speaking children in English' (p. 80). He also reports that parents have showed an unwillingness to transmit the language to their children (see also Mackinnon, 1977; Withers, 1982). It is interesting to note that, although Scotland (unlike Wales) was never conquered by the English, the shift from the original language was more complete. Today, with the resurgence of interest in local administration associated with the devolution movement, it is also true that there is not the relationship between Gaelic and the Scottish National Party that exists between Welsh and *Plaid Cymru*. We have already seen, of course, that the religious factor distinguishes the Welsh and Scottish cases. The different degree of association between language and nationalist political parties is discussed by Nairn (1981; see also Agnew, 1981b; Birch, 1977) and Durkacz (1983), who notes that Scots Gaelic could not so easily 'fuse' with nationalism since, unlike Welsh, it reflected only a small, economically backward part of the country. Welsh, although lacking a strong urban base *per se* was associated – through the Industrial Revolution – with the coal-mining valleys; this was a vitally important factor, as Saunders Lewis pointed out in his famous 1962 lecture on the fate of the language. [11]

Welsh is perhaps the strongest of the surviving Celtic languages, although here, too, decline has been continuous (see generally Raybould, 1984; Stephens, 1973). Thomas (1982) notes, for example, that the number of Welsh speakers has decreased by about five per cent every decade from 1901 to 1971; now, there are about 600,000 who speak the language (about 20 per cent of the total population). As noted above, industrialisation actually supported Welsh; Lewis (1980) reports that, in Glamorgan, industrialisation began in the strongest Welsh-speaking areas, and attracted people from similar areas elsewhere. This is what led Thomas (1962) to his observation that the Industrial Revolution kept Welsh alive (and it was to Thomas' work that Saunders Lewis referred). However, Lewis (1980) feels that this view is short-sighted, and neglects the rapid anglicisation which followed (see also Williams, 1976). A predominantly English workforce proved too much for Welsh to assimilate. Thus, Jones (1981), drawing upon the first official census of the Welsh language (Southall,

1895) and some earlier estimates, outlines a rapid decline of Welsh speakers – from about 70 per cent to 55 per cent – between 1870 and 1890.[12] This is thus another example of in-migration contributing to language decline. Nonetheless, Welsh remained stronger than other Celtic languages in Great Britain, aided by the presence of religious material in the language (see above; and Durkacz, 1983). In 1891, Welsh speakers were still in the clear majority in almost all areas, although this census is the only one to show the language in this position (Jones, 1981).

The decline of Welsh and the perceived threat to cultural identity led to the formation of *Plaid Cymru* in 1925 by Saunders Lewis and others. In 1962, Lewis' broadcast on the fate of Welsh (*Tyn Ged yr Iaith*) had no small part to play in the foundation of *Cymdeithas yr Iaith Gymraeg* (the Welsh Language Society).[13] A useful sketch of the development and activities of *Plaid Cymru* and the Welsh Language Society can be found in Williams (1976). The changing emphasis in the former – which altered from a mainly cultural pressure group to one which more and more stressed the economic underpinnings of nationalism – contributed to the establishment of the Language Society which, of course, is principally concerned with Welsh itself. Perhaps its most notable recent success has been in pressing for a Welsh television channel.[14]

In 1979, the Conservative Government reversed an election pledge to provide a channel for Welsh, and proposed instead that Welsh-language programmes be split between the new channel and an existing BBC one. This was seen as a blatant breach of faith by the Welsh Language Society and, in May 1980, Gwynfor Evans (the president of *Plaid Cymru*, and a member of the Society) announced that he would fast to the death, beginning in October, unless the Government returned to its original intention. His threat received more attention in August, as the parliamentary debate on the new channel entered its final stages. At the same time, the Welsh Language Society led a campaign of protest in which some 2,000 people refused to pay their television licence fees, several of them going to gaol. In mid-September the new channel was finally approved, and the Government returned to its promise regarding Welsh. Thus, in November 1982, *Sianel Pedwar Cymru* (Channel Four Wales) went on the air, providing 22 hours of prime-time, Welsh-language programming weekly. It now broadcasts to all 2.7 million inhabitants of Wales. Reports have recently appeared on the first-year viewing figures for Channel Four; a *Sunday Times* article noted that:

In the beginning the week's top rated Welsh programme was attracting as many as 221,000 viewers. But that had fallen to about 150,000 by April, 100,000 by mid-summer, and 55,000 in last week's BARB (British Audience Research Board) figures: a two per cent share of those served by S4C and only a pitiful 10 per cent even among Welsh speakers who were supposed to be as keen as mustard for programmes in their own tongue during peak hours. Since that is the week's top rating the size of audience for S4C programmes lower down the list scarcely bears thinking about. (30 October 1983)

The great attention given to television is not accidental (see also Dodson & Jones, 1984). It is an extremely powerful medium and minority-language presence is obviously important. At the same time, it can transmit foreign language and culture to the continued detriment of the threatened variety. As a Welsh language nationalist recently explained in a television interview, the medium has itself become a language domain.

THE CELTIC LANGUAGES: SUMMARY AND IMPLICATIONS

Even this brief survey of Irish and the other Celtic languages allows a number of important points to be made, points which are generalisable both within and beyond the Celtic context.

1 Languages in decline characteristically have a predominance of middle-aged or elderly native speakers. This reflects a lack of transmission of the language to the younger generation and *this*, in turn, usually represents a pragmatic decision in which another variety is seen as more important for the future. The voluntary contribution to language shift can only be denied through a wilful continuation of the simplistic 'us-and-them' argument in which oppressors and oppressed are neatly defined and pigeonholed. The fact that original languages are not retained for communicative purposes reflects real-life exigencies which may leave symbolic linguistic values intact, and may even enhance them. In this way, an evolutionary group identity may continue to have some sort of linguistic component – although it is unlikely that this can be rekindled into an instrumental medium.

2 Languages in decline are often confined to rural areas in which associations are made between the language and poverty, hardship and ignorance. The lack of an *urban* concentration of speakers is very important. The out-migration from linguistic heartlands obviously weakens the language but, in some cases (where at least part of the heartland is industrially strong) *in*-migration of foreign speakers is also a weakening factor. Attempts to strengthen shrinking heartlands usually founder because of the powerful socioeconomic currents which contributed to the decline in the first place.

It is often the case, of course, that strong ethnic and nationalist sentiments are urban phenomena, and that individuals (and groups) concerned with language maintenance and revival are middle-class, city-dwelling intellectuals. Such persons are generally atypical of the heartland native speakers, have in fact assimilated successfully into the majority mainstream (or *are* majority-group members), have often romantically rediscovered their 'roots', and often evoke little interest from native speakers in the heartland.

3 Bilingualism is often only a temporary phenomenon, to be replaced with dominant-language monolingualism. When a language possesses no more monoglots, the process of decline has very often begun. Bilingualism *can* be a stable condition, but only when there exist important domains of use for each language. The evidence assembled so far shows that domains specific to

the minority variety are often encroached upon, and eventually taken over, by the more powerful language. The rule of the day here is again pragmatic: people do not maintain two languages for ever, when one is sufficient in all contexts.

4   Language decline cannot be usefully considered in isolation from other important social phenomena, nor should it be seen as a single dependent variable influenced by a combination of other features seen as independent variables. All are interrelated. It follows that attempts to intervene on behalf of one feature alone – language, for example – are not likely to succeed.

5   Desires to stem the decline of threatened languages are usually active only in a minority within the minority group. It has proved difficult to interest ordinary group members themselves in language-maintenance efforts and, in some cases, revivalist movements have not made much of an attempt.

6   Language-revival efforts have often led to a growth in the number of people knowing the language. However, 'secondary' bilinguals, for whom the minority language is not the maternal variety, are less vital elements for the continued life of the language than are native speakers. Relatedly, the 'numbers game' often involves confusion between those who *can* speak the language – and the *degree* of fluency is clearly important here too – and those who *do so* regularly. Again, these groups are not equally relevant for the survival of the language.

7   Many cultural activities originally associated with a language may continue long after that language has declined drastically. As well, various non-linguistic manifestations of groupness are often stressed in ethnic celebrations and revivals. It is usually a mistake to think that these can be used as a base for language restoration, or even that those most involved in them are neces-sarily committed to the language in any active way. Cultural activities often retain their appeal precisely because they provide desired links with tradition which are easy, not requiring substantial alterations to equally desired assimilative shifts which have occurred.

8   General linguistic evidence (see Edwards, 1979b) suggests that women are more likely to be favourably disposed towards prestigious varieties (including dialects *within* a language) than are men. This can be an important factor, given women's traditionally important role with children, in the decline of languages in contact with powerful, higher-status rivals (see above).

9   The media are two-edged swords for declining languages. On the one hand, it is clearly important that such languages are represented in them; on the other, the seemingly inevitable importation of foreign-language elements, coupled with the increasing, global levelling of culture which the media (particularly television) present, can obviously contribute to the decline.

These are some of the important points which can be extracted from my analyses of the Celtic languages. I will be adding to them when I consider, in the next section, a number of other language situations around the world. Indeed, it is my contention that the generalities already made will be seen to have a very broad application. Before leaving the Celtic world, however, it makes sense to give some brief attention to other comprehensive analyses of Celtic language decline – for the sake of completeness and to reinforce the argument. I turn, then, to the work of Hechter, Birch and Durkacz, each of whom has made significant contributions to our understanding of Celtic language and identity.

Hechter (1975) ascribes the decline essentially to his now well-known theory of *internal colonialism*. Modernisation proceeds unevenly over a state territory, minority and majority groups become differentiated and social comparisons increasingly favour the latter. There thus develops a core–periphery dichotomy; the advanced core group dominates the periphery politically, exploits it and condemns it to subordinate status. Nationalist movements in the Celtic periphery are, at least in part, a response to this, drawing naturally upon objective and subjective markers of difference as rallying points in the struggle to regain some degree of autonomy. However, the influence of education and industrialisation has eroded language and made it a rather unlikely marker. Hechter, in defending his model, thus notes that linguistic homogeneity:

might appear to weigh against the internal colonial model, which predicts the maintenance of indigenous cultural identity in the periphery despite heightened exposure to the core culture...However the internal colonial thesis need not insist on maintenance of the peripheral culture in all its forms, but in at least one. It is the existence of a social boundary which defines the peripheral group, and not the particular cultural stuff that it encloses. (1975, p. 207)

In his last observation, Hechter is referring to Barth's (1969) ideas on groups and group boundaries (see chapter 1); he goes on to suggest that religion, rather than language, serves the boundary function for the Celtic periphery.

Hechter opposes his internal colonial theory to a *diffusion* model of national development which 'suggests that ethnic solidarity should wane among groups having long experience in the industrial setting' (p. 312). Hechter's dissatisfaction with this model is based, of course, upon the various types and forms of ethnic resurgence which challenge it – it is the internal colonial approach which better explains the 'bitter sea which separates England from the Celtic fringe' (p. 341). Although noting that ethnic resurgence in the British Isles has included language-revival efforts, Hechter acknowledges again that language maintenance has faded in the Celtic areas, while correctly observing that 'a group's ethnic identity need not rest solely on its linguistic distinctiveness' (p. 345).

It is beyond my purpose here to offer a thoroughgoing critique of Hechter's general thesis. It is possible, however, to note that the diffusion model does seem to explain linguistic decline. While Hechter believes that other ethnic features have remained as markers of distinctiveness (and these may better be explained by *his* model), there is clearly room for *both* perspectives. The decline of the Celtic languages is not adequately dealt with by the colonial model. We might also want to question Hechter's evocation of a 'bitter sea' dividing centre from periphery. It is quite possible to hold that such ethnic distinctiveness as remains – apart from that retained and promoted by minority groups within the Celtic areas – has for the most part co-existed reasonably amicably with centrist culture. Again, we see the possibility for a combination of Hechter's approach with the diffusion view. In a review of Hechter's work, Agnew (1979) also notes that it tends to ascribe action to the core and only *reaction* to the periphery, and it assumes a self-conscious and intended domination of the periphery by the core. The latter seems altogether too neat, while the former downplays the dynamics *within* the periphery. Still, it cannot be denied that colonisation of a sort, mixed with blundering and benign neglect, has been a feature of the scene. It is with the alleged implications of internal colonialism that problems arise. This is obviously true for language matters.

Birch (1977) points out that Hechter's model is an attempt to explain the survival of local loyalties, whose demise had earlier been generally predicted. Its two main features, according to Birch, are that the dominant group excludes persons from the periphery from prestigious state positions, and that industry in the periphery is controlled so that it becomes highly specialised and dependent upon export. Birch believes that neither assumption applies to the United Kingdom and, needless to say, is highly critical of the internal colonial model. Indeed, he considers the search for a predictive model useless in the inexact domain of politics.

As regards language, Birch's analysis of history leads him to the observation that it 'can no longer serve as a basis for national self-consciousness, except among a rather small minority' (p. 117; he refers specifically to Welsh here but, since this is the strongest of the languages, his remark can obviously be applied to the others as well). And unlike Hechter, for whom English intentions seem calculated and aimed explicitly at bringing the periphery to heel, Birch feels that recent English attitudes at least are essentially 'tolerant, ill-informed and insensitive, and generally complacent' (p. 138). This is not a flattering description but it is, perhaps, less reprehensible than active oppression.

Finally, Birch's own explanation for the survival of ethnic loyalties is simple. First, such loyalties are enduring features of life, are natural to it and thus – although they may be overlaid with other sentiments – they remain. If circumstances change, such that wider state loyalties lose some of their attractions or advantages, these initial group ties may expand in importance. Second, Birch suggests three recent developments which relate to this: (a) the decreasing importance of belonging to a sizeable state for defence and security reasons; (b) the development of cross-national bodies (like the EEC) which can provide economic viability to small regions; and (c) the impact of television, which brings majority culture with it and provokes immediate and angry response.

Durkacz (1983) charts the process of the decline of the Celtic languages – particularly for Scots Gaelic – from the Reformation. He stresses the important relationship between language and religion. Thus, the Reformation in Wales produced a Welsh prayer-book and bible and the language became established in religious life. Scots Gaelic and Irish, however, remained linked to Catholicism, which did their fortunes no good in times in which few political, religious or linguistic compromises were allowed, or thought possible.

Durkacz also discusses the educational treatment of the Celtic languages, where suppression was often less a factor than neglect. Where the languages *were* given a place in education, it was usually with a view to expediting the acquisition of English. Only in the nineteenth century did the realisation dawn that English instruction might be meaningless for many children, for whom education was often a parrot-like exercise. This was also the age, however, of increasing parental desire for English. It is very important to note here that this parental acquiescence in language shift is *not* simply one facet of a general docility in the face of English pressure. Durkacz demonstrates that on other issues (e.g. land measures) local populations were quite able to put up resistance. So, again, we see the importance of not downplaying the voluntary element in the shift to English.

Overall, Durkacz rejects the simplistic notion that nineteenth-century education was the main culprit in linguistic decline – the process began very much earlier, for essentially economic reasons. In a context in which English was the language of commerce and utility, and where the Celtic varieties were increasingly restricted and lacking in prestige, education alone was much less important than some might think; there are surely important lessons here for modern linguistic nationalists, many of whom continue to pin their hopes on schools. Indeed, in such a context, both teaching and *not* teaching the less-powerful language tend to lead to linguistic assimilation by the stronger (Edwards, in press b).

It cannot be assumed, of course, that people's pragmatic option for English meant that they lost their attachment to their own language; it retained a strong symbolic value. The association of the Celtic languages with 'childhood, song and dance' and of English with 'emigration, employment and prosperity' were not, however, of equal power in the lives of most ordinary people. Durkacz shows that, essentially, people made their decisions in the light of day-to-day needs and, in this 'they knew their own interests better than the professors of Celtic, the émigré Gaelic speakers in the various highland societies, and the Lowlanders who learned everything they knew about the Highlands from the novels of Sir Walter Scott' (1983, p. 224).

OTHER LANGUAGE SITUATIONS

I have given a reasonably detailed account of the course of Irish, and briefer attention to the other Celtic languages. However, in order to further establish my argument, I want to consider – more briefly still – some other linguistic contexts. There are, of course, many case-studies available in the literature, and the present effort is not meant to add significantly to these *per se*. Rather, it is my purpose here to broaden the base from which conclusions may be drawn. As with Smith's (1981) study of ethnic revival, the intent is not to add more descriptive bricks, for their own sake alone, but to use some brief sketches as illustrations of general points.

With this in mind, I have been particularly anxious to include information from non-European settings. Not only does this counter-balance the material already presented on the Celtic languages, it also goes some way to correct an imbalance often commented on in the minority-language literature generally. It has been all too easy for a writer's generalities about small or threatened languages to be criticised on the grounds that information is taken from too restricted or selective a sample. I provide material here from 47 language contexts around the world. Most of the notes are very brief indeed, but each case has been selected to contribute something to the overall picture which I obviously hope will have a scope broader than usual. There are, of course, many interesting situations not represented here. Not all of the examples involve minority groups, but all reflect language contact. I have attempted to use the most recent sources available, and I have provided many references for further study. The 47 sketches themselves will be found in the Appendix; this is in the interests of brevity and the continuity of the main text. What I attempt in this section itself is to bring out the important generalisations which these diverse sketches suggest, under five broad geographical headings – Africa, the Americas, Asia, the Pacific and Europe.

Before turning directly to these, however, I should like to call attention to a number of *general* works bearing upon the topic (i.e. works discussing minority languages generally, describing a number of languages under certain headings, etc.).

General works of interest

I have categorised the material here into three groups, although this is merely a rough arrangement, trying to include the most useful, recent work which deals generally with processes relating to group identity, language maintenance and shift. I have not, by and large, referred to edited and other works here which are cited in, or can be traced through, the language sketches themselves (see Appendix).

The first category deals with minority groups and languages. Adler (1977a), for example, treats 13 European varieties, with an emphasis upon Welsh. There is useful information presented but it is flawed by his weak analysis of factors contributing to language survival and death. Another Adler production (1977b) – on *lingue franche* – is also less than entirely satisfactory although, again, it contains useful material. Alcock *et al.* (1979) present nine good chapters on many of the important features affecting minority groups. Allardt's monograph (1979) is a useful overview of the Western European linguistic-minority scene, but there is a lack of generality: Allardt tends to stress the differences among groups and, while each situation obviously presents unique characteristics, one of the points I am emphasising here is that there *are* recurring generalities across contexts (see Williams, 1980, for a critique of Allardt's work). Anderson (1979) provides a comparison of linguistic minority situations and, in a later work (1981), comments on the minority language conference reported in Haugen *et al.* (1981). Ellis and Mac A'Ghobhainn (1971) discuss 20 small languages, giving what is perhaps a too optimistic account of language revival. Fishman's classic work on languages in the United States (1966) remains important, not least because it demonstrates that the great diversity within the American context can be profitably examined by those interested in situations elsewhere. Foster's (1980) collection deals with European minorities; Haarmann (1973), Haugen *et al.* (1981), Krejčí and Velímský (1981) and Straka (1970) are also worth consulting here. The bibliographies of Price (1969) and Williams (1971) are also useful; the former treats 13 minority languages in Western Europe, the latter provides 1,000 references on bilingualism. C. Williams (1980, 1982) presents data on ethnic separatism, Paulston and Paulston (1980) deal with ethnolinguistic boundary maintenance, and Hamp (1978) discusses aspects of multilingualism. A recent report by the Linguistic Minorities Project (1983) is concerned with minority groups in England, and the final work to be mentioned here, Stephens (1976), is probably the best-known work to date on Western European minorities.

A second broad category comprises works that are not restricted to minority-language settings; they all, however, provide information bearing upon language contact and shift. Lewis (1976) presents a readable account of bilingualism across the centuries. Pattanayak (1981) discusses multilingualism in India in a manner which makes the material relevant for other contexts. Lambert and Freed (1982) edit a collection on factors contributing to language loss. Weinstein's (1983) book treats the general theme of language choice as a political issue, and is a particularly wide-ranging work. An older study, that of Rundle (1946), is of historical interest, considering as it does language issues facing mid-twentieth century Europe; it gives about 100 pages to data on European languages. More recent treatments are those of Haarmann (1975) and Héraud (1968, 1979–82). Bourhis (1982) and Carranza (1982) provide notes on the state of the French- and Spanish-speaking worlds respectively, while Wood (1981) and Rogers (1981) survey linguistic nationalism within Germanic and Romance languages. Wood (1978) also gives us a mammoth review of 21 books dealing with language matters in Scandinavia. Fishman *et al.* (1968) edit a valuable collection on the particular problems of developing nations; LePage (1964) also looks at national languages in 'new' countries. Finally, four recent studies document the linguistic situation in Africa (Greenland, 1981; Scotton, 1978, 1982; Treffgarne, 1981).

The third group consists of works more general still, dealing with ethnicity, pluralism and nationality. Some have relatively little to do with language itself, but all are worth the attention of the student of ethnolinguistic issues. Breton (1981) and Héraud (1974) provide general treatments of European ethnic populations. Tudjman (1981) discusses modern European nationalism. There is useful material here, but the treatment of Celtic minorities, in particular, is poor. Tudjman takes a simplistic view of English dominance in Ireland, for example, and he also tells us that there are 60,000 Manx speakers on the Isle of Man and 350,000 Cornish speakers in Cornwall! An old classic in the nationalism literature is the report of the Royal Institute of International Affairs (1939/1963), which is still worthwhile reading; the language notes are particularly sensible. Two useful pieces on European nationalism are those of Deutsch (1968) and Jakobson (1968), and Van der Plank's article (1978) on assimilation pressures on minorities makes some reasonable points. Books on ethnicity which deal adequately with language matters include those of Bell and Freeman (1974), Dashefsky (1976), DeVos and Romanucci-Ross (1975), Schermerhorn (1970) and Shibutani and Kwan (1965). The third is particularly useful for notes on the communicative–symbolic language distinction. Du Toit (1978) has a collection dealing with ethnicity in Africa, and a Russian view of contemporary ethnic issues may be found in Grigulevich and Kozlov (1981). Francis (1976) is good on ethnic relations, and Esman's collection (1977) on ethnic conflict has some reasonable chapters. Finally, there are two books which deal centrally with the Australian scene but which also provide general comments on language, pluralism and group identity: Bullivant (1981a) and Smolicz (1979b). The first author adopts a cautionary tone in discussing the pluralist 'dilemma'; the second is an advocate of cultural and linguistic pluralism.

Africa

African linguistic situations are characterised primarily by issues arising from contact between colonial languages and native varieties. An important feature here is the degree of linguistic homogeneity or heterogeneity existing within states. In Somalia, for instance, the rapid expansion of Somali in the post-colonial era is in part a function of the country's linguistic homogeneity, and in part because of the existence of a standard Somali pre-dating colonial times (English and Italian remain important, however, particularly at higher levels of education). In Burundi, on the other hand, there also exists linguistic unity, in that Kirundi is the mother-tongue of more than 95 per cent, but this language has not achieved the standardisation of Somali and French continues to dominate.

Morocco and Tunisia also demonstrate the continuing importance of a colonial language, even though Arabic competence is almost universal; and, in this case, the native mother-tongue is itself a language with a long and celebrated history encompassing both arts and science. The general point here would seem to be that linguistic uniformity can be of great importance for the establishment of an indigenous national language but the degree of modernisation/standardisation is also highly relevant. It goes without saying that *any* variety can be adapted to adjust to new demands and needs but the question is often a pragmatic one, involving the presence of an already-modernised language. The colonial languages have great advantages here and, in addition, offer ready-made links to the outside world. Their prestige may be compromised by historical associations, but the answer here often lies in bilingualism in a widely spoken mother-tongue and the colonial form. Even in Somalia it is hardly conceivable that Italian and English, particularly the latter, are in danger of disappearance.

In societies in which linguistic heterogeneity is the norm, the attraction of external varieties becomes, of course, even stronger; however, demands still remain for a national language of one's own. There may be tendencies to go for the strongest or most widely spoken language here, but these can alienate other linguistic groups and, in any event, the strongest variety may not be the most useful across within-country settings or for the purposes of external communication. In Cameroon, for example, the lack of one common, educationally acceptable vernacular has caused the government to opt for English-medium schooling. Again, one could argue on purely linguistic grounds that the lingua franca, Cameroon Pidgin English, might be brought to national-language status (cf. the situation in Papua New Guinea). However, the strictly linguistic feasibility of such an exercise is of little account compared to the social perceptions of Cameroon Pidgin which recognise its utility but continue to consider it unworthy of a larger role. And, once more, the presence of a highly developed variety already on the scene is of great significance.

In Nigeria, on the other hand, there is linguistic heterogeneity but there also exist widely spoken indigenous languages, Hausa being the most important. Hausa is in a better position than Cameroon Pidgin as an acceptable educational medium but, again, internal ethnolinguistic rivalries must be kept in mind. In such circumstances, more 'neutral' lingue franche may provide a solution to the national-language issue. In Kenya the desire to have, on the one hand, an African language as the national form while, on the other, to avoid ethnic conflict, led to the proclamation of Swahili as the officially approved variety. English remains important in Kenya, but Swahili is receiving more and more attention; indeed, is is hoped that a particularly Kenyan form of Swahili will emerge. In Tanzania, Swahili has also proved a workable national language, for although it is the mother-tongue of fewer than ten per cent most now have it as a second language. Swahili, with its historical lingua franca status, thus functions as a 'supra-ethnic' variety (cf. the role of English in Singapore). It does not, of course, reign supreme in all contexts. In Zaire, for example – which is near the historical limits of the range of Swahili – the language has *co*-official status with other varieties. A final African context of linguistic heterogeneity is South Africa, where English and Afrikaans have been the prestige colonial varieties. The native populations are, if anything, more skilled in English – the contemporary and historical associations with Afrikaans make it an emotionally more troubling form – but Afrikaans remains central in many practical domains.

Overall, the African settings reveal the familiar potential clash of nationalistic demands with pragmatic concerns for communicative and educational efficiency. The obvious answer is bilingualism. But internal complexities, rivalries and heterogeneity often mean that *tri*lingualism is required – mother-tongue, neutral or indigenous lingua franca, and colonial language. So far, some stability has proved possible here but it may be that smaller mother-tongues will be increasingly threatened if their domains – family, village life, etc. – are disrupted by urbanisation, modernisation and out-migration. We should emphasise here the powerful political pressures which influence the course of language, besides which purely cultural or educational currents are very much weaker. The wealth of language diversity – in Nigeria, for example, where 80 million people speak 400 varieties – is, historically, a reflection of immobility and stasis. The contact which mobility brings inevitably puts stress on linguistic (and other) manifestations of group life. It seems unlikely that this mobility – physical, social, psychological – can be totally resisted; more importantly, it often seems to be welcomed by those most directly involved.

The Americas

By and large, the situation affecting many South and Central American countries is the same as obtains in Africa: contact between indigenous varieties, which are often low in prestige and unstandardised, and colonial languages. A familiar pattern is the Mexican one in which Indian languages are declining in the face of Spanish, where bilingualism is often an impermanent state and where parents, for practical reasons, want their children educated in Spanish. Similarly, in Peru, Bolivia and Ecuador, Quechua and Aymara are downgraded *vis-à-vis* Spanish, and their speakers are increasingly assimilated into an urban or semi-urban life style where Spanish dominates.

There are also analogies in South America to the campaigns elsewhere which aim to standardise and modernise indigenous languages, so strengthening them against colonial forms. This is being attempted in Suriname, for example. However, the conflict remains an unequal one in that a fully standardised Saramaccan would still not provide the same scope as Dutch. Language planners can work on languages but they cannot create a 'language of wider communication' (as it is sometimes called) out of a variety with relatively few speakers in relatively isolated settings. Another interesting case is the Haitian. There is a high level of linguistic homogeneity – about 90 per cent are monolingual speakers of Haitian Creole – but those few who also know French are in no hurry to help the masses become bilingual. Any language planning in this context will be secondary to somewhat more thoroughgoing social reform.

An interesting example of language contact is found in Paraguay. It demonstrates, as does the Somalian case (see previous section), that indigenous languages are not inevitably doomed in the face of powerful external varieties.

Guaraní competence in Paraguay is high, the language has a relatively long written history, and there are current efforts to develop it more fully as a *lengua de cultura*. Many Paraguayans consider Guaraní an important element of their identity, and parental rejection of the native variety at school, while present, seems not as marked as it is elsewhere. It is entirely possible that bilingualism here will be a stable phenomenon, although the long-term view may still favour Spanish.

Asia

The language situation in much of Asia also involves strong colonial languages but, as well, there are powerful indigenous forms, many of which have standardised, literary traditions. The problems are similar, however, since whatever the provenance of the languages, the old pull between communicative efficiency and nationalism still exists. In some cases, there are strong internal contenders for national-language status, in some a 'neutral' or 'supra-ethnic' variety is more useful, and in still others a form may be promoted which is a *particular* variant – but not necessarily the mother-tongue for most of those affected – of a widely spoken language.

In China, Taiwan and Singapore, for example, much effort is being directed towards the promotion of Mandarin. On mainland China this is essentially the prestige variety of the capital. In Taiwan, however, a good case might have been made for the modernisation of Fukienese, a southern Chinese variety. The *political* aims of the Taiwanese, however, clearly favour Mandarin. Although Fukienese remains dominant at home, some have expressed concern that official moves on behalf of Mandarin may gradually erode the base of Fukienese. In Singapore, too, Mandarin is actively promoted as the prestigious Chinese variety, even though it is the mother-tongue of only 0.1 per cent. Hokkien and other varieties have been downgraded and the present situation is one in which, although Mandarin, Malay, Tamil and English are all official, only the first and last are stressed. Indeed, as the only supra-ethnic variety in Singapore with obvious national and international prestige, English remains of great importance; it may, in fact, increase in importance as many parents push for English-medium schooling. Similarly, parents in Hong Kong are opting for English education, even though the population is overwhelmingly Chinese, Cantonese is the lingua franca, and government policy has been to encourage Cantonese at school.

In Indonesia and Malaysia, Malay is official although its replacement of the previously dominant colonial language has been more successful in the former. Indonesia is a huge country of 125 million people and 250 languages, but there is religious unity (most are Islamic) and Malay has long been the lingua franca. For purposes of national unity the language in Indonesia was termed Bahasa Indonesia, while the Malay of Malaysia is called Bahasa Malaysia. English has remained stronger in Malaysia than Dutch has in Indonesia, and this is partly due to the greater heterogeneity there. In particular, the Chinese population is nearly the same size as the Malay, and this tends to make the retention of a 'neutral' language more likely.

The linguistic diversity in India is vast, but there are 15 'recognised' languages, and it is clear that government policy is for Hindi and English as the two great lingue franche. There is, of course, a great deal of multilingualism in India although, as one might expect, language competence is often restricted to particular domains. Among the major Indian varieties is Tamil, spoken mainly in the south by some 35 million people. It is also, however, a minority language in Sri Lanka, and recent events have demonstrated increasing animosity and violence between Tamils and Sinhalese. Official policy seems to be rather ill-informed; moves have been made to downgrade Tamil, and recent state approval has been given to Buddhism, the religion of the majority. As elsewhere in the region, English is an important supra-ethnic variety. A similar lack of well-considered policy has characterised the Nepalese scene. Although Nepali is clearly an important mother-tongue and lingua franca, other varieties are also strong; yet, the government has essentially followed a Nepali-only policy.

The final context to be noted here is the Russian. Recent moves to 'Russify' the republics are reminiscent in intent, if not in approach, of Tsarist policies. The post-revolutionary tolerance of indigenous varieties was at least partly based upon the assumption that they would decline with the increase in Russian competence – Russian was seen as the great lingua franca and, indeed, world language. Recent moves aim to actively promote Russian although, unsurprisingly, the stronger indigenous languages have resisted, some quite successfully.

The Pacific

Yet again, dynamics here most often involve indigenous and colonial varieties. In smaller territories, like Ponape, Samoa and Vanuatu, the influence of colonial languages is great, although indigenous forms often retain dominance in domestic domains, and some are now receiving increased attention. As elsewhere, much depends upon the unity within the indigenous community. Linguistic unity for Samoan, for example, is greater than that existing on Ponape, where no one variety dominates. In Vanuatu, Bislama is a lingua franca whose pidgin status has decreased its acceptability; there are, besides, *two* powerful external varieties (English and French). In Guam there have been recent moves to promote Chamorro, but it is unlikely that the displacement of English is at hand. Although there *does* appear to be an increase (among the educated, at any rate) in the perceived importance of Chamorro for Guamanian identity, most remain pragmatic; support for Chamorro does not imply a desire to oust English. Maori in New Zealand was historically downgraded but is also now receiving some support. However, it is a shrinking quantity, and there exist the familiar small-language characteristics: more outsiders than insiders are *actively* concerned with its retention, and there continues to be a decline in its transmission to children.

In Papua New Guinea, the major interest derives from the increasing status of New Guinea Pidgin, by far the most important lingua franca in a region where 700 varieties are spoken, and undergoing creolisation. Admittedly, New Guinea Pidgin still suffers from colonial associations and perceptions of it as 'improper' speech. However, its great practical value, coupled with the creolisation process, means that it may well become the national language.

One of the most fascinating language situations is that found in the Philippines. Here, independence and nationhood were achieved without the support of a common language. This is, of course, also the case for other 'new' countries (particularly in Africa) but it has been argued that, in the Philippines, there exists a strong sense of national identity – not necessarily allied to Pilipino – which is lacking among the populations of other states. English is extremely important in the Philippines, and will continue to be so. Official support exists for Tagalog (renamed Pilipino for obvious reasons) as the national language but it has not transcended its specific ethnic association *as* Tagalog. Again, English acts as an acceptable supra-ethnic form.

Europe

I shall be briefer here than the complexities really allow, since the European context has been relatively well-studied. All of the examples discussed below deal with minority languages – indigenous or immigrant – and all reveal, once more, the struggle between pragmatism and group sentiment.

The situation of the Swedes in Finland involves a minority which is generally well-treated (in a country which was part of Sweden for a very long time), has educational facilities available (including at university level) and is close to the homeland. Although relatively few in numbers, the Finnish Swedes are concentrated, and bilingualism has been stable. However, Swedish is declining, not because of any active suppression but because social forces are decreasing the desire to maintain it. Similarly, the Finns in Sweden are moving from Finnish monolingualism to Swedish–Finnish bilingualism, and some children are now no longer learning Finnish. The language is increasingly restricted to home and leisure domains, and (interestingly) children are often given Swedish names. Yet it is important to note that this language shift co-exists with the maintenance of affective ties with Finland itself. The Saami people (in Finland, Norway, Sweden and Russia) are also a bilingual group, faced with pressures of out-migration and declining transmission to children. A Saami Language Board was established in 1971 and this, of course, shows concern (at some level at least) for the language; it must be also noted, though, that such agencies (with other forms of linguistic interest) are often signs that languages are in grave danger.

There is great interest in the lexicography of North Frisian dialects, at a time when their erosion is perhaps unstoppable. In the Netherlands there are some half-a-million Frisians, but their heartland is strongly influenced by Dutch media and there is non-Frisian in-migration. No longer does Frisian dominate across domains; it is now largely restricted to domestic settings.

Recent Dutch tolerance has been with the understanding that the 'problem' is a provincial matter, not a national one. In Germany, the difficulties of the North Frisians of Schleswig-Holstein are even more pronounced. A small population in a small area is divided by dialect variation and by political affiliation. Out-migration of Frisians and in-migration of others, lack of grassroots activity for the language, and a government generally antipathetic to minority-language matters – these are the familiar elements here.

If we turn to France and Spain, we observe interplay between essentially centralist regimes, which are now bending slightly towards their indigenous minorities, and groups increasingly at risk of linguistic assimilation. Among Occitan speakers, for example, we see the old association between the language and backwardness; we also note formal moves for the language actively supported by only a few within the community itself. Also characteristic is a cultural revival effort in which language is not a central component (cf. the Breton case). As with the Occitans, so with the Basques and Catalans. The Basques now have some regional autonomy and their language has some degree of official status – but it too has become a language of hearth and home, is not essential to Basque nationalism, and is decreasingly transmitted to the next generation. Catalonia, like parts of the Basque country, is industrially strong and this has meant a dilution of the language by Spanish-speaking immigrants.

Yugoslavia and Romania have fairly good records of tolerance of indigenous minorities. The Hungarian speakers of Banat and Transylvania have media representation, and Hungarian–Romanian bilingualism is reasonably stable. Yugoslavia has been forced, by its composition, to come to terms with heterogeneity and has been at pains to promote linguistic and cultural rights, while restricting those of nationality. Obviously, the aim here is to strike a balance in which pluralism does not lead to fragmentation. The status of languages is a matter for each region to determine; Serbo-Croatian, which many speak, is perhaps the only real contender for overall national-language status.

The language situation in Belgium is one of regional dominance, with a north/south divide between Dutch and French speakers. The matter is complicated by the presence of a large and growing francophone Brussels *north* of the boundary. A Belgian federalism involving the two main groups is the prevailing scenario since the country is, historically and linguistically, really two states in one. Switzerland is also well known for its regionalisation of language dominance, but Romansh and Italian are very much less important than French which, in turn, is less important than German in the overall national picture. In Luxemburg, on the other hand, a country-wide triglossia exists with German, French and Lëtzebuergesch. Linguistic domains seem well-defined and, so long as this remains the case, we should expect the three varieties to continue in their present stable relationship. Finally, Malta provides an example of an indigenous variety tenaciously clung to over centuries of foreign domination. Discussions of Maltese and the influences upon it suggest a strong linguistic solidarity function, made possible by homogeneity. The role of Maltese as a vernacular is unchallenged, although it co-exists with English for written purposes and in the media.

Summary

The generalities extractable from this brief survey of language situations around the world support and reinforce, I believe, the points made in the more detailed summary of the Celtic languages.

1   We note again a powerful concern for linguistic practicality, communicative efficiency, social mobility and economic advancement. This is the largest single advantage possessed by internationally dominant varieties. Coupled with nationalistic demands, linguistic practicality often leads to bilingualism but, in many areas, the progress of group aspirations and sociopolitical factors make this an unstable condition, particularly in the long-term.

2   Competence in more than one language is required in many, if not most, settings, but the increasing power of supra-ethnic or ethnically 'neutral' varieties restricts this competence to highly specific situations. Even mother-tongue maintenance becomes a matter of group will more than anything else. Language planning itself can do little to stem the usually desired processes of urbanisation, modernisation and mobility – and these are the factors which *have* caused language shift and which will continue to do so. To put it simply: a decline in the existence and attractions of traditional life styles also inexorably entails a decline in languages associated with them.

3   Relatedly, support for given languages becomes problematic when many exist within state boundaries. It is common (and sensible), therefore, to adopt a lingua franca – either a strong internal variety or a prestigious external one. The latter is usually one which has historical associations with the area, even though this can also mean a continuing reminder of colonial status. Supra-ethnic or 'neutral' varieties are often chosen to reduce possible ethnic antagonisms and it is sometimes possible for these forms to become indigenised, as it were. Kenyans are attempting to promote a particularly Kenyan Swahili, for example and, in other contexts, local Englishes emerge.

4   Standardisation and modernisation of internal varieties is always theoretically possible, but not always practical. When such varieties *are* developed to national-language status (Somali, Guaraní, etc.), the process rests upon a complex of historical variables which are not, and have not been, manipulable in any isolated fashion. There is, therefore, obvious scope for language planning here, but only in the sense of adjustments to linguistic phenomena made possible themselves by forces quite outside the boundaries of conscious planning.

5   Even where indigenous varieties have achieved a developed status they are still not necessarily equal in all senses to external languages. Standardised Guaraní and Somali are very much less useful, in a broad perspective, than are Spanish or English, particularly given the desired social mobility and modernisation which now seem to be global phenomena.

6   Environments change, people move and needs and demands alter; and it is much more natural for language-use to change, or for linguistic contact to emerge and recede, than to have linguistic stasis. The evidence suggests that it is more reasonable to consider group and individual identity *altering*, in the face of changing social (and linguistic) environments, than it is to see the abandonment of original or static positions as decay or loss.

LANGUAGE REVIVAL

Eastman (1983) has suggested that language revival includes both the restoration of a language to its previous standing and the resuscitation of a dead language. Revival, as the information already presented implies, is a difficult business yet interest in it continues, particularly in the current climate of concern for small groups and their identities. The matter is confused because of the vagueness attaching to key terms (e.g. when is 'revival' a more appropriate label than 'restoration'; when is a language 'dead'?). We can at least agree with Nahir (1977), who notes that there is little scholarly literature on linguistic revival because the number of revival efforts is itself small. The chief obstacle is that by the time languages are seen to be in need of sustenance, their position is often irretrievable. Further, language decline does not occur in a vacuum but is accompanied by changes in the entire social fabric. To attempt to revive a language *per se* is thus difficult because the milieu in which it once flourished has irrevocably altered. We have noted, for example, the specious argument that, since the British schools had killed Irish, Irish schools could revive it; even if the first part of the analysis were true (which it is not), the second does not logically follow, because it neglects sociocultural evolution.

All language revival efforts have failed, according to Nahir, with the exception of that of Hebrew. Some of the unsuccessful ones he lists are Irish, Welsh, Provençal and Breton. However, many have held that these (and other) situations are ones of *successful* revival. Ellis and Mac A'Ghobhainn (1971), for example, describe some 20 small-language settings in which successful revivals have occurred. But what are the criteria of success here? In a debate on Irish, Tierney (1927) observed that 'analogies with Flemish, Czech or the Baltic languages are all misleading, because the problem in their cases has been rather that of restoring a peasant language to cultivated use than that of reviving one which the majority had ceased to speak' (p. 5).

If we restrict consideration to attempts to revive languages in which the number of speakers and domains has shrunk to minority status, and if we count success to mean the revival of such varieties to widespread and regular communicative use, then it does appear as if Hebrew is the only real success. It *has* been claimed that Cornish, like Hebrew, has been revived; it was certainly dead enough by the end of the eighteenth century. There are now a number of people who speak it, but it can hardly be said to be a common vernacular. Even George (1984), who recently presented the case for revived Cornish, stated that it is a living language but not a living *community* language – a curious distinction and one which could fuel still more terminological wrangling. Price (1984a) has argued, conversely, that Cornish is dead, and what is now revived is a modern, pseudo-Cornish (which he calls *Cornic*), a 'twentieth-century invention in its orthography, its pronunciation, its vocabulary, and even its grammar' (p. 142). In short, there is no revival here (see also Edwards, 1977c, in press b). Limited success might also be claimed, in some areas, for some minority languages, in Europe particularly, but, in terms of societies generally, efforts seem to have, at best, decreased the rapidity of language decline.

Why has the revival of Hebrew succeeded where others have not? Nahir (1977) suggests that, with the state of Israel receiving a linguistically heterogeneous population, a communicative need existed. This is not unique to Israel, of course, but there *also* existed in this case an old language with a psychological claim on the population. This is quite unlike the Irish situation, where the attempted revival of the ancestral variety did *not* coincide with communicative need. Nahir rightly stresses the importance of this need, without which linguistic movements – that must then call upon religious, national or political sentiments – are severely hampered.

Furthermore, it is possible that the Hebrew case is not quite as remarkable as it is often made out to be. Fellman (1973a, b, 1976) points out that Hebrew was never a dead language; indeed, he says there is *no* attested historical case in which a truly dead variety has been revived. Hebrew was a living community language in Palestine until about AD 200, although it had been abandoned by Jews outside the homeland several centuries before. However, it continued as a religious language and, in some communities, also as a secular one for certain purposes. Among European Jews in the Middle Ages there were many who were literate *only* in Hebrew. By the nineteenth century, Hebrew was indeed dormant for Jews in Western and Central Europe, but it still existed in a diglossic situation for Eastern European Jews. When, in 1879, Ben-Yehuda first advocated the use of Hebrew as the national tongue in Palestine, there still existed, therefore, a base of Hebrew. 'Through Eastern European Jewry, in particular, then, the revival of Hebrew could – and did – proceed apace, *without any overriding or insurmountable difficulties* (Fellman, 1976, p. 17; original italics).

Indeed, given the particular circumstances surrounding Hebrew, it is unsurprising to find that the actual impact of Ben-Yehuda's famous 'seven steps' for revival was slight. The setting up of the first modern, Hebrew-speaking home (his own) had little effect on the general revival, as did the second step, the appeal to the Jews of the diaspora to adopt the language – the appeal was not heeded. The formation of Hebrew-speaking societies likewise had only minor importance, and the Hebrew dictionary and the establishment of a Language Council came *after* the early, critical years. Ben-Yehuda's Hebrew newspaper is judged to have been more important, but the most important feature of the revival was the Hebrew class. Here, although Ben-Yehuda certainly advocated school Hebrew, his contribution was slight. He played no significant teaching role himself; he was based in Jerusalem and not in the agricultural areas where most of the educational revival took place, and the original idea of language classes was not his anyway.

As Nahir so rightly observes, the communicative need is what distinguishes the Hebrew revival from others. Without it the revival would simply not have happened; with it, the success or failure of *particular* programmes of language planning (e.g. Ben-Yehuda's 'seven steps') becomes of secondary, technical interest. In fact, the Hebrew case demonstrates that the power of language planning tends very much to depend upon existing social forces, and in most cases planning involves the tidying up (often a substantial task admittedly) of processes put in train or made possible by these larger forces.[15]

LANGUAGE PLANNING

Planning a language revival is clearly a dubious undertaking. However, short of this, there are many aspects of language which can be consciously planned. In the last 20 years or so, language planning has become a formal topic in its own right within applied sociolinguistics, although planning efforts of various kinds obviously have a long history. There now exist two journals devoted to it, *Language Problems and Language Planning* and *Language Planning Newsletter*, several others which publish relevant material (including *International Journal of the Sociology of Language, Language in Society* and *Journal of Multilingual and Multicultural Development*), and a number of books (two of the most important here being Fishman, 1974b and Cobarrubias & Fishman, 1983). A sign of the field's coming of age is the publication of a general introductory text (Eastman, 1983). There has been, then, a fairly dramatic rise of a language planning 'paradigm' (Neustupný, 1983).

The major features of language planning were presented in a model by Haugen (1966a). More recently (1983), he has stated that during the intervening years he has 'seen nothing in the literature to make me reject the model as a framework for the starting points of language planners everywhere' (p. 269). There are four aspects to the model: norm selection, norm codification, functional implementation and functional elaboration. Here, selection and implementation are extra-linguistic features, societal in nature; codification and elaboration, on the other hand, deal directly with language itself. The operation of language planning along these lines is, theoretically at least, quite straightforward. A linguistic problem arises, such that a choice has to be made between or among varieties. Following this, standardisation is often needed to codify the chosen variety – to give it a written form and to regularise its grammar, orthography and lexicon. Implementation simply involves spreading the variety through official pronouncements, education, the media, etc. Various evaluation procedures are often employed at this stage to monitor the degree of acceptance of the chosen norm. Finally, elaboration means keeping the norm viable in a changing world; obvious necessities here include lexical modernisation and expansion.[16]

Linguists, particularly those concerned with the historical dynamics of large languages, have traditionally viewed the very idea of language planning as futile or undesirable, or both. Language *change* is a constant and natural process; language *planning* is a distasteful and possibly damaging one. Consequently, the idea of actively intervening in the course of language has not generally appealed. Recently, for example, the linguist has had this traditional unease with planning and prescriptivism reinforced by a stream of popular outpourings on 'good' English by writers seen not as explorers but rather as 'amateur do-gooding missionaries' (Quirk, 1982). Nonetheless it is abundantly clear – historically and currently – that language planning *happens*, and the examples I have already presented in this book demonstrate this.

It can be noted, however, that the purely linguistic aspects (codification and elaboration) of planning are very much less important than the social ones (selection and implementation). In this sense, language planners essentially engage in technical activities, *after* important decisions have been taken by others (although, to be sure, linguists may be consulted at initial stages; but see below). It is, of course, an important task requiring a great deal of skill to attempt linguistic codification and elaboration but language planners should not delude themselves into thinking that they are prime movers here. In fact, in some ears at least, language planning has an altogether too grandiose ring about it. Those involved *do* usually realise that their work does not occur in isolation, but it is not always so clear that they appreciate the radical difference of magnitude between their contribution and that of the *real* planners – politicians, administrators and rulers.

It is not always recognised, either, that language planning is a value-laden exercise. Many of the situations it addresses, for example, involve small languages perceived to be at risk, the establishment of a lingua franca, or a high level of linguistic diversity, i.e. contexts riddled with opinion, prejudice and emotion. Haugen (1983) thus observes that any language planning theory has to 'take a stand' on values, and Neustupný acknowledges that it is 'unrealistic to maintain that language planning theory could or should be a value-free politically neutral discipline... [it] has always been governed by socioeconomic value judgements' (1983, p. 27). Yet Cobarrubias (1983a) holds that theory here does *not* have to involve values. It would seem, however, that theorising can remain value-free only when it stays at the most abstract level; unlike other theories, its application immediately involves judgements of opinion and value. Indeed, given his hopes for value-free theory, it is interesting that Cobarrubias (1983b) remarks that working for linguistic change is not 'philosophically neutral' and that 'the ethical criteria a given society is willing to adopt seem to depend upon certain ideologies the group in control wishes to endorse. Language-status planning is ultimately contingent upon such ideologies' (p. 41). Theory aside, the language planner *cannot* be neutral – at least not in the field – since he has been called in to assist in a process of social change.

It is heartening to see that many leaders in the area recognise that language planning is not an isolated exercise and is always subject to other matters. Fishman (1983a, p. 383) notes that it is 'often but the plaything of larger forces' and is secondary to more basic socioeconomic, political and cultural currents. Similarly, Eastman (1983) notes that language plans are initially made by government authorities, and that planners then work at their behest. Still, it seems to be a feature of the area – perhaps inevitably – that those working in it come to see their labours and interests as potentially independent and free-standing.

Kloss (1984), writing on language shift and death, asks planners to consider whether survival is desirable, or possible, as well as whether language shift can be 'channelled in an adequate fashion. We even may romantically ask whether we might not take over precious subtleties from at least some of the doomed languages and, even more romantically, whether there are not some few languages so precious as to make us try to keep them alive permanently' (p. 66). These are heady sentiments, and language planners may well want to reflect on them. What they should not do, however, is to imagine that their considerations and actions are likely to significantly affect the state of affairs – unless, of course, these coincide with powerful extra-academic views (see below). Indeed, in some contexts (see chapter 5) there exists the possibility that intervention may cause distress to its intended beneficiaries, if it proceeds in a 'romantic' vein.

It is worth mentioning here that successful language planning does not only depend upon the approval of those in power; it also requires some acceptance from those whose linguistic repertoires are under discussion. This seems an obvious and unnecessary comment, but it is the case that language-planning policies commonly proceed without adequate investigation of the attitudes of those most directly involved (see chapter 5). Gonzalez (1980), in his assessment of the Philippine situation, concludes that the 'consensus of society' is needed. Bentahila (1983a) claims that the practical needs of ordinary people are often ignored among North African language planners, although here, in fairness, the culprits are not so much linguists as government officials, for policies tend to come 'direct from the ministry'. Language planning ultimately should be a function of the needs of the population (see Haugen, 1966b).

While language planners can congratulate themselves on the 'relevance' of their endeavours, the increasing establishment of their work as an academic area in its own right implies the possibility of disembodied, pedantic and naive analysis. It is important, at the simplest level, to understand that language planning is subservient to the demands of other, non-academic interests with very real social and political axes to grind. This should make us think more about the provenance of language-planning policies. Haugen (1983) observes that, as we have noted already, planners are usually called in 'after the fact' to work out the technical details for the implementation of policies desired by those in power. It is not language planners themselves, nor the results of academic argument, which sway the real policy-makers. As in other areas of public life, 'experts' are called as needed, and their recommendations are either implemented or gather dust according to how well they support or justify desired positions. Bell (1976) has likened the language planner to the 'management scientist' who rarely takes real decisions, but is rather employed to organise and analyse data; the 'decision-maker – manager or politician – takes the result of this work into account along with other information which he considers important' (p. 186). In the world of language planning, such 'other information' usually encompasses far more than language alone.

Further, Williams (1981) has pointed out that 'it is high time that we recognize that language planning is undertaken by those who are in a position of power to undertake such policies and is therefore designed to serve and protect their interests' (p. 221; see also de Terra, 1983; Dhillon, 1984). Language planners would also do well to consider Kedourie's comments; here, he is dealing specifically with the rationalisation of linguistic frontiers:

Frontiers are established by power, and maintained by the constant and known readiness to defend them by arms. It is absurd to think that professors of linguistics and collectors of folklore can do the work of statesmen and soldiers. What does happen is that academic enquiries are used by conflicting interests to bolster up their claims, and their results prevail only to the extent that somebody has the power to make them prevail. He who exercises power exercises it while he can and as he can, and if he ceases to exercise power, then he ceases to rule. Academic research does not add a jot or a tittle to the capacity for ruling, and to pretend otherwise is to hide with equivocation what is a very clear matter. (1961, p. 125)

All of these points notwithstanding, language planning has a very real utility. It may be, as Haugen (1983, p. 276) points out, that it is still 'largely descriptive and has not reached a stage of "explanatory adequacy"' but this stage of development can itself provide fascinating insights into social change viewed from a linguistic perspective. It may be possible, once sufficient data have been assembled and analysed, to offer, if not a theory, at least a manual of likely scenarios. Modesty, patience and an awareness of the intricacies and scope of the subject matter will stand language planners in good stead.

I have been briefer here than some may think appropriate, given the breadth of language planning. However, my purpose has been only to illustrate some important general ponts. The specific linguistic situations which I have already presented reveal language planning at work or, at least, contexts within which it may be attempted; these can be referred to for more specific details.

LANGUAGE AND ECONOMICS

Gellner (1983) asks us to consider how important language is, compared to other social factors, for a 'typical burgher in an agrarian society' who heard one morning that

the local Pasha had been overthrown and replaced by an altogether new one. If, at that point, his wife dared ask the burgher what language the new Pasha spoke in the intimacy of his home life – was it Arabic, Turkish, Persian, French or English? – the hapless burgher would give her a sharp look, and wonder how he would cope with all the new difficulties when, at the same time, his wife had gone quite mad. (p. 127)

In another work, Gellner (1964) observes that:

life is a difficult and serious business. The protection from starvation and insecurity is not easily achieved. In the achievement of it, effective government is an important factor. Could one think of a sillier, more *frivolous* consideration than the question concerning the native vernacular of the governors? Hardly: and men have seldom had time or taste for such curious frivolity. The question they *have* in the past asked is rather like that commended at the end of Kedourie's book: whether 'the new rulers are less corrupt and grasping, or more just and merciful'. (p. 153; the Kedourie citation is from his 1961 book, p. 140)

However, the once-frivolous question about the language of the rulers is now important, Gellner notes, for it has increasingly become the 'crucial sign as to whom the new power will favour' (1983, p. 128).

The change in the importance of language here is due to the rise of nationalism, according to Gellner. Nationalism is seen as a possible protective response to modernisation and industrialisation, particularly to their uneven diffusion across society, in which some differentiating characteristics exist to allow apparently 'natural' divisions. Thus, 'men do not in general become nationalists from sentiment or sentimentality, atavistic or not, well-based or myth-founded: they become nationalists through genuine, objective, practical necessity, however obscurely recognised' (Gellner, 1964, p. 160). Nationalism itself could thus be seen as grounded in economics.

However, Gellner does not consider that language *per se* is especially important here since, unlike other characteristics, it is relatively easy to change. If language were all that kept men apart, in the uneven flow of modernisation, then there would be little problem; or, 'if switching of language were the only problem, no new divisive nationalism need ever arise' (1964, p. 165). Gellner outlines his linguistic analysis here very succinctly: 'Changing one's language is not the heart-breaking or soul-destroying business which it is claimed to be in romantic nationalist literature' (1964, p. 165). In this way, the language issue can be as unimportant for contemporary, post-agrarian man as it was for his predecessors.

The general point I wish to establish here is that linguistic matters are dependent upon other sociopolitical factors, and can be best understood in terms of pragmatic adjustment to new requirements; indeed, the reader has no doubt observed how many times I have already used the word *pragmatic* in the discussion so far. In its analysis of essentially tolerant regimes, the Royal Institute of International Affairs (1939/1963) noted that people *will* shift languages if necessary, and learn a new variety: 'Although it will be learnt in the first instance as a subsidiary language, subsequent generations will tend to use it increasingly for all purposes. There will be a tendency to use the dominant language both in literature and commerce on the ground that it has the wider appeal' (p. 287). Apart from echoing Gellner, this statement can be justified on the evidence of language situations presented in this book. The Institute's report goes on to observe that practical considerations bearing upon freedom, security and good government will tend to outweigh purely cultural matters (we have seen evidence for this too), although lack of coercion in these vital issues itself means that strongly held group differences can be maintained. However, retention of an original language, in its communicative form at least, is often seen as detrimental, not so much because of external sanctions but because of internal desires. We should thus expect language shift in tolerant societies, but we should also expect retention of other group markers (see also chapter 4), markers which are not perceived to interfere with social mobility and advancement.

Dorian (1982) has pointed out that 'language loyalty persists as long as the economic and social circumstances are conducive to it, but if some other language proves to have greater value, a shift to that other language begins' (p. 47). One can appreciate that the reduction of language shift to essentially economic motives is not a popular position among linguistic nationalists or supporters of minority languages generally. Although Williams (1979) has observed that 'language allegiance is firmly rooted in the economic order rather than in any independent cultural order' (p. 58), Fishman (1984) has protested against 'economic reductionism', and Ridler (1984) has discussed the 'priceless' nature of language and identity.

My view is that economic considerations are of central importance. There *are* cases in which the application of simple cost–benefit analysis does not explain language shift or retention. One of these relates to groups in which language is indissolubly tied to a central pillar of life – religion being the obvious example. Indeed, the retention of religious beliefs has been so vital for some groups that they have been willing to undergo privation, suffer persecution and even make the ultimate sacrifice. This is surely 'uneconomical' of them. However, if we substitute 'pragmatic' for 'economic', then the argument still holds, i.e. even these sorts of groups are obeying what, for them, are practical imperatives. Given sufficient strength of religious belief, what could be more practical than to obey *its* tenets when these are in conflict with purely temporary and mundane considerations? Such groups, however, are increasingly rare; and even historically, despite much glorious rhetoric, we find other-worldly considerations to be, given enough worldly pressure, completely compelling for only a minority within the group itself.

There is a second and more common instance in which simple economics do not seem to apply to language matters. Groups and individuals can be found who support the retention of linguistic and cultural markers, where this does not materially advance them and where there is no link to something as central as religion. This *is* uneconomical, and there is not even some metaphysical pay-off. How can it be explained? The important feature here is that such retention may not contribute to material improvement but, equally, it does not lead to material loss. Groups in this category are secure enough to have, as it were, some psychological and economic capital to spare. Higham (1975) has thus noted that cultural pluralism appeals primarily to those who are strongly positioned within society; Linton (in Weinreich, 1974) observes that 'nativistic tendencies will be strongest in those classes of individuals who occupy a favored position' (p. 101). Such individuals tend to form minorities within groups and are atypical of the ordinary group members for whom, on occasion, they presume to speak (Edwards, 1977a, 1984a). This has been recognised even among those academics who themselves support language retention and cultural pluralism *per se*, e.g. Greeley, an ardent supporter of the 'new ethnicity' (see chapter 4), admits that the 'ethnic revival' in the United States has been more intellectual than popular (1978; see also Edwards, 1981a).

For most groups and for most individuals within them, pragmatic or economic issues have top priority. It is for this reason that language shift occurs and that calls for the retention of language (or other markers of groupness) are usually without broad appeal. In this way, at least, people demonstrate a firmer grip on reality than do many academic apologists for pluralism and language maintenance. It should be noted that this grip is an unself-conscious one, particularly where language use is concerned, and in that sense more natural than the highly self-conscious attention to language and culture which is so much a part of nationalistic appeals. There is often, therefore, a gap between group 'spokesmen' and their alleged constituents, e.g. as we have seen in the Gaeltacht, where native Irish speakers themselves were hardly in the vanguard of the language movement. Gellner (1964, p. 162) reminds us of a general point here: 'The self-image of nationalism involves the stress of folk, folklore, popular culture, etc. In fact, nationalism becomes important precisely when these things become artificial. Genuine peasants or tribesmen, however proficient at folk-dancing, do not generally make good nationalists.'

It is quite clear, I think, that pragmatic considerations – of power, social access, material advancement, etc. – are of the utmost importance in understanding patterns of language use and shift; by extension, they are also the primary determinants of success for any language-planning exercise. For linguistic minorities in particular, economic considerations militate against language retention in several ways. A region that is economically depressed often becomes one where the language is associated with penury and backwardness; the 'paradox of the Gaeltacht' means that it is extraordinarily difficult to significantly affect language in this situation. Government intervention, it should also be noted here, usually necessitates the drawing of boundaries (e.g. to define just what the Gaeltacht comprises), and those just outside may become resentful of special attention directed to those within – particularly if the outsiders, too, are disadvantaged but lack the cachet of possessing a threatened language (see also O'Brien, 1979). Sometimes, as we have seen, regions having languages at risk are *not* economically depressed – parts of the Basque country (around Bilbao) and Catalonia (Barcelona) fall into this category. But here a strong economic base also leads to linguistic dilution because of the influx of foreign speakers.

Thus, in both depressed and more well-off areas, the minority-within-a-majority scenario bodes poorly for language retention, and the economic forces at work are difficult to stem. The artificiality of economic intervention on behalf of purely linguistic and cultural goals usually manifests itself in temporary or isolated measures. Success would require an effort of sustained political will from those most directly involved. While this will may be latent – for which group would not, if it could, retain *all* its distinctive markers if at the same time it could achieve material well-being and upward mobility – history shows simply that most groups have always been willing to make alterations if these were seen to be in their best interests. Note here how patronising and naive are attempts to preserve people as they are, on the grounds that they are really better off if only they knew it, that progress is not all it is made out to be, etc. This stems from, and reinforces, a romanticised view of the peasant, the tribesman, the minority-group member which involves an unrealistic admiration of the past or of social stasis, and which can continue to encapsulate or 'ghettoise' people. Little wonder, then, that sensible populations themselves do not accept this line, and that the major proponents of the view are usually securely ensconced within that very segment of society they rail against.

In recent literature critical of ethnic and cultural pluralism (e.g. Patterson, 1977; Stein & Hill, 1977; Steinberg, 1981), the economic basis of group dynamics has again been stressed. Commenting on the American scene, for example, Steinberg (1981, p. 256) notes that ethnic groups have maintained some form of pluralism where this was advantageous, but 'have been all too willing to trample over ethnic boundaries – their own as well as others – in the pursuit of economic and social advantage'. Economic advancement *has* certainly been potent here, but surely Steinberg errs in his use of the word 'trample', for this indicates a mindlessness which is an inaccurate description of what are, in fact, reasonable decisions to alter course. Steinberg does acknowledge that the 'compromising' of ethnic-group membership has typically involved difficult choices and cultural losses. Choices are certainly required, and some things (particularly visible markers) are lost; still, the fact remains that most have been willing to 'compromise'. This is the phenomenon that invites analysis (see chapter 4), more so than the pious wishes of group spokesmen and academic apologists.

Patterson (1977), although wavering from time to time, also emphasises the power of economic considerations:

There is no a priori reason to believe that individuals always choose ethnic identification over other forms of identification. The primacy of economic factors over all others has been demonstrated . . . people never make economic decisions on the basis of ethnic allegiance, but, on the contrary . . . the strength, scope, viability, and bases of ethnic identity are determined by and are used to serve the economic and general class interests of individuals. (p. 145)

Connor (1980) has criticised Patterson's work, and it is true that the latter's claims are oversimplified. People may well make decisions on the basis of ethnic allegiance, and probably prefer to do so if they can. The point is that ethnic allegiance in most cases is but one factor to be considered, and it is certainly rare when decisions can be made on this basis alone.[17]

Steinberg, Patterson and others have essentially reacted against the romanticised view of ethnic-marker retention which has characterised much of the recent literature, particularly that dealing with the American 'new ethnicity' (see chapter 4). In so doing, they stress social-class considerations as having greater explanatory power (see also Sowell, 1978; Wilson, 1978). This may imply a greater emphasis upon group mobility than some pluralists apparently advocate. Certainly, the following quotation (Fishman, 1980b, p. 171) seems a rather curious one:

Stable bilingualism and biculturism cannot be maintained on the basis of open and unlimited interaction between minorities and majorities. Open economic access and unrestricted intergroup interaction may be fine for various practical and philosophical purposes. Indeed, they strike most of us as highly desirable legal and social principles; but they are destructive of minority ethnolinguistic continuity.

This suggests that the price of stable diversity is higher than most have evidently been willing to pay, and that ethnolinguistic continuity depends upon a static compartmentalisation which, again, does not reflect the actual historical record. It is remarkable, too, that open economic access and group interaction are merely seen as 'fine' – they are, of course, central to life in a free society, not just for 'various purposes' or as 'desirable' principles. For immigrant groups in particular they are often the very things which lead to immigration itself (see also Anderson, 1975; Edwards, 1981b). If these are the features which destroy ethnolinguistic continuity, then that commodity is very much in danger, and rightly so.[18]

SUMMARY

I hope that what I have said so far has illuminated some of the important factors of language, identity and their relationship. The course of language is indeed dynamic and while we may reject the old notions that language is itself organic, it is certainly inextricably linked to the social determinants of human life. As a marker of identity, language is of great importance, but history shows that language shift is the rule, not the exception. Indeed, while we lament the decline of some contemporary minority language we often forget that if we took a long enough perspective we would see that virtually *all* groups have language shift somewhere in their past. Does this mean that *everyone's* identity is reduced? This would seem to be the logical extension of those arguments which place language at the centre of identity.

Surely the reasonable view here is that identities *alter*. Given that all aspects of the social environment change, this should seem neither surprising nor inevitably damaging. It is true that adopting an immediate perspective only makes change look like loss. Indeed, some things *are* lost, and points of transition are always upsetting. But the fact of the matter, as I have repeatedly implied, is that change and transition are social realities for most people. The alternative is a stasis which very few have been prepared to accept. Change may not always be welcomed, of course. Adjustments made for perceived advancement are not without cost, but usually the cost is less than that which would ensue if change were not made. [19]

It is important to realise that change does not mean that all connections with the past are severed, all cultural continuity eroded. The choices involved in adapting to new requirements are often made in terms of the least possible disruption to existing life style; elements which can remain in position without incurring penalties do so. Thus we see the importance of Barth's (1969) idea that, ultimately, a sense of identity depends more on the continuation of group boundaries than it does upon specific elements within them. Most people at most times are committed to maximising material well-being, and it follows that a great deal of cultural 'stuff' is expendable. The contest between survival and tradition – if it comes to a contest – can be a very uneven one. We should always bear in mind the timescale here. It is to be expected that groups will resist change and they may do so for some time without great disadvantage. But if pressures are persistent and strong enough, shifts will occur. The fluidity of identity is a very real asset here because it allows group continuity in the midst of change. As I have already hinted, it should be expected that groups changing some aspects of identity in response to social pressures will do so in a non-random manner (see chapter 4). Specifically, those markers of difference which are visible will tend to disappear (or be retired from active service at least) faster and more completely than those that are intangible, or restricted to limited and private domains. Language, for example, may remain longer in religious and family rituals than in regular communicative use. The more private an ethnic marker is, the more it is exempt from external pressure and the more likely to survive. It should be noted here that these markers are exactly those which neither need nor benefit from active intervention, however well-intentioned.

Language in its communicative sense is, then, an element of identity very susceptible to change. We may lament the fact, we may wish it were not so – but it is. To expect otherwise is tantamount to asking for change itself to cease. This does, indeed, seem to be the view or hope of some, of those whose reading (or ignorance) of history has failed to demonstrate that change is natural, of those who want to impose some unnatural stasis on groups for what seem to be purely cultural reasons, and of those who yearn for some romanticised past. [20] Looking backwards has been a favourite sport for disaffected intellectuals for a long time, but actually *moving* backwards has not been so popular. Indeed, for most people, the past is unrecapturable anyway: 'Mankind is irreversibly committed to industrial society . . . The charms and horrors of the cultural and political accompaniments of the agrarian age . . . are simply not available' (Gellner, 1983, p. 39). Even if there were a possibility of returning to our 'roots', we can be quite sure that there would be very few takers. We have already seen that, where some sort of cultural revival has occurred, it rarely involves renunciation of contemporary life. There is usually not much learning of the original group language either; this is too unrealistic a step for most, even among those otherwise attracted by the past.[21] If the romantic look backwards has any substance, it is usually in simpler manifestations (dancing, singing, folk-art, etc.) which cause no appreciable ripple in the contemporary stream.

Of course, it is obvious to many concerned with threatened languages that a return to the past is not possible and, indeed, quite undesirable. Often some sort of stable linguistic pluralism is envisaged which, although sometimes conceived in artifically static terms, at least does not necessitate a rejection of the present. But here too the problems of language retention are great. The very fact that a language is seen to be at risk demonstrates that it has been subject to the powerful social evolutionary forces discussed. Can we then hope to intervene successfully on behalf of language alone? Language revivals have been notably *un*successful – the Irish case showing particularly well how difficult it is to induce people to shift again once they have already shifted to a variety which serves all their communicative needs and where, consequently, the only appeals can be made on grounds of tradition and culture.

It seems that language interventions have, at best, stemmed the rapidity of decline, but this is not usually very dramatic and generally represents but a small bump on the curve of the inevitable. The chief difficulty is that all such efforts attempt to isolate language (and sometimes other markers) from the prevailing social currents. My point is merely that language cannot be seen in such isolation. It is also worth recalling here that, since speakers of threatened languages themselves typically do not become as exercised over decline as do group leaders or concerned outsiders, there is a very real danger of interventions becoming programmes in which planners try to orchestrate the lives of others. This is usually with well-intentioned motives, but it can also be condescending and naive.

Overall then, the currents which in real life affect language are mundane ones deriving from social contexts and their evolution. Official government coercion in matters of language and identity is morally indefensible, and linguistic prohibitions are generally unwise and often inexpedient (see Potter, 1975). Tolerance, on the other hand, is both just and practical. Identities clearly survive language shift and it is naive, ahistorical and, indeed patronising to think otherwise. The essence of group identity is individual identity and the essence of individual identity, ultimately, is survival, personal security and well-being. To the extent to which a language hinders these things, it will be deemed a negotiable commodity. We can, with Dr Johnson, regret the loss of *any* language but it is not at all certain that we can do more, unless we (and, more importantly, those whose language is at stake) are willing to alter the entire social fabric which has evolved with and around language.

4

The Ethnic Revival and the New Ethnicity

INTRODUCTION: REVIVAL OR NOT?

In recent years there has been much discussion of an ethnic revival. Steinberg (1981) notes an ethnic 'resurgence' in the United States, beginning in the 1960s. Mann (1979) outlines how the so-called 'White ethnic' movement was fuelled by the awakening of Black consciousness, and how it presented itself to an unprepared American public. He quotes Greeley:

One of the most extraordinary events of our time has been the resurgence of tribalism in a supposedly secularized and technocratic world. Science and economic rationalization had been expected to reduce, if not eliminate, man's attachment to ancient ties of common ancestry, common land and common faith, but suddenly ties of race, nationality and religion seem to have taken on new importance. (pp. 17–18)

Khlief (1978) discusses the ethnic 'awakening' in the First World, Novak (1980) talks of the resurgence of 'ethnic consciousness', Rokkan and Urwin (1983) describe the 'pronounced and sudden increase' in peripheral protest, and Allardt (1979) documents a 'recrudescence' of ethnic mobilisation throughout western Europe.

Fishman (1983b) also discusses ethnic revival, but his stance is a curious one. The title of his piece refers to the rise and fall of the revival, yet he puts 'ethnic revival' in quotes and suggests that perhaps revival is not an apt term at all. Ethnic revivals, he observes, are 'ethnicity repertoire changes'; this is not unlike the emphasis I have already made. He also seems to agree with Smith (1981; see below) that there will be no 'non-ethnic tomorrow'. Yet Fishman also states that, in the United States at least, revival was but a temporary 'alienation from the central ethos and institutions of mainstream society' (p. 28). If the revival is temporary, it can indeed 'fall'; if there will be no non-ethnic tomorrow, then the revival, as 'repertoire change' would seem a more enduring feature. In general, Fishman's view seems to be that some aspects of the revival (e.g. language maintenance) are unsuccessful, but that ethnic continuity is assured. Thus, the ethnic 'sidestream' will continue to exist and interpenetrate the mainstream. The liberal expectations of ethnicity's disappearance are confounded by this co-existence, but the 'innumerable and mighty mainstream forces' (p. 29) *have* made many features of ethnicity secondary and have permanently altered others.

Smith (1981) has devoted a volume to the ethnic revival. Ethnic ties, he notes, have become more deeply rooted than ever, shocking many liberals, academics, rationalists and Marxists who not only expected a decline in ethnicity, but welcomed it. For many, then, there has been a 'systematic underestimation' of the ethnic revivalist trend, and the hoped-for evolution – the dissolution of ethnic ties and a transition from nationalism to an ever-widening internationalism – has not come to pass. It should be pointed out that the disappointment and the unpreparedness here were essentially academic phenomena inasmuch as they reflected the dashing of theoretical predictions. Furthermore, those *most* surprised by the 'resurgence' were professional ideologues of one stripe or other. Many more comprehensive assessments were not, in fact, so upset by apparently strange new trends, for the simple reason that these were not really new (see below). Smith himself describes the 'new' ethnic trend as part of a broader current beginning in the eighteenth century; the major element which distinguishes it from still earlier variants is the power of modern nationalism (and, we might wish to stress particularly, *linguistic* nationalism). In any event, the new ethnicity is at least two centuries old (see also Edwards, 1984c).

The post-War variety has profited greatly from a new tolerance for national self-determination (still coupled, of course, to a continuing concern for the power and self-interest of dominant groups). Smith (1981) claims that the ultimate, probably lasting, impact of the ethnic revival is to create a tension between 'state and community'; we are fated to live within a 'dynamic spiral' of this tension because 'the ethnic revival is now too deeply entrenched to be easily reversed or eroded, at any rate for many decades; but so is the scientific state' (p. 196).

Smith's discussion suggests that the 'persistence' of ethnicity would be a more accurate reflection of the facts than 'revival'. Mann (1979) notes here that the more enlightened academic observers, of the American scene at least, had been interested in ethnicity long before its popular rediscovery: 'they did not have to be reminded of the persistence of ethnicity' (p. 44). Indeed, our discussion so far – and the particular observation that language and other visible characteristics can be altered or lost in the face of changing circumstances, without the loss of identity – does suggest that ethnic *persistence* accords best with history.

The ethnic 'revival' and the 'new ethnicity' refer to a phenomenon which is neither new nor revived: *ethnicity is an enduring fact of life.* [1] It may be that ethnicity is more visible at present than it has been for some time, but this is due to the changing environment; there is now greater tolerance of diversity, coupled with a pervasive cultural relativism which, within academic circles and officialdom (to some degree), has permitted the ethnic factor to surface – albeit primarily via group 'spokesmen' – with less penalty than has been the case previously.

In a more liberal context, ethnicity is freer to express itself. It might be argued, then, that a revival *does* exist, that a real resuscitation of ethnic markers has occurred. Indeed, some elements *can* be brought back into some degree of prominence, for some people at least. Where this occurs, however, the elements are typically those which do not hinder mobility or adversely mark group members. Many of them – particularly the more 'colourful' ones – become things to be enjoyed not only by group members but by others too. Far from encapsulating groups, or marking them off, these may actually contribute to, and become part of, that cosmopolitan society which is supposedly destructive of ethnic continuity. Relatedly, the notion of ethnic revival often connotes the bringing forward of characteristics in some unaltered and pristine state; this neglects the social evolution which affects all groups and all cultural 'stuff'. Sowell (1978) reminds us that the 'distinctive' cultures of American ethnic groups are largely 'creations growing out of their experiences on American soil' (p. 233; see also Gleason, 1984, on 'groups reshaped by the assimilative forces of American society', p. 243; see also Glazer, 1981; Glazer & Moynihan, 1963; Yancey *et al.*, 1976).

In any event, I am suggesting here that the most important aspect of the ethnic revival has more to do with overall societal dynamics – particularly the degree of tolerance within dominant circles – than it has with any volcanic upsurge from ethnic groups themselves. The greater visibility of group markers and customs is a product of social change, and reflects revised perceptions of what is possible, and desirable, without placing in jeopardy the benefits of social advancement and accessibility. It is often suggested that an important feature of the revival is the rejection of faceless technocracy and a renewed search for more personal, intimate and valuable roots. If this were true, incidentally, it would itself demonstrate general social tolerance; one has to be allowed to reject modernity, or be able to opt out without punishment. Birch (1977) has suggested, mildly enough, that ethnicity may surface when the larger society loses some of its attractions; indeed, if this occurs within a reasonably tolerant society, then we might well expect heightened ethnic visibility. However, many proponents of the new ethnicity have gone further and have waxed poetic over the idea of a return to earlier and simpler times of strong spiritual and ethnic values, values now submerged in the flood of modern, secular, urban life (e.g. Donahue, 1982, cites the 'mechanization, routinization, impersonalization, meaninglessness and valuelessness' of modern urban existence). We have noted already, however, that there is no 'going back' for most people; it is just not an available option. As well, a romantic view of the past disguises harsh realities, and a mindless admiration for contemporary poor, underdeveloped or peasant societies cannot explain the eagerness many have to leave them. There is no evidence at all that people *en masse* wish to escape modernity, least of all the 'ethnics'. In fact, as Sowell (1978) suggests, the intellectually pretentious sport of romanticising past (or present) 'simpler' societies often affronts the desires and hopes of ordinary people. While not unaware of the depersonalising and negative aspects of modern life, most obviously prefer it to some vaguely construed return to roots.

The tolerance which allows a relative flourishing of diversity is itself a product of security and affluence. To the extent to which these may be impermanent themselves, we should expect changes in perceptions of ethnicity and, therefore, in its visibility. There is plenty of historical precedent for repression emerging from societies under pressure, societies having hitherto had good records of tolerance. Indeed, there is emerging at the moment a predictable backlash against pluralism and intra-societal diversity (especially regarding the treatment of diversity, and ethnic minorities, at school; see chapter 5). Also, the notion of cultural relativism is being re-examined and this process may in time affect the open expression of ethnic difference. It is probably inaccurate, however, to think that – in Western society at least – there will be a return to truly repressive policies. In part this is because society itself has altered so much that turning the clock back in this way would entail a more wholesale and undesired regression: we should not forget here that many minority-group members have long been citizens and have more or less successfully penetrated social institutions. It is also the case that most members of most ethnic groups are, *pace* the pluralists and revivalists, increasingly visibly 'unmarked'.

It must be admitted in all this that the question of the *meaning* of the current ethnic manifestation is not entirely answered simply by saying that it reflects a more permanent presence than the term *revival* implies. Given that ethnic visibility is now more possible in many societies, why has it become an *actual* presence? First, we must note that its force is somewhat less than academic interest, media attention, curiosity value and group 'spokesmen' might suggest; ordinary group members are, as we shall see, rather more 'assimilationist' than we are sometimes led to think. Second, however, there *are* dissatisfactions with the bureaucracy and impersonality of modern life, and these may cause people to consider the possibility of having their cake and eating it. Patterson (1977) sees things in altogether too black and white terms here when he outlines a necessary choice between modernity and 'pre-industrial' culture: 'We demand the rewards of industrial civilization but we are not prepared to worship at its shrine. We still want the solace of the old gods and the old faith' (pp. 278–9). Apart from his over-emotional tones here, Patterson is simply wrong in thinking that, within limits, we cannot have both. It is one of the themes of this book that identities alter with contexts, and that the alterations are not haphazard but, rather, reflect the hope of maintaining continuity in the face of changing circumstances. The fact that group boundaries persist while the content they enclose changes indicates that is is normal for groups to come to some accommodation with *both* modernity and tradition.

One of the interesting questions then becomes, Which aspects of the old faith will be kept and which will not? I have suggested that the rule of thumb here is a pragmatic one; while groups may maintain some traditional features in altered circumstances, it is rare that they can keep them all or, indeed, that they would wish to. Language, in its ordinary communicative sense, is often one of the features that must be set aside.

PLURALISM AND ASSIMILATION

A simple dichotomy between pluralism and assimilation has often been assumed by revivalists and apologists for language retention.[2] Not only is the polarisation seen in theoretical terms but, more importantly, it is considered a moral one as well (Gleason, 1984). The almost Orwellian incantation of *pluralism good* and *assimilation bad* has animated many critics of the melting pot (a fusion of diverse elements into a new homogenised whole) and has led to the conclusion that the rendered ethnics must be unmelted.

The basic distinction, as understood by many, is between the melting pot and a maintenance of diversity within the larger system (cultural pluralism). Both of these terms, however, admit of some ambiguity, and both have strong emotional connotations. Gleason (1979) has pointed out that current reference to the melting pot is almost always negative, because of the presumption that the homogenising process is coercive. In addition, however, many go on to hold that the melting pot never really existed anyway (in the United States, at least):

Not only do most writers reject this melting pot with vehemence, they go on to deny that it even had any reality. The conventional wisdom is thus twofold: an an ideal or goal the melting pot is reprehensible, but in the practical order (fortunately, one presumes) it didn't exist, never happened, failed to melt, and is a myth. (Gleason, 1979, p. 15)

Opposed to the conception of a forced melting are those supporting the 'new ethnicity' (e.g. Greeley, 1974; Novak, 1971). Gleason cites Novak, for example, on this new wave:

It stands for a true, real, multicultural cosmopolitanism. It points toward a common culture truly altered by each new infusion of diversity...Struggling to be born is a creature of multicultural beauty, dazzling, free, a higher and richer form of life. It was fashioned in the painful darkness of the melting pot and now, at the appointed time, it awakens. (1979, p. 17)

Readers will note that this poetic expression itself seems to advocate some form of melting; Gleason comments that this is typical of the general confusion.[3] In the minds of many pluralists, however, there seems to be a clear distinction between melting (bad) and pluralism (good).

We should note that *assimilation* has many connotations, two of which are conformity to the dominant culture and complete homogenisation. The first, in the English-speaking world, is often termed *anglo-conformity;* here, ethnic groups adapt themselves to the prevalent culture which, itself, remains stable. This is not a melting pot in the true sense, but it is what the melting pot has meant to many. The second main connotation is a truer reflection of the melting pot image – *all* elements, indigenous and immigrant, minority and majority, intermingle to produce a new identity *for all*. This has been seen as superior to anglo-conformity and Zangwill himself (whose play, *The melting pot,* introduced the phrase and reinforced the theme in modern times) was in favour of this process. But this form, like anglo-conformity, has been criticised as a surrender of identities before some New-World juggernaut.

The plot (or pot) is further thickened by the assertion of pluralists that, awful as it is, the melting pot has not worked (see above). Much is made of Glazer and Moynihan's (1963) statement to this effect. However, we have Gleason (and others) to thank for making it clear that Glazer and Moynihan did *not* mean that assimilation had not occurred. In fact, these writers acknowledged that assimilation had indeed eroded some aspects of ethnicity (language among them), although other group manifestations had endured. The position of Glazer and Moynihan in *Beyond the melting pot* cannot be taken as a simple endorsement of the cultural pluralist position, since the authors' analysis demonstrated a symbiotic relationship between pluralism and assimilation. Misunderstanding has also occurred with Gordon's *Assimilation in American life* (1964), particularly concerning his distinction between cultural and structural pluralism. Gordon argued that cultural pluralism (including linguistic features) was increasingly rare; however, *structural* pluralism, which indicates that some groups have not fully penetrated mainstream institutions, remains somewhat more evident. Gleason (1984) implies that advocates of the ethnic revival were too quick or too incautious to see this important distinction.

It becomes obvious that, in discussions of pluralism and assimilation, there is much room for confusion. Some clarification of basic terms and ideas may be found in Driedger (1980), who outlines six theoretical positions on ethnic groups in majority societies. Two of these (assimilation and amalgamation) assume the gradual disappearance of ethnicity in the face of urbanisation and modernisation; two more (multivariate assimilation and modified pluralism) allow for the retention of some ethnic characteristics, perhaps in altered form; the final two (ethnic conflict and pluralism) predict the maintenance of a relatively unchanged identity.

Assimilation (here signifying conformity to the mainstream) has been a major assumption within sociology for some time. Minority groups would, in the end, melt more or less completely into the dominant milieu. A major proponent of this view was Park (e.g. Park, 1930; Park & Burgess, 1921/1969). However, even here – as Gleason (1984) notes – there was some latitude in the concept and Park himself adopted a view that assimilation really signified the achievement of *sufficient* 'cultural solidarity' to get on in the larger society. *Amalgamation*, the true melting pot, implies that *all* groups fuse and intermingle (see above).

Multivariate assimilation is, Driedger notes, the central pillar in Gordon's (1964) influential study of American life. Here the possibility exists for assimilation to proceed in different ways and at different rates. As noted above, assimilation along cultural lines (language, dress, etc.) was seen as more rapid and more pervasive than that along structural ones. Gordon's position also allows for less assimilation in private spheres (religion and family) than in public ones. *Modified pluralism* reflects Glazer and Moynihan's (1963) observation that groups may retain distinctive features but that these are not the ones originally possessed (i.e. groups change over time, and the content within boundaries is inevitably affected by social dynamics; see Sowell, 1978).

Ethnic conflict sees group differences leading to competition, confrontation and, sometimes, outright hostility (see also the section Ethnic separatism). There exists here a 'dialectic of incompatibles' (Driedger, 1980, p. 297). *Cultural pluralism* itself allows, like its modified variety, the continuation of group distinctiveness. Here, however, there is more emphasis placed upon the transmission and maintenance of original, ancestral group culture. The original architect of cultural pluralism was Kallen (1915, 1924). His argument was rather obscure, but it has been admirably analysed by Gleason (1984). Kallen held that there was no overarching American nationality but rather a collection of distinct groups who would perpetuate themselves indefinitely. The prospects for the future were, in the best of all worlds, ones involving group harmony. Modern cultural pluralists – if they have considered history at all – have looked to Kallen's notion of permanent, harmonious diversity as the ideal. Kallen was never crystal-clear about the actual operation of cultural pluralism, but he assumed that harmony would be automatic. However, Kallen *also* made provision for assimilation; after all, harmony in diversity requires some consensus. As Gleason (1984, p. 224) observes: 'Kallen thus made tacit provision for the *Unum* of the national motto, although his rhetorical stress was altogether on *Pluribus*.' [4]

These theoretical positions on group dynamics accord quite well with the actual possibilities available to minority groups, and they have been dealt with by many writers on the subject. Berry (1981a,b) and Berry *et al.* (1981), for example, present a matrix of group-relations options bearing upon unity and diversity in a larger society. Thus, if traditional identity maintenance is desired but positive relations with mainstream society are too, then *integration* results; here we find voluntary pluralism. If, on the other hand, relations with out-groups are *not* sought, then *segregation* occurs. The other two possibilities in Berry's scheme involve the loss of identity markers and, again, the maintenance or rejection of positive group relations – here we have *assimilation* or *marginality*. [5]

Smith (1981) has also listed a number of strategies available to ethnic groups living in 'polyethnic' states. They are: *isolation* (i.e. segregation, forced or chosen); *accommodation, communalism* and *autonomism* (all varieties of pluralism); *separatism* (the 'classic political goal of ethnonational self-determination'); and *irredentism* (consolidation by means of reunification and recovery of dispersed parts of the community; a cross-state version is the 'pan' movement).

It seems clear that, for most, some form of *multivariate assimilation, modified pluralism* or *accommodation* is the preferred option. These approaches allow both participation in mainstream society *and* maintenance of group cohesion. At the same time, they allow for a dynamic interplay between minority and mainstream, so that groups are not locked into the preservation of all original markers; the 'content' to be maintained is itself changeable. Outright amalgamation or assimilation are not so evident as some might think; certain group markers can be kept for a long time. We have noted how Kallen acknowledged some accommodation within pluralism and Park some cultural maintenance within assimilation. More extreme responses such as separatism, marginality and segregation are usually desired by very few indeed, or are forced upon groups.

If some *form* of pluralism has the widest appeal, it is not the case that pluralism itself is an easy state to maintain nor that there is one level of participation-plus-diversity which will attract all. Gleason (1984) has shown that while pluralism, for a large part of its history, has presumed a considerable degree of accommodation – representing for many 'an enlightened and liberal means of achieving the goal of assimilation, a harmoniously united society' (p. 228) – there have been more militant varieties too. The new ethnicity has often presupposed a simple dichotomous relationship between pluralism and assimilation, and militant pluralism has gained ground here over the last 20 years. Ethnic activists have rejected all forms of 'assimilationist values' and have glorified ethnicity as standing apart. The 'monoculture' and modernity are viewed as technological evils and pluralism as the hope of recapturing what is true, free and human; interestingly, Gleason points out that while militant pluralists advocate the elimination of racist treatment of minority groups, they themselves uphold group classifications based largely on ancestry.

A recent academic response to this tendency has been provided by Gordon (1978, 1981). He views the more militant pluralism as a threat to the social fabric, particularly with its insistence on *group* rights. He calls this stance *corporate pluralism,* and rejects it in favour of *liberal pluralism* (i.e. a participationist version), where 'members of minority groups...make as much or as little as they please of their ancestral cultural heritage. There are no "bonus points" for perpetuating it and no penalties for drawing away from it' (Gordon, 1981, p. 185).[6] Gordon is not alone in rejecting a perspective which places group rights above those of individuals. I noted in chapter 2 Porter's (1975) criticism of the notion that liberal, assimilationist views are too rational, secular and universalistic, that they swamp modern man under a flood of technology. For Porter, the ethnic revival is an anachronistic effort, particularly in the primacy it places upon group rights and the legitimacy of minorities making 'claims *qua* minorities' (p. 295). An important and positive modern social development has been the organisation of societies based upon individual citizenship; for Porter, it would be retrogressive to abandon this (see also Alter, 1972; Glazer, 1983; Isaacs, 1972; O'Brien, 1973; Podhoretz, 1972).

There often exists in pluralist philosophies a sense of a permanent change which, when made, will endure forever. The ethnic populations, now callously homogenised, will return to their unmelted positions and stay there. It is a ludicrously static conception which assumes that once some balance has been achieved things will remain in an unaltered equilibrium (see Edwards, 1977a,

1980a). There is here a naive reliance upon ethnic solidarity, commitment and even boundaries which is belied by history generally and, more specifically, by the social movements which created many ethnic mixtures in the first place. It is probably incorrect, generally speaking, to see cultural pluralism as a state which can be preserved intact. Van den Berghe (1967) has observed that 'cultural pluralism frequently tends to reduce itself as a result of prolonged contact' (p. 133) and, indeed, such a reduction accounts for many societies which are now more or less homogeneous.

Van den Berghe goes on to note that cultural pluralism is not always conducive to democratic order, that pluralistic societies are often held together by political coercion and economic interdependence. It is interesting to consider that many opponents of assimilation feel that unequal social relationships can be amended by pluralising power, when many plural societies are themselves patchworks of inequality. Van den Berghe bluntly observes that 'pluralism and tyranny, though complexly related, have tended to go together' (1967, p. 139; see also Rabushka & Shepsle, cited in Connor, 1980, on the incompatibility of democracy and the 'multinational' state). Higham (1975) notes that 'particularism' and 'fragmentation' may emerge from pluralistic societies, and Stein and Hill (1977) see in pluralism a redefined caste system.

Gleason (1984) supports the view that a general understanding of the real implications of the more strident forms of pluralism will bring about 'a strong reaffirmation of the traditional values of democratic universalism and a frank espousal of assimilation' (p. 253). Less militant pluralism, on the other hand, has much to recommend it if it permits participation. 'Liberal' or 'modified' pluralism is a useful concept at both academic and real-life levels.[7] It prescribes a reasonable course to follow and, more importantly, accurately reflects what most members of most groups *do* anyway. Here, we should recall that most ethnic group members are 'more main-stream and assimilationist than generally believed by language planners' (Drake, 1979, p. 226). Alba (1981), in his studies of American Catholics, notes that the ethnic revival was largely an 'eye-of-the-beholder' effect, and that the enduring elements of ethnicity are mainly symbolic (see also Alba, 1976; Alba & Chamlin, 1983). Gaarder (1981) too has referred to the almost complete lack of resistance to assimilation among American ethnic groups (see also Weinfeld, 1978).

But, does not a participationist pluralism simply represent a stage on the path to complete assimilation? This is a point of criticism which has been raised; two answers suggest themselves. First, even if total assimilation awaits at the end of this road, it is difficult to see how it could be avoided. Second, and more positively, there is the likelihood that private aspects of ethnicity will remain for a long time – exactly as long, in fact, as groups and individuals wish them to. In replying to the question of how post-third-generation groups can keep a sense of identity, Glazer (1980) said that it is, on the contrary, hard to see how it will disappear.

Participationist pluralism – in which some ethnic 'content' is lost or altered – should not be seen as some blind turning away from roots, under pressure from an overarching majority. There is every indication that groups desire change (or, at least, the advantages which they hope it will bring). Indeed, groups often demand greater expedition here than their 'leaders' might like. We often note a gradual decline in affiliation with group societies, schools, churches and media as these become unwanted or unneeded. For example, Lemaire (1966) has documented the growing gap between Franco-American societies and Franco-Americans themselves, and Rumilly (1958) showed how French-speaking parishioners and parents asked for more English at church and in school. Fishman's (1966) work demonstrates that these trends are not unique to Franco-Americans by any means.

The general implication here is that 'de-ethnicisation' occurs because of the formidable attraction of mainstream life. Thus, we can agree with Ravitch (1976) who notes that the process of Americanisation (read also Canadianisation, Australianisation, Anglicisation, etc.) is one sponsored by ethnic groups themselves. To assume that they have been indoctrinated by some mass conspiracy is to credit them with little intelligence or self-interest. The fact that the melting pot does not entirely render ethnicity and that some elements – private, personal, symbolic – remain is evidence that a selection takes place in which some aspects of former life are retired. This is not a traitorous repudiation, but good sense.

Multiculturalism

Multiculturalism, a term favoured in the British, Australian and Canadian contexts, is another name for cultural pluralism, and the issues surrounding it have essentially been dealt with above. I intend to give a very brief outline of the Canadian experience here, however, to reinforce some points already made by presenting information from another important minority-group context. The Canadian setting is particularly interesting given the so-called 'French fact'.[8]

A Canadian policy of multiculturalism within a bilingual framework was first outlined by the Government in response to the report of the Royal Commission on Bilingualism and Biculturalism. In October 1971, Prime Minister Trudeau stated that it would become policy to assist Canadian cultural groups in their efforts to develop and to contribute to society as a whole, to help them overcome cultural barriers to participation in mainstream society, to promote 'creative encounters' among groups, and to assist immigrants in learning at least one of the two official languages. From this flowed the Canadian Consultative Council on Multiculturalism, and the Multiculturalism Directorate within the Department of the Secretary of State.[9]

Burnet (1975) points out that the Government's intention was not to encourage *cultures*, but rather ethnic groups; the aim seems to be to help in the preservation of ethnic identity insofar as this does not interfere with the recent sacred quest for a Canadian one. The phrase 'within a bilingual framework' refers to the fact that only the two 'charter' languages are to be stressed – meaning that others are not (see O'Bryan *et al.*, 1976). There is thus an apparently enduring difference between the status of ethnic groups and that of the French and English. Burnet summarises the possibilities of multiculturalism as follows:

Multiculturalism within a bilingual framework can work, if it is interpreted as intended – that is, as encouraging those members of ethnic groups who want to do so to maintain a proud sense of the contribution of their group to Canadian society. Interpreted in this way, it becomes something very North American: voluntary marginal differentiation among peoples who are equal participants in the society. If it is interpreted in a second way – as enabling various peoples to transfer foreign cultures and languages as living wholes into a new place and time – multiculturalism is doomed. (1975, pp. 211–12)

Burnet herself is in favour of the first interpretation which, of course, represents a participationist pluralism (see above).

Some have claimed that the policy is, in fact, a myth, and Burnet (1979) addresses herself to this issue. [10] Her view is that multicultural policy is *not* a myth, although it leads to the creation of myths. One of these has to do with the misinterpretation of the policy's intent, noted above. Burnet also discusses the myth of 'early arrival', the idea that having arrived first in Canada establishes special claims; this is a dangerous and foolish idea, as I have noted elsewhere (Edwards, 1980a). Burnet refers, too, to the myth of British villainy, the idea that solace can be found in the definition of an overarching oppressor. This, she notes, is very oversimplified. Indeed, Burnet makes the salutary observation that ethnic groups are not more or less virtuous than others: 'We must forego the pleasure of regarding some ethnic groups as more virtuous than others, and look instead in a detached way at the kinds of things people – all people – do in various situations' (1979, p. 55). Most groups have been both oppressors and oppressed and it does no good to try and make mileage from the fact that, at some carefully selected time and place, they were either one or the other.

There have been objections to multiculturalism in Canada, the most vociferous of which have come from the Francophone community (see Lambert & Curtis, 1983). Some have feared that the French will be reduced to the status of the 'other' ethnic groups, losing their traditional position as one of the two dominant partners in the country. It could be argued, of course, that multiculturalism would have this effect on the English as well, but this group is not seen to be in the same precarious position as the French. In fact, a cynic could suggest that some of the English support for multiculturalism exists precisely because it may have a defusing effect upon the French 'problem' in Canada. Rocher's criticisms (cited in Bullivant, 1981b) illustrate typical French apprehensions over multiculturalism. The policy, it is felt, may jeopardise the future of bilingualism which, itself, may lose its cultural connotation. Multiculturalism and national unity may be incompatible (a point of view obviously shared by some Anglophones). Most generally, multi-culturalism may be a backward step for the French who have their own traditional concerns about dominance and equality in Canada.[11]

It might be thought that the Canadian context – in which there are two 'charter' groups, one of which, however, is in a minority position – is unique since the struggle of the French to maintain and improve their position undermines multiculturalism in a manner not to be found elsewhere. The Canadian scene certainly presents its own features, but inter-minority rivalries are common in all heterogeneous societies. Much special pleading is done for *particular* groups under the mantle of a *general* regard for pluralism itself (Edwards, 1984a).

Ethnic separatism

Ethnic separatism, as noted above, is a possible strategy for resolving group tensions and fulfilling group needs; because of its extremity it is a fairly rare commodity. Still, Smith (1981) reminds us of the nineteenth-century Eastern European movements, the Bengalis in Bangladesh, the Eritreans, Kurds, Ibo and, in a more contemporary context, the efforts of the Scottish National Party and the Parti Québécois (see also Smith, 1982; Williams, 1982, 1984).

Williams (1984) has provided a useful overview of separatism, or *autonomist nationalism,* supplementing his theoretical outline with case studies of the Welsh, Basques, and Québécois. Citing Smith (1979a), he notes the 'watchwords' of separatism – identity, authenticity and diversity – and the three basic preconditions for its development. These are a core territory, group markers (particularly language and religion) and 'opposition groups' (concentrated regionally or in terms of power or dominance). These three conditions often exist not only for indigenous minorities but also for immigrant populations (especially newly-arrived ones). As I have noted elsewhere (Edwards, 1984c), it is interesting that, where these conditions no longer exist or where they are weak (e.g. increasingly among most American minority groups), cultural pluralists and group leaders often try to re-establish them. The idea of a common homeland (or past) is invoked, attempts are made to reinvigorate group markers (like language) and a 'we-them' opposition is postulated (difficult when group members – and particularly the leaders themselves – have often penetrated at least some way into the corridors of power). Thus, while separatism itself may be unlikely in many contexts, and is often not wanted, we observe that the important factors are not unlike those underlying less extreme ethnic movements.

SYMBOLIC ETHNICITY

In the first chapter I referred to the distinction between communicative and symbolic aspects of language and throughout the book I have mentioned differences between public and private manifestations of ethnicity generally. With regard to language the point is that while, ordinarily, communicative and symbolic facets co-exist, they are separable. Among mainstream populations the language of daily use is usually also the variety which carries and reflects group culture and tradition. Among minority groups, or within groups in which language shift has occurred in the reasonably recent past, the value of language as a symbol can remain in the absence of the communicative function (see Edwards, 1977a). The Irish example demonstrates a continuing attachment for a language no longer widely spoken, whose communicative revival is neither feasible nor generally desired. Eastman (1984) has argued, similarly, for the notion of an 'associated' language which is connected with group identity but which is not used regularly or, indeed, known at all (see also Eastman & Reese, 1981).

Ignorance of the communicative–symbolic distinction can lead to lack of clarity and misdirected effort. If revivalists emphasise language mainly in communicative terms when mounting their campaigns, and if their appeals are directed towards groups where shift has occurred, then they: (a) will be unsuccessful in the promotion of language use; (b) may reintroduce, under the mantle of pluralism, a sort of *anomie* (see Riesman, 1965); and (c) may promote a cynical view of any and all efforts on behalf of group identity. In 1976, for example, I described a bilingual education programme for French children in Vermont. As part of the study of the effects of this programme, parents (who spoke French) were asked to rate themselves along linguistic lines. About 55 per cent saw themselves as mainly English; another 13 per cent felt they were in some transitional period between French and English. There were other families in the programme who did not meet the criterion of speaking French at all. Yet the project had been established, by well-meaning outsiders, precisely to bolster communicative French usage. The most cursory survey of the area showed that most families were well settled – originally from Quebec, they were not new immigrants – thought of themselves as Americans and retained French for private purposes. The programme, in its ignorance, attempted to sustain a changing identity through public language use, via the children. When it ended, because of local unwillingness to pick up the financial reins from the federal funding agency, it left in its wake a cynicism which extended to all forms of active intervention in defence of identity. It seemed too, that this failure to influence a public marker of groupness actually weakened the desire for private elements – especially among the children, whose increasing lack of interest in the language transferred itself to other features of their French background.

A distinction between communicative and symbolic language mirrors a more general one between public and private ethnic markers. It is the force of the argument so far that, for practical reasons, we should expect public and non-symbolic charateristics to be relatively early casualties in assimilative or modified pluralistic contexts. Private and symbolic markers, on the other hand, continue to exist because they promote the continuation of group boundaries without hindering social mobility and access. It should be noted that *some* public markers persist for a long time; this is because they are both public *and* symbolic. Dress, ornamentation, dance, song – these may disappear as ordinary markers of group life while persisting (or re-emerging) as symbolic markers, albeit public ones. In this case, their appearance is often limited to special festivals, 'days' and the like, may be linked to commercial interests, and can become available to anyone interested, group member or not. [12]

A very useful discussion of symbolic ethnicity, to which I have already briefly alluded, has been provided by Gans (1979). He states that the new ethnicity has not affected basic processes of acculturation and assimilation, but there *is* a new interest in 'roots'. This is not intense enough to lead to any revival, but it does give rise to renewed ethnic symbolism. This, in Gans' words, is 'an ethnicity of last resort, which could, nevertheless, persist for generations' (p. 1). Ultimately, however, even this will disappear, according to Gans. Consequently, there has been no essential disruption of so-called 'straight-line theory', i.e. that which predicts the gradual absorption of minorities. However, because of upward mobility, ethnic groups have become more visible and have adopted ethnic symbols; this has led to attention from 'journalists and essayists' who have been largely responsible for propounding the idea of an 'ethnic revival' (see also Hinton, 1981). All of this implies that Hansen's (1952) famous notion of the third-generation 'return' to ethnicity is, if true, essentially limited to symbolic manifestations, e.g. the returning grandsons do not often want to learn the ancestral language (see Edwards, 1977a; Fishman, 1966; Smolicz, 1979b).

If symbolic ethnicity and private markers are the aspects which remain, it follows that active intervention on behalf of minority identity may be non-productive or, indeed, counter-productive. There is no evidence to suggest that meaningful aspects of ethnicity can be held in place for any reasonable length of time by such action, much less the ones that are usually dealt with (like language), which are visible and public markers highly susceptible to change. It is instructive here to consider that Greeley – clearly in favour of ethnic persistence – acknowledges that the 'core of ethnic residue' endures precisely because 'little if any self-consciousness about ethnic heritage is required and because behavior patterns are intimate and interpersonal' (1981, p. 146), that residual characteristics remain because they do not evoke social penalty, and that groups 'will rather quickly relinquish ethnic characteristics that are an obstacle to American achievement' (p. 147). [13]

It can of course be argued that a trade-off between public and private, symbolic and non-symbolic ethnicity is bad if all that remains to a group is some symbolic 'residue'. Thus Smolicz (1979b) observes that 'residual ethnicity obscures the fact of ethnic cultural degeneration...ethnic culture gets steadily shallower' (p. 87). But is change degeneration? Does Smolicz bewail the inevitable? The force of history suggests simply that the transition to residual ethnicity occurs widely and that it is not a phenomenon fought against by most ordinary group members. Retention of public, visible markers is unlikely, with or without official support and encouragement, given the social realities bearing upon majority–minority relations – except, of course, where group segregation is preferred (rare) or enforced (indefensible).

CULTURAL RELATIVISM AND THE FORCE OF MODERNITY

In the social movements which lead to the erosion of certain group markers, one fact stands out: most people are animated by the desire for material well-being and advancement, and are thus inexorably drawn towards the technological, in-dustralised mainstream. They may not welcome all the changes required, but their cost–benefit analyses indicate that they should be made. Mankind, Gellner (1983) observes, is committed to industrial society, and in pursuit of its rewards will alter traditional life-styles. In an earlier work, Gellner (1968) clarifies why this is a reasonable course to follow:

The cognitive and technical superiority of one form of life [i.e. the 'scientific-industrial'] is so manifest, and so loaded with implications for the satisfaction of human wants and needs – and, for better or worse, for power – that it simply cannot be questioned. If a doctrine conflicts with the acceptance of the superiority of scientific-industrial societies over others, then it really is out. . . The cognitive and technical superiority does not im-ply or bring with it superiority in any other field. What it does do is to bring along the *possibility* – no more – of a certain material liberation. (p. 405)

The import of Gellner's remarks, apart from the general approval of modernity, is to question the idea of *cultural relativism*. This, in turn, is important for present purposes because cultural relativism underlies much of the argument (particularly in its more extreme forms) for cultural pluralism. If we were able to say that culture A is superior to culture B, then we might not feel obliged to support the latter. But it is part of the rhetoric of pluralism that *all* cultures are valuable and worthy of support.

Cultural relativism has been a received idea in much of the social sciences for a long time, but it does present certain difficulties. Musgrove (1982) notes, for example, that the fact of Nazi Germany dealt a severe blow to the concept; could it be that there was, after all, 'no rational way of deciding between the ethics of a Roosevelt and the ethics of Hitler?' (p. 123). O'Brien (1973) reminds us that the respect for group culture inherent in relativism may lead us to accept and support an acceptance of castes, brutal treatment of women, religious intolerance, etc. Honey (1983) adds Stalinist Russia, cannibalism, child prostitution and slavery to the list.

All of this convinces Musgrove of the 'repugnance of relativism', and it is, indeed, difficult to reconcile an all-embracing respect for different cultures with practices abhorrent to us. Thus we search for what Musgrove calls 'transcenden-tal criteria and yardsticks against which all cultures. . .could be measured, valued, and placed in order' (p. 126). Several have been suggested, including Clive Bell's 'good states of mind', Steven Lukes' 'law of non-contradiction', and the degree to which societies permit self-criticism. Yet none of these *logically* refutes cultural relativism, and Gellner (1968) doubts whether the problem *has*

The Ethnic Revival and the New Ethnicity

such a solution. Still, as we have seen, he comes down on the anti-relativism side; he argues this way, not from logic, but from the evidence of the real world: 'It is worth noting that it is intuitively repellent to pretend that the Zande belief in witchcraft is as valid as our rejection of it, and that to suppose it such is a philosophical affectation, which cannot be maintained outside the study' (p. 388). The evident superiority of the scientific culture is reinforced by the fact that it is the only one which 'castigates itself for being ethno-centric and indulges in cultural relativism' (Musgrove, 1982, p. 128). [14] For Gellner, the most important argument against relativism is that, while it holds that cultures cannot be judged one with the other, or against themselves at different times, *they in fact do so*. Social evolution involves judgement, evaluation, repudiation and change. Implicit in progress is the notion that change is for the better, that the society of a later time is superior to itself at an earlier one. The scientific society is pre-eminent here because it is the product of such evolution, it permits (though by no means ensures) greater individual freedom and, in Musgrove's words, simply allows for more human decency.

Now, all of this may seem at some remove from matters of minority adjustment to larger societies, particularly when the groups in question originate, themselves, from more or less 'scientific' societies. But an extension of the anti-relativist argument is that all cultures or subcultures in contact *should* change, in some social survival-of-the-fittest scenario. Thus, Musgrove cites with approval the views of Chazan (1978) – whose work deals with Jewish education and culture in Great Britain – that 'survivalism' for its own sake is dysfunctional and that traditional culture should persist only where it continues to have relevance in the contemporary context. The danger of relativism (particularly in education: see chapter 5) is that, out of a misplaced and unselective respect, it may freeze cultures and people, keeping them in primitive, deprived or powerless states or perhaps segregating them in some kind of 'folk museum'.

I must say I find Gellner's position a compelling one, and parts of Musgrove's thesis are also valuable. An outright cultural relativism *does* lead to horrendous real-life problems, whatever the difficulties in finding logical cross-cultural yardsticks. After all, the pragmatic adjustments to group identity which I have been stressing here as eminently sensible do, themselves, suggest that ordinary people are quite able and willing to make value judgements about societies and cultures.

However, I also find that *anti*-relativism poses problems, especially concerning language. Both Musgrove (1982) and Honey (1983) have attempted to say that some languages are superior to others and that the assumptions of linguists – that languages and dialects cannot be compared in terms of 'better' or 'worse' – are suspect because they rest upon linguistic relativism. I have argued elsewhere in favour of the idea of linguistic relativism (see Edwards, 1979b, 1983b, in press d) and have accepted the evidence of linguists and anthropologists that there are no 'primitive' or 'debased' varieties, that all are sufficient for their users' needs, and that no variety is logically superior to another.

The flaw in the perspective of the anti-relativists is essentially that, since the concept of cultural relativism is suspect and open to error, *all* elements of it are seen to be unlikely. My position, simply, is that *relativism is itself relative*, i.e. *relative to specific cultural manifestations and practices*. I take it for granted that a society which condones female circumcision and believes in witchcraft is inferior, *in these respects*, to one which does not. I accept Gellner's claim for the general superiority of the scientific-industrial society over all others, including itself at an earlier stage of development. I do not see that this constrains me to accept, as well, that language A is superior to language B, even if B-speakers eat their enemies while A-speakers turn the other cheek. It is a very large and vexing question as to why some societies do not 'develop' as much as others, why 'cultures are extremely unequal in their cognitive power' (Gellner, 1968, p. 401). Physical environment is doubtless the most important distinguishing feature here, promoting or retarding social evolution. But we must recall, with Cole and Scribner (1974), that although cognitive capacities are differently developed, the same underlying potentials are found in all cultures. My conclusion is that linguistic relativity is unshaken as a basis for understanding language variation precisely because – whatever the degree of development of other cognitive skills in other areas – the development of adequate *language* is a universal. [15]

SUMMARY

The notion of an ethnic revival is a dubious one. True, there has been more ethnic visibility of late, particularly of ethnic *symbols*, but *persistence* seems a more accurate term than *revival*. Ethnicity has become more manifest because of changes in the amount of tolerance of diversity and the increased social mobility and success of ethnic groups themselves. In important ways, however, the assimilative process continues, This should not be wondered at, for, in America and elsewhere, the adoption of mainstream values is perceived as a necessary move; it is a very strong drive, both in indigenous minorities and among immigrant groups who, in making moves entailing very real psychological and material costs, obviously wish these to prove worthwhile.

Yet all is not lost. Not all elements of ethnicity are flung beneath the juggernaut of mainstream society, of urban modernity; not all features are melted down. Typically and unsurprisingly, one finds a need and a willingness to make alterations in those visible markers of groupness which might compromise chances of success; at the same time, more private and symbolic elements are retained without penalty. The theoretically appealing position here accords with reality and can be termed *participationist pluralism*.

This variety of pluralism also accords with what I have discussed here as *relative relativism*, for the latter also involves selection. I emphasised the importance of being able to retain the concept of *linguistic* relativism, while rejecting the position that *all* values and practices of *all* cultures are above criticism and judgement. Questions of relativism are probably not, as Gellner notes, logically answerable, but the force of reality nevertheless compels us to some accommodation with a concept which, if pushed to extremes, confronts us with practices and ideas which most in the world find repellent.

Porter (1972, 1975) has expressed very well the fear we have encountered in Musgrove's anti-relativism, with its celebration of modernity, of 'cities, literacy, cognitive skills, and schools; scientific rationality, mobility, and educated elites' (p. 173). Porter feels that ethnicity is atavistic in an industrial world, fears that it elevates group rights above those of individuals, and rejects the view that cultures have automatic rights to existence and equal claims on our moral support. In short, Porter's view is that ethnicity is an anachronism (see also Lipkin & Lawson, 1978; Vallee, 1981). My view, as noted above, is that Porter, Musgrove and others like them are both right and wrong. They are right to celebrate the evolution of scientific rationalism and to point out that ethnicity can be a regressive force. Yet they err in underestimating and misjudging the continuing power of ethnicity and, indeed, its value.

The value of ethnicity is, increasingly, as a complement to scientific-industrial life rather than as an alternative to it. Some form of modified pluralism, some retention of ethnic symbolism – these are the keys to this complementarity. In an out-and-out struggle with modernity, ethnicity is the loser, but traditional elements can be successfully maintained within contemporary life. It may be that, for some ethnic and pluralist extremists, altering ethnicity is tantamount to destroying it. Such views, however, have never had much currency among those most directly involved.

The dilemma posed by the conjunction of minority and majority, of tradition and modernity, is one of 'roots and options' (Rokkan & Urwin, 1983) or of 'civism and pluralism' (Bullivant, 1981, 1984b), or of 'state and community' (Smith, 1981). The position adopted in this book is that people sort out this dilemma according to their own best interests, within the constraints of the context, and often in a way which permits cultural continuity to exist alongside full social participation. They realise only too well that 'domination by roots alone may end up in social, cultural and even economic serfdom. The multiplication of options may result in anomia' (Rokkan & Urwin, 1983, p. 115). These authors also put the matter another way: 'A policy of alliance and acceptance increases the risk of inexorable loss of cultural identity; a policy of self-assertion may simply lead towards trivialization and a folklorization of the peripheral population' (p. 95).

Adjustments made to resolve this dilemma occur in a real world and thus do not always accord with the desires and ideals of group spokesmen, cultural pluralists, language revivalists, and the like. Two important factors suggest themselves. First, supporters of pluralism often seem to want a more highly visible, distinct sense of group differentiation than is envisaged by group members themselves. Second, they wish to accomplish their ends by deliberate intervention in the social fabric. This does not accord particularly well with the powerful evolutionary processes described above. We should not forget, too, that proponents of pluralism are often concerned for *specific* groups and 'are not primarily interested in understanding what is going on, but in getting something for their constituents' (Gleason, 1979, p. 18).

In short, *pluralistic integration* (modified pluralism, liberal pluralism, etc.) appears more attractive and reasonable than more militant forms of cultural pluralism in that it represents a more natural social process. It also allows us to conceive of a population willing and able to decide its own adaptations. Many supporters of cultural pluralism are atypical of those they supposedly represent, leading one to think that theirs is an elitist movement which does not trust in its constituents' capacity to look after themselves.

5

Language, Education and Identity

INTRODUCTION

Access to education, once a privilege, is now a right. Indeed, children in most places *must* go to school until a determined age. The school must therefore cater for large numbers of children who do not always come from similar backgrounds. This simple fact means that pressures of many kinds are endemic within the educational process. There are of course different ways in which schools can respond to issues raised by the heterogeneity of populations, but perhaps it is not unfair to see these as falling into two main categories. The first involves pupils adapting to the ideas and methods of the school; the second, the adaptation of the school to its pupils. Present-day education in many parts of the world shows at least some tendencies towards the second, and is generally more flexible than has historically been the case. Inflexibility clearly involves potential damage to children who are forced into pre-existing moulds. However, the apparent advantage of greater flexibility on the part of the school can be offset by the possibility that children may not be exposed to things which will fit them for participation in the wider social milieu. Since many minority-group families see their children's future directly related to success in the mainstream, too much accommodation may be actually unwelcome. We do not, more generally, wish to see education *limiting* children's chances.

Minority-group accommodation to the mainstream is, as we have seen, a valuable process. At the same time, we have also seen that cultural continuity is possible under some variety of participationist pluralism. What is the role of education here? In particular, what is the function of the school in the maintenance of group identity and of group language? While I shall briefly discuss matters of strictly pedagogical import, it should be clear from the beginning that schools have always been considered to have great extra-academic significance. Indeed, it is not putting things too strongly to say that education has often been perceived as the *central* pillar in group-identity maintenance, providing an essential support for linguistic nationalism and ethnic revival.

The discussion so far has suggested that schools do *not* possess the power attributed to them by many; experiences in Celtic and other contexts demonstrate that the school reflects strong social currents more than initiating or leading them and that – in situations in which dominant languages threaten weaker ones – either teaching or *not* teaching the subordinate variety can serve the assimilative process. The 'ultimate prospects of survival' (Greene, 1981, p. 6) are not primarily influenced by what goes on in school. It might be argued then, that little need be said of education specifically. However, it is worth attending to here for at least three reasons: (a) it allows me to bring out more interesting and generalisable details from the fascinating North American scene; (b) whatever history may suggest, pluralists continue to place their best bets on education, and we should, consequently, pay some particular regard to it; (c) I want to show that emphasis upon *communicative language* maintenance at school is, following the argument thus far, often a misguided notion.

It is apparent that, regardless of purely pedagogical factors, educational programmes can be seen as potential servants to the cause of cultural pluralism; schools can be instruments of ethnic or nationalist policy. This has interesting, not to say disturbing, ramifications. For example, Kedourie (1961) states that:

On nationalist theory...the purpose of education is not to transmit knowledge, traditional wisdom, and the ways devised by a society for attending to the common concerns; its purpose rather is wholly political, to bend the will of the young to the will of the nation. Schools are instruments of state policy, like the army, the police, and the exchequer. (pp. 83–4)

Ravitch (1981) notes that schools in the United States have reeled under the impact of social policies they are supposed to effect; the role of the schools as educational institutions has been increasingly rejected in favour of seeing them as 'sociological cookie cutters'. While not denying that schools may have many additional purposes, Ravitch remarks that their first concern should be to encourage, guide and promote intelligence. Of course, *all* education is political, but presumably there are degrees. Bullivant (1981a) touches upon the same theme. In a study of six plural societies he discusses the dilemma of 'civism' and 'pluralism' at school. The modern stress on individualism, he notes, has weakened the school's transmission of essential common elements, and he thus emphasises the need for a general-knowledge core curriculum – this is what will really help minority students function and succeed in the wider society. In a statement referring specifically to Great Britain, but having a broader significance too, Bullivant states: 'It seems to me inevitable that the composition of the core elements in the curriculum must be related to the dominant society, even though this might be interpreted as a form of ethnic hegemony' (1981a, p. 39). As well, Bullivant demonstrates how attention to educational programmes can distract from the solution of real sociopolitical problems of minority groups. We can imagine how this is most often an emphasis promoted by unthinking but well-meaning supporters of diversity; it is also possible to conceive of a more sinister variant, in which governments may adopt a pluralistic stance as a way of keeping minorities subordinated while *appearing* to attend to their needs (see e.g. Breton *et al.*, 1980). If governments pay groups to retain aspects of public ethnicity and if they support school promotion of various ethnic manifestations, may they not be doing groups a disservice (see chapter 4)?

As I implied in the last chapter, Musgrove (1982) has come down firmly against education *for* culture. His argument is basically that – with the rejection of relativism as 'repugnant' – we are not obliged to respect all possible cultures and we are certainly not required to help transmit or maintain them at school. Indeed, we should stress and promote the scientific-industrial society; the school has an essential part to play here in helping to liberate people from those contexts in which needed skills and opportunities are lacking. The value of education lies precisely in its ability to take learning *out* of specific contexts: 'The critical weakness of in-context teaching [is]...it suppresses both curiosity and intelligent understanding' (p. 62). Musgrove acknowledges that recent 'liberal' currents which have encouraged multiculturalism at school are valuable insofar as they reflect a sympathy for other cultures 'often worthy of respect and support' (p. 115); multiculturalism makes sense when it means that pupils' origins are taken into account. But schooling is to 'open windows onto wider worlds' and the 'culture concept closes them' (p. 133). Thus, Musgrove's view of education is one in which minority and mainstream cultures both have a place; they are, after all, both social facts of life. But, the *role* of the school is not to transmit them but to transform them. Underlying all must be a firm base of scientific rationality, e.g. there is no question of presenting witchcraft as merely a *different* approach to that of science.

I have already indicated that, while there is much that is commendable in Musgrove's thesis, it does lead to some dubious conclusions (e.g. concerning language). As well, many of the 'other' cultures Musgrove considers are considerably farther removed from the scientific-industrial mainstream than are those of concern to pluralists in Europe, North America and Australia. However, his basic point – that education should strive to accommodate and transform cultures in contact, not to transmit them *in toto* – is clearly of significance in all contexts.

BILINGUAL EDUCATION IN THE UNITED STATES

Throughout this discussion I shall refer to bilingual education in a broad sense,[1] along the lines of a definition provided by Andersson and Boyer (1970, p. 12): 'Bilingual education is instruction in two languages and the use of those two languages as mediums of instruction for any part or all of the school curriculum. Study of the history and culture associated with a student's mother tongue is considered an integral part of bilingual education.' The definition stems from guidelines for the federally supported programmes in the United States, on which most of my comments here will be based. The reader should be aware, however, that many different actual and potential programmes exist under the general rubric of bilingual education (e.g. Gaarder, 1967; Mackey, 1970).[2]

Historically, the decline of the ethnic-group-initiated schools paralleled the course of assimilation generally. Immigrant groups which established their own schools, churches, societies and newspapers came to feel the need of them less and less. It is important to understand that the decline of these institutions reflected this decreasing need and desire and was not due to abdication of responsibility on their part. Historical consideration of early bilingual education in America has been rather slight. As Schlossman (1983a, b) has pointed out, there *have* been historical references made in current debates over bilingual education, but these have been 'politicized', based upon poor research and used essentially to score debating points; 'jingoism' has often been a substitute for dispassionate analysis (see also Edwards, 1980a, 1984a, c). In his two articles, Schlossman considers early controversies in bilingual education for the two groups for whom it was most salient: the Germans and the Mexicans.

In the nineteenth century, only concentrated settlements of Germans in rural areas received much vernacular instruction; in cities, German was more a token offering. Those non-Germans in favour of German at school were motivated by desires to prevent the continuation of ethnic enclaves; instruction in the language would at once foster family cohesion *and* promote assimilation (see chapter 3). There were strong feelings that, although private school arrangements should certainly be allowed, the public system was under no legal obligation to provide anything other than English instruction. Indeed, Schlossman notes that there was little parental protest when such German as existed in the public sector declined, and he suggests that parents never considered public schools as preservers of identity. Schlossman observes that German schooling was subject to much curricular change – an 'unending process of local improvisation and conscious experimentation' (1983a, p. 158) – and contrasts this with the modern desire for a 'best' solution to bilingual education. Overall, his analysis suggests both an extraordinary potential for educational provision for minorities and the increasing popularity of the view, among Germans themselves, that adjustment to mainstream society was a desirable process.

When he turns to consider some early currents in the education of Hispanic Americans, Schlossman again notes that the 'self-evident remedy' of bilingual education for Spanish children in the United States today shows little historical continuity. The views of George Sanchez – the 'most distinguished intellectual predecessor' of modern Hispanic-American education (1983b, p. 873) – are examined and we note that, in the early decades of this century, he advocated Hispanic socioeconomic advancement over language/culture maintenance *per se*, saw schools as the modernisers of Hispanic culture (see Musgrove, 1982) and the key to 'assimilation and success', and viewed Spanish in classrooms as 'at best, an unfortunate necessity' (p. 899). By the time Sanchez made his final observations on Hispanic education, in 1966, the movement for the 'self-evident remedy' had become vociferous, even though disagreement within the Hispanic community has always existed over the 'transition-maintenance' distinction (see section below). As Schlossman points out, consideration of Sanchez's ideas is not without contemporary merit, particularly because they illuminate the inadequacy of extreme stances – for and against – on current bilingual education.

I think the general value of Schlossman's work lies in its demonstration that minority-group desires concerning public education are not unrelated to larger social aims; indeed, they reflect them. Since I have already stressed that, with regard to 'visible' markers at least, assimilation has proved by far the most popular option (see chapter 4), it is not at all surprising that German-Americans accepted the gradual decline of the language at school, or that Spanish educators, acutely concerned for their group's well-being, stressed and welcomed the modernising, indeed anglicising, role of the school. This does not mean that bilingual education *per se* was, or is, without value, but it does suggest that some transitional form commanded the widest general appeal.

From about the time of the First World War until the early 1960s there was very little bilingual education in the United States (Andersson, 1971; Andersson & Boyer, 1970; Fishman, 1966). The contemporary phase began in 1963 with the establishment of a Spanish–English programme in Miami catering for a substantial Cuban population (Richardson, 1968). But the major recent impetus for bilingual education came with the passage of the Bilingual Education Act in 1968 (Andersson & Boyer, 1970; United States Commission on Civil Rights, 1975). This legislation, while emphasising the primary importance of English, aimed to assist children of limited English-speaking ability by providing them with instruction in their own language, especially during the early school years. Many thousands of children have participated in hundreds of programmes under the auspices of this legislation (Cooper, 1978b; Troike & Pérez, 1978; see also Thernstrom, 1980, for general notes on bilingual legislation). Most programmes have been directed towards Spanish-speaking children but they have also been established for speakers of many other languages.

Perspectives: for and against

From the beginning, it is apparent that contemporary American bilingual education was not a disinterested exercise but a programme of social policy and ideology. Sowell (1978) pointed out, for example, the distortion caused by commentators' 'moralistic-ideological imperatives'. Drake (1979) also refers to ideological colouring affecting supposedly objective discussion (see also Van den Berghe, 1967). Some examples here will establish the point.

A relatively early view held that bilingual education was 'the noblest innovation in American education' (Gaarder, 1970, p. 13). More recently, Swanson referred to it as the 'greatest undertaking in American education during our life-time' (1978, p. 139). Fishman (cited in Spolsky, 1978) stated to a Senate committee that 'our national genius and our national promise depend upon a more conscious and a better implemented commitment to a permanently culturally pluralistic society' (p. 274). Hernández-Chávez (1978, p. 547) noted that 'we urgently need to seek a policy of bilingualism in this country that supports the maintenance, development, and full flowering of the ethnic languages.'

De Valdés (1979) discusses bilingual education for Spanish children in the United States. She sees an America 'fraught with xenophobia' (p. 408; see also Troike & Pérez, 1978), a 'mass media campaign to discredit ethnicity' (p. 409) and a 'textbook demonstration of an orchestrated development of public opinion with planted articles, news items, and television features' (p. 411) designed to oppose bilingual education and cultural pluralism (see Edwards, 1980a). Nieves-Squires refers to the 'onslaught of cultural imperialism' (1977, p. 98). Blanco (1977) discusses, on the other hand, the 'salutary climate for cultural diversity' and 'America's recognition of its pluralistic society' (p. 2). He also states that the community has 'rallied to the aid of bilingual education' (p. 52) and that, in its handling of pluralism and bilingual education', America has the chance to 'prove its mettle' (p. 63). Advertising to the need for objective presentation of findings on bilingual education, Blanco observes that 'it is not possible to lend credence to the negative reports concerning bilingual education' (p. 61), although positive findings can be supported because they have met strict research criteria. Positive findings, incidentally, are not always regarded as being of such a reliable nature (see Venezky, 1981) and Epstein (1978a) has referred to the attempted suppression of negative findings. On a grander scale altogether, Troike and Pérez (1978) see bilingual education as supporting nothing less than 'the continued leadership and security of our nation' (p. 79). Parker and Heath approvingly cite the view that bilingual education can help 'the true spirit of American democracy' to be freed from the 'shackles of prejudice, discrimination, and wasted manpower' (1978, p. 50).

These are views of supporters of American bilingual education; some are doubtful, some are grandiose, some are distastful. They give a flavour, however, of the climate within which proponents of pluralism have seen education as a servant to their cause. It is equally the case that *critics* of bilingual education have reacted emotionally. However, it is worth observing at this juncture – and it is not without interest extending well beyond American shores – that the emotional opposition to bilingual education and cultural pluralism has come largely from the popular press, whereas the emotion on the favourable side can be found among the academic constituency.

An editorial in the *New York Times* (28 October 1975) dealt with the allegedly disruptive aspects of bilingualism in Canada, a phenomenon seen as perpetuating differences along an 'ethnic tightrope'. In the Canadian experience, the editorial concluded, there was a lesson for the United States: the sooner immigrants learned English and assimilated, the better for them and the country. About a year later (22 November 1976), the same newspaper published another editorial on the 'bilingual danger'. Again, the Canadian situation and the Quebec separatist movement introduce the piece. While endorsing bilingual education as facilitating non-English-speaking children's assimilation, the editorial opposed programmes which would maintain a language (Spanish in this case) in a more permanent manner at school. This, it is feared, would lead to 'linguistic separatism' which would, in turn, condemn 'to permanent economic and social disadvantage those who cut themselves off from the majority culture'. [3]

Parker and Heath (1978) draw our attention to an article in *Time* (13 February 1978) dealing with the 'swamping' of English by Spanish in Miami, and to a *Washington Post* editorial (27 September 1974) which fears that bilingualism will weaken the 'common American glue' which can bind diverse groups, who should now develop an 'American inheritance'. Similarly, Blanco (1977) refers to a piece in the *New York Times* (3 November 1974) in which it is claimed that, while recognising diversity, Americans still want the schools 'to be the basis of an American melting pot'.

A lengthier and more cohesive article against bilingual education is that of Bethell (1979). He begins by noting, with astonishment, the large number of languages catered for in current bilingual education. Many of these can hardly be said to approach major status in terms of use (as Mackey has pointed out elsewhere: 'Only before God and the linguist are all languages equal. Everyone knows that you can go further with some languages than you can with others', 1978, p. 7). Still, Bethell states, most bilingual education is directed towards Spanish speakers – 'more or less the Hispanic equivalent of affirmative action' (p. 30). What began as a transitional programme to help children at school has grown into one of indefinite maintenance of maternal languages. Bethell is against this, for the familiar reason that it promotes fragmentation within society by overemphasising minority languages and weakening basic English skills.

Such emotional journalistic attacks on bilingual education are not the only ones. There have been more sober, critical appraisals as well, although these have been rather fewer in number than the overenthusiastic academic writings in support of bilingual education. [4] Not long after the Bilingual Education Act was passed, for example, Roeming (1970) wrote about bilingualism in America; although he has not been referred to very much by subsequent writers, his comments remain important. Roeming noted that: (a) bilingual education came about without general agreement on a definition of bilingualism; (b) there was an assumption made in some quarters that the Act *established* an interest in bilingualism; (c) the Act was essentially an anti-poverty measure. Roeming expanded upon these points in a second article (1971) in which he stated that there was only the *illusion* of a national concern for bilingualism and, somewhat cynically perhaps, that it was very much in the interests of second-language teachers to sustain support for language study. Bilingual education, he observed, was a measure to help poor people of limited English-speaking ability and any real bilingualism which resulted should be considered a useful but secondary by-product. Those who see in bilingual education a vehicle for promoting pluralism and permanent diversity are misguided: 'The reasons why this country is English-speaking are obvious to any student of history, and no attempt by us to make it anything else will succeed unless we can change all the economic, social, and political forces' (p. 74). Krug (1976) took a similar line: 'The United States will not become a multi-ethnic and multi-cultural society. Those who make such demands are unrealistic and impractical' (p. 83; see also Postman, 1979, who sees no possibility of the country becoming a 'truly bilingual polity').

Roeming's points are still relevant. The establishment of bilingual education before enough attention had been given to definitional and other matters reflects the bandwagon effect which has been part of the programme from the start. Second, there *has* been too facile an assumption that legislation equals national interest or concern. Shuy (1978a) described bilingual education, for example, as a 'realization of a value which got litigated in the courts and legislated in the government' (p. 592). It is reasonable to ask for whom bilingual education was valued. Shuy goes on to note that the legislation reflected 'an expression of a moral value partly derived from a great deal of intuition but with very little empirical research' (p. 593). Roeming's final point – that the Act was an anti-poverty measure – has also proved thorny. The original phrasing of the legislation does imply such a thrust, and amendments do not appear to have greatly altered this (see Edwards, 1976). Of course, this direction has not proven popular with apologists for pluralism and diversity, whose hopes for bilingual education go somewhat further. The distinction between 'transitional' bilingual education (essentially of a compensatory nature) and 'maintenance' programmes is a recurring theme, and I shall turn to it below.

Drake (1979; see also 1984) has also considered bilingual education. While not taking an opposing stance, he does observe that the programme has been erected upon the assumption of a major value shift in the United States from assimilation to pluralism, and this he feels to be a shaky foundation. He points out that there may well exist greater tolerance towards ethnic groups but that this cannot be equated with favourable and active dispositions towards pluralism. In fact, Drake thinks that current opposition to bilingual education may be seen as an attempt to force this distinction upon those who have hitherto been unwilling to recognise it.

The final account to be mentioned here is one which has aroused considerable reaction. In a monograph produced at the invitation of academics, Epstein (1978b) presents a journalist's view of bilingual education and ethnicity it (it should not be classed however, with newspaper and magazine accounts). He discusses many of the issues associated with the topic: the uncertain pedagogical impact of bilingual education, the transitional–maintenance distinction, the melting pot–cultural pluralism debate, etc. His major concern is whether the promotion of ethnic interests should be subsidised by government. Epstein attempts to distinguish between tolerance for difference and state-supported maintenance of diversity; this is a valuable point (see also Epstein, 1978a). He concludes with these questions:

Is *the national government* responsible for financing and promoting attachments to ethnic languages and cultures? Would federal intervention result in more harmony or more discord in American society? Would it lead to better or worse relations between groups? Better or worse relations *within* groups? More democracy or less? Greater separation or greater integration? What is the federal role? (p. 70)

The fact that Epstein ends on an interrogative note is, I think, to his credit. His work usefully adds to the debate, without presuming to give too many hard and fast answers. This seems to be the view of Orfield, whose response is appended to Epstein's report. The other response which is attached to the monograph is by Cardenas. He accuses Epstein of 'missing the boat' and making 'erroneous' and 'opinionated' statements. Others too have criticised Epstein. De Valdés (1979) claims that he 'equates ethnicity to a social disease'; since Epstein has given us a journalist's survey and not a 'study' his work is *ipso facto* less valuable. Fishman (1976c) calls Epstein's work 'journalistic muckraking'. González (1979) dismisses Epstein as a 'non-specialist'. This is interesting, since many who might be termed specialists are not without strong personal biases themselves.

One observes then, that bilingual education has been a most controversial issue (see Lewis, 1978). While there are intrinsic pedagogical issues here (see below), most of the debate has centred upon the perceived social implications of bilingual education. On the one hand, an increased tolerance for diversity has allowed schools to adapt more to minority groups. On the other, some have felt that the pendulum has swung too far and that schools actually have the potential to promote social fragmentation. It is particularly galling to some critics that this process is being underwritten by tax–payers. It is important now to consider how the *type* of bilingual education affects the argument.

Transition and maintenance

In discussions of bilingual education involving minority groups, two broad themes recur: transition and maintenance. The first of these refers to an educational process by which a child receives early instruction in the maternal language until such time as he or she can participate without academic loss in the regular curriculum. There are, of course, questions here as to when the time for this switching occurs; we require accurate assessment of children's linguistic skills, and this has not always been well done. Nevertheless, the philosophy of transitional bilingual education is clear enough. It is of a temporary, bridging nature, its success is measured by the ease and timing of its termination, and it includes a large element of instruction in the majority language. Maintenance bilingual education, on the other hand, is seen as a more permanent fixture. The desire here is *not* to move the pupils into some majority-language-only mainstream, but rather to retain bilingual instruction throughout the school career (or, at least, a substantial part of it).

Otheguy and Otto (1980) have recently commented on maintenance education, noting that it may be of a static or developmental kind, i.e. the aim may be either to preserve the maternal language at the initial competence level possessed by pupils or to develop first-language ability as well as majority-

language competence. The authors point out that where maintenance programmes have existed in the United States they have typically been of the static
preservation variety. Indeed, many who support bilingual education seem to
have the view that it should merely preserve the original language; Otheguy
and Otto, however, feel that development of the first language is both intrinsically useful and supports progress in the second.

The primary thrust of the Bilingual Education Act of 1968 was part of the
larger 'war on poverty' (Di Pietro, 1978). Given that English was viewed as
prepotent, the Act has a definite compensatory tone and was clearly not meant
to overturn the melting pot or to institutionalise cultural pluralism. Amendments and further legislation have continued this tone (see Teitelbaum & Hiller,
1977; Venezky, 1981). It is no surprise, therefore, that most of the programmes
financed by the Act have been of a transitional nature. Gaarder (1970) reviewed
the first 76 of them, finding that 54 were located in primary schools only.
Blanco (1977) reported that in 1975-6 only 83 of 406 programmes existed at
secondary-school level. Both the reports show, then, that about three-quarters
of the bilingual education programmes were *not* of a maintenance variety.
Similarly, Kjolseth (1972) reckoned that over 80 per cent of the programmes
he reviewed were of the 'assimilation' type and the remainder were not strongly
committed to pluralism; there is little reason to think that this situation has
since changed markedly (Hernández-Chávez, 1978). At a state level, similar
findings exist. Vázquez (1978) noted that 'of the 19 states which have established either legislative or executive provisions for bilingual education, 17 have
indicated explicitly the transitional intent of their programs' (p. 69; see also
Seelye, 1977). In summary, it is transitional bilingual education which is most
prevalent and probably the most supported among those of the general public
who have at all considered the matter.

However, much of the academic community concerned with bilingual education is opposed to the transitional philosophy (see Alatis, 1978; Center for
Applied Linguistics, 1977-8). The general view is that transitional education
actually expedites assimilation. Most writers on bilingual education are also
proponents of a continuing pluralism; since language retention is seen to be
a major feature of ethnic continuity, bilingual education is considered a potentially powerful agent. It can only be so, however, in its maintenance mode.
It is easy enough, therefore, to imagine the frustration of some pluralists; there
does exist bilingual education, which *could* (in their view, anyway) help to
promote pluralism, but it is currently of a type not likely to do so. Much effort
is based upon the hope and desire that bilingual education will undergo a
'metamorphosis' into some better, maintenance form (e.g. Fishman, 1977a).

Are there any purely pedagogical grounds on which we might favour either
transition or maintenance? Cummins (1981) reviewed research findings on
lanaguage proficiency and concluded that, for language development *per se*,
there was little to recommend transitional bilingual education for minority-
group children. The assumption that children must be placed in regular
classrooms as soon as possible in order to fully develop their knowledge of

the mainstream language was seen not to be supported by available evidence. It is debatable, however, whether this assumption is at all operative for those in favour of transition; it is more likely that most considerations are of a sociopolitical nature (i.e. the desire to maximise minority-group participation and to avoid social fragmentation). In any event, Cummins' remarks are generally to the effect that transition to the mainstream is not *necessary* for the development of literacy skills in the majority language, not that transition will, of itself, prove harmful. If one could show the value of transitional bilingual education on grounds of, say, social cohesion, advancement or access – or conversely, demonstrate that maintenance education was potentially socially undesirable or generally unwanted – there would not appear to be substantive psychological damage involved. It should also be pointed out here that some have claimed that prolonged mother-tongue instruction for minority-group children *does* hamper their chances for majority language and social success, and that is not required to combat the intriguing but ill-conceived notion of 'semi-lingualism' (see Cummins & Swain, 1983; Edelsky *et al.*, 1983; Martin-Jones & Romaine, 1984).

An interesting variety of maintenance education is the 'immersion' programme in which children receive their schooling entirely through a second language. This approach has not been directed towards minority-group children but caters, rather, for mainstream populations whose first language and cultural identity are secure, but whose parents (usually middle-class, well-off and highly motivated) want them to acquire a fuller second-language competence than that provided in traditional school-language curricula.[5]

In Canada, where immersion programmes originated for English-speaking children, results have generally been encouraging (Stern, 1981).[6] However, Mackey (1981) has pointed out that immersion classes employ a 'somewhat artificial French' since they are composed of pupils who regularly speak English at home. 'Such pupils as they become more and more adult tend to shy away from the play-acting language of childhood in favour of the everyday language of the adult world. Such "bilingual" uni-ethnic schools do not in themselves tend to promote societal bilingualism' (p. 13). One notes here how important is the milieu in which learning occurs, and how real-life contexts tend to dwarf what goes on in school. Genesee (1981a) has recently shown that differences between immersion students and those studying French in more traditional ways are very slight. The former do little French reading and, like their counterparts, report essentially instrumental rather than integrative reasons for learning French. Although more likely (unsurprisingly) to use more French in personal encounters, the immersion students do no more than the others to seek them out or initiate them. Thus, the much-vaunted differences between immersion and traditional instruction, in terms of acquired competence, may not be carried through to *use* of the competence. This, presumably, is a large part of what the whole exercise is supposed to be about.[7]

MULTICULTURALISM AND EDUCATION

Discussions of the multicultural education question in societies like Canada, Australia and Great Britain have had to grapple with the same pluralism–assimilation controversies which have animated the American bilingual education scene.[8] The difficulty to be contended with in education is that same 'dynamic spiral' of unity and diversity which I have already discussed in the larger social context (see chapter 4). There are, of course, extreme positions here. On the one hand, some have argued that education should make few accommodations to non-mainstream groups. This is a view which is generally weaker now than it once was; liberal tolerance increasingly decrees that differences should be recognised and not actively discouraged. On the other hand, the argument that education in the service of pluralism should make radical accommodations to diversity has to combat the view that along this way lies social fragmentation, maintenance of ethnic enclaves and possible suppression of minority-group advancement. Consequently, and realistically, most of the important debate over multicultural education centres upon a middle ground in which there is some balance between unity and diversity. This, of course, can be seen to recapture exactly that modified pluralism, or pluralistic integration, already described. The matter takes on special interest in the educational domain, however, because, while it may be argued that pluralistic integration generally is a more or less natural reflection of social forces, school policy here must be more self-consciously planned.

What is under discussion, essentially, is the formulation of educational policy which will affect individual and group identity. Language is often seen as central here. Even among those who understand that original group language is not, itself, a required component of identity, the idea often exists that when language goes, other features tend to follow. Thus, Rokkan and Urwin (1983) observe that language loss leads to further cultural 'erosion' (see also Reitz, 1980). Craft (1982) argues that mother-tongue loss weakens culture and may lead to 'intergenerational stresses' and loss of identity. I have tried to show that language (in its communicative aspect) is almost inevitably abandoned in minority–majority contexts but that other (symbolic and/or private) ethnic markers remain. The fallacy apparently accepted by the authors just cited is that language loss *leads to* further marker erosion, that language is somehow instrumental here and that, therefore, if its loss could be prevented, other elements would remain in place. This last point is true enough but the important fact of the matter is that language and other elements of ethnicity are *simultaneously* acted upon by social forces; some succumb, some do not. Although, for obvious enough reasons, language continues to be seen as the central linchpin of identity and, consequently, something which schools should attend to, the assumption is as inaccurate (and likely to lead to just as few successful interventions) within education as it is in the larger society. If language contact is such as to lead to language decline, it is most unlikely

that schoools can significantly affect the situation; the historical evidence here
is overwhelming.[9]

But if schools cannot alter strong social currents, particularly linguistic ones,
there is no reason why they cannot reflect the heterogeneous society of which
they are a part. Even Musgrove (1982), who, as we have seen, argues so strongly
against relativism, acknowledges that minority cultures have a place in the
curriculum, that children must not be made ashamed of their origins when
they go to school, and that schools should 'at least start from where they are'
(p. 128). The question is, assuming a respect for difference, exactly what
education can and should *do* in terms of curriculum. Can acknowledgement
and respect concerning cultural variation co-exist happily with education for
social mobility, for that 'civism' which Bullivant (1981a) argues for, for
Durkheim's 'collective conscience' (1953)?

My view here has no doubt been anticipated. On questions of language and
identity generally, there is no reason to suppose that schools alone can
significantly affect maintenance. While education offers itself as a visible and
often manipulable resource, its power here has been much overrated. Schools
can, however, provide tolerant atmospheres which do not act against the
expression and continuation of groupness. Practically speaking, it is unlikely
that their contribution can be much greater.[10] Attempting to do more is likely
to be unsuccessful and may be counter-productive insofar as it may detract
from provision of much-needed 'core' curricula for *all* children.

Stone (1981) has argued this in the British context, with regard to West
Indian children. West Indian herself, she takes a stance not unlike that of
Musgrove. Schools should stress core knowledge and skills, not the vague
'affective' goals of self-expression and self-fulfilment which are so much a part
of many multicultural curricula. In fact, Stone questions much of the rationale
for such education by noting that lack of self-esteem, low self-worth and
psychological insecurity are *not* best combatted by 'culturally adapted' schools.
Indeed, as Figueroa (1984) observes, explanations of minority-group
underachievement in terms of such variables are rather tenuous.[11] Stone's work
has led her to state that 'the West Indian children's unfavourable view of their
teachers' feelings towards them did not correlate with an unfavourable view
of themselves' (1981, p. 214). And why, asks Jeffcoate (1984), do other groups
(e.g. Asians in Great Britain) do relatively well at school, particularly when
compared to West Indians, when they too suffer the racism which contributes
to feelings of inadequacy and self-doubt? Indeed, differences *among* West
Indian children themselves are greater than those between them as a group
and other groups.[12] We can appreciate then, the strength of Stone's disdain
for education programmes which emphasise supposed cultural repair jobs over
the transmission of basic skills and literacy: 'I want to suggest that MRE
[multiracial education] is conceptually unsound...while at the same time
creating for teachers, both radical and liberal, the illusion that they are doing
something special for a particularly disadvantaged group' (1981, p. 100). We
can also understand Woodford's comments (cited in Tomlinson, 1984, p. 149):

'Black parents don't want black studies or multicultural education for their children – that is for white children; black pupils need to be good at science, history, geography – at what society thinks of as things of worth.'

If, therefore, schools cannot (and perhaps should not) make such active efforts on behalf of minority cultures – because these may be counter-productive or ineffectual – what, if anything, is left to a multicultural curriculum? Is it all simply a matter of providing a tolerant atmosphere while stressing a core curriculum? Is the school to look after civism and let pluralism look after itself? I think the answer is yes. Craft (1982), though clearly a supporter of pluralism in education, seems to take this view, claiming that to take account of diversity does not necessitate adding new elements to the curriculum 'but simply a greater *awareness* of pluralism' (p. 20). [13] Not only is this approach practical in that it allows a common, central curriculum for *all* children, it is philosophically satisfying because it reflects that larger social process of pluralistic integration.

I suggest, in fact, that *all education worthy of the name is multicultural.* It should be part and parcel of education generally to show an awareness of diverse cultures and to develop an appreciation of human difference (although respect for diversity should not be so all-encompassing and unselective as to rule out the possibility of value judgement; see chapter 4). This is even more desirable when a given classroom is itself culturally heterogeneous. However, I agree with Musgrove (1982; see also Lipkin & Lawson, 1978) to the extent that the school's role is not one of cultural transmission. Schools reflect society, of course, and cultural transmission occurs in the sense that majority standards and values inform the curriculum; this is unavoidable and desirable. But much of the strength of education – particularly with regard to those aspects most desired and accepted by minority groups – lies in material which is (or should be) relatively culture-free or material which, although (originally, at least) culture-specific, has some claim to superiority (see chapter 4). For the rest – in the education I am arguing for here, with its awareness of cultural difference – material can be presented in ways which make clear that is is not the *only* presentation possible, but simply one which reflects the society's historical traditions. To the extent to which these traditions still have force *outside* the school, it makes sense for them to be presented and explained within it. As society changes – often due in part to ethnically based diversity itself – so schools and their curricula will inevitably alter. School can do little to accelerate or retard the social processes outside its gates, but it can ensure that they are accurately reflected in the classroom. Schools *can* lead society in the promotion of tolerance and understanding, and to abdicate responsibility here would be to renege on the basic goals of education itself. To attempt more active intervention, to engage in programmes specially planned to bolster minority-group identity – this is neither desirable nor practical.

NON-STANDARD LANGUAGE AND EDUCATION

I have noted that schools should be tolerant of linguistic cultural diversity, that they should at least 'start from where children are'. My argument to this point is that, while bilingual education (in its maintenance form) and the sort of multiculturalism based upon an unrealistic culture-transmission approach are not the necessary consequences of tolerance, one *can* make a good case for transitional bilingual education and for a wide-ranging multiculturalism which I have suggested is, and always has been, an essential feature of *all* good education.

So far, however, I have discussed education for different cultures and linguistic groups. What is the situation for *sub*cultures whose linguistic differences are ones of dialect rather than language? What is the school's role in dealing with children whose speech patterns are non-standard and low-prestige variants of the mainstream language?[14] We have seen (in chapter 1) that all dialects, like all languages, are valid systems; all are capable of reflecting and carrying group identity. There are no *sub*standard varieties, although the realities of class and dominance do make the term *non*-standard an appropriate one. Equally, however, one realises that academic and linguistic enlightenment does not always mean general acceptance of dialect varieties, and it is precisely because of social prejudice that *different* dialects are commonly viewed as deficient.

Traditionally, the school has been a strong supporter of 'proper' language, and implicit in this role was the belief that some children arrived at school with substandard forms which needed to be eradicated. As a powerful and visible institution, the school typically gave great weight to standard dialects, those spoken and accepted by the dominant mainstream. There has been, it is true, some question as to whether the school really *is* a middle-class bastion, particularly with regard to language matters (see e.g. Feagans & Farran, 1982), but there is little doubt that, overall, schools reflect and encourage the values and standards of this segment of society (Edwards, 1983d). Schools have certainly felt that some language styles were simply wrong, reinforcing the view that non-standard dialect is substandard; they have been so successful here that speakers of non-standard varieties themselves have usually come to accept this judgement (Edwards, 1979b). Rist (1970) discussed a 'self-fulfilling prophecy' here: children arrive at school speaking a variety which is considered deficient; teachers, acting from the best of motives, aim to replace this with a standard form (they also very often make attributions, based upon their perceptions of pupils' speech, about the children's intelligence and educability; see Edwards, 1977d, 1979b, c); children, treated differently because of presumed deficiencies, come to perform less well than others. It must be admitted that much of the work on teachers' expectations and their effects upon children is speculative. It is exceedingly difficult to know to what degree perceptions affect performance; it seems unlikely, however, that there is *no* effect on school achievement, and there is certainly a very real possibility of damage to children's sense of identity. This is all particularly unfortunate, of course, when we consider that damage here may result from inaccurate or biased views of language and dialect.

Schools are now more tolerant of linguistic variation, demonstrating again their mirroring of wider social perceptions. However, ideas about 'poor' language can hardly be said to have disappeared. Linguistic evidence does not work very fast or very completely on popular stereotypes, and attitudes, by their nature, are singularly resistant to fact. Even the limited gains made within the educational arena cannot be taken for granted.

Within the academic world itself, the non-standard but not substandard view continues to be assailed. Several contributors to the volume edited by Feagans and Farran (1982) – all of whom can be assumed to be well-informed on the relevant research – consider that the deficit position may not be totally without merit. And, a recent monograph by Honey (1983; see also Edwards, 1983b) attacks the 'difference' viewpoint, claiming that linguistic evidence supporting it is without firm basis. When he considers current educational practice, Honey errs in supposing that acceptance of the difference stance necessarily entails active school promotion of non-standard varieties (which, of course, he rejects). But it does not. My position – as will be clear by now – is that schools must accept non-standard forms as valid. Teachers should not attempt, then, to stamp them out and children should not be penalised for using them. However, because of social, not linguistic, realities, schools should continue to provide standard models and to promote awareness and use of this form, within an atmosphere of tolerance and respect for all other dialects (see Edwards, 1979b).

Among teachers, however, the view that non-standard varieties are deficient continues (buttressed by certain strains of academic writing). Edwards and McKinnon (in preparation), for example, recently surveyed about 100 teachers in Nova Scotia on their views of student disadvantage in general and language in particular. They typically pointed to poor grammar, vocabulary, articulation and reading as important features of educational disadvantage. Differences were seen as deficits, and some representative comments illustrate this:

Disadvantaged children have a lack of experiences, poor language development... usually disorganised.

Children often cannot articulate their thoughts and feelings in such a way that they satisfy both themselves and their audience.

The common element of experience among disadvantaged children is infrequent interaction with adults in discovery activities where opinions and experiences can be shared.

Both receptive and expressive skills seem to have low levels of value and priority when it comes to developing accuracy and fluency.

One notes here beliefs which correspond strikingly with views expressed in the language-deficit literature. Children are seen to be unable to communicate adequately, they lack the experience and interactions which are necessary for developing language skills and, indeed, it is suggested that their 'receptive and expressive' talents are not greatly valued anyway. All of this is quite reminiscent of the miguided sentiments of deficit theorists of the 1960s (Edwards, 1979b).

Teachers were not unsympathetic to language 'problems' but, although they viewed language differences as springing from varied home backgrounds (true), they also saw them as necessitating some sort of compensation (dubious). Where teachers were in contact with minority-group children, the speech patterns of these were singled out for attention. Many put Black and French-Acadian children at the top of the list of those having language problems. A fairly general view was expressed by one teacher as follows: 'Blacks have a slang language all their own. They will not use proper English when the opportunity arises.'

Thus we can see that work remains to be done in the promulgation of the view that *all* normal children come to school with a well-formed system of language. We cannot expect schools and teachers to change general social attitudes about non-standard varieties; we can hope that they will not exacerbate the situation. We can also agree with Halliday (1968) that school contexts which make children ashamed of their language are morally and linguistically indefensible.

What can schools do if they (correctly) reject the linguistic-deficit argument, yet still see a need for children to acquire a standard form approved by society at large? The old policy, essentially one of language *replacement*, can no longer be supported. How can repertoire *expansion* be effected? Certainly, children should be allowed to use their own dialect at school without penalty, but what is the best way to gradually add knowledge of the socially approved and useful standard? Language drills and other formal exercises can hardly be used without suggesting that the maternal variety is, after all, deficient. Textbooks written in non-standard dialect have not been shown generally useful in bringing about a smoother transition to standard-language editions (Edwards, 1977e) and there is often opposition from parents (see e.g. Covington, 1976; Wilby, 1984). In fact, any active process which highlights differences between standard and non-standard forms is liable to lead to stigmatisation of the latter.

It must be remembered here that the children under discussion are not living entirely apart from mainstream society; they are, in fact, inundated with standard-speaking models. Furthermore, evidence has shown that children speaking non-standard varieties are quite able to understand the standard, even if they do not customarily use it, from an early age. The issue is not so much one of comprehension of the standard as it is of its *production;* the child has a choice whether or not to use it, although home and peer pressure may militate against the standard. The teacher in particular acts as a model from which the child can gradually come to understand in which contexts the standard is most appropriate and where, therefore, its use is likely to be most beneficial. As in other important aspects of life, much must be left to the discretion of those most directly involved. Thus, the Bullock Report made the sensible recommendation that 'the teacher's aim should be to indicate to his pupils the value of awareness and flexibility, so that they can make their own decisions and modify these as their views alter' (Great Britain: Department of Education and Science, 1975, p. 143). This does not mean that the teacher cannot act as a guide, but the process of becoming *bidialectal* – if this is desired – is not one which responds well to force or even strong suggestion. Lest it be thought that all of this is much too *laissez-faire*, it should be remembered that any more formal apporach is likely to be unsuccessful and may widen a gap which already too often exists between the non-standard-speaking child and the school.

Finally here, it is interesting to compare school treatment of non-standard-speaking children with that of children whose *language* is different, in terms of effect upon identity. I have suggested, for the latter, that school promotion of their own language is not likely to be a useful contribution to group maintenance. School policy here should consist of tolerance for linguistic difference and may involve some form of transitional bilingual education coupled with mainstream-language instruction. For those speaking a non-standard variant of the majority language we see that, again, a tolerant atmosphere is required, with no stigmatisation of the mother-tongue form, within which standard-speaking models (and written material of course) may lead to bidialectalism. Bidialectalism in these circumstances need mean no assault on identity, just as bilingualism itself need not damage it. [15] In both cases, the appropriate educational position *vis-à-vis* identity involves tolerance for language and cultural variation co-existing with the provision of needed linguistic repertoire expansion. In this sense, we see again a compromise between civism and pluralism.

SUMMARY

It is now common to read that current American bilingual education is on its way out, having had a lifespan of about 15 years (Bickley, 1980; Schlossman, 1983b). Certainly, change may be in the air. Bickley noted that further federal funding might be available only for ESL (English-as-a-second-language) programmes. Recent articles by Gray (1982a, b, c) indicate that this restriction is indeed the intent. Kirp (1983) notes the diminishing federal presence under the Reagan administration and a desire to eliminate special bilingual-education funding *per se* and to divert resources into programmes intended to move children into the English-speaking mainstream. Formal changes may occur after the present Act expires in 1984 but the writing already seems to be on the wall. Kirp claims that the government – in promoting, at best, a purely transitional education – is apparently shifting from its earlier stance; however, as we have seen, the *original* intent was also a transitional one, and it might be argued that those who thought otherwise are now being reminded of this. The original legislation was not meant to overturn the melting pot and hopes that bilingual education could metamorphose from transition to maintenance were never strongly supported at official levels.[16]

As will have become obvious, I think that government reaction against education as a servant to pluralism is well-founded. However, there is a real danger that the pendulum may swing too far backwards, eliminating useful transitional programmes altogether and, in effect, returning to old 'submersion' methods. For example, much of the impetus behind the current drive against bilingual education derives from a desire to have English officially enshrined as the language of the United States; language rights have not, so far, been explicitly outlined in the constitution. Hayakawa (cited in Gray, 1982c), a linguist and a senator, has proposed this; he believes that bilingual programmes have 'strayed from their original intent of teaching English', prefers ESL instruction and, generally, notes that the bilingual education debate reflects the broader issue of 'what language will be used in the United States' (p. 5). As of June 1984, the Congress was studying an amendment to make English the official language, and it is clear that supporters feel that bilingual education has undermined assimilation processes by which immigrants learn English (see Tucker & Crandall, 1984). It is worrying that what might be a reasonable rejection of excessive school attention to language and identity maintenance may degenerate – because of pressure from 'old-style' assimilationists – into an erosion of the valuable aspects of some forms of bilingual provision in education.

In Great Britain too, multiculturalism is under attack. As Wilby (1984) notes, there is increasing criticism of the idea that it is part of the school's function to teach minority languages and cultures; these are seen to be the responsibility of communities themselves. Multicultural education is seen as regressive insofar as it stresses differences over similarities. Similarly, in Australia, multiculturalism has become a subject of increasingly strident debate. Bullivant (1980a) wrote a paper entitled *Multiculturalism – No* and has since expanded his ideas in a series of articles and books. Smolicz (1980), on the other hand, wrote a piece called *Multiculturalism – Yes* and has contributed further views about pluralism, the 'core values' of ethnic groups, and the role of the school in promoting stable diversity.[17] A useful overview of the Australian scene is provided by Shafer (1983). The question, as always, revolves around the civism-pluralism dilemma, the most appropriate balance to be struck, and the role (if any) of schools and other agencies in actively intervening on behalf of minority cultures perceived to be at risk. In Canada, as we have seen, the multiculturalism debate is exacerbated by the dominance, among non-English minorities, of the Francophones who, indeed, are a *majority* group within Quebec and who fear that multiculturalism may relegate them to the status of other minorities and erode their 'charter' position.

As with the criticism of American bilingual education there is, I believe, much that is sensible in current reappraisals of what were, in many cases, overenthusiastic, faddish and value-laden approaches to multiculturalism (see also Edwards, 1983a). Again, however, one hopes that the present climate will not lead to a rolling back of a very welcome awareness and tolerance for ethnic diversity. While there have been many unlikely and regressive aspects to modern thinking on pluralism and identity – particularly where language in education is concerned – earlier school policies were certainly flawed. A middle course, one in which modified pluralism is reflected at school, has the most to recommend it (see Eggleston, cited in Wilby, 1984).

Overall, there is no doubt that, in failing to understand the dynamics of ethnic minority life, in failing to accord to groups themselves any real appreciation of linguistic and cultural values, and in having a static or selective historical awareness, promoters of pluralism through education have been sadly misguided. If my analysis so far is at all accurate, it should be clear that education is most unlikely to significantly alter perceptions of self-identity or to expedite the progress of cultural pluralism. Specifically, it is hoped that educational programmes can support identity through language maintenance. Yet, communicative language-use is one of those visible manifestations of identity most susceptible to change and decline. Attempting to prop it up in the school therefore runs counter to powerful social trends. There is a further, more general point as well, given that schools tend to follow and reflect these trends. Even if we judged cultural pluralism to be an unalloyed good, language to be essential to the continuation of identity and ethnic minorities to need externally supported expertise to help them know themselves, we still could not assume that school projects would do the trick.

Promoters of cultural pluralism (and maintenance-bilingual education) tend to ignore information salient to their cause and, in particular, pay too little attention to the needs and wishes of the potential beneficiaries of their policies. Given a reasonably tolerant society and educational system, minority groups should and will define themselves *vis-à-vis* the mainstream as they think proper and in aspects of their life ranging from language use to cuisine. If bilingual education and other programmes can truly be seen as responses to appeals from the people themselves then they are, in effect, part of this self-definition process. If they are not, they run the risk of being wasteful, ill-conceived and possibly harmful. Comparisons, in terms of desired public-school programmes, between early and contemporary education in America, and between transition and maintenance forms, make it reasonably clear that the wishes of intended beneficiaries are generally some way removed from those of their vocal and visible 'spokesmen'.

'Ethnics' themselves are more likely to support transitional language programmes than maintenance ones. Fishman (1980c) contrasts the 'numerous' and 'tragically destructive' transitional programmes currently prevalent in the United States with the better ones sponsored by the ethnic communities themselves, these being few in number and 'weak'. We know why the former type thrives – it has Government backing. But why are the self-sponsored programmes few and weak? Is it not for the same reasons that the earlier ethnic schools declined? – i.e. the paucity of ethnic schools reflects the fact that there is no longer the demand for them that there once was. When Fishman concludes his paper by seeing the United States as the poorer for the weakness of the 'parochial' schools, he is simply indicating a preference for a life style which most contemporary group members simply do not share. It is true, as Steinberg (1981) observes, that schools traditionally ignored immigrant languages in the United States and that the ethnic groups' own schools were limited to a small part of the potential constituency. Yet we should ask why more forceful demands were not made on public-school systems for minority-language instruction, especially given that there were few real legislative obstacles in the United States. We must also ask why the parochial efforts were not more expansive initially and why they typically declined from the base of importance which they did have. We can also extend the argument and ask why current transitional programmes are not more widely criticised. The answers here have already been given.

While transitional language programmes are reasonable activities deserving of public support – although there are many practical difficulties relating to resources, number of languages to be catered for, etc. – maintenance education is not so easy to defend from an all-society point of view. It involves direct administrative involvement in identity retention, i.e. it reflects the idea that diversity is not only to be approved of, it is to be promoted to the level of official policy. There is no evidence to suggest that any meaningful aspects of ethnicity can be held in place by outside intervention, much less ones which are visible markers (like language). There is also no evidence that such an intervention policy is supported in any active sense by large segments of the population, minority or majority (see also chapter 6). The only language-maintenance programmes which make sense are those which are restricted to a small minority within a minority (or to groups who voluntarily segregate themselves: usually a religious phenomenon). Such programmes have existed, and continue to exist, both within public educational systems and on a parochial basis. Their longevity is always in doubt and they cannot reasonably be seen as any sort of basis for a generally pluralistic society.

6

Language Attitudes, Behaviour and Research

INTRODUCTION

So far, I have discussed language matters largely from a broad social perspective, stressing sociological, historical and sociolinguistic currents. In this chapter I turn to a consideration of issues on a more psychological level. There has been an ever-increasing amount of research interest in language and identity within social psychology over the last 25 years or so, much of it centring upon language attitudes, perceptions and evaluations. I am particularly interested here in determining the extent to which experimental and theoretical work confirms real-life observation, offers new insight, supports work from other disciplines, and permits correlations to be made between individual and group behaviour; I have noted elsewhere (Edwards, 1982a) that the relating of empirical findings to behaviour as revealed in the sociological and historical record is vital. On the one hand, the confirmation of macro data by carefully controlled experiment would clearly be of great use; on the other, an appreciation – by social psychology in particular – of the real contexts which affect behaviour is long overdue. This is a general matter of concern for social psychology, but it takes on special relevance when the discipline attempts to comment on language and identity which, as we have seen, are most susceptible to large social forces. Indeed, we can go further and say that a social psychology of language which neglects contemporary and historical trends, and which insulates itself from useful information in other fields, is likely to be empty and misleading.

Central to much of what follows here is the concept of *attitude* which, though widespread in social psychology, is not one about which there has been universal agreement. At a general level, however, one might agree with Sarnoff (1970) who views attitude as 'a disposition to react favourably or unfavourably to a class of objects' (p. 279). This disposition is often taken to comprise three components: thoughts (the cognitive element), feelings (affective) and predispositions to act (behavioural), i.e. one knows or believes something, has some emotional reaction to it and, therefore, may be assumed to act on this basis (see e.g. Secord & Backman, 1964). Two points should be made here. First, there is often inconsistency between assessed attitudes and actions presumably related to them (one reason, incidentally, for seeking confirmatory data). Second, there is often confusion between belief and attitude; strictly speaking, *attitude* includes *belief* as one of its elements. A subject's response to the question, Is a knowledge of French important for your children?, indicates a belief. To gauge attitude would require further probing into the respondent's *feeling* about the expressed belief, e.g. someone could believe that French *was* important for his children, yet he could loathe the language and all its associations. Many attitude questionnaires are largely, in fact, ones which measure belief.

In a way, of course, I have been discussing attitudes throughout the book. We might consider it possible, at least, to deduce underlying attitudes or beliefs from material already presented on language shift, nationalism, revival, etc. The emphasis of this chapter is upon a more direct, experimentally-based examination of language attitudes. Before turning to this, however, I should like to briefly outline some perspectives on language, pluralism and identity which, directly or indirectly, reveal attitudes. This can be seen as a summary of information already discussed and real-life prologue to what follows.

SOME VIEWS OF LANGUAGE AND IDENTITY

In this section, I refer to five important groups, not all mutually exclusive: ethnic-group members, group spokesmen, mainstream populations, academic constituencies and official policy-makers.

Ethnic-group members

Although the lives and views of ordinary group members are clearly of the greatest importance in understanding *their* language, identity and social relationships, we do not have much formal information here. Fishman (1977a) has noted, for example, that 'the only aspect of bilingual education that has been even less researched than student attitudes and interests is that of parental attitude and interests' (p. 45). Nevertheless, the informal record is useful. In the United States, we have noted the gradual lessening of the influence of specifically ethnic institutions and societies as group need for them decreased (Edwards, 1977a). As regards ethnic language itself, there has not been much legal or official pressure on ethnic-group speakers to abandon the mother-tongue; the important factor here has typically been the perceived advantage of life in the mainstream. The few moves to suppress immigrant languages in the last century were unpopular and soon revoked (see Dinnerstein *et àl.*, 1979; Mann, 1979; Teitelbaum & Hiller, 1977). This is not to say that minorities would not have preferred a Utopian society with mainstream accessibility *and* complete cultural and linguistic retention. Choices had to be made. These were not always easy or welcomed in themselves but it is clear that communicative language, at any rate, was a dispensable commodity for most groups. However regrettable this may be, we must remember that, in areas generally untouched by legal compulsion, immigrants Americanised of their own volition, to the extent desired or made necessary by attractive options (see Ravitch, 1976). Providing we acknowledge the public–private and communicative–symbolic distinctions (see chapter 4), we can see that American groups have been largely assimilationist in their attitudes.

The picture for immigrants in other settings is not unlike that obtaining in the United States. Changing attitudes in Great Britain have inexorably affected linguistic transmission, even where the first generation remains committed. Just as the culturally active Chinese immigrant in San Francisco laments the lack of interest in Chinese among children (Morrison & Zabusky, 1980), so Mascarenhas (1983) reports that the editor of a Punjabi weekly newspaper in Great Britain does not have Punjabi-speaking children. The Asian vernacular press in Great Britain is shrinking, despite a good deal of concern and interest, and the young Asian boy who delivers Urdu newspapers in Birmingham does not read the language himself.

So far as indigenous minorities are concerned, perceptions of ordinary group members confirm what is mentioned above. It is true that group languages have suffered persecution (but see Petyt, 1975) or, at least, ignorance. But even here we should not neglect the elements of choice and volition. Languages may, through force of circumstance, come to play a very reduced communicative role or only a symbolic one, and only group members themselves can save them (Fennell, 1981; Price, 1979); but, we observe that ordinary group members are not, typically, language activists. They are not generally swayed by abstract or romantic appeals which cannot compete with more immediate exigencies; the attitudinal stance is clear.

Most minority groups are, above all, pragmatic and this usually implies a considerable assimilationist sentiment (see Gaarder, 1981). A recent book provides some first-hand accounts which support this. Morrison and Zabusky (1980) interviewed 140 first-generation immigrants to the United States and one is struck by the overwhelming desire to learn English. Many of the interviewees had regrets connected with emigration and not all of them preferred to describe themselves as American – although many, even in this first generation, did so – but the pragmatic desire to make the act of emigration worthwhile is clear.

A lengthier description of adaptation to life in the larger society is given in an autobiography by Rodriguez (1983; see also 1980a, b). He discusses the public–private distinction I have discussed here: home was Spanish and outside was English. Rodriguez considers that having to learn English at school, although painful, established his right to speak the language of *los gringos*. This, as he makes quite clear, created a loosening of ties with parents and relatives who remained Spanish-speaking, for as his English improved his Spanish declined. For Rodriguez, 'public individuality' (via English) caused a diminished 'private individuality' (via Spanish). Whether this need be so for all ethnic group members is doubtful, and Rodriguez's case might be taken as an example of the need for bilingual education. If so, however, it would be of the transitional variety, for he is critical of those who reject assimilation; they are 'filled with decadent self-pity...they romanticize public separateness' (p. 27). Besides, Rodriguez was to find that family life and intimacy could indeed be expressed through English – 'intimacy is not created by a particular language; it is created by intimates' (p. 32). His linguistic cost–benefit analysis will not be to everyone's taste but it is an honest account and, I think, generalisable.

Less temperate reactions by other 'ethnics' towards policies intended to affect their language and identity can also be found, often in the popular press. Thus, Zolf (1980) proclaimed himself against the Canadian multicultural policy: 'I don't need a multiculturalism grant to be Jewish' (p. 6). Multiculturalism, he feels, is a political sop to ethnic voters, encourages fragmented loyalties, and attempts to maintain what can only be sustained by groups themselves. Hayakawa (1980), commenting on bilingualism in the United States, states that it is a good thing in itself, but should not be *officially* supported. He is particularly exercised by politicians stressing their own ethnic roots.

In general, the adjustments made by minority groups – as revealed in the historical record and discussed in this book – give a rather clear assessment of attitudes towards language and identity. At the risk of belabouring the point, I note again that their views are the products of altered environments. In this sense, and especially during periods of transition, they may not always reflect ideal preferences. They *do* reflect practical and necessary choices.

Ethnic-group spokesmen

I have already discussed the gradually increasing gap between the lives of ethnic-group members and the societies, churches and schools which were once so important to them. The fact that these institutions remain means that there exist persons who feel themselves to be group spokesmen and leaders, but who may also be some way removed from grassroots sentiment. These individuals, furthermore, are often ones who have prospered in the larger society; indeed, their role as spokesmen often reflects an admired ability to straddle two cultures. Relatively secure, these activists endorse cultural pluralism because they feel that 'permanent minority status might be advantageous' (Higham, 1975, p. 211; see also Edwards, 1977a; Riley, 1975; Weinreich, 1974). The reader will also recall here the results of the Irish survey (Committee on Irish Language Attitudes Research, 1975) which found markedly different viewpoints held by ordinary people and those involved in pro-Irish activities. All of this is not to deny that spokesmen may reflect the wishes of less articulate or visible group members and that they may galvanise latent desires – leaders are always a minority, after all. But it is surely worth noting that, in an area as sensitive as language and identity, care should be taken to see how far and in what form enthusiasm extends.

Mann (1979) has outlined in some detail the distance between group spokesmen and the masses. Noting that rank-and-file ethnics in the United States were not swept into the cultural renaissance, he cites the view of Myrdal that, far from being a people's movement, the new ethnicity is supported by well-established intellectuals and writers. While they may be sincere, they are hardly typical. Mann suggests that they are too ready to see mass support for their ideas in public ethnic activities and festivals – celebrations which have in most cases become thoroughly Americanised. The fact that intellectuals and leaders present an articulate, powerful and visible source of influence should not confuse us into thinking that they represent large-scale opinion (see an interesting article here by Lowy *et al.*, 1983).

The mainstream population

What do majority-group members think of cultural pluralism and of the retention of minority language and identity?[1] Historically, the evidence shows little tolerance or concern for such matters at all and, as we should expect, such a stance is still prevalent in many quarters. Reactions in the popular press to issues relating to ethnic diversity show a continuing fear of social fragmentation (see Edwards, 1980b); the title of one of Greeley's books, *Why can't they be like us?* (1971), surely summarises the view of many.

There is, however, a more recent tolerance for diversity. The surveys of O'Bryan *et al.* (1976) and Berry *et al.* (1977) on unofficial languages and multiculturalism in Canada demonstrate a growing awareness that diversity can be a strength. A similar interpretation could be placed upon the findings of the report of the Committee on Irish Language Attitudes Research (1975). In fact, we might say that in many parts of the world a liberalism which is, at least in part, the product of relative affluence and security is now ready to accept ethnic diversity. This is not always based upon a great deal of knowledge, however – many people surveyed in the Canadian work knew very little about multiculturalism *per se* (see also Edwards & Chisholm, in preparation). When we reflect further on the meaning and implications of tolerance for diversity, we should consider at least three important questions: (a) is current tolerance necessarily a stable quantity; (b) does tolerance extend equally across all majority–minority and minority–minority relationships; and (c) can we equate tolerance with active support for diversity, especially in language matters?

Tolerance for diversity has not been something which minority groups could always count upon. The findings of scapegoats when times are bad has been a regrettably common occurrence and it surely needs no documentation here. As well, the sort of tolerance which Skutnabb-Kangas (1984) discusses in the case of European guest-workers – where, when industrial productivity slows, workers are retained to serve as a cushion for economic shocks at the lowest end of the social hierarchy – operates from a base of self-interest and not from one of altruism. We should be careful, therefore, if we attempt to erect an enduring social policy upon public attitudes which may shift quite rapidly. At the very least we should be concerned not to build false hopes, and not to dash minority-group expectations which have been encouraged to rise on unstable foundations.

We should also understand that, while there may be a greater degree of tolerance by majorities of minorities in general, this does not imply equal tolerance for all groups. Nor does it imply uniformity of goodwill within and across minority groups themselves. Kopan (1974) notes that antipathy to new immigrants in the United States came from those who had been new immigrants themselves only a little earlier. Kolack (1980), in a study of ethnic communities in Massachusetts, refers to the often violent feelings between minority groups (see also Dinnerstein *et al.*, 1979). Again, inter-minority hatred does not require extensive documentation here.

Finally, we should not equate tolerance for diversity with a desire to see *active* promotion of ethnic-group interests (especially where support comes from government sources). Where there is general support for bilingual education, for example, it is for a compensatory or transitional variety. Drake (1979) feels that there has *not* been a shift towards active support for pluralism in the United States (see also Mann, 1979; Sowell, 1978). The implications of accepting the equation are obvious (see Edwards, 1982b).

The academic constituency

Many group spokesmen (see above) are also academics; this is, of course, a quite reasonable combination of roles, providing that the academic stance is not confounded with more subjective advocacy. I have suggested elsewhere (Edwards, 1980b, 1981a, 1982b) that unfortunately this confounding does occur and in some areas it is now almost to be expected. Drake (1979), Sowell (1978), Van den Berghe (1967) and others have drawn attention to the colouring of academic argument with 'moralistic-ideological imperatives'.

We do have, however, more disinterested academic views of language, identity, diversity and pluralism. Much of the relevant information here has already been discussed (see Glazer & Moynihan, 1963; Gleason, 1984; Gordon, 1964; Higham, 1975; Mann, 1979; Parrillo, 1980). One important feature of these views is the attempt to understand, describe and assess the realities and implications of majority–minority relations for *all* segments of society and for society as a whole. This, of course, is not a value-free exercise; changing notions of pluralism and the changing society within which these ideas are formulated are interrelated. But, given these limits, there have been many admirable efforts to document important current issues and to place them in historical perspective. The most successful of these have, above all, pointed to the relative nature of group interactions and have emphasised their dynamic qualities (as opposed to the static absolutism so often a part of pluralist rhetoric). There has been, in fact, a laudable effort in recent years to counter the deluge of polemical material on pluralism. Mann (1979) notes that academics, having studied the matter for a long time, 'did not have to be reminded of the persistence of ethnicity' (p. 44); they became increasingly concerned with the oversimplifications and distortions associated with the 'new ethnicity' which over-emphasised, as Gleason (1984) might say, the *pluribus* and trivialised the *unum* of the American motto. This desire to restore balance has led to works re-examining the pluralism–assimilation relationship, the explanatory value of social class, the relationship between ethnicity and social inequality; such writings can be seen as responses to more advocatory publications (e.g. Greeley, 1974; Henk *et al.*, 1972; Novak, 1971; Schrag, 1971).

Official policy-makers

Official views of pluralism and, especially, language retention have followed a predictable pattern in many areas of the world. As the general aim of government is to ensure society's survival and prosperity (if only for Machiavellian motives), it is not surprising to observe a concern for homogenisation and standardisation and a corresponding fear of particularism and social fragmentation. It would be easy to assemble illustrative quotations from world leaders past and present. In the name of unity, however, many misdeeds have been done, and discrimination and persecution blot the histories of *all* societies. An increasing tendency to tolerance is therefore welcome. It should come as no shock, however, to see that government action on behalf of enduring diversity does not generally extend as far as some proponents of pluralism would like. The present stance of many governments reflects a continuing concern for social integrity, alongside a newer acknowledgement of the value of diversity. This combination is not static, or uniform across contexts, or insensitive to currents of opinion and this is as it should be. However, if we acknowledge that some currents of opinion present themselves more forcibly and more vocally to officialdom than do others, we can see that government action may be swayed inappropriately.

An American example of this involves the Ethnic Heritage Studies Act of 1972. Mann (1979) remarks that it was a response to 'ethnic ideologues' and it sanctioned their claim 'that their own intense feelings of ethnicity applied to Americans as a whole' (p. 167). Mann is of the opinion that the best governmental policy here would have been none at all, on the grounds that matters of ethnicity are best left to those directly concerned. This is a position with which I agree. It is important to note that many see lack of government legislation as ignorance or discrimination. They fail to understand that, as Mann implies, lack of response (in legislative terms) is itself a government action. My view is that a refusal to legislate on matters of ethnicity is a reasonable response which can be supported by the sorts of evidence I have assembled here. This presupposes, of course, a real tolerance (and *this* could well be endorsed in law) for groups to define themselves as they see fit (see also Isaacs, 1972).

LANGUAGE ATTITUDES

In sociolinguistics and the social psychology of language, attitudes have traditionally been of great importance. This is because people's reactions to language varieties can reveal their perceptions of the *speakers;* in this way, language attitudes are linked to views of identity. Useful reviews of the topic in general can be found in Agheyisi and Fishman (1970), Cooper and Fishman (1974) and Giles and Powesland (1975); these writers also discuss the methods used to elicit and assess language attitudes – questionnaires, interviews, scaling techniques and various indirect approaches (of which the 'matched-guise' format is perhaps the best known and most used; see next section).

One important use to which language-attitude information has been put is in connection with the learning of a second language. I shall not discuss this here, since it is peripheral to my concerns, but the general view is that, *ceteris paribus,* positive attitudes are likely to facilitate second-language acquisition (see Gardner, 1982; Gardner & Lambert, 1972). Variations in the context of second-language learning and in the perceived functions of that language often, however, interact significantly with the importance and type of positive attitude (see Carroll, 1978). Macnamara (1973) appeared to take an opposing view, asserting that attitudes were of *little* importance in language learning. His argument is worthy of some brief attention here, since it leads to considerations relevant to all types of language attitudes.

First, Macnamara notes that necessity may overpower attitude; this is obviously true. He discusses the adoption of English by the Irish population, a shift not accompanied by favourable attitudes. Indeed, as we have seen, most historical changes in language-use owe much more to socioeconomic and political pressures than they do to attitudes *per se.* However, Macnamara does acknowledge that attitudes of a sort – instrumental attitudes – may play a part in language shift, e.g. a mid-nineteenth-century Irishman may, initially at least, have hated English and what it represented, yet, in the face of his perceptions of the sociopolitical climate, may have realised the necessity and long-term usefulness of the language. An instrumental motivation need not imply an integrative one (i.e. one based upon a desire to become part of another group). There may be a useful distinction here between *positive* and *favourable* attitude; to stay with the Irish example, we might say that the language attitudes towards English were positive and instrumental, but not necessarily favourable or integrative. It is, however, interesting to consider that once language shift has been accomplished the instrumental–integrative distinction may break down.

Macnamara also contends that language learning at school has typically been an unreal and artificial business in which communication is subordinated to an appreciation of language as a purely academic subject. It is this lack of communicative purpose, not children's attitudes, which underlies poor language competence among pupils, according to Macnamara. I would agree that a great failing in language classrooms has been the absence of realistic usage, but I do not think that this implies that attitudes are of small importance.

Overall, Macnamara's article usefully focuses attention on language attitudes and their place in the larger scheme of things, but I do not agree with his judgements of the minor significance of attitudes. In the cases of mass language shift and individual necessity, the point is not that attitudes are unimportant but that they are instrumental, even if unfavourable. In the school context, the argument that the situation is artificial is a condemnation of traditional approaches, and does not of itself indicate that attitudes are trivial. In fact, attitudes may be of considerable importance precisely *because* of artificiality, i.e. given that a context is *not* perceived as pertinent to real life or is *not* based upon necessity, attitudes may make a real difference. If we return once more to the Irish situation we can see that the notion of artificiality can extend beyond the classroom. With the establishment of the Irish State in 1922, and the subsequent emphasis upon schools as agents of Irish restoration, there arose a disjunction between official aims regarding the language and actual social linguistic behaviour. An ever-decreasing level of native competence has been accompanied by an increasingly widespread minimal competence in basic skills, produced entirely through education. It can therefore be argued that schools – and the attitudes towards Irish which they have encouraged – have been of the greatest importance in sustaining the language, weak and artificial though this may be (and however much criticised by revivalists); see chapter 3.

Language-attitudes research

In 1960, Lambert *et al.* introduced the 'matched-guise' technique as a means of assessing language attitudes.[2] Judges evaluate – on a number of dimensions – a tape-recorded speaker's personality after hearing him or her read the same passage in each of two or more language varieties. That the speaker is, for all 'guises', the same person is not revealed to the judges and, typically, they do not guess this. Their judgements are then considered to represent stereotyped reactions to the given language varieties, since potentially confounding elements are constant across guises. While the technique has been criticised, mainly for its alleged artificiality, it does seem to provide useful information which can be confirmed by other means (e.g. by questionnaires, or by ratings of actual speakers *not* adopting guises). In general then, the technique presents to the listener samples of speech which are thought to act as identifiers allowing the expression of social stereotypes.

The study by Lambert *et al.* considered reactions towards French and English guises in Montreal. The English-speaking judges generally reacted more favourably to English than to French guises; more interestingly, the French-speaking evaluators *also* rated English guises more favourably. Lambert and his colleagues concluded that the findings demonstrated not only favourable reactions from members of the high-status group towards their own speech but also that these reactions had been adopted by members of the lower-status group. This 'minority group reaction' is a revealing comment on the power and breadth of social stereotypes in general, and on the way in which these may be assumed by those who are themselves the objects of negative stereotypes.

A study by Giles (1970) investigated reactions of British secondary-school children to a variety of accents, including the non-regional RP (Received

Pronunciation), Irish, German and West Indian. In terms of status, aesthetic quality and communicative content (a measure of the perceived ease of interaction with the speakers), RP was rated most favourably, regional accents (e.g. South Welsh and Somerset) were in the middle ranks, and urban accents (e.g. Cockney, Birmingham) were at or near the bottom of the scale. These results agree largely with an earlier suggestion by Wilkinson (1965) that there exists in Great Britain a tripartite accent prestige hierarchy: at the top is RP, then come various regional accents and, finally, accents associated with heavily urbanised areas (see also Trudgill, 1975a).

Earlier, Lambert (1967) had introduced a refinement which seems to clarify this work. He categorised the many personality dimensions on which judges typically rate speech and speakers into three groups. Thus, some are seen to reflect a speaker's *competence* (e.g. dimensions like intelligence and industriousness), some *personal integrity* (helpfulness, trustworthiness) and some *social attractiveness* (friendliness, sense of humour). An investigation by Giles (1971) considered reactions to RP, South Welsh and Somerset accents along these lines. Although RP received the highest ratings in terms of *competence*, the other two were perceived more favourably on *integrity* and *attractiveness;* the assessments were made by judges who were themselves from either South Wales or Somerset. In a later study, Giles (1973) presented the same three accents, plus a Birmingham variety, to groups of South Welsh and Somerset schoolchildren whose views on capital punishment had earlier been ascertained; the guises in this study all presented arguments against capital punishment. Giles was interested to measure both the children's views of the quality of the arguments presented, and any changes in their stance on the topic. It was found that the higher the status of an accent, the more favourable were the ratings of the quality of the argument. However, in terms of attitude change among the children, only the regional accents proved effective. The study thus suggests that messages can be seen as high in quality without necessarily being persuasive; or, to use Lambert's terminology, accents judged as reflecting high speaker *competence* need not always have greater influence upon listeners than regional varieties associated with *integrity* and *attractiveness* (see also Giles & Powesland, 1975).

Carranza and Ryan (1975) studied the reactions of Mexican-American and Anglo-American students to speakers of Spanish and English. Although the topic discussed by speakers had some influence upon the ratings, English was generally rated more favourably than Spanish on both status-related and *solidarity* (i.e. integrity and attractiveness) dimensions. However, Spanish *was* seen more favourably on the solidarity than on the status traits. Similar results were found in a study by Ryan and Carranza (1975) in which evaluations of standard English and Spanish-accented English were made by Mexican-Americans, Blacks and Anglos (i.e. White, English speakers). Arthur *et al.* (1974) found that White, Californian college students downgraded the so-called 'Chicano' English on several personality dimensions. Ryan *et al.* (1977) have also shown that the *degree* of accent may affect ratings; as Spanish-American 'accentedness' increased, reactions of English-speaking students became less favourable (see also Brennan & Brennan, 1981a, b; Ryan & Carranza, 1977).

Studies involving Black speakers in the United States have also shown that language-attitude ratings reveal social perceptions. Tucker and Lambert (1969) presented a number of American English dialect varieties to northern White, southern White and southern Black college students. All groups rated 'Network' speakers most favourably – 'Network English' being roughly equivalent here to British RP – and Black speakers were downgraded (see also Fraser, 1973). Irwin (1977) found that White judges perceived Black college students less favourably than their White counterparts on dimensions of voice quality, fluency and confidence. We could also note here the work of V. Edwards (1979), since her studies of evaluations of Black speakers in Great Britain show a similar pattern – both teachers and West Indian adolescents perceived West Indian speakers less favourably than they did working-class and middle-class English speakers.

Overall, these studies of language evaluation show that speech can evoke stereotyped reactions reflecting differential views of social groups. Standard accents and dialects usually connote high status and competence; regional, ethnic and lower-class varieties are associated with greater speaker integrity and attractiveness. The trust and liking apparently reflected in such varieties may be related to conceptions of ingroup solidarity. It is important to remember in all this that the social context in which evaluations occur is not a static entity; as it changes, one should expect to see alterations in attitudes too. Recent movements like the new ethnicity, French-Canadian nationalism and 'Black pride' can, for example, be expected to reveal revitalised group perceptions through linguistic evaluation.

However, the process by which speakers of nonstandard varieties adopt the stereotyped views of the majority continues (Edwards, 1979b). We do not observe, though, the large-scale defection from these varieties to which this might be expected to lead. In this connection, we should recall that *all* varieties – standard or non-standard – can serve that bonding or solidarity function which is a part of group identity; we now see that this is reflected in evaluations along *integrity* and *social attractiveness* dimensions. There may also, of course, be practical difficulties and psychological penalties involved in attempts to leave one dialect group and join another (see Carranza & Ryan, 1975; Edwards, 1979b; Ryan, 1979). Finally here, we can note that an association between lower-class speech patterns and masculinity accounts for a 'covert prestige' (in the United States and Great Britain at least) attaching to non-standard speech (see Labov, 1966, 1972; Trudgill, 1974a, 1975a, b). This phenomenon seems to cross class lines; middle-class speakers often report using *more* non-standard forms than they actually do. In any event, it appears that the overt downgrading of non-standard varieties may co-exist with more latent positive connotations.

Recently, Ryan *et al.* (1982; see also Ryan *et al.*, 1984) have attempted to summarise language attitude studies by providing an 'organisational framework'.

They suggest that there are two determinants of language perceptions: *standardisation* and *vitality*. A standard is one whose norms have been codified and is associated with dominant social groups. Vitality (see also next section) refers to the number and importance of functions served, and is clearly bolstered by the status which standards possess; it can also be a feature, however, of non-standard varieties, given sufficient numbers of speakers and community support. There are also two main evaluative dimensions: *social status* and *solidarity*. We have already noted that standard varieties usually connote high status, while non-standard ones may reflect group solidarity. Finally, the authors suggest three major measurement techniques: *content analysis* and *direct* and *indirect* assessment. The first of these is seen to include historical and sociological observation, as well as ethnographic studies. Direct assessment usually involves questionnaire or interview methods, while the 'matched-guise' approach is the best example of indirect measurement of language attitudes.

There is obviously a need for a combination of approaches to language-attitude assessment; in particular, given the decontextualised nature of much social psychological work, both direct and indirect methods should be supplemented with real-life observation. This is a theme I have considered important throughout this book, and I have argued elsewhere for an eclectic, 'triangulation' approach (see Edwards, 1978, 1982a).

LANGUAGE BEHAVIOUR AND IDENTITY

The study of language attitudes reveals, with some regularity, that different varieties evoke different perceptions, i.e. speakers' identities are evaluated largely in terms of status and solidarity. The discussion so far has indicated that, in minority–majority contexts, language shift occurs. With regard to dialect and accent, however, where language assimilation need not happen, it is apparent that retention of negatively stereotyped varieties is at least partly due to the continuing value they possess for group solidarity and identity (see Ryan, 1979). Still, there are many examples of people 'losing' such varieties once they move away from the contexts where these are vernaculars. It is also the case that many speakers of non-standard forms become, to a greater or lesser degree, bidialectal, retaining the original variety while adding another for instrumental purposes. Individuals may thus alter their dialects depending upon the situations they are in.

I have suggested (see chapter 5) that expansion of the dialect repertoire can be a feature of education. The point here is that, while *bilingualism* is often a transitional stage on the way to language shift, *bidialectalism* can be a much more permanent phenomenon. The reason is simply that two dialects (one reflecting group solidarity, the other instrumental needs caused by desired group contact and social mobility) can be maintained at much less cost than can two languages. Dialects often imply mutual intelligibility, after all, and share many common features. As Labov (1976, p. 64) puts it: 'the gears and axles of English grammatical machinery are available to speakers of all dialects.' As well, dialect speakers do not represent a separate culture so much as a different *sub*culture, one which, again, overlaps to some extent with that of standard speakers. Thus, dialects remain where languages do not.

However, as noted above, there is the fact of dialect (or accent) mobility, whereby speakers can select from their repertoire according to their perceptions of situational constraints and demands. This has been studied within social psychology under the rubric of linguistic *accommodation* and merits some consideration here. For, if language attitudes *per se* allow some insights into the perception and presentation of identity, as revealed through group dialect/accent markers, then study of acommodation may illuminate adjustments made in this presentation.

The investigation of accommodation has been most thoroughly explored by Giles and his colleagues and, although their perspective is not the only one on the matter, I shall consider it here because: (a) there is a fairly large amount of published material to examine; (b) there are useful linkages and continuities between attitudes and accommodation in Giles' work; and (c) most importantly, there are some grounds for believing that this perspective is the most comprehensive to date. Street and Giles (1982), for example, examine some other formulations and note that the accommodation model is superior inasmuch as it takes into account language listeners/recipients as well as speakers, acknowledges the importance of subjective perceptions of speech as well as objective markers, has the potential to treat wider ranges of speech behaviour, and can deal with interpersonal encounters as inter*group* situations. One assumes, of course, that Street and Giles will be naturally biased in favour of their own model, but my own examination of the relevant literature leads me to the conclusion that, generally, the points they make above are reasonable. [3]

Linguistic accommodation

Giles and Powesland (1975) suggest that the essence of the theory of speech accommodation derives from social psychological studies of similarity-attraction and social exchange. Byrne (1971), for example, describes a series of studies demonstrating that personal similarity increases the likelihood of attraction and liking – we like others who are like ourselves. This insight was supplemented by findings that reduction of existing dissimilarities will lead to more favourable evaluation. Since the desire for social approval is 'assumed to be at the heart of accommodation' (Giles & Powesland, 1975, p. 159), we see that the model involves reducing linguistic differences in order to be better perceived by others. However, accommodation means change, and change costs something; consequently, Giles and Powesland draw upon the social-exchange literature (e.g. Homans, 1961) and note that accommodation will only likely be initiated if a favourable cost–benefit ratio can be achieved.

Thus, 'accommodation through speech can be regarded as an attempt on the part of the speaker to modify or disguise his persona in order to make it more acceptable to the person addressed' (Giles & Powesland, 1975, p. 158).

Three more relevant points are brought out by Giles and Powesland. First, the speaker is not necessarily 'consciously aware' of his accommodative plan. Some strategies may be quite overt, but covert accommodation is also possible and here the *listener* may not always detect its operation either. Second, accommodation can imply divergence as well as convergence; just as a speaker may become linguistically more like the listener whose approval is desired, so divergent accommodation can occur where dissociation is wanted. Third, convergent accommodation does not *always* lead to social approval. Giles and Powesland cite an example in which an English-speaking European addresses an East African official in Swahili. In this case, accommodation is seen as condescension and implies that the official is incapable of dealing in English.

In terms of the mechanics of accommodation, Giles and Smith (1979) observe that obvious 'intralingual convergences' are those of pronunciation (i.e. accent), speech rate and message content. They also acknowledge the importance of Tajfel's theory of intergroup relations and social change, particularly with regard to divergence (see e.g. Tajfel, 1974, 1978, 1981). This is outlined further in Giles *et al.* (1977). Tajfel proposed that groups in contact compare themselves, and want to see themselves, as distinct and positively valued entities. Members of a subordinate group, in trying to achieve a more positive identity, have a number of strategies available to them (assuming, of course, that any changes are seen as actually possible). They may move into the other group (assimilation), may redefine negative qualities as positive (e.g. negatively marked group features like colour or dialect may become positive, in a process of revitalised group pride), or may create altogether new evaluative dimensions which will favour their group. Outright group competition is also seen as a possibility.

Speech accommodation, as discussed by Giles and his colleagues, can thus be seen – in either its divergent or convergent mode – as an identity adjustment made to increase group status and favourability. A summary of speech accommodation theory is found in Thakerar *et al.* (1982). *Convergence* reflects a desire for approval, occurs when perceived benefits outweigh costs, and varies in magnitude according to the extent of the available linguistic repertoire and the degree of need for approval. It is favourably received by listeners (i.e. where they are conscious of its operation; Giles and Powesland, 1975) to the extent to which positive intent is attributed. *Divergence* (or at least speech maintenance) reflects a desire for personal dissociation or an emphasis upon positive ingroup identity (if the encounter is defined in intergroup terms). Magnitude constraints are as above and unfavourable reactions can be expected when listeners perceive negative intent.

Ethnolinguistic vitality

For present purposes, the accommodation model is most interesting as it relates to a further development, that of *ethnolinguistic vitality*. Giles *et al.* (1977) outline three variables pertinent to group vitality: status (particularly socioeconomic), demography (number, concentration and proportion of group members) and institutional support (e.g. the use of group language in education, government, religion, etc.). When the notion of vitality is connected with Tajfel's theory of group relations and with the accommodation perspective, the authors propose that a unified model for understanding language and ethnic group relations emerges. Thus, Tajfel provides the primary conceptual framework of group strategies, these are examined in their linguistic contexts through accommodation theory, and the vitality factors provide the social background.

The next important treatment is that of Giles and Johnson (1981). Here a theoretical approach to language and ethnic identity is given, having four components. The first is Tajfel's theory of social identity and group relations (see above) which involves strategies of social creativity (i.e. in the redefinition of negatively valued dimensions or the creation of new ones) and social competition. The second is *perceived* ethnolinguistic vitality (see also Bourhis *et al.*, 1981; Giles & Byrne, 1982), i.e. in addition to the actual variables affecting vitality (above), Giles and Johnson now append group members' perceptions of vitality; they suggest that while objective and subjective conceptions of vitality often overlap, they need not always do so, and subjective assessments may prove a revealing refinement. Third, Giles and Johnson refer to the distinctiveness, strength and value of group boundaries; taken together, these are seen to contribute to the perceived 'hardness' or 'softness' of boundaries. Boundary permeability, in turn, affects the strength and potential changeability of group membership. Fourth, Giles and Johnson acknowledge that ethnic-group membership is not the only salient category in people's lives and may not, therefore, be of explanatory value in all social interactions. Thus, they discuss the importance of *multiple*-group membership.

Giles and Johnson then propose that individuals are more likely to define encounters with outgroup members in ethnic terms, and will try to maintain positive linguistic distinctiveness (i.e. maintain identity) when they: (a) identify strongly with an ethnic group which has language as an important group dimension; (b) are aware of alternatives to their own group status; (c) consider their group to have high vitality; (d) see their group's boundaries as hard and closed; and (e) identify strongly with few other social categories (see also Edwards & Giles, 1984, where these propositions are outlined as they relate to *dialect* rather than language). It follows that, when the alternative to each of these propositions is considered, linguistic attenuation is to be expected, and possibly assimilation by the outgroup.

Bourhis *et al.* (1981) present further information here and produce a 'subjective vitality questionnaire'. The authors claim that the objective measures of status, demography and institutional support already permit a rough classification of speech communities 'as possessing low, medium or high vitality' (p. 146), but acknowledge that group members may minimise or exaggerate group vitality in given circumstances. Thus, the addition of subjective to objective data may be useful. In particular, it may help in assessing the group's survival chances and in providing 'advance indication' of group mobilisation or attempted revival 'not otherwise forseeable solely on the basis of "objective vitality" information' (p. 147). A 22-item questionnaire is appended to the article as a pilot instrument; the questions largely reflect the three objective dimensions of vitality.

A further development of ethnolinguistic vitality theory has been to use it as a basis for a better understanding of second-language acquisition. Thus, when the *alternatives* of each of the five propositions above are in force and when, as we have seen, Giles and Johnson (1981) suggest the possibility of attenuation and assimilation, Giles and Byrne (1982) propose that a strong motivation will exist to learn the outgroup language for *integrative* reasons. Conversely, when the propositions themselves (listed as (a) to (e) above) apply, second-language learning is hindered. Giles and Byrne claim this will be so, 'even assuming instrumental value' (p. 35) attaches to the second variety. Giles and Byrne (see also Beebe & Giles, 1984) make clear that the vitality approach has more to say about the facilitation of language learning (i.e. the achievement of native-like proficiency) than about some learning–no learning dichotomy. [4]

Husband and Saifullah Khan (1982) have recently criticised the vitality concept, focusing particularly upon work outlined in Giles *et al.* (1977), Bourhis *et al.* (1981) and, with specific regard to its application to second-language acquisition, Giles and Byrne (1982). The most important objections are that the three dimensions of objective vitality are gross and inexact, not independent of one another, and are given no differential weighting. Perceived or subjective vitality, inasmuch as it rests upon the objective measures, is thus equally flawed. As a basis for understanding second-language learning, the propositions outlined are seen to imply that such learning is obtained at the cost of group independence. Vitality is grounded in social psychological theory which is itself weak and decontextualised. The 'attractive, but illusory conception of "vitality"' (p. 196) exists without adequate theoretical background and thus the way is open for 'years of fruitless, speculative factor analytic fishing expeditions' (p. 195).

Johnson *et al.* (1983) have replied to these criticisms. They begin by noting that their earlier work was unlike mainstream social psychological treatment precisely because of their 'insistence on publishing demographic, historical and sociopolitical accounts of the ethnolinguistic groups' under study (p. 256). Vitality then emerged because of a need to formalise the placement of social psychological processes in 'socio-structural' context. The authors acknowledge that the three vitality dimensions are interrelated, but suggest the value of proposing 'a certain degree of orthogonality' (p. 257) until specific empirical links can be made. They also acknowledge that the relationship between vitality and larger social variables is a dynamic one. They stress again the social value of investigating perceived vitality and make the point that while low vitality may undercut a group's survival chances it may also spur efforts at group maintenance and revival. However, there are probably 'points of no return' here and 'as yet little is known about the minimal objective and subjective vitality needed for the survival of ethnolinguistic groups and their language' (pp. 262-3). Johnson *et al.* (1983) also respond to Husband and Saifullah Khan's questioning of their definition of 'group', claiming that self-identification should be the vital determinant. This 'may be based on a common set of ancestral cultural traditions, or may stimulate the creation of a unique set of traditions' (p. 263). The authors reject their critics' claim that vitality theory makes assimilation the price of integrative language learning; here they note their emphasis on the holding of multiple group memberships.

SUMMARY

I have little to say by way of summary concerning the first two sections of this chapter. Investigations of language attitudes tend to confirm the information already presented at a more sociological level. The status and solidarity dimensions found to be important in psychological studies relate very well to the tensions and attractions existing between mainstream and minority groups. Attitudes to dialects reveal something of the reasons for the persistence of non-standard and negatively stereotyped varieties while, at the same time, show with some regularity the status-linked attractions of standard forms. Given the dynamics of standard–non-standard relationships, and realising the overlap between dialects which does not apply at the level of language, we can understand how bidialectalism is a more likely and more endurable condition than bilingualism.

When we look at the extrapolations from language-attitude studies to those dealing with accent/dialect mobility and group vitality, points arise requiring discussion here. The theories of intergroup relations and social identity (Tajfel) and speech accommodation (Giles) probably represent the most comprehensive approach available, within social psychology, to the presentation and manipulation of language and identity. An important question is whether or not the theories advance our understanding of the processes discussed or simply restate or formalise, from a particular perspective, existing knowledge. The answer, as is usually the case within social psychology, is the latter. This does not mean at all that the approaches are without value, but it does mean that we can and should check the insights claimed against other evidence. Accommodation theory, for example, clearly does not account for all the possible complexities of speech interaction (e.g. the Swahili example above) and it is easy to imagine encounters where accommodation occurs not for social approval *per se* but for a wide range of quite different Machiavellian or opportunistic reasons, often with highly conscious motivation,[5] or, indeed, at a purely automatic level, for communicative efficiency or because it is normative. The danger (again endemic to much of social psychology) is that theoretical perspectives may become prematurely solidified, with a great deal of internal coherence at the expense of on-the-ground explanatory value. Things are often made neater than they really are. As well, an awareness of this difficulty can lead to what often appear to be potentially infinite embroideries on a theme, to the 'fishing expeditions' noted by Husband and Saifullah Khan above (1982). It sometimes seems as if the final, if unattainable, goal of social psychology is destined to be some 1:1 map which essentially reproduces social reality. This is clearly an undesirable state of affairs which itself prompts the often premature, altogether too simplistic, but eminently understandable drive to 'theory'.

Perhaps a way out of the dilemma lies in attaching social psychological work to other perspectives and disciplines. For, although the psychological approach clearly has something to offer, it is likely to be as a complement to other avenues of inquiry. And, in fairness, it must be noted that more macro approaches to language and identity are often less than completely satisfying precisely because they cannot attend to processes at an individual level. Up to this point, as the emphasis in this book makes clear, I believe that the additional insights afforded by social psychology into the language–identity process have been rather slight.

The work of Giles and his colleagues has the potential to make more useful the linkages between social psychology and other information. As Johnson *et al.* (1983) observe, they *have* been concerned with the demographic, historical and social contexts, and the recent development of interest in factors affecting ethnolinguistic vitality attests to this. Still, there is a continuing need to broaden the scope here and Husband and Saifullah Khan are right to note this. It can be argued that the information seen to influence group vitality is already available, in a much more detailed form, in history, sociology and the 'real-life record' generally. Husband and Saifullah Khan point to the dependence of group vitality upon economic, social and political currents, and there is a danger that vitality theory, as presently construed, involves little more than superficial attention to these. The sorts of prediction presently derivable from vitality theory are rather restricted. Relatedly, the claim by Johnson *et al.* (1983) that criticisms of the atemporal, ahistorical character of vitality theory are met by having questionnaire respondents give their assessments of group vitality in the past, and predictions of future vitality, is not a strong one. Questions along these lines can be interesting but they are less useful than intelligent deduction from the historical record itself.[6]

There are also problems with the interdependence and weighting of the dimensions of vitality. The authors acknowledge this but want to allow empirical research to make the necessary links and establish relative importances. However, it is not clear that experimental findings can themselves do this. In any event, more attention to context might allow, at *this* stage, some reasonable approximations concerning these matters. Without this, dimensions may become ossified and artificial.

Still, in all of this, I think that Giles and his colleagues are moving in a useful direction. They are clearly aware of the difficulties I have mentioned so far and there does exist the possibility, through vitality research, of a real social psychological supplement to existing information. This is particularly so when we consider developments along the lines of *subjective* vitality. For here there is something which is suited to psychological inquiry and which is less likely to be directly reflected in sociological or historical accounts. [7] There is clearly a great need, however, to draw upon context more fully in the establishment of subjective vitality variables which, as they now exist (see Bourhis *et al.*, 1981), reflect too directly and too simply underlying objective factors deemed to be important. A specific problem which affects this approach too, is that questionnaire formats do not generally permit variable weighting or the assessment of relative item importance. Some questions may be of intense interest to respondents; others may suggest themes of little importance or ones not previously thought of at all. Summarising results, by simple addition along dimensions of *a priori* relevance to experimenters, may obscure more than clarify. In particular, the overall tenor of the format may suggest 'groupness' as the underlying factor of importance. Generally, the fact that questionnaires usually impose a framework on answers is a vexing one.

The investigation of subjective vitality should always, therefore, involve consideration of context. And, as with social psychological work generally, care should be taken in not overemphasising the value and applicability of findings. To claim that vitality data can predict group survival chances or the likelihood of revivalist mobilisation (Bourhis *et al.*, 1981) is probably overly sanguine. Johnson *et al.* (1983) note that 'vocal élites' may have more accurate perceptions of vitality than less 'mobilised' group members or, alternatively, may over- or underestimate it; they also claim that as yet we know little about the minimal vitality needed for group survival. But, in fact, on all these matters a great deal *is* known, although the knowledge may not be in a form acceptable to social psychology. Still, there is no excuse for psychology ignoring existing insights, or expending a great deal of energy reinventing them under new auspices.

The authors' conception of the ethnic group itself, and criteria for membership, would also profit from deeper awareness of the non-psychological literature. Their definition is itself built upon social psychological work, and emphasises *self*-identification which *may* be based on a common background. While they are right to stress the essentially subjective nature of ethnic identity, it is not so accurate to see a common ancestral tradition as optional. At some point in the past, there must exist shared, tangible group markers (see chapter 1). Similarly, the idea that group identification may 'stimulate the creation of a unique set of traditions' fails to come to grips with the definition of the group in the first place, although it is quite true that *existing* groups often invent traditions (see e.g. Hobsbawm & Ranger, 1983).

The final point I want to make here concerns the proposition of Johnson *et al.* (1983) that low vitality may actually spur group maintenance efforts. They give three examples: (a) individuals learning Scots Gaelic perceived it to have low vitality but were still interested, perhaps because of this, to know and support it; (b) Welsh speakers who identified strongly with their group were found to be more committed to it and the Welsh language when vitality was perceived to be low; and (c) fears for French in Quebec led to the election of a pro-independence government and to the adoption of a French-language charter.

First we should note that, as the theory stands, low vitality can lead either to assimilation to group mobilisation. As we have seen, the authors claim that we need to know more about the matter before predictions are possible. Yet (see above), information is already available from history which allows us to understand something at least of the dynamics of group-language shift. Second, the cases noted above rely too much upon the view of vocal, visible but minority groups within minority groups. I have already discussed the inaccuracies which result from overattention to group spokesmen and to those consciously committed to culture and language. I also have data about Gaelic learners, in Nova Scotia, which suggest strong commitment based upon perceptions of low group vitality (Edwards, 1982c). But any attempt to extrapolate from these views and concerns to more general linguistic maintenance would be wholly misleading. In fact, when looking at any minority-language situation, one must always be aware that those still speaking the language are very often, by that fact alone, atypical. This is not to say, of course, that no psychological interest attaches to these individuals – quite the contrary – but information gained from them may not say much about more widespread group dynamics. As to the Quebec case discussed by Johnson *et al.*, two points might be made: (a) it is questionable that a group's vitality is very low if it has the official wherewithal to promulgate a government charter; and (b) the election of the Parti Québécois in 1976 had at least as much to do with a desire for good government generally as it did with the endorsement of the party's stance on Quebec independence.

I have gone into some detail discussing the work of Giles and his colleagues because, on the one hand, there are promising directions here while, on the other, it demonstrates weaknesses inherent in the social psychological approach to language and identity and shows very clearly the continuing need to incorporate in a thoroughgoing manner work in other disciplines. I think there is no question that the idea of directly collecting data about perceptions of group language, identity and vitality is a very good one. It would be extremely regrettable if the exercise were to be vitiated through the lack of a broad perspective, since it is as the psychological addition to sociology and history that the venture is worthwhile.

7

Summary and Conclusions

INTRODUCTION

I began this book by noting that questions of language and identity are complicated; I hope that, over the last six chapters, I have been able to throw some light on the topic and, perhaps, to have reduced some of the confusion attaching to this emotional area. The simple conclusion is that, while language is commonly held to be a highly important or, indeed, essential component of group identity, it is not *necessary* to retain an original variety in order to maintain the continuity of a sense of groupness. While various agencies have concerned themselves with supporting language so as to prop up threatened identities, language *per se* has typically not been of the greatest concern to people possessing these identities. I have been particularly interested here in presenting historical documentation which shows that identities can and do survive the loss of the original group language.

The overall message is at once negative and positive. There is, I believe, a general inevitability to language shift under certain conditions, and no amount of revivalism or educational support can significantly affect the powerful social currents which produce shift. This can be construed as a negative, unfavourable occurrence – after all, something once common is now lost and the group is obliged to adopt another's language. I would emphasise, though, that to see this as negative implies a static conception of history which is, simply, unrealistic. It is much more useful to consider language shift as *alteration;* this accords with social dynamics and, in any event, there is never a question of a loss, pure and simple, with nothing to replace the abandoned form. Another language comes to serve and, in the transitional period, bilingualism is the usual bridge. Then, given sufficient time, the adopted language becomes a new group language, fulfilling all the requirements once met by the original variety. Is there any group in history for whom this is not so? Surely not, provided we take a long enough perspective. In this sense, much of the contemporary debate over the fate of 'small' languages and cultures can be seen to represent that volatility which always accompanies periods of transition.

However, all of this notwithstanding, there is also a much more positive interpretation to be placed upon language and group dynamics. I hope, in fact, that the message of this book can be seen as an *optimistic* one: Social continuity can be, and is commonly, maintained through and beyond the transitional times made inevitable by social evolution. Groupness is a tenacious quantity and is capable of surviving the loss of any objective marker, including language. Change there is, of course, but change need not imply loss. I suggest that the historical record shows, again and again, that ordinary group members – much better than spokesmen, pluralists, revivalists and others – understand this. The adjustments made in order to maximise social well-being, access and advancement are seen to be necessary and to involve cultural adaptation. But, at the same time, marks of distinction are retained which contribute to continuity without hindering social progress. I do not mean to imply that people consciously calculate cost–benefit ratios or cold-bloodedly determine which markers are to be kept in place and which must be retired. The power of concepts like 'pluralistic integration' or 'modified assimilation' resides exactly in the fact that they describe a socially *natural* process of accommodation which represents a gradual evolution through many choice points. How different this is from the psychologically understandable but sociologically and historically naive exhortations and hopes of consciously committed apologists for group and language maintenance. Their actions reflect, in Dr Johnson's words, 'the triumph of hope over experience'.

I do not suggest, of course, that the idea itself of intervening in the social fabric is inevitably useless. Far from it: the development of cultures is the result of constant and cumulative alteration. My point here is one of degree and complexity. Social adjustments reflect social needs and the overall pattern is a tightly woven one. Alterations may begin as small adjustments, but their success or failure in contributing to, and changing, the pattern depends very much upon the degree to which they recognise and accommodate to the contemporary state of things. Put simply, are they seeds which, given the earth available, will bear fruit? Of course, we very often do not know but history can teach us things and, with regard to language and identity, the lesson is clear: they reflect the workings of powerful economic and social forces and cannot be attended to in isolation. Language revival or maintenance, cultural pluralism, stable bilingualism – these cannot be instituted by fiat. If languages and cultures are seen to be at risk, it is because of a finely meshed social evolution. To remove them from risk would entail wholesale reworking of history, a broad reweaving of the fabric; except for a very few people, this has never been even considered as a practical exercise.

Again, the optimistic line here – and one in which optimism is firmly based in social reality – is that the essential element of groupness need never be at risk. More specifically, group continuity can survive the most radical changes, if its maintenance is desired by group members themselves, because the core requirements are intangible and private. They need not conflict with social progress, but neither are they amenable to intervention. On the other hand, visible markers like language are highly susceptible to change in the face of altered environments and, although their visibility invites intervention, there is no evidence to suggest that they can be maintained for any substantial length of time through active and usually isolated efforts.

SUMMARY

I began in chapter 1 by noting the serious lack of intercorrelation among disciplines treating language and identity and by announcing my intention to try and establish a balanced view that would attend to information from several quarters. The sociology of language is an obvious meeting point here – it can be argued that its central concern is, basically, the language–identity link; in order for it to be fully meaningful, it must necessarily encompass many more specific approaches.

In examining the concept of ethnic identity, I pointed out: (a) that *ethnic* need not imply *minority;* (b) that an emphasis upon group boundaries was more valuable, in the long run, than accenting the cultural 'stuff' these boundaries enclose (because the former deals better with social dynamism); (c) that both objective and subjective factors are important in matters of identity; and (d) that ethnic symbols are more potent than we may sometimes believe. An analysis of these elements led to a definition of ethnic identity which stressed boundary continuity and the intangible yet vital sense of groupness. Nationalism was then seen as ethnicity combined with a desire for full or partial group autonomy. Throughout the discussion I noted that language was a common but not necessary marker of groupness.

Language and dialect were themselves examined in the opening chapter. I was particularly concerned to note the communicative–symbolic distinction within language and to demonstrate that while the two aspects often co-exist (e.g. in majority groups), they are separable (e.g. among minority groups undergoing, or having completed, communicative language shift). There are many examples of groups retaining an important symbolic attachment to a language no longer regularly used. I also outlined in this section the arguments – now I think fairly well-understood – against the idea of 'better' or 'worse' languages and dialects. Any variety, whether standard or non-standard, is adequate for its speakers' needs, and can be a valid constituent of identity.

In chapter 2, I turned to a consideration of the relationship between language and nationalism. While an original language is not a necessary component of identity, it has clearly been seen as such by many, past and present, and consequently requires further attention. I began here by outlining the powerful German influence on the burgeoning association between language and nationhood. Fichte, Herder and others made it abundantly clear that language was to be conceived of as an almost sacred concomitant of nationality. They also demonstrated, however, how this can often lead to a denigration of other groups and other languages. Just as the early eighteenth century gave rise to a still-potent association of language with groupness, so it also established a continuing darker side of nationalism.

Antedating but supporting linguistic nationalism was the idea of keeping languages 'pure'. Indeed, given the perception that language is vital for the continuity of the group essence, nothing could be more natural than endeavouring to keep this well-spring undefiled. The European academies – particularly the Académie Française – concerned themselves with this, producing grammars and dictionaries and giving rulings on acceptable and unacceptable terms, neologisms and foreign borrowings. It is not at all surprising that, in times of perceived linguistic threat, these academies would become particularly active. It is interesting that the idea of official bodies established to safeguard language was, although advocated by some, not a popular one in Great Britain and the United States. Still, these countries were also in need of language standard-isation and regulation and the answer in both was a one-man, unofficial academy. I refer, of course, to the great English dictionary-makers, Webster and Johnson. Both men were at once aware of the need for rules and wary of the undesirability and likely impossibility of an academically imposed stasis. I concluded this section by remarking upon the continuing popular concern for standards, on the refusal of many linguists to enter the debate at a popular level, and on the need to chart with greater precision the uncertain middle ground between academic linguistics and public language.

I also gave some brief attention to the matter of lingue franche. While these – whether naturally occurring or constructed varieties – are obviously of greatest importance at a purely communicative level, they are still a part of the overall linguistic scene and are capable (at least potentially) of becoming carriers and reflectors of identity. Pidgins that become creolised, powerful natural lingue franche which first command attention solely for instrumental reasons, and so-called 'artificial' languages – all can assume symbolic as well as com-municative value. Indeed, it is interesting to note that constructed forms like Esperanto were, at least in the eyes of their originators, intended to transcend instrumental utility and to become carriers of some transnational identity.

Having added in this chapter a discussion of the linguistic features of nationalism to the introductory material on the subject in chapter 1, I thought it useful to conclude with a consideration of evaluations of nationalism. From the middle of the last century, criticism of nationalism has centred upon its inward- and backward-looking perspective, its elevation of feeling over rational-ity, and its ability to constrain people within boundaries; relatedly, it has been seen to promote hatred, disdain or dismissal of other groups. Many have con-sidered nationalism to be a blatantly chauvinistic and increasingly anachronistic doctrine. Furthermore, by its emphasis upon groupness it can work against the recognition and liberation of the individual. Nevertheless, nationalism continues to exercise a powerful force. There is no doubt that it has produced important cultural manifestations, but the major reason for its endurance is a need which persists for a sense of allegiance, groupness and 'roots'. National-ism was thrust into life by revolutionary modern developments and is maintained by modernisation (particularly where this is an unevenly distributed quantity; see also chapter 3) and industrialisation. Whatever the balance-sheet shows, the force of nationalism is likely to be with us for some time to come.

In the third chapter I focused upon language dynamics, supplementing general observation with details drawn from a wide variety of real-life contexts.

I began by examining language decline and death, noting that the most familiar pattern here involves language shift occasioned by essentially economic forces. Where pragmatic reasons for maintenance are not forthcoming, language is placed in jeopardy. This simple fact alone poses great problems for most maintenance and revival efforts, since these are generally unable to stem the practical pressures which conduce to shift and must, therefore, base their appeal on other, cultural grounds, grounds which are usually much less potent than economic ones.

My case study of the Irish language and my notes on Scots Gaelic, Breton, Welsh, Cornish and Manx led me to suggest a number of generalisable points:

1 Declining languages often have a predominance of older speakers. Lack of transmission to the younger generation is obviously the most direct contributor to language loss and this is brought about more by perceptions of economic advantage than by official anti-language measures. Nevertheless, decline in communicative language may leave symbolic significance in place.
2 Weakening languages are often confined to poor, rural areas; attempts to strengthen these, so as to shore up language, are obviously fraught with difficulties.
3 In language shift, bilingualism usually represents a bridging phenomenon and is itself a dispensable commodity.
4 Language decline cannot be understood, assessed or halted if it is treated in isolation from the more general social fabric and without appreciation of the processes of social evolution which have created contemporary conditions.
5 *Active* desire for language maintenance or revival is felt by only a small, unrepresentative minority.
6 Bluntly speaking, successful language maintenance is highly unlikely.
7 There is ample evidence that group identity survives language shift.

When I went on to consider more far-flung linguistic contexts, some further generalities emerged which complement those just outlined. Thus:

1 Economic success and communicative efficiency militate against the viability of 'small' languages in contact with powerful ones. These are factors of great weight, accompanying social processes like urbanisation, modernisation and social access which are very difficult to combat (even if this were generally desired, which it is not).
2 Attempts to 'upgrade' small, threatened or local varieties are always linguistically possible, but very often they are not socially, economically or politically expedient.

I amplified some of these points when turning to consider, more specifically, language revival, language planning and the relationship between language and economics. Language restoration – the bringing back into regular use of a variety spoken by a minority – is difficult; halting and then reversing linguistic decline is an unlikely proposition. How much more difficult it is, then, to revive a dead language no longer regularly used by anyone. Dead languages stay dead, at least as ordinary communicative mediums. The classic example of 'revival' is, of course, that of Hebrew in Israel. However, this was a unique setting in which a real communicative need existed alongside a variety with strong psychological claims on a linguistically diverse population. Furthermore, there is evidence suggesting that Hebrew was not previously so moribund as some have assumed. It remained throughout the diaspora, of course, as a religious medium; it also served, however, as a secular tool among elements of East European Jewry.

Language planning involves the selection and codification of a variety, followed by its implementation and further elaboration. However, as I noted, selection and implementation are usually dependent upon powerful policy-makers; language planners themselves, i.e. professional linguists and others, are most directly concerned with linguistic codification and elaboration, and their input is very much secondary to that of the real planners. The main point I was anxious to clarify here was simply that language planners are not prime movers and that they are better seen as important technicians, skilled in making adjustments to something set in motion by others.

The relationship between language and economics is, I believe, a very strong one, and practical considerations underlie most linguistic patterns and alterations. Naturally, this view has been downplayed by nationalists and apologists for linguistic pluralism, who have a vested interest in elevating language to sacred status. Nonetheless, the historical evidenc is clear: with some easily explained exceptions, economic (or at least pragmatic) motives determine language use. Indeed, some have seen nationalism itself as the result of practical necessity. All of this suggests interesting differences between pluralists and nationalists and more ordinary group members (see below). If we compare the rhetoric with the reality, there is no question at all that the latter group have more accurately understood their social world than those who try to interpret it for them.

Generally, in chapter 3, I tried to point out the large forces affecting language shift, how shift usually reflects an adaptation sought for instrumental reasons, and how difficult it is to stem language decline. Yet through it all identities continue, and it is precisely because they are *not* irrevocably bound up with objective markers like language that they can persist.

In chapter 4, I considered the alleged revival of ethnic feeling in contexts like North America. I argued essentially that, given a *persistence* of ethnicity, distinguished primarily by symbolic and/or private markers, the modern phenomenon represents an altered environment in which ethnic visibility is now more accepted than has hitherto been the case. There is no evidence for a widespread desire for a real return to ethnic roots; indeed, it can be argued that current ethnic manifestations are largely the product of assimilation, security and even some degree of affluence. The discussion of symbolic ethnicity in particular shows that contemporary groups can arrange an accommodation which permits both the benefits of modernity and the continuation of boundaries. It is an egregious error to think that the 'new ethnicity' has altered the basic underpinnings of acculturation and assimilation. Further, if it is the case that symbolic manifestations are what allow the desired accommodation, it follows that ethnicity is not now likely to be significantly affected by self-conscious attention to *non*-symbolic markers. The risks involved in misunderstanding the grounds upon which current ethnicity exists (in Western contexts at least) are obvious and I refer to some of these in the next chapter.

I also tried in chapter 4 to illuminate the sometimes-confused area of assimilation and pluralism. Assimilation – anathema to pluralists – has not so completely rendered ethnicity as many have thought; indeed, there are many positive aspects to it, most of them desired by minority groups. Pluralism has meant many things to many people, varying from a simple-minded and complete rejection of assimilation to a conception of group harmony which can co-exist with assimilation. At any rate, assimilation and pluralism should not be thought of as polar opposites. As will be plain by now, my interpretation of the historical evidence is that most have preferred what is, in fact, the most reasonable course here, a course which allows group continuity *and* mainstream participation. Thus, pluralistic integration or participationist pluralism represents a sensible middle road between the Scylla and Charybdis of segregation and homogenisation. Implicit in this view is the idea that, despite the claims of those who presume to know better, ordinary group members make, in the main, intelligent adaptations to changing circumstances. At the simplest level they realise, for example, that change is required but they can be relied upon to retain what is possible without active and essentially artificial policies of support. If, in fact, given markers of group identity are seen to require support, this probably indicates that they cannot be retained anyway (in unchanged form at least).

Finally here, I discussed cultural relativism – another difficult area and one currently undergoing some questioning. On the one hand, out-and-out relativism may lead to support for morally repugnant features of group life and may contribute to that superiority of group over individual rights which can be so threatening. On the other hand, anti-relativism seems to lead to value-laden judgements in which whole cultures are condemned and where world perspectives are ignored or trampled upon from prejudiced and ethnocentric viewpoints. My solution here was to see cultural relativism as relative itself and to acknowledge that value judgements may be applicable in some areas but not in others, e.g. most educated people would condemn cannibalism even though it cannot be proven to be wrong, while also accepting that linguistic evidence largely eliminates value judgements in questions of 'better' or 'worse' languages and dialects.

In chapter 5, I considered the educational implications of pluralism and assimilation and the impact of school programmes upon group identity and language. The dilemma in the school treatment of minority groups is to provide programmes which allow some reconciliation of core-curriculum 'civism' with some pluralistic acknowledgement of heterogeneity. I argued that schools should not be asked to transmit cultures *in toto*, that they should respect and illuminate diversity and that, in fact, all good education is multicultural.

Bilingual education in the United States is a particularly fascinating arena when considering the school role in group and language maintenance. The historical record shows a gradual decline in the desire for programmes in and on ethnic-group language on the part of the beneficiaries themselves. So, we should not be surprised that most contemporary bilingual-education pro-grammes are of a transitional type. I tried to communicate some of the flavour of the rhetoric surrounding bilingual education; it is clear that in this American context – as in many others – education has been seized upon, unrealistically, as the main support system for groups and languages perceived to be at risk. The transition–maintenance debate illustrates rather neatly that a general tolerance for diversity and, indeed, a willingness to help minority groups does not necessarily also mean a desire to actively promote or sustain diversity. For reasons now obvious, maintenance bilingual education is most unlikely to significantly affect group identity (and may in fact damage it), while transitional forms can be seen to reflect those adaptive patterns followed and promoted by group members themselves.

In turning to the position of non-standard language in education, I discussed matters to which I have given detailed attention elsewhere (Edwards, 1979b). Non-standard varieties, like standard ones, reflect group identity and solidarity and must be respected by the school. This is particularly so since the linguistic evidence is clear that there is noting instrinsically deficient about these forms: non-standard is not substandard. Still, just as it is not the role of the school to transmit cultures or to maintain minority languages, neither is it appropriate for education to teach in non-standard varieties or to decrease the emphasis upon socially accepted standard forms. I argued in this section that the thrust of the school is one of dialectal repertoire expansion, not replacement; this is a course which recognises both the psychological claims of the maternal, non-standard form and the practical necessity for continued exposure to the standard.

At the conclusion of chapter 5, I suggested that we must be careful not to allow criticism of some of the ill-founded ideas about education and identity to turn back the clock. For instance, the greater educational tolerance for linguistic diversity is a welcome commodity – one which reflects an open society and accords with an ideal of pluralistic integration. If there have been excessive claims about the school's potential to affect identity, there are also now retrogressive views abroad which would return schools to a greater inflexibility in the face of heterogeneous student bodies. The only way to strike an appro-priate balance is, as always, to sift through the arguments on all sides, reject the empty, grandiose or prejudiced sentiment, and consider what reasonable options remain.

In chapter 6, I treated language attitudes and the contribution of social psychological reserch to the topic. I began by summarising the views of several groups on language and identity. When considering ordinary group members, I stressed their practical concerns, their willingness to make adjustments without altogether abandoning group continuity, and the necessary decline in visible group markers over time. Group spokesmen, I suggested, were often atypical of those they supposedly represent; they are often well-ensconced individuals who now have sufficient psychological capital to allow themselves the luxury of considering ethnicity as some (unrealistic) static quantity. Group leaders may also be particularly intellectually committed to permanent diversity. In either case, while an interesting phenomenon in themselves, they contribute very little to the overall canvas. Mainstream populations have often been traditionally intolerant of diversity; nowadays, in many contexts, they are less so. However, their tolerance cannot be permanently taken for granted, nor does it necessarily proceed from purely altruistic motives, nor does it generally extend to active encouragement of social heterogeneity. The academic constituency is usually a major source of group spokesmen; it also, however, continues to provide disinterested assessment of language, identity and pluralism which takes into account the entire social fabric. Official policy-makers reflect the mainstream view, inasmuch as greater tolerance for diversity is usually balanced by traditional concerns for homogeneity and fears of social fragmentation. I suggested here that lack of government legislation on ethnic matters need not mean ignorance or discrimination; it may reflect the view that such affairs are best treated outside officialdom. Lack of response here can be, itself, a policy statement.

When considering the psychological research on language attitudes, I pointed out again that all language varieties can reflect identity. There is a regularity in research findings here: non-standard forms attract high ratings in terms of group solidarity, while standard ones are seen to reflect higher competence. Thus, even dialects lacking in social prestige retain a claim upon their speakers. In this sense, a bidialectal person is like one for whom bilingualism is a stable quantity – identity can be carried in an original variety while another is added for essentially instrumental reasons. This might be taken as a dialectal analogue to the more general process of pluralistic integration. Indeed, the data presented on linguistic accommodation suggest this strongly. Dialectal adjustment according to the perceived demands of context reflects a motivation for success *and* original marker retention. For obvious reasons – since we are dealing here with social *sub*groups – bidialectalism can be a more permanent feature for groups under the same overall language umbrella than bilingualism often is for groups from different language communities altogether.

The final aspect of the social psychological contribution to the language– identity link which I discussed was the notion of ethnolinguistic vitality. Here, a broader approach to the understanding of groupness is advocated, in which objective data on group vitality are supplemented with information about perceived or subjective vitality. I argued that psychology is particularly well-suited to give us insights into the latter dimension, but should always be viewed in concert with knowledge available from other sources. As for social psychological treatment of objective vitality, there are grounds for thinking that this has not, as yet, been particularly well done. Psychological enquiry should be able to usefully add to our understanding of group identity but it must been seen as an adjunct to other approaches, should resist the temptation to invent a wheel which already exists – and which perhaps rolls better for other drivers – and should pay more attention to the real-life record.

CONCLUSIONS

Johnson *et al.* (1983), in their discussion of psychological work on ethno-linguistic vitality, note that 'there is as yet no grand theory for the study of language, ethnicity and intergroup relations' (p. 258). Husband and Saifullah Khan (1982) observe that 'a theory of language and ethnic-group relations is an important but mammoth task' (p. 199). In presenting what follows here, I can hardly claim to have accomplished this mammoth task; I do suggest, however, that the information assembled in this book allows some theoretical observations to be made. These are most useful, perhaps, because they: (a) take into account the findings from a variety of sources and disciplines; (b) draw upon and thus reflect a wide range of real contexts; and (c) allow connect-ions to be made between large-scale and more individual treatments of social identity. In fact, as the points summarised above imply, I have become convinced that some *general* theoretical ideas can be advanced because, although the specifics of language, group and identity obviously vary with context, the basic elements are remarkably similar. To put it another way, I would suggest that there are important generalities across situations, even though the patterns or configurations of these may vary (see also Ferguson & Dil, 1979).

Theoretical points

1   History is dynamic and so are group processes; change, rather than stasis, is the order of the day. Furthermore, change is usually seen to be necessary and is often welcomed. There are very few groups that voluntarily maintain self-segregation for any substantial period. The continuity of groupness thus occurs despite the loss of given objective markers; indeed, it could not occur if it were dependent upon an historically unreal retention of visible features.
2   Relatedly, identity is an evolving concept. Its essence is a sense of groupness which is vital precisely because it survives radical change. Boundaries outlast the cultural manifestations they enclose. Traditions can be invented and history can be altered, but there must exist, at however distant a remove, some links to a real common past. It is possible to create social atmospheres within which identities can be maintained, and tolerance is always to be desired, but it is unlikely that identities can be actively fostered, however well-meaning the attempts here may be. Groupness resides, ultimately, in individual identity

and this, in turn, is highly related to personal security and well-being. It follows that, at both the individual and the group level, markers will be altered and practices adjusted to the extent to which they are seen to interfere with these quantities.

3   Boundary continuation in the face of social change suggests that there is a middle, desired course embracing elements of assimilation *and* pluralism. It is possible to ascertain which elements of group culture are most susceptible to change and which are likely to remain the longest. Here, the public–private, overt–covert and symbolic–non-symbolic dimensions are particularly important.

4   A middle course of pluralistic integration allows the practical and necessary alterations to be made without loss of groupness itself. As opposed to the recommendations of some apologists for diversity, it appears as a *natural* process. Economic and pragmatic motives are, without any doubt whatsoever, the most important where this middle course is concerned.

5   A good case can be made for officially sponsored social tolerance, but it is less easy to argue for active official involvement in identity itself. Refusal to legislate on cultural and linguistic matters, particularly, seems an appropriate stance.

6   A similar argument applies to educational involvement in group-identity maintenance. While all education worthy of the name should promote multicultural awareness, it is not the role of the school to take an active part in promoting diversity itself. While it is easy to understand why schools have traditionally been used to support pluralism and, particularly, language, their position here is much weaker than many have liked to acknowledge. Proponents of the educational support of language and identity would do well to consider the historical record, as well as the contemporary attitudes of the proposed beneficiaries of such support.

7   Language shift and decline have an historical inevitability and have proved impossible to halt or reverse without widespread, draconian or undemocratic methods. As an objective marker of groupness, language is highly susceptible to change; despite its obvious claims on our attention, its continuation is not necessary for the continuation of identity itself. There is evidence to suggest that the communicative and symbolic aspects of language are separable during periods of change, such that the latter can continue to exercise a role in group identity in the absence of the former. Failure to recognise this separability and inaccurate notions of the indispensability of communicative language for group continuity may lead to unwise and fruitless intervention attempts.

8   Thus, language maintenance and revival efforts are usually artificial – in the sense that they are removed from a realistic overall appreciation of social dynamics – and doomed to failure. It is not surprising that they are initiated by persons atypical of those for whom they allegedly speak and that they usually fail to enlist the active support of the intended beneficiaries.

9   Language planning can contribute to codification and elaboration, but the real policy-making, in terms of language selection and implementation,

depends upon powerful, official sources which, themselves, are susceptible to political and economic pressure. It is an error to think that academic language planners are of primary importance or that purely cultural considerations carry much weight in the planning process (see also the interesting hypotheses advanced by Ferguson & Dil, 1979).

10 Individual behaviour in matters of language and identity, as studied in psychological research, can be seen to reflect more large-scale social dynamics.

Further research

The material assembled here suggests that interesting new work could be done in studying the importance and perception of the language–identity link among many groups. These could, at least, include those discussed above: minority groups, mainstream populations, officials and legislators, group leaders and spokesmen, and educators. We should aim always for a broad and inter-disciplinary scope; although I have singled out psychology here as an area in need of expanded vision, it is likewise true that other approaches will benefit from awareness of work undertaken elsewhere. This will contribute to that 'relevance' which is so much demanded within social science these days. However, in addition, we should ensure that relevance is not bought at the expense of depth and scholarship. Some more specific suggestions are as follows:

1 We clearly need much more information about perceptions of identity from ordinary group members. Particularly important here, both intrinsically and with regard to multicultural and pluralistic policy-making, is the study of symbolic and non-symbolic markers, and their perceived role in identity continuation.

2 More specifically, we must gather more information about perceptions of the importance of language, since this is clearly going to continue to be viewed by many spokesmen and academics as the central pillar of group identity. Research which illuminates perceptions of language *without* suggesting beforehand, however indirectly, that is the central feature of investigation would be particularly valuable (see Dorian, 1982).

3 Examination of the views of group spokesmen, apologists for diversity, and language activists would be interesting in itself, and would permit a greater insight into current ethnic revivalism.

4 More attention should be given to the desired and actual effects of educational programmes intended to affect group culture and identity.

5 More analysis is needed of official views, intentions and policies concerning language and identity.

6 Studies could be mounted to chart the speed, degree and type of group-marker decline, as this occurs within the overall society. Work here could be carried out on contemporary situations as well as on past dynamics.

7 Relatedly, we should have more information about marker retention over time and the continuity of the sense of groupness in changing circumstances.

Appendix
Language Issues Around the World:
A Brief Guide

AFRICA

Burundi

Burundi has, unlike many of its African neighbours, an historical linguistic unity in which Kirundi has been the only Bantu language spoken throughout the country. Today, in a population of about three million, all but 50,000 or so have Kirundi as a mother-tongue. As well, about half a million know some Swahili. French, of course, was the colonial language and, from independence in 1962, it retained co-official status with Kirundi. Most government, education and media work is in French, and relatively little effort has been given to modernising and standardising Kirundi.

(Source: Verdoodt, 1979.)

Cameroon

In Cameroon, among more than 200 ethnic groups, French and English are official languages; Cameroon Pidgin English is without official recognition but acts as a lingua franca. There are also several large African languages (including Hausa), and Arabic is valued for its religious and cultural significance. There is, however, no one common vernacular and there is no one very large ethnic group. Consequently, the policy has been to give *no* education in an vernacular language; since 1958, all education has been through English. An argument could be made for the educational use of Pidgin, but many do not consider it prestigious enough for school use. Todd (1984) argues that the policy here is an eminently sensible one. Indeed, although not reflecting the UNESCO (1953) recommendations regarding mother-tongue education, the policy seems more one of pragmatism than of some simple continuation of a colonial mentality favouring 'world' languages.

(Source: Todd, 1984.)

Ethiopia

After Egypt and Nigeria, Ethiopia is the most populous country in Africa. About 70 languages are spoken among its 32 million inhabitants. Recent acknowledgement of this linguistic diversity is shown in the replacement, in 1976, of Haile Selassie's Amharic Language Academy with an Academy of Ethiopian Languages.

(Sources: Cooper, 1978a; Cooper & Carpenter, 1972; Fellman, 1983; Ferguson, 1970.)

Kenya

Swahili is a lingua franca spoken by about 25 million people all over East Africa, from Somalia to Mozambique, and west to the Congo. Sometimes described as a compromise between Arabic and Bantu, Swahili is structurally Bantu but has many Arabic words.

In July 1974, Kenyatta proclaimed that Swahili was to be Kenya's national language. In Nairobi particularly, however, Kikuyu would have been a more obvious choice in terms of number of speakers, and English is still the prestige variety. But, for its purposes, the Government wanted an African language and hoped that Swahili would prove ethnically 'neutral'. Now, both Swahili and English are offical in Kenya, although the former retains national-language status, and moves are underway to standardise a variety of Swahili that will be particularly Kenyan.

(Sources: Eastman, 1983; Harries, 1968, 1976; Kanuri, 1984.)

Morocco*

Four languages dominate the Moroccan context. Before the French arrived in 1912 and imposed their language (especially at school), Morocco was a bilingual Berber-Arabic country – Berber being the indigenous vernacular before the seventh-century Arab invasion. Berber has been maintained for reasons of identity, helped by its mountainous isolation. However, there also exists great respect for Arabic, and here there is diglossia with the Classic and Moroccan varieties. Since independence (1956) Arabic has achieved official status. French has not been rejected, largely for practical reasons, although it is not the mother-tongue of any sizeable section of Moroccan society. Arabisation is Government policy, but French is recognised as important. Thus, both French and Classical Arabic are prestige varieties (although for quite different reasons), while Moroccan Arabic is the vernacular, although often considered low in status.

*See also Somalia; Tunisia.
(Sources: Bentahila 1983a, b.)

Nigeria

In Nigeria 80 million people speak about 400 languages. About half, however, speak one of the three major varieties – Hausa, Igbo and Yoruba – and English is a well-established and widespread second language; of the three native languages, Hausa is the most important as a lingua franca. Educational issues are complicated by the fact that mother-tongues vary greatly in terms of standardisation. Some are unstandardised dialects within large language families (e.g. Ibani); some are partly standardised forms (e.g. Shuwa Arabic, Abua); some are fully standardised (e.g. Efik, Idoma). The two main streams of educational thought can be characterised as mother-tongue unilingualism or 'straight-into-English' and, given the linguistic complexity, it is not immediately apparent which is more appropriate; no doubt strong cases can be made for each, according to particular contexts.

(Sources: Akere, 1981; Amayo, 1984; Brann, 1979a, b, 1983; Paden, 1968; Zima, 1968.)

Senegal

Of the 4.7 million inhabitants, 44 per cent have Wolof as the mother-tongue, 21 per cent Pulaar (Fula) and 16 per cent Sereer. However, Wolof is a national lingua franca, with about 80 per cent of the population knowing it, and Dakar and other big towns have a Wolof majority. French remains very important and has been the official language since independence. Many urban dwellers, at least, are trilingual in their mother-tongue, Wolof and French.

(Source: Mansour, 1980.)

Somalia*

Somalia's population is largely homogeneous and Somali-speaking, and the country's linguistic problems can be seen as relatively minor compared to others in Africa. Arabic, English and Italian have also been important in Somalia and after independence in 1960 literacy and education were associated with English in the north and Italian in the south. Only in 1972 was Somali made official; moves were then made to formalise it. Remarkable gains have been achived here, and Somali is now the medium of instruction for all pre-university education.

*See also Morocco; Tunisia.
(Sources: Andrzejewski, 1980; Laitin, 1977.)

South Africa

For practical reasons, English is the most widely used languaged in South Africa and, with Afrikaans (developed from the Dutch of early Cape settlers), is official. English, Afrikaans and bilingual speakers total about six million. The most important indigenous language groups are the Nguni (Zulu, Xhosa, Swazi, Ndebele) and the Sotho (Tswana, Sotho), with about nine million and five million speakers respectively. Others (including Tsonga and Venda) have about 1.5 million speakers. About half a million people speak Indian languages (Tamil, Hindi, Gujerati, Urdu, Telugu) and several hundred thousand speak other immigrant languages.

Among the White population generally, English is associated with commerce and Afrikaans with administration; these are both important domains and so bilingualism is stressed. English speakers tend to be concentrated more in the middle and upper class, while Afrikaans speakers are more evenly distributed. Among Black South Africans, Afrikaans is associated more with oral skills and practical needs, English with reading and writing: thus, the latter is favoured as a school medium and is generally viewed as more prestigious. Urban Blacks use more English than do their rural counterparts but, even in rural areas, Blacks read English better than Afrikaans, and English speaking is on the increase. English is slightly more predominant among Black women than among Black men.

(Sources: Hauptfleisch, 1977, 1978; Kachru, 1978; Lanham & MacDonald, 1979;
(Schuring, 1979; Van den Berghe, 1968; Van Wyk, 1978.)

Tanzania

As a second language for large segments of the population, Swahili dates only from the mid-nineteenth century. As a standard language, it goes back only to the 1930s. Today, with less than ten per cent of Tanzania speaking Swahili as a mother-tongue, it is the national language. English has been, and continues to be, very important but (especially since independence in 1961) the status of Swahili is growing, and it is now the second language of most. The Institute of Swahili Research (established in 1964) is an important force in the development of the language.

(Sources: Harries, 1968; Mkilifi, 1978; Whiteley, 1968.)

Tunisia*

Virtually everyone in Tunisia (population: 6.2 million) speaks Tunisian Arabic as a mother-tongue. At school, both French and Classical Arabic are taught; about three-quarters of subjects are given in French by the end of secondary school. Thus, three varieties are important in the country. Classical Arabic is important for religious reasons and for pan-Arab unity; Tunisian Arabic is the vernacular and, although sometimes considered to be lacking in prestige, possesses 'covert' status; French is required for modernisation, but is sometimes seen as a threat to national unity. Since independence in 1956, the official goal has been Arabisation, but practical demands have meant that this has had to be put aside, or postponed at least, in favour of French-Arabic bilingualism.

It is interesting to note that, unlike many Third-World countries, Tunisia is not substantially affected by ethnic rivalries, almost all speak the same language, and Arabic has historically been a language of *both* scientific and cultural expression (i.e. it is not a 'restricted' local variety). Still, French remains a powerful linguistic influence in the modern Tunisian scene.

*See also Morocco; Somalia.

(Sources: Ghrib-Maamouri, 1984; Stevens, 1983.)

Zaire

In this country of 26 million, there is a great deal of linguistic heterogeneity, although many speak Bantu languages. Historically, there have been three main lingue franche: Monokutuba and Lingala in the west, and Swahili in the east. French has been the prestigious, official language used (with Swahili) in education. Since 1973, four languages have had 'national' status, Kikongo, Lingala, Swahili and Ciluba. Of these, Lingala is perhaps the most important.

(Sources: Goyvaerts *et al.*, 1983; Ndoma, 1984; Polomé, 1968.)

THE AMERICAS

Haiti

Diglossia exists between Haitian Creole and French in Haiti but only for a few as 90 per cent of the population are monolingual Creole speakers. Resources are too scarce to make all bilingual, and many are excluded from those formal, public domains where French prevails. Any standard should probably be based upon Port-au-Prince Creole, but the inequality and power structure of the country mean a continuing resistance to the demotion of French from its official-language position.

(Sources: Comhaire, 1984; Valdman, 1968.)

Mexico

Among the 55 Amerindian languages of the country, the general pattern is one of linguistic decline. There is decreasing monolingualism in these languages and bilingualism (with Spanish) is more and more tending towards Spanish *mono*lingualism. As in other situations, the native speakers themselves are often not the ones most interested in language maintenance and there is a general desire to have Spanish taught at school, rather than Indian languages.

(Sources: Lastra de Suárez, 1978; Modiano, 1968.)

Paraguay

In Paraguay, Spanish is official but Guaraní is recognised as a national language. The former has tended to be the more prestigious, especially in the capital city of Asunción, while the latter predominates in rural areas. Yet, there is a high degree of bilingualism (among more than 50 per cent of the population generally, and among about 80 per cent in Asunción), many Paraguayans identify with Guaraní (although not necessarily with its Indian heritage), and Guaraní is a "language of intimacy" often used abroad even by those who normally speak Spanish at home. Thus, unlike many Indian languages in South America, Guaraní is not generally looked down upon.

Guaraní has had written status since the time of the Jesuits in the sixteenth century and now efforts are being made to promote general Guaraní literacy. Since 1973, it has been accepted in classrooms, there exists an Academía de Cultura Guaraní, and there is hope for the development of a Guaraní *lengua de cultura*. It remains the case, however, that upward mobility is associated with Spanish, and many Guaraní-speaking parents prefer Spanish education for their children. Still, Guaraní is in a strong position (e.g. compared to Aymara in Bolivia, Quechua in Peru, Bolivia and Ecuador, or the Indian languages of Mexico), and bilingual education may prove a valuable linguistic support in Paraguay. At the moment, the dynamics are unclear, for it is suggested, on the one hand, that Guaraní is strengthening in rural areas while, on the other, that transitional bilingual education (where Guaraní is used to facilitate the acquisition of Spanish) may be lessening the use of Guaraní in such contexts, where it was thought strong enough (at an oral level at least) to survive such programmes.

(Sources: Corvalán, 1983; Engelbrecht & Ortiz, 1983; Garvin & Mathiot, 1968; Rubin, 1968a, b, c, 1978.)

Peru

Spanish is the dominant language for the White and *mestizo* majority, which is largely urban and coastal. Quechua and Aymara are the languages of the large indigenous minority of the Andean sierras. Despite recent declarations of 'respect' and encouragement for these varieties, the present policy aims at Spanish literacy (although it is acknowledged that, in some areas, Quechua/Aymara literacy may expedite this process). A clear status distinction separates the Spanish *patrons* from the peasants, many of whom are becoming assimilated into urban economic life. In contrast to Paraguay, Peru is not a very bilingual country. Of the total population (about 15 million, as of 1972), 60 per cent are Spanish speakers, 35 per cent Quechua and four per cent Aymara. The low prestige attaching to the last two also applies to these varieties in Ecuador and Bolivia (where the numbers of Spanish, Quechua and Aymara speakers are more or less the same). There is general acceptance of the necessity for Spanish, and of the presumed retarding effects of Quechua/Aymara monolingualism; one observes, again, parents insisting upon Spanish education for their children.

(Sources: Albó, 1979; Burns, 1968; Escobar, 1983; Hill & Coombs, 1982; Weichselbaum, 1978.)

Suriname

Dutch is both prestigious and official in Suriname, but there now exists a campaign to promote literacy in Saramaccan. This is in response to the tradition in which vernacular speakers have repressed their own mother-tongue, a situation viewed by some as detrimental to personal and group self-esteem.

(Sources: Glock, 1983; Koefoed *et al.*, 1984.)

ASIA

The People's Republic of China

In mainland China, 94 per cent of the population are said to speak a Han language – either the common standard, Putonghua, or one of the others (classed here as dialects, although most are not mutually intelligible). The largest number, mainly in the north and west, speak varieties of Mandarin; in the east, many speak Wu dialects; in the south-east, Cantonese, Fukienese and Hakka are important.

Putonghua (a variety of Mandarin; the name itself means 'common speech') was officially endorsed in 1956, and embodies the Peking pronunciation and northern Chinese grammar generally. The national aim is to promote Putonghua, simplify the written characters, and create and popularise a phonetic alphabet. However, the constitution (1954) protects national minorities and their languages (the major ones being Mongolian, Tibetan, Korean, Uighur and Zhuang). English is the most important second language taught.

(Sources: Barnes, 1983; Dilger, 1984; Lehmann, 1975; Light, 1980.)

Hong Kong

In this colony, whose future is now the subject of much concern and debate, about 98 per cent of the five million inhabitants are Chinese, and Cantonese is the lingua franca. English is of great practical value and figures in much local administration and education. Daily speech often comprises a mixture of Cantonese and English, e.g. students are more likely to use a mixture than either Cantonese or English, even though they may perceive the mix as low in social status. In Hong Kong, then, where the high-status variety is English, the 'solidarity' function is not always served by the variety (i.e. mix) most often used.

Cantonese recently gained official status, alongside English, and there is official support for more Cantonese at secondary school (90 per cent of children already receive primary education in Cantonese). However, parental pressure has been *against* this on practical economic grounds. Schools have been left to choose for themselves and Cantonese-medium schools have declined. Thus, English officialdom is encouraging Cantonese, while Cantonese parents continue to insist on English.

(Sources: Bolton & Luke, 1984; Gibbons, 1982, 1983.)

India

The linguistic heterogeneity of India is vast. The 1961 census classified more than 1,000 mother-tongue varieties into about 200 languages – these representing some 440 million people. At a much more minor level, there were another 530 'unclassified' languages, as well as more than 100 languages of foreign origin. In this diverse linguistic scene there are two important lingue franche, English (26 per cent of all bilinguals claim it as their second language) and Hindi (22 per cent). The former is particularly important at the inter-state level, but there have been some fears of English eroding other varieties and some moves to stress Hindi as the preferred bilingual option.

The Indian constitution recognises 15 languages (Sanskrit plus 14 'modern' varieties) which, it is claimed, reflect almost 90 per cent of the population. Most state governments are reasonably tolerant of multilingual areas but there are those who have pushed for the replacement of 'grassroots' pluralism with mandatory bi- or trilingualism. Thus, the so-called 'three language formula' of 1956 recommended that schools teach the mother-tongue, Hindi and English to non-Hindi speakers; and Hindi, English and another Indian language to Hindi speakers.

Pandit (1979) has provided an interesting insight into the stable bi- and multilingualism so common in India; his point is that linguistic competence is often restricted to the minimum usage required in specific settings. He gives the example of a Bombay businessman whose home language is a Kathiawari dialect of Gujerati. He uses Marathi in the local markets and Hindustani at the railway station (this variety, Pandit notes, is used in 'non-elite' pan-Indian contexts; thus, it is appropriate on the railways but not to an air hostess on an internal flight). At work – the businessman is a spice merchant – the language used is Kacchi. At leisure, he may watch films in Hindustani or English and probably reads a newspaper written in a Gujerati more standard than his own mother-tongue form.

(Sources: Apte, 1979; Bhatia, 1982; Brass, 1974; Das Gupta, 1975; Ghosh, 1984; Khubchandani, 1977, 1978, 1979, 1983, 1984; Krishnamurti, 1979; LePage, 1964; Pandit, 1979; Schermerhorn, 1978; Suresh, 1984.)

Indonesia

Dutch continued to be powerful here even when, from the start of this century, demands began for political and national rights. A nationalistic youth congress held in Jakarta in 1928 called for Malay – the existing lingua franca – to be the official national language. In the 1945 constitution, Malay was given this status and, although hopes that it would completely replace Dutch have not been realised, it *has* unified the archipelago of 125 million people (90 per cent of whom are Islamic) and 250 languages. Further moves on behalf of Bahasa Indonesia (as the language was termed) were put in train with independence in 1947, but it still requires modernisation and standardisation.

(Sources: Alisjahbana, 1977; Furnivall, 1939/1967; Jaspars & Warnaen, 1982; Rubin, 1977.)

Malaysia

Before independence in 1957, English was the official language; afterwards, the new Federation of Malaya adopted Malay. However, official policy was to retain English for ten years, during which time it was accepted that it would continue as the main legislative instrument. In 1963, Malaysia came into being, incorporating the Federation, Sarawak, Sabah and Singapore (which opted out two years later). Malay continues as the lingua franca, but English remains strong. In 1969, for reasons of national unity,

Malay was officially termed Bahasa Malaysia. It is to be expected that English will continue to have importance, particularly since the Chinese population is only slightly smaller than the indigenous Malay (about 37 per cent and 45 per cent respectively). As well, the intensification of Malay promotion has meant hardship and some resentment for those who are monolingual in other languages.

(Sources: de Terra, 1983; LePage, 1964, 1984; Platt, 1981; Watson, 1980a, b.)

Nepal

About 40 languages are spoken in Nepal. The national language, Nepali, is the mother-tongue of just over half the population and acts as a lingua franca. An education report of 1956 stressed Nepali and downgraded other varieties, although some (notably Hindi and Newari) are important; the Government has yet to implement any official language policies.

(Sources: Davies, 1984; Sonntag, 1980.)

Singapore*

Making up Singapore's 2.5 million population are Chinese (76 per cent), Malays (15 per cent), Indians (7 per cent) and others. There are four official languages – Mandarin, Malay, Tamil and English (the last understood by almost half the population although this varies with age, the younger understanding more than the older). It is official policy in Singapore to promote Mandarin, which is spoken natively by only about 0.1 per cent of the populace, and to downgrade Hokkien, a major lingua franca which is functionally and lexically restricted (cf. Fukienese and Mandarin in Taiwan). Thus, the 1979 campaign of Mandarin promotion pointed out that 'dialects cannot communicate your educated thoughts and refined feelings'. Kuo (1984) reproduces some of the signs and posters used. One of these ('Use English between different communities. Use Mandarin within the Chinese community.') indicates the continuing concern for English proficiency. Historically, English has been very important, and it remains the only high-status lingua franca acceptable in virtually all domains.

Mandarin and English are, then, the prestigious varieties; Hokkien and the so-called 'Bazaar' Malay are low in status and the number of speakers is declining. Tamil plays a minor role. Nonetheless, Malay remains the national language (a reminder, if nothing else, of Singapore's brief incorporation in Malaysia from 1963 to 1965) and is a widely understood lingua franca. Complicating matters further is the assignment of all Singaporeans to one of the four groups (Chinese, Malay, Indian, English) and a rather confused national stance in which, one the one hand, a Singaporean identity is important while, on the other, people are urged in various ways to maintain their place within one of the four official categories. Mother-tongues are 'assigned' to individuals on the basis of their category and this means that many do not speak their designated 'mother-tongue' (particularly, of course, within the Chinese community). At school, about 85 per cent of children start in a language which is not that of their home. And there is extra-educational confusion too; Altehenger-Smith (1980) reports a case of a civil servant, ethnically Chinese but with Malay as a mother-tongue and English as a second language, who was refused permission to sit an examination in Malay because it was considered 'only natural' that one should be competent in one's mother-tongue – designated here as Mandarin.

Generally, the educational policy seems to be more and more in favour of bilingualism (mother-tongue plus English), but the confusion already noted above and the increasing power and status of Mandarin may indicate future difficulties. As well, since English remains the high-status supra-ethnic lingua franca, many members of *all* groups have switched their children to English-medium programmes.

*See also Taiwan.
(Sources: Altehenger-Smith, 1980; Clammer, 1982; Harrison, 1980; Kuo, 1980, 1984; LePage, 1984; Platt, 1977, 1980; Platt & Lian, 1982; Platt & Weber, 1980.)

Sri Lanka

Language is a major cleavage in Sri Lanka. There are about nine million Sinhalese, Buddhist Sinhala speakers, and over 2.5 million Tamils. Some of the latter descend from settlers who came from south India a thousand years ago, some from mid-nineteenth century immigrants who arrived to work on tea and rubber estates. These Hindu people speak Tamil.

Under British rule (from the end of the eighteenth century until 1948), English became the official and prestigious language. Prior to independence there existed a *swabhasha* movement for 'own language' which embraced both Sinhala and Tamil. However, a national resurgence among the majority Sinhalese community led to a 'Sinhala only' thrust which culminated in the 1956 declaration of Sinhala as the sole official language of the island. Naturally enough, Tamil resentment was great, and their sense of being a beleaguered minority increased. On the other hand, it was pointed out that Sinhala was spoken *only* by the nine million on Sri Lanka, while Tamil was a large and powerful language in southern India (with more than 40 million speakers).

The scene since then has been one of increasing polarisation and, indeed, there has recently been considerable violence and the development of a Tamil separatist movement which demands autonomy in the Jaffna peninsula where the overwhelming majority of Tamil speakers live. Official response to Tamil protest has often been less than diplomatic, e.g. the 1972 constitution not only reaffirmed the dominant position of Sinhala but also gave state blessing to Buddhism.

(Sources: Dharmadasa, 1977; Gair, 1983; Kearney, 1976; Suseendirarajah, 1980.)

Taiwan*

A diglossic bilingualism exists on Taiwan, where 15 million speak Fukienese (Taiwanese), one million speak Hakka, and about two million have other native languages (including Mandarin). It is Mandarin, however, which is the official national language and which acts as the lingua franca. Most are bilingual in Mandarin and another variety, most commonly, of course, Fukienese. It is not perhaps readily apparent why Mandarin rather than Fukienese has received official recognition; however, given the linguistic policy on the mainland (cf. China), the Nationalists on Taiwan have felt it necessary to promote Mandarin as a marker of their legitimacy as the rightful Government of *all* China.

This curious situation involves official disapproval of Fukienese and Hakka in public life. They are permitted at school only in the very earliest stages; otherwise, their use is proscribed. Mandarin competence now extends to about 95 per cent of the population, but fears have been expressed that Fukienese and Hakka are threatened with extinction because of draconian government measures. The current situation is a clear diglossic distinction: Mandarin in public, Fukienese (or another) at home. This may well be a stable phenomenon since, while Fukienese is not developed enough to challenge

Mandarin in public domains, the Mandarin policy does not aim to replace the existing home-based dominance of Fukienese and Hakka.

See also Singapore.
(Sources: Cheng, 1979; Kaplan & Tse, 1982; Tse, 1982.)

USSR

The Russification policies of the Tsars were deliberate attempts to use the Russian language as the 'cement of empire'. Although there were a few who called for the use of other national languages in school (see e.g. the views of Academician Ianzhul, cited by Kumanëv, 1979), no real change occurred until after the Revolution. Leninist policies rejected compulsory Russification and supported the linguistic rights of minorities, in an effort to improve literacy rates and as a fundamental article of equality. However, the Leninist line clearly hoped that literacy in the various national and minority languages would be but a step towards competence in Russian. Russian would then become, first, a universal lingua franca and, later, a potential world language.

Thus, in 1938, the Government made Russian lessons compulsory in all schools and, although the earlier views have continued to be officially in force (e.g. as reflected in a 1973 law concerning freedom of choice for languages of instruction), some have suggested that a new wave of Russification has been underway for some time. From Stalin to Brezhnev, the status of Russian has been amplified. The aim, again, is for Russian to be the lingua franca *and* the central element in a common supranational identity.

Some of the stronger linguistic groups – Georgians, Ukrainians, Armenians – have opted for Russian as a second language, but smaller speech communities have increasingly adopted it as the language of instruction at school, largely for reasons of perceived economic advantage. A recent official pronouncement is that the Soviet people have voluntarily adopted Russian as the language of communication between nations, but there obviously exists some tension between pressures for Russification and legal safeguards for minority languages. These pressures may be expected to increase, with increasing Russian concern about internal unrest (e.g. pan-Islamic movements).

Official statistics now show that more than 80 per cent of the total population are fluent in Russian. Generally, the contemporary position is one in which official hopes are for increasing assimilation, but where the stronger national languages continue to thrive. The interesting question here, as elsewhere, is whether or not bilingualism will be (or will be allowed to be) a stable condition.

(Sources: Allworth, 1980; Central Statistical Board of the USSR, 1982; Comrie, 1981; Creissels, 1979; Goodman, 1968; Grant, 1981; Haarmann, 1979; Kravetz, 1980; Kreindler, 1982; Kumanëv, 1979; Lewis, 1971, 1980, 1983; Pipes, 1975; Shorish, 1984; Tollefson, 1981b; Wixman, 1984.)

THE PACIFIC

Guam

In two articles, Riley (1975, 1980) discusses the linguistic situation in Guam, one of the Mariana Islands. In 1975, about 82 per cent were Chamorro–English bilinguals, 15 per cent were bilingual in English and another language, and the rest were monolingual English. A survey of college students revealed little ethnocentrism: 78 per cent (of 194 respondents) felt that Chamorro should have official status with English, 82 per cent felt that students should support Chamorro, but 68 per cent considered that a knowledge of Chamorro was not necessary to be a 'proper' Guamanian. The students reflected the linguistic pragmatism which has characterised the community, where English has traditionally had high status. While it remains the medium of instruction and dominates in public life, there have been some recent moves to encourage Chamorro. The latter is now taught as a subject in some schools and has figured in experimental bilingual programmes (not, however, without arousing some opposition from non-Chamorro ethnic groups). Thus, Riley's later survey (1980) revealed that 91 per cent of students thought that Chamorro should be supported and there was a drop to 50 per cent who felt that it was unnecessary for full Guamanian identity. Riley sees this as the start of a major attitude change, but recent experiences elsewhere would suggest a longer perspective is necessary.

(Sources: Combs & Jernudd, 1981; Riley, 1975, 1980.)

New Zealand

In 1976 the population of New Zealand was about 3.3 million, 90 per cent of whom were *Pakeha* (English-speaking Europeans). Most of the rest are Maori (about 250,000), and there are about 70,000 European and Pacific Islands immigrants. The population has intermingled considerably and many Maori are no longer visually distinctive. Many still identify themselves as Maori, even though they speak only English (there are no Maori monoglots remaining, although Maori is still spoken by at least 70,000).

Traditionally, Maori has been downgraded and it still lacks prestige despite recent increases in school support and promotion of Maori culture generally. It is a familiar feature of declining languages that, once provisions are made for teaching them, many learners are 'outsiders'; many studying Maori now are *Pakeha*. Still, from the 1960s Maori has had a small place at primary school. Most Maori are now urban-dwelling, most use English (even at home), there is the familiar generation gap and, generally, there is not a great deal of *active* community support for programmes aimed at supporting the language and culture. The language retains lingua franca status in some communities and some domains in others but it is recognised that, with or without bilingual programmes at school, the number of native speakers will continue to shrink.

(Sources: Benton, 1979a, b, 1980b, 1983a, b; Kaplan, 1981.)

Papua New Guinea

More than 700 native languages are spoken in Papua New Guinea: 200 Austronesian (among 20 per cent of the population, mainly in the islands and along some of the coast) and 500 Papuan (among 80 per cent, largely in the interior and on much of the coast). However, among the three million inhabitants there are three important lingue franche: English, Tok Pisin (New Guinea Pidgin) and Hiri Motu (Police Motu).

The southern part of Papua New Guinea was run by the British from 1884 to 1906; the northern was a German colony from 1884 to 1914. Australia took over both parts, fused them into a single administration in 1946, and the region gained independence in 1975. From 1946, English was official, and Tok Pisin and Hiri Motu were widely used. Today, all three have official status but government proceedings are in English. The situation of interest in Papua New Guinea does not involve conflict among actual vernaculars so much as the dominance of a lingua franca. New Guinea Pidgin is the most important of the two native varieties and has about five times as many speakers as Hiri Motu (although many are competent in both). Further, adding to its potential as the national language, New Guinea Pidgin is now undergoing creolisation. Against this is a degree of functional restriction, an association with colonial days and (in the eyes of some) low status as a 'debased' form of English. Still, many believe New Guinea Pidgin to be the strongest contender for national-language status.

(Sources: Bickerton, 1984; Brennan, 1983; Feather, 1981a, b; Taylor, 1981; Wurm, 1968, 1977, 1978, 1979.)

The Philippines

A population exceeding 50 million speaks more than 70 languages in the Philippines. Tagalog and Cebuano are each natively spoken by about a quarter of the population, Ilocana and Hiligaynon by more than ten per cent each. Bikol and Waray by about five per cent each. In all, there are some three dozen mother-tongues having more than 30,000 speakers. There is a high degree of bi- and multilingualism, particularly in the Manila area, but degrees of competence are not well-known. An example is provided by Kaplan (1982) of a Manila taxi-driver who is a native Cebuano speaker married to a Waray speaker. He uses these two in family settings, but Tagalog (Pilipino) with his children and in daily life, and English with some customers, in some shops and for some leisure activities.

Before the Americans established English as the language of education in 1900, Spanish had been the colonial variety, although it was learned by only an elite among the Filipinos. Since 1900, English increased its hold and it is estimated that by the time of the Second World War about one-quarter of the population had some competence in it. The major internal rivalry has been between Tagalog (the language of the capital) and Cebuano. With independence (1946), Spanish, English and Pilipino (as Tagalog was now termed) became official, although English continued to dominate in many spheres, e.g. it has a major place in the broadcast media and the biggest newspapers are in English.

The renaming of Tagalog was for the sake of national unity, but non-Tagalog speakers were, in some cases, annoyed with this rather transparent operation. Tagalog – officially proclaimed as the national language in 1937 and renamed Pilipino in 1959 – has nevertheless become more and more accepted. It is now used by more than half the population and is certainly the lingua franca of the country. But, many refuse to see it as *the* national language (particularly on Cebu Island), and it has clearly not transcended its particular ethnic roots. English thus continues as the supra-ethnic variety. Furthermore, moves to 'purify' Pilipino have alienated some of its own speakers. Another complication here is the official lip-service paid to the development of a 'new' national language – Filipino – which may mean nothing more than a second renaming of Tagalog. Still, there is clearly an ongoing desire for an indigenous national language.

The 1973 constitution makes both English and Pilipino official, also stressing the formulation of Filipino, and the National Board of Education supports English–Pilipino bilingualism at all but the very earliest levels; this policy, of course, excludes the mother-tongues of most of the population. Yet English still has official priority in any 'case of conflict' and for international communication, science and technology. This would suggest the possibility of a stable diglossia in which Pilipino would dominate in sociocultural life. However, for non-Tagalog speakers, other varieties will continue to occupy the family domain, at least where migration and urbanisation do not entail a shift to Pilipino.

It has also been suggested that, except among urban dwellers where opportunities exist for the use and reinforcement of English, the general aim of upgrading Pilipino often means a decline of English; *this* would further favour Tagalog speakers and city dwellers generally. The Manileños might then become the new bilingual elite and the rural populace (and the urban poor) would be left with their own vernaculars and, increasingly, Tagalog. Indeed, estimates put the number of Tagalog speakers in the year 2000 at about 97 per cent of the population.

Whatever the future, the history of the Philippines shows that the achievement of nationhood is not dependent upon a common language. Indeed, 'short of a massive social upheaval or a radical change in the politics of the region, the Filipino will continue to be multilingual, [or] at least, trilingual' (Gonzalez, 1980, p. 157). The relationship between English and Pilipino will continue to be an interesting one too, given that, despite efforts to augment the status of the latter, many have a low regard for Tagalog/Pilipino. 'Filipino shoppers in downtown Manila who speak Pilipino to the clerk get little attention or receive haughty stares. One gets prompt service when he [sic] speaks English, and prompt, polite service when he speaks Spanish. Some Filipino parents object to their children being taught their mother-tongue on the grounds that they have learned the language at home' (Ramos, cited in LePage, 1964, pp. 26–27). (Sources: Asuncion-Lande, 1978; Asuncion-Lande & Pascasio, 1979; Benton, 1980a; Gonzalez, 1977, 1980, 1982; Kaplan, 1982; LePage, 1964; Llamzon, 1977; Luzares, 1982; Miller, 1981; Pascasio, 1977; Pascasio & Hidalgo, 1979; Sibayan, 1984a, b; Yabes, 1977.)

Ponape

Ponape is one of five island groups in the Carolines. There are two important dialects of the language, with subdialects. However, no one variety commands the most prestige and the main linguistic rival is English. The Americans have administered the territory since the end of the Second World War. Generally, there is a widespread desire to acquire English and it is predicted that, within a few decades, most will have it as a second language.

(Source: Fischer, 1979.)

Samoa (American)

Most of the 30,000 population are bilingual, to some extent, in English and Samoan. There exists here the familiar love–hate relationship with English, which is feared for its potential destructive power but desired for pragmatic benefits. Most daily business is conducted in Samoan and it is the language of the home. English is dominant in other contexts however, notably in the media; official forms and legal proceedings are bilingual. The Government aim is to improve the standing of English, but it must also recognise the desire to maintain (and, in some cases, regain) Samoan.

(Source: Baldauf, 1982.)

Vanuatu

It is claimed that in this Pacific island there are more indigenous languages per capita than anywhere else in the world (108 varieties among 100,000 people). Bislama, a Melanesian pidgin, is the lingua franca and many see it as a unifying force, although it is not official in education or law. The official languages are French and English, i.e. Vanuatu possesses *two* colonial varieties. There are separate French and English school systems, each having a roughly equal share of the population. The English schools have been established longer than the French, but the French system is free whereas the

the English is not. Also, French financial aid to Vanuatu is dependent upon the maintenance of the school system. The most recent development was a 1981 conference recommending more room for Bislama (and other local varieties) in education.

(Sources: Charpentier, 1984; Lindstrom, 1983; Topping, 1982.)

EUROPE

Belgium

In Belgium, a 1,000-year-old language boundary separates Dutch-speaking Flanders in the north from French Wallonia in the south. Traditionally, the French region and language have been dominant, although French speakers have always been numerically fewer; now, however, the Flemish (constituting about 56 per cent of the country's 10 million inhabitants) have the stronger economy. Power imbalances have meant that, to an extraordinary degree, Belgian political life is dominated by the language issue and what it reflects. Governments have fallen on the matter (e.g. in 1968 over the Louvain University crisis).

French was the dominant national language until the 1932 legislation which gave Dutch official status in Flanders. However, the continuing (and most painful) thorn for the Flemish is the presence and expansion of Brussels, which is largely a francophone city but which is *north* of the linguistic divide. It is now difficult to ascertain language dynamics since no census data on language have been gathered since 1946, but there is no doubt that the Flemish continue to know more French than the Walloons do Dutch. This reflects the differential status and perceived utility of the two languages – nationally and internationally – and is of particular interest in the continuing shift to French among the Flemish of Brussels.

In 1963, language laws fixed the linguistic boundary, restricted the metropolitan Brussels area and essentially broke up the unitary Belgian state. This schism had, of course, been a *de facto* matter for some time – many Walloons had always looked to Paris for 'cultural guidance' and many of the Flemish to The Hague – but the situation is now such that many commentators propose federalism as the only realistic bond. The continuing 'Belgian dilemma' as Donaldson (1983, p. 31) puts it, is that 'it is an artificially created country, founded a mere 150 years ago but divided in two by a linguistic frontier which has existed for over 1000 years.'

(Sources: Baetens Beardsmore, 1980, 1983; Bourhis, 1982; Bourhis *et al.*, 1979; Donaldson, 1983; Edwards & Shearn, in preparation; Halls, 1983; Hamers, 1981; Lorwin, 1972; Petersen, 1975; Swing, 1982, 1983; Willemyns, 1984; Zolberg, 1977.)

*Finland**

In 1970, Swedish speakers in Finland numbered about 300,000 (i.e. about seven per cent of the population). Swedish is an official language and bilingual organisation is relatively easy since speakers are largely found in three, well-defined coastal areas: the Åland Islands, the south coast around Helsinki, and the west coast around Vaasa. Swedish speakers are virtually all bilingual, are often willing to use Finnish wherever possible, and show signs of increasing assimilation. Swedish is more and more restricted to home environments, older people use it more than do younger ones, and it has been suggested that the declining position of Swedish in metropolitan areas has passed the point of no return. Still, given the numbers, Swedish remains viable, and benefits from the historical fact that Finland was part of Sweden for six centuries and that Swedish retained dominance in Finland until the mid-nineteenth century. There have been calls for a Swedish television channel, Swedish is compulsory in all schools, and education is available in Swedish at all levels (there is a unilingual Swedish university in Turku/Åbo). Generally, the Finnish authorities are well-disposed towards the minority language and thus the most important factor seems to be the desire of the Swedish-speakers to maintain the language.

*See also Lapland.
(Sources: Laurén, 1980; Liebkind, 1982; Reuter, 1981.)

France

Traditionally, France has had a very centralist orientation. In 1539, Francis I ruled French to be the sole language of his dominion and, in the following centuries, many could be found to dispute Renan's statement (1947/1882): 'Un fait honorable pour la France, c'est qu'elle n'a jamais cherché à obtenir l'unité de la langue par des mesures de coercition' (p. 899). In the modern era, one observes a continuing concern for the status of French, now perceived as losing international ground to English, in spite of some apparently growing tolerance of indigenous minority languages.

In 1951, the *Loi Deixonne* did provide some educational status for regional varieties, in particular, Basque, Breton, Catalan, Corsican, Alsatian, Flemish and Occitan. A 1978 survey showed that 72 per cent of the population were in favour of maintaining this diversity, 47 per cent wanted educational support/development and 35 per cent actually spoke or understood one or more regional languages. However, the tolerance of minority forms in France is still rather restrained.

As an example here, we can consider the situation of Occitan (or Provençal).* It has been receding in the face of French for centuries and today, while there may be as many as eight million who *can* speak it, perhaps only 1.5 million use it regularly. Factors including restrictions on its use at school and its association with rurality and backwardness have meant that, over the past two generations at least, Occitan has not been systematically passed on to children. In 1945, the *Institut d'Estudis Occitans* was established, but the enthusiasms of language militants are not always a good barometer of more general attitudes. As in other minority-language contexts, one finds more of a rejection of Occitan by women than by men; the former are often more conservative, linguistically, than the latter but, given competition between a prestigious variety and one whose status is diminishing, are often more likely to opt (for themselves and for their children) for the form seen to be linked to upward mobility. Other features found elsewhere include a recent emphasis by linguistic nationalists on the 'reconquest' of the urban young (obviously an important group for the future of the language) and a relative neglect of the remaining native speakers, who are increasingly associated with traditionalism, clannishness and poverty. Enmity also exists between speakers of traditional Occitan and those seeking to formulate a standard. Publications and classes in Occitan have little impact for most native speakers; the leaders here are usually native speakers themselves but their followers in the movement are mainly not. Culturally, there is more general success with singing and acting than with actual language learning or revival (cf. Timm's comments on Brittany, 1980).

*Discussion of the Breton situation will be found in chapter 3.
(Sources: Dalby, 1983; Field, 1981; Schlieben-Lange, 1977; Tabouret-Keller, 1981; Weinstein, 1976.)

West Germany *

In Schleswig-Holstein, near the Danish border, is the region of North Frisia *(Nord-friesland)*. In an area of about 800 square miles, there are five languages in regular use: High and Low German, Danish, Jutish and Frisian. The last of these is divided into ten major dialects, some of which are not mutually intelligible, e.g. *Father* (German: *vater*) is *taatje* in the Mooring dialect, *aatj* (Fering), *faader* (Sölring), *foor* (Halunder) and *heit* (Frysk). And all of this linguistic diversity is found within a group of only 10,000 Frisians!

Despite recent efforts in support of Frisian, the language is in a state of decline. Important features here (not unique to this context by any means) include: poor literacy levels, shrinking language domains, out-migration, in-migration (post-War refugees and, latterly, tourists), parental disinclination to transmit the language, general linguistic apathy and, of course, a large degree of dialect diversity within a small population. On this last point, it is interesting to note that the body promoting Frisian is called the *Nordfriisk* institute, where the *friisk* is meant to be a dialectally 'neutral' term. Similarly, a magazine edited by some young people is given a Latin title, *Frisica Nova*, to maintain neutrality and to avoid dialect choice. The great diversity also poses problems with, for example, school materials. It is difficult to produce a book in six dialect editions, print only 1,000 copies in total, and sell it anywhere near a price that would cover costs – yet this has recently been done.

Another complication is that some Frisians are oriented towards West Germany, others towards Denmark. There are thus 'German Frisians' and 'Danish Frisians'. There are fewer in the latter group but they are more active in language promotion. Consequently, there has arisen a general association of Frisian with Danish, with negative repercussions for the whole Frisian movement since the regional government in Kiel (capital of Schleswig-Holstein) is fearful (or claims to be) of Frisian separatism. Frisians are not, in any case, considered a minority officially, since they do not constitute what the authorities conceive of as a *national* minority (unlike, for example, the Danes in Schleswig-Holstein).

*I restrict myself here to the Frisian situation; see also the Netherlands.
(Sources: Boelens, 1976; Walker, 1980a, b, 1984.)

Lapland (Finland, Sweden, Norway, the USSR)

The Saami people live in four countries: there are about 20,000 in Norway, 2,000 in Russia, 10,000 in Sweden, and 3,000 in Finland (Keskitalo, 1981, puts the last two figures at 17,000 and 5,000). The highest densities are in northern Norway and Finland and in some municipalities the Saami constitute a majority. However, they hardly exceed ten per cent in any midland districts. Finland is the only one of the four countries where an official definition of Saami is in force but the group has no official language rights. In 1971, a Saami Language Board was established, and this may be taken as an indication of concern for the language. Most Saami are bilingual (at least) and there exist the familiar difficulties of out-migration and declining language transmission to children. Historically, educational aims have stressed the learning of the majority language.
(Sources: Keskitalo, 1981; Korhonen, 1976; Reuter, 1981.)

Luxemburg

In courtroom proceedings in Luxemburg, evidence is often given in Lëtzebuergesch (a German dialect and the country's vernacular), lawyers argue the case in French (a prestigious variety) and the written verdict is presented in Standard German (a language of practicality and convenience). This illustrates the trilingualism/triglossia which exists in the region. All speak Lëtzebuergesch as a mother-tongue, many have Standard German, and some (particularly the middle and upper class) have French. Schools teach all three, with German as a medium of instruction in primary school and French at the secondary level. However, the strength of Lëtzebuergesch has not been eroded and it remains a vehicle for identity and solidarity. Still, 'only lunatics' would consider giving it sole official-language status.

(Sources: Hoffman, 1979, 1981; Jakob, 1981.)

Malta

The language situation in Malta has not received much outside attention, but it is a fascinating one. Maltese is a Semitic language, with many Romance and English borrowings. There has been an interesting debate concerning the *type* of Semitic roots which it possesses. Members and supporters of the Maltese Labour Party (generally pro-Arab) encourage the importance of Arab roots – these date from the ninth to eleventh centuries – and there is some mutual intelligibility between Maltese and Arabic. Those who are anti-Arab support a Hebrew influence, which dates from late Roman times; this is the stance of many in the National Party. Some older Maltese stress earlier Phoenician roots. All these allegiances are complicated by religious and socioeconomic status differences. Finally, Italians have claimed that Maltese is a variety of their language!

While the British arrived in Malta in 1801, Italian continued to be the prestigious variety until the early twentieth century. In 1934, Maltese was given official status, recognising its vernacular role. Now it is the language of state, church and conversation, though still not of literacy (written material is largely in English). Two of the three receivable television channels are Italian; the other is half-English, half-Maltese. Some areas can also receive Libyan television. Generally, as a vernacular, Maltese is in a strong position. It is much-discussed as an identity symbol and there is some resentment of foreigners speaking or understanding it.

(Sources: Dench, 1975; Gullick, 1974.)

The Netherlands*

In this country of 15 million, Dutch is the mother-tongue for over 90 per cent of the population. The most numerous minority groups are the Moluccans (about 30,000, speaking Malay), Surinamese (250,000, Sranan or Sarnami), Dutch-Indonesians (about 250,000 repatriates) and Frisians (about 500,000 in Friesland – 70 per cent use Frisian regularly and more understand it). As well, there is a *gastarbeiter* population of some 200,000.

The Frisians are by far the largest indigenous minority and, recently, have had their language-maintenance efforts supported in school. Frisian literacy is at a much lower level than oral competence and consequently school programmes are seen as vital. The region is characterised by non-Frisian in-migration, weakness of the language outside the home, and the influence of Dutch media. Feitsma (1981) notes that 'the homogeneous Frisian-speaking village does not exist any more' (p. 168). It may be that activity on behalf of Frisian is coming too late and, in any event, the Dutch want to limit any official recognition of bilingualism to Friesland itself (i.e. to keep the phenomenon at a provincial level).

*See also West Germany.
(Sources: Appel, 1983; Boelens, 1976; Feitsma, 1981; Gorter, 1981; Pietersen, 1976, 1978.)

Romania

Before the 1948 constitution, there was job discrimination against minorities generally, and particularly within the civil and armed services. However, the general tenor of Romanian history has been one of tolerance and lack of linguistic oppression. Since 1948, cultural pluralism has been officially acknowledged, all have language rights, and there is media coverage in the larger minority languages. Almost all of the population (17.5 million in 1956) speak Romanian, the official language; other important varieties include Hungarian, German, Russian, Ukrainian and Serbo-Croatian. About ten per cent of the population are of Hungarian provenance, mainly in the areas of Banat and Transylvania, which adjoin Hungary, and this long-standing minority group is the single most important.

(Sources: Kellogg, 1984; Petyt, 1975.)

Spain

Basques   The Basque country (Euskadi) is found in the four northern Spanish provinces of Vizcaya, Guipúzcoa, Alava and Navarra (with other Basques living in the French Pyrénées-Atlantique region). Within this area is a population of about 2.5 million. The core of the territory is largely mountainous, but also contains major industrial centres (principally around Bilbao) and tourist resorts.

It is estimated that, in 1860, more than half the population spoke Euskera; in 1970 this had declined to about 20 per cent (450,000). The decrease can be partly attributed to lack of generational transmission and to high in-migration of Spanish speakers. There has been a history of suppression of Basque language and culture, particularly during the Franco years. From about 1950, however, tolerance has increased and, in 1979, some regional autonomy and status for Euskera came into effect. It is now increasingly recognised that people should know and use both Euskera and Castilian. However, literacy among Basque speakers is low. A 1975 report showed that although 43 per cent *could* read Euskera, only about 20 per cent did so regularly, and only 12 per cent wrote it. It is also a language increasingly associated with the family domain. It is, generally, difficult to ascertain the degree to which the language itself serves as an important rallying-point for Basque identity; it certainly is one for activists, but it has been suggested that Basque nationalism is not, overall, closely allied to the use of the language.

(Sources: Azurmendi, 1981; Clark, 1980; Connor, 1977; Greenwood, 1977; Medhurst, 1982; Williams, 1984.)

Catalans   Catalonia, like Euskadi, has an industrially developed heartland and Barcelona has important shipping and textile operations. And, like the Basque situation, this has meant a dilution of Catalan through an influx of Castilian-speaking Spaniards. Historically, Catalan (related to Occitan/Provençal) has occupied a central position in the region. From the fourteenth to the eighteenth centuries it was the 'official' language, although the growing hegemony of Castile had eroded Catalan as a language of culture, and the Bourbon monarchy repressed the language. By the late nineteenth century, there was a fully fledged Catalan nationalism, constructed from an earlier, highly romantic renaissance.

The modern history of Catalan is, again, like that of Basque – oppression under Franco, followed by a gradual increase in tolerance and regional autonomy. It is estimated that now about half the population speak and use Catalan, but the Spanish in-migration and the standardising effects of Western culture generally are bringing about a change from diglossia to a more impermanent bilingualism.

(Sources: Argente *et al.*, 1981; Llobera, 1983; Pi-Sunyer, 1980; Rees, 1981; Ros i Garcia & Strubell i Trueta, 1984; Sala, 1981; Siguan 1980; Strubell i Trueta, 1982; Tabouret-Keller, 1981.)

Sweden*

The Finns in Sweden fall into two main categories: the border minority living in the Torne valley in northern Sweden (about 50,000), and about 200,000 Finnish immigrants who live mainly in industrial centres in central, western and southern Sweden. Many, in both groups, are monolingual Finnish speakers – the Torne valley group because of their isolation and the immigrants because of their 'passive self-segregation'. The former are still closely connected to Finland but, among the immigrants too, ties are strong with the homeland: there are regular contacts and many view their time in Sweden as temporary.

In both groups, bilingualism is increasing, there sometimes exist inferiority feelings about speaking Finnish and a generation gap is developing in which children are not learning Finnish. In the Torne valley, about 40 per cent now speak mainly Swedish, children are often given Swedish names and, generally, Finnish is becoming associated with a 'dated' culture. A telling note, gleaned from observation of social clubs, is that Finnish is used when refreshments are served, Swedish to record the minutes.

*See also Lapland.
(Source: Jaakkola, 1976.)

Switzerland

Among Swiss *citizens*, German is the major mother-tongue (74 per cent), followed by French (21 per cent), Italian (four per cent) and Romansh (one per cent). However, among the population as a whole, the first three percentages alter to 69 per cent, 19 per cent and ten per cent. Thus, although the Romansh figures remain unchanged, there are obviously many foreign Italian speakers in Switzerland. Indeed, there are more of them than the Italian-speaking Swiss, who are thus a minority within their own language group in their own country (about 90 per cent of all Italian-speaking Swiss live in the canton of Ticino).

Romansh is also largely confined to one canton – Graubünden – where, in 1979, 23 per cent (about 40,000) spoke it. There has been a 20 per cent decline since the 1950s and familiar features here include an age gap, a sex difference (women move away more from the minority language) and social-status and urban-rural distinctions (Romansh is associated with rurality and poverty). Some have suggested more attention should be paid to popular culture, to attract the young back to things Romansh, but evidence from other minority-language contexts indicates that this often does little for the language itself.

(Sources: Billigmeier, 1979; Matthews, 1979; Peterson, 1975; Williamson & Van Eerde, 1980.)

Yugoslavia

In this country of six republics (Bosnia-Herzegovina, Croatia, Macedonia, Montenegro, Serbia and Slovenia) and two autonomous provinces (within Serbia: Kosovo and Vojvodina), the official aim is to separate linguistic from nationality rights, to promote the former and restrict the latter. *National* status is conferred on the groups dominant in the republics, while *nationalities* comprise other, non-dominant groups; two of these, however, have some status as dominant groups in the two provinces – Albanians in Kosovo and Hungarians in Vojvodina.

All languages have some degree of status, but each republic or province determines which will be officially recognised. There is no *single* official language, with Serbo-Croatian, Macedonian and Slovenian having recognition. Serbo-Croatian is perhaps the main contender for 'national' status inasmuch as many speak some form of it.

(Sources: Dorotich, 1978; Radovanović, 1983; Štrukelj, 1978; Tollefson, 1980, 1981a, b.)

Notes

CHAPTER 1 SOME BASIC CONCEPTS

1 There are recent indications that links among ethnicity, nationalism and language are going to be more fully explored (see e.g. Brass, 1976; Fishman, 1984; Paulston, 1984).

2 No apologies are needed though for descriptive and pre-theoretical efforts, given the often premature rush to grandiose but empty theorising in social science generally. As well, although many existing treatments are lengthy and complex, I am not always convinced that they clarify; indeed, they often obfuscate (see generally Andreski, 1973).

3 This is perhaps abating; see the editorial in the first issue (1982) of *Journal of Language and Social Psychology*, an outlet designed to reinstate language within social psychology.

4 In this and following sections, definitions presented should be seen as brief and introductory. Further remarks on the concepts discussed here will be found, as necessary, in later chapters.

5 Paulston (1984) has referred to a 'continuum' between nationalism and ethnicity, while acknowledging that the two are not synonymous.

6 There is, of course, much confusion over the terms *nation* and *state* (see Connor, 1978; Fishman, 1972).

7 'Objective' need not always mean 'involuntary', of course, but it usually does.

8 Fishman (1972) claims that Baron's definition of nationalism as 'organised ethnocultural solidarity' does not necessarily involve political goals (e.g. independence). He approves of this, and presents the term *nationism*, to be used when these goals are desired. This seems an unnecessary elaboration because most of those who use the term *nationalism* include the idea of national self-determination and, if nationalism is not to include this goal it largely reduces to ethnicity. There is certainly nationalism without the desire for full independence but the term, if it is to be useful, always implies a desire for autonomy in at least some spheres.

9 Renan also notes, however, that 'language may invite us to unite, but it does not compel us to do so' (Fishman, 1972, p. 53).

10 The question of language origins proved so vexing and fruitless that, in 1866, the Linguistic Society of Paris forbade its discussion. The matter seems now to have been reopened: in 1981, in Paris, a UNESCO-sponsored conference heard 35 papers on 'glossogenetics'.

11 The time element is important here, e.g. we would no longer expect English speakers to attach any significance to Pictish.

12 It is, of course, possible for *some* linguistic markers to remain after language shift. Giles *et al.* (1977) note, for example, that groups like the Irish and Scots retain distinctive *accents* and are proud of them. This is an obvious example of solidarity (see chapter 6) but we should also remember that many distinctive accents *(within* English, say) are retained without any conscious intent (see also Giles, 1979b; Giles & Johnson, 1981; Gumperz, 1982a, b).

13 For a discussion of the 'Whorfian hypothesis' on the relationship between language and thought, see Edwards (1979b). (See also Cole & Scribner, 1974; and chapter 2.)

14 Some are willing, of course, to do this, but it has not generally been within the social-scientific tradition. An interesting recent discussion is found in Musgrove (1982). (See also chapter 4.)

CHAPTER 2   LANGUAGE AND NATIONALISM

1 A contemporary example is found in the agonising over a Canadian identity, which has often taken the form of describing ways in which Canadians are *unlike* Americans. Perhaps this is an inevitable consequence of a close geographical and/or historical relationship between groups of unequal power.

2 Not only were German romantics xenophobic. French culture thought highly of itself and, as well, had friends in high places. Frederick the Great praised French literature over German, and Hertz (1944) tells us that Voltaire, visiting the court in Berlin, felt very much at home: 'French was spoken exclusively and German was only fit for the horses. The king's brother advised a Prussian nobleman to learn French since he surely could not want to be a "German beast" ' (p. 84). Voltaire's own words were as follows: 'Je me trouve ici en France. On ne parle que notre langue. L'allemand est pour les soldats et pour les chevaux: il n'est nécessaire que pour la route' (Waterman, 1966, p. 138).

Earlier German rulers had also downgraded German. Charles V (1500–58; reigned 1519–58) is supposed to have said that he spoke Spanish to God, Italian to women, French to men and German to horses. It is an historical curiosity that this has been mis-attributed to an earlier Charles V, Charles the Wise of France (1337–80) and misquoted: Lord Chesterfield (1694–1773) wrote in a letter of 1750 that Italian was perceived as useful for one's mistress, French for men, and *English* for horses!

3 Kedourie, 1961, p. 59. Ernst Arndt was contemptuous of German affectation in the use of French and, in 1818, called for his countrymen to 'hate the French strongly'. Friedrich Jahn, at about the same time, thought that Germans who allowed their daughters to learn French were giving them up to prostitution. And, Herder himself also said that 'a so-called education in French must by necessity deform and misguide German minds' (Fishman, 1972, p. 53).

4 There seems to be a revival of interest in the early influence of European academies. A conference was held in 1983, for example, on the emergence of linguistic national consciousness in Renaissance Europe, with papers on Italy, Germany, France, Spain, Portugal and England (Center for Medieval and Renaissance Studies, Los Angeles).

5 Hall (1974) puts the founding date at 1572 (p. 179) and, later, at 1546 (p. 234); this latter date is endorsed by Bowen (1970). There is room for debate since unofficial bodies and town academies in Italy date from the mid-fifteenth century.

6 Nokes (1984) presents an interesting portrait of Dr Johnson, 'the man behind the caricature'. Johnson's proposals for a dictionary were welcomed, and his patron,

the Earl of Chesterfield, hoped that he would be an 'absolute dictator of standards'. However, Johnson followed Locke who had said that he was 'not so vain as to think that anyone can pretend to perfect reforming the languages of the world, no, not so much as his own country, without rendering himself ridiculous'. Thus, according to Nokes, Johnson's dictionary was an 'expression of a unique attempt to convey the living force of the language, rather than the museum-piece of formality that Chesterfield had envisaged'.

7 For a useful discussion of American prescriptivism from about the time of Webster, see Drake (1977).
8 See also the next chapter for examples of lingue franche.
9 Useful general notes on lingue franche will be found in Goodman (1968), Hall (1972, 1974), Issawi (1981), Kahane and Kahane (1979), Samarin (1968) and Toynbee (1956).
10 McQuown (1982) has been one linguist, however, who has written about what Ornstein-Galicia (1982) calls the 'taboo' topic of constructed languages. Lieberman also makes an even more general observation, relating to the overall theme of this book: 'Why has so little been written about language and identity?' (p. 101).
11 Anderson (1983) notes that it is worth remembering nationalism's 'love-inspiringness'. He also points out, rather naively perhaps, that it has generally promoted little hatred of others.
12 See also Patterson's rejection (1977) of Smith's attack on Kedourie.
13 See also p. 45, however. Fishman's comments here refer specifically to ethnicity and do not mention nationalism. I have extended his range here because he explicitly attacks the Acton–Kedourie line which of course deals with nationalism.

CHAPTER 3   LANGUAGE MAINTENANCE AND LANGUAGE SHIFT

1 Languages have certainly suffered persecution in Europe but Petyt (1975) has questioned how typical this was in reality. He notes, for example, that the Ottoman and Habsburg empires were not noted for linguistic intolerance. Much more common surely, are settings of benign neglect; this certainly characterises much of the British attitude to the Celtic languages, for example. After all, from the point of view of a central authority, power need not necessarily concern itself with the *languages* of subject peoples.
2 I have also stressed the limitations of objective analysis in another emotion-laden area, that of linguistic and educational disadvantage (see Edwards, 1979b; Edwards & McKinnon, in preparation).
3 Other useful discussions here include those of Dorian (1982) and Kahane and Kahane (1979).
4 For a comprehensive listing of relevant references, see Edwards (1983c).
5 The Gaelic League has recently become rather more active again. This is partly due to an international resurgence of interest in 'small' languages and partly as a response to perceived government inaction over the past 20 years or so.
6 The Gaelic League condemned the abolishing of the compulsory Irish pass. Its position is that, in this and other matters, the Government is severely hindering – if not actually working against – the progress of Irish. Andrews (1978) has presented a highly critical view of official educational policy, claiming that recent history demonstrates disdain of Irish; he was particularly exercised over Government inaction

194 *Notes to Pages 66–96*

following the publication of the report of the Committee on Irish Language Attitudes Research (1975).

7 The classic treatment of languages in contact is that of Weinreich (1974). Dorian has done useful recent work here; e.g. in her studies of grammatical change in a dying Scots Gaelic dialect she points out the reduction of grammatical and lexical options, large-scale borrowing from English, and syntactical simplification (1973; see also Dorian, 1977, 1978, 1981). Andersen (1982) presents a thorough analysis of the linguistic attributes of language decline and provides an extensive bibliography. Further bibliographic details and a summary of research on language loss will be found in Williamson (1982). Dorian's general comment (1977, p. 24) is that 'on the whole, the assumption that the reduced use of a language will lead also to a reduced form of that language seems realistic' (see also Dressler, 1972; Dressler & Wodak-Leodolter, 1977).

8 It is beyond my scope here to delve further into the very important relationship between religion and the decline of the Celtic languages; see the admirable treatment by Durkacz (1983) and, with regard to Wales in particular, that of Glanmor Williams (1979).

9 See Edwards (1979b) for a discussion of the greater female adherence to prestigious varieties, an interesting topic in its own right.

10 Further notes on Breton can be found in Stephens (1984), Timm (1973, 1982) and Van Eerde (1979).

11 This work was influential for Irish as well. It was translated into that language by Ó Cadhain in his *Bás nó beatha (Death or life);* see Breatnach, 1969.

12 Southall (1895) presents a Welsh-language census for 1891; he also published a work dealing with the situation ten years later and, earlier, a book on the Welsh language generally, with some reference to Cornish and Irish (see Southall, 1892, 1904).

13 It is interesting that after many years as an activist, as one who claimed (in 1962) that only revolutionary action would save Welsh, Saunders Lewis was given an honorary D.Litt. from the University of Wales – for contributions to Welsh literature and literary criticism.

14 There was a lot of Irish interest in this (see also Citizens for Better Broadcasting, 1976; Edwards, 1984b, in press (a); Jones, 1974).

15 Further useful material on Hebrew (and Yiddish) may be found in Cooper (1983), Fishman (1974a, 1976a, 1980a, 1981), Fishman and Fishman (1978), Nahir (1984) and Saulson (1979).

16 To some extent at least, this fourfold classification of language planning overlaps with Nahir's (1977) 'five aspects' – purification, revival, reform, standardisation and modernisation. Haugen has been more concerned with formalising what steps planners follow, while Nahir attends primarily to the possible applications of language-planning policies.

17 An example of the interaction between ethnicity and economics is provided by Kedourie (1961). A Hungarian statesman, visiting a district whose status was disputed by Czechoslovakia and Poland, asked how many Poles there were there. He was told that the number varied between 40,000 and 100,000. He was further told that the figures varied because 'the people of certain villages are changing their nationality every week, according to their economic interests and sometimes the economic interests of the mayor of the village' (p. 124).

18 In fact, as we shall see in chapter 4 (and as has already been noted in chapter 1), group continuity can survive very well in contexts of open access and interaction.

Specific markers of identity may be discarded or altered, and language is often one of these.

19 Fishman (1983b) acknowledges that identity can survive language loss but claims that the loss does 'exact a huge price in terms of ethnocultural authenticity and continuity' (p. 24). This is putting it too strongly. Group continuity is often maintained quite well, and the idea of 'ethnocultural authenticity' is a very vague one, with perhaps more than a hint of patronising.

20 I do not intend, obviously, to demean the concept, but a 'culture' divorced from real-life exigencies is surely not a living culture.

21 It *is* a step sometimes taken by the atypical minority-within-a-minority. It is noteworthy how many language activists, incidentally, are *not* themselves members of the group in question.

CHAPTER 4   THE ETHNIC REVIVAL AND THE NEW ETHNICITY

1 One of the very few clear statements about this is that of Birch (1977) who notes that 'ethnic and local loyalties are enduring features of social life. No elaborate reasons are necessary to explain why people retain an attachment to their own ethnic group…These attachments may be overlaid by an acquired loyalty to a wider society and its political institutions, but the attachments remain' (pp. 172–3). Birch goes on to describe how changes in the wider society account for the apparent revival.

2 Useful reviews of the American scene include Abramson (1980) and Walzer (1980).

3 Alter (1972) takes Novak to task for his elevation of feeling over rationality (see also Musgrove, 1982, on 'Utopian nostalgia').

4 Much later, Kallen (1956) moved even further towards an assimilationist position.

5 In an earlier paper, Berry (1974) doubled the number of cells in his matrix by considering, additionally, whether or not groups themselves had free choice concerning identity maintenance and social relations. Obviously, all four patterns shown here can be voluntary or imposed.

6 This view is apparently endorsed, somewhat surprisingly perhaps, by Novak (1980): all can maintain what they want, while taking what is desired from the 'superculture'. Indeed, emphasising the 'humanistic tradition', Novak claims its first priority is to defend the *individual* (but see Alter, 1972). Greeley, another prominent supporter of the new ethnicity has also remarked that ethnicity is optional, not obligatory (1981). There is indeed confusion in the pluralist camp (see Gleason, 1979).

7 See also the concept of 'pluralistic integration' (Higham, 1975); and, further, Higham (1982) on 'hard' and 'soft' pluralism. Higham also presents a valuable discussion of the emergence of new writings dealing dispassionately once more with assimilation, now that 'the passions of hyper-ethnicity' (p. 11) have cooled.

8 Recent assessments of multiculturalism in Canada may be found in Cummins (1984), Driedger (1978) and Palmer (1975); see also Berry *et al.* (1977). For Great Britain and Australia, see V. Edwards (1984) and Bullivant (1984a) respectively.

9 Official pronouncements in favour of multiculturalism are sometimes interesting. Fleming (1982), then the Minster of State for Multiculturalism, noted that 'multiculturalism in Canada isn't a weakness, it's a strength. It forces people to be tolerant of differences and eccentricity' (p. 9). Forcing people to be tolerant is an odd thing to recommend, and the Minister may have not found the *mot juste* in 'eccentricity'.

10 Moore (1979), for example, saw a possibility that government, with the aid of well-ensconced and secure ethnic 'spokesmen', could essentially co-opt minorities and do them a disservice by attending to some aspects of group life (cultural manifestations) while side-stepping *real* problems (socioeconomic, political, etc.); see footnote 12 and chapter 6.

11 French-Canadian fears have some basis in fact. Castonguay (1984) has analysed recent census data to show that the increasing assimilative power of English, coupled with declining birth-rates and economy in Quebec, is slowly 'smothering' the French-speaking population. He advocates a territorial bilingualism policy (cf. Belgium, Switzerland) and the reindustrialisation of Quebec. Current discussions of Quebec legislation supporting French are found in Bourhis (1984) and C. Williams (1984).

12 The tourist value of ethnic symbols can extend to language itself. Alastair Walker has told me that, in some quarters, the maintenance of Frisian dialects is encouraged as a quaint tourist resource. More generally, it is feared that officially supported ethnicity may do nothing more than encourage rather empty manifestations of difference. Comeau (1981), the Director of the Nova Scotia Acadian Federation, has noted that official multiculturalism may simply encourage ethnic groups to become more visible. Skvorecky, a Czech-Canadian writer, has also lamented Government tendencies: there is no money for book publishing, but funds are available for dressing up in native costume (Stuewe, 1981).

13 Greeley goes on, however, to state that is is unclear whether groups must necessarily abandon their languages in order to succeed in the United States; this seems a rather obtuse conjecture. It is remarkable in the light of what I have presented here and Greeley's own comments, that he can still observe that 'we do not know exactly how much of its cultural heritage an ethnic group has to give up to be successful in American life' (p. 152); curiouser and curiouser (see footnote 6).

14 Musgrove's work – predictably enough, I suppose – has been reviewed unfavourably by those who have simplistically charged him with ethnocentrism (Moodley, 1984; Sidel, 1983).

15 Geertz (1984) discusses relativism and anti-relativism; he writes with precious erudition.

CHAPTER 5   LANGUAGE, EDUCATION AND IDENTITY

1 My discussion here prescinds from treatment of the 'mechanics' of bilingual education, nor am I concerned with such important issues as the relationship between bilingualism and intelligence. I emphasise, rather, the social and cultural factors associated with school programmes.

2 A consideration of the sociocultural aspects of bilingual education, in the United States and beyond, is facilitated by several 'state-of-the-art' publications (e.g. Alatis, 1978; Center for Applied Linguistics, 1977–8; Edwards, 1983a; Fishman, 1976b; Lewis, 1980).

3 A reply by Fishman (1977c) – which the *New York Times* did not publish – emphasises the 'unfailingly unifying' character of bilingual education and points to the larger social issues which are really responsible for economic and social disadvantage. Bilingual education is seen as potentially linking together populations 'that might otherwise be totally estranged' because of 'English-dominated inequality' in the United States.

4 Thus, Ornstein (1979) and King (1979) called for some 'devil's advocates' in the area; Fishman (1977a) drew attention to the fact that 'few (if any) integrative efforts along rejective lines have appeared in print...although many of the advocates of bilingual education claim to have encountered opposition/rejection from one audience or another and react to such in their work' (p. 6).

5 Indeed, immersion in a second language would be 'submersion' for minority-group children. This is seen to hasten assimilation, representing as it does the sink-or-swim scenario traditionally presented by the school to such children.

6 Useful summaries of immersion education may be found in special numbers of *Canadian Modern Language Review* (1976, *32)* and *Language and Society* (1984, *12).* See also Genesee (1983), Mackey (1984) and, for a criticism, Olson and Burns (1983).

7 A similar problem affects modern Celtic contexts too, e.g. Welsh-medium schools are not leading to the hoped-for *use* of the language (Raybould, 1984).

8 Useful overviews of multiculturalism can be found in Bullivant (1984a), Cummins (1984), V. Edwards (1984), James & Jeffcoate (1981), Linguistic Minorities Project (1983), Little (1978), Lynch (1981), 1983), Saifullah Khan (1980), Samuda *et al.* (1984), Tsow (1983) and Young (1979).

9 A contemporary example within the Canadian multicultural context is discussed by Lupul (1978). He notes that ethnic groups have often been indifferent to learning their own languages; even the Ukrainians, a relatively strong minority, 'have had an annual struggle to maintain enrolments' (p. 47).

10 I have not even alluded here to difficulties of scale (e.g. decisions about how many and which groups can/should be catered for, teaching staff, adequate resources, etc.).

11 Radical criticism blames underachievement on the capitalist system's desire to reproduce an 'under-class' (see e.g. Skutnabb-Kangas, 1984). The point is clearly an interesting one, although I think it flawed inasmuch as it assumes an altogether too neat transmission of intent from power centres, through schools and teachers, to children. For *really* monolithic systems, we should look outside the capitalist world. In any event, my purpose here is not to explain underachievement but simply to note the objection to multiculturalism as its remedy.

12 A recent survey of 5,000 British adolescents indicated that, allowing for class and ability, West Indian and Asian children are *not* under-achieving, and there are few group differences in terms of self-esteem. Thus, 'there is little support for the supposition made about "racism" in schools, negative teacher attitudes, inappropriate curriculum or low expectations' (Wilby, 1984, p. 13; see also Flather & Wilby, 1984).

13 Craft seems not entirely consistent in his views however. He acknowledges the civism–pluralism dilemma but claims that 'schools have a prime responsibility to recognise and to further' social diversity (p. 13). What I have argued for here, and what Craft himself seems to approve of at the end of his monograph, certainly supports *recognition* of diversity. But, I am obviously much less easy with the idea that schools should work to *further* this.

14 Expanded notes on the subject of non-standard language and education will be found in Edwards (1979b) and Edwards and Giles (1984).

15 I have not dealt with the bilingualism–identity relationship here; the thrust of this book is to show that a shift from language A to language B occurs because shift – rather than stable bilingualism – makes sense, *not* because the addition of B to A need itself cause the slightest psychological affront to identity. *Anomie* should only be expected at stages of transition from A to B which are impermanent, or

when language shift/addition occurs through completely unwanted coercion. Even in the latter case, however, we would expect identity to survive. In most cases, bilingualism reflects an instrumental expansion of the linguistic repertoire and does not entail any sort of 'schizophrenic' identity pattern, although there are many intriguing possibilities here (e.g. Steiner (1975) claims to be a perfect trilingual, to have three mother-tongues!); see also Genesee (1981b).

16 It is interesting to consider the ambiguity surrounding the very *beginning* of American bilingual education in which, *pace* Fishman (1977a), there are grounds for thinking that legislation was a response to vocal spokesmen and not to any real grassroots pressure (see Di Pietro, 1978; J. Edwards, 1976; Haugen, 1978; Parker & Heath, 1978; Shuy, 1978a, b; Spolsky, 1978; Vázquez, 1978).

17 The positions of Bullivant and Smolicz are not, however, as opposed as these blunt titles suggest. Bullivant supports a modified pluralism and Smolicz is not unaware of the appeal and value of core curricula. Still, he asserts (1979b) that schools have an active role to play in language and culture maintenance because families, on their own, cannot arrest the decline. See also Bullivant (1980b, 1981a, b, 1982a, b, 1984a, b), Smolicz (1979a, 1981a, b, 1983), Smolicz and Harris (1977) and Smolicz and Lean (1979, 1980).

CHAPTER 6   LANGUAGE ATTITUDES, BEHAVIOUR AND RESEARCH

1 I am not unaware of recent writings which claim that the notion of a mainstream is not a clear one in heterogeneous societies where assimilation of various groups has taken place. However, it is mere academic affectation to consider that there is no essential continuity to the dominant strands in societies like the United States, Canada, Australia and Great Britain. The private and symbolic aspects of ethnicity which may remain among those largely assimilated endure because they can be added without cost or liability, not necessarily because they become generally shared by all.

2 Here I draw mainly upon the English-language experience; see also Bourhis (1982) and Carranza (1982) for French and Spanish data respectively. See also generally Edwards (1979b) and Giles and Edwards (1983).

3 I shall, of course, refer to difficulties with the accommodation perspective as and when necessary.

4 In outlining the usefulness of vitality theory, Giles and Byrne (1982) criticise earlier approaches to second-language learning (eg. Clément, 1980; Gardner, 1979) for not sufficiently considering the importance of ethnic identification or the social milieu generally. Gardner's model, for example, is seen to operate in an 'intergroup vacuum'.

5 Perhaps the theorists would want to claim that these motivations still involve listener approval but, if so, a deeper analysis of 'approval' seems to be indicated. I must point out, however, that my summary of accommodation theory has necessarily omitted many fine points and qualifications.

6 Such questions are not new, of course, within social enquiry; I have used them myself (see Edwards, 1982c; Macnamara & Edwards, 1973).

7 However, group perceptions *are* discernible within these perspectives. The advantage of the psychological approach is that it can address them more directly.

References

Abramson, H. Assimilation and pluralism. In S. Thernstrom, A. Orlov & O. Handlin (eds), *Harvard encyclopedia of American ethnic groups*. Cambridge, Massachusetts: Harvard University Press, 1980.

Acton, J. Nationality. In J. Figgis & R. Lawrence (eds), *The history of freedom*. London: Macmillan, 1907 (original, 1862).

Adams, G. Language and man in Ireland. *Ulster Folklife*, 1970, *15/16*, 140–71.

Adler, M. *Welsh and the other dying languages in Europe: A sociolinguistic study*. Hamburg: Helmut Buske Verlag, 1977. (a)

Adler, M. Pidgins, creoles and lingua francas. Hamburg: Helmut Buske Verlag, 1977. (b)

Agheyisi, R. & Fishman, J. Language attitude studies: A brief survey of methodological approaches. *Anthropological Linguistics*, 1970, *12*, 131–57.

Agnew, J. Review of *Internal colonialism* (M. Hechter) and *Political integration and disintegration in the British Isles* (A. Birch). *Language Problems and Language Planning*, 1979, *3*, 172–7.

Agnew, J. Language shift and the politics of language: The case of the Celtic languages of the British Isles. *Language Problems and Language Planning*, 1981, *5*, 1–10. (a)

Agnew J. Political regionalism and Scottish nationalism in Gaelic Scotland. *Canadian Review of Studies in Nationalism*, 1981, *8*, 115–129. (b)

Aitchison, J. *Language change: Progress or decay?* London: Fontana, 1981.

Akenson, D. *The Irish education experiment: The national system of education in the nineteenth century*. London: Routledge & Kegan Paul, 1970.

Akenson, D. *A mirror to Kathleen's face: Education in independent Ireland 1922–60*. Montreal and London: McGill-Queen's University Press, 1975.

Akere, F. Sociolinguistic consequences of language contact: English versus Nigerian languages. *Language Sciences*, 1981, *3*, 283–304.

Alatis, J. (ed.) *Georgetown University Round Table on languages and linguistics*. Washington DC: Georgetown University Press, 1978.

Alba, R. Social assimilation among American Catholic national-origin groups. *American Sociological Review*, 1976, *41*, 1030–46.

Alba, R. The twilight of ethnicity among American Catholics of European ancestry. *Annals of the American Academy of Political and Social Science*, 1981, *454*, 86–97.

Alba, R. & Chamlin, M. A preliminary examination of ethnic identification among whites. *American Sociological Review*, 1983, *48*, 240–7.

Albó, X. The future of the oppressed languages of the Andes. In W. McCormack & S. Wurm (eds), *Language and society: Anthropological issues*. The Hague: Mouton, 1979.

Alcock, A., Taylor, B. & Welton, J. (eds) *The future of cultural minorities*. London: Macmillan, 1979.

Alisjahbana, S. The present situation of the Indonesian language. In B. Sibayan & A. Gonzalez (eds), *Language planning and the building of a national language*. Manila: Linguistic Society of the Philippines, 1977.

Allardt, E. Implications of the ethnic revival in modern, industralized society: A comparative study of the linguistic minorities in Western Europe. *Commentationes Scientiarum Socialium*, 1979, *12*.

Allworth, E. (ed.) *Ethnic Russia in the USSR:* New York: Pergamon, 1980.

Altehenger-Smith, S. Language planning in Singapore: Promote the Use of Mandarin campaign. Unpublished paper, 1980.

Alter, R. A fever of ethnicity. *Commentary*, 1972, *53(6)*, 68–73.

Altoma, S. Language education in Arab countries and the role of the academies. In J. Fishman (ed.), *Advances in language planning*. The Hague, Mouton, 1974.

Amayo, A. The place of language in the national development process in Nigeria. Paper to the Seventh World Congress of Applied Linguistics, Brussels, 1984.

Andersen, R. Determining the linguistic attributes of language attrition. In R. Lambert & B. Freed (eds), *The loss of language skills*. Rowley, Massachusetts: Newbury House, 1982.

Anderson, A. The survival of ethnolinguistic minorities: Canadian and comparative research. In H. Giles & B. Saint-Jacques (eds), *Language and ethnic relations*. New York: Pergamon, 1979.

Anderson, A. The problem of minority languages: Reflections on the Glasgow conference. *Language Problems and Language Planning*, 1981, *5*, 291–303.

Anderson B. *Imagined communities: Reflections on the origin and growth of nationalism*. London: Verso, 1983.

Anderson, C. Equality of opportunity in a pluralistic society: A theoretical framework. *International Review of Education*, 1975, *21*, 287–300.

Andersson, T. Bilingual education: The American experience. *Modern Language Journal*, 1971, *55*, 427–40.

Andersson, T. & Boyer, M. *Bilingual schooling in the United States*. Washington DC: United States Government Printing Office, 1970.

Andreski, S. *Social sciences as sorcery*. London: André Deutsch, 1973.

Andrews, L. *The decline of Irish as a school subject in the Republic of Ireland 1967–77. Dublin: Conradh na Gaeilge, 1978*.

Andrzejewski, B. The implementation of language planning in Somalia: A record of achievement. *Language Planning Newsletter*, 1980, *6(1)*.

Appel, R. Minority languages in the Netherlands: Relations between sociopolitical conflicts and bilingual education. In B. Bain (ed.), *The sociogenesis of language and human conduct*. New York: Plenum, 1983.

Apte, M. Region, religion and power: Parameters of identity in the process of acculturation. In W. McCormack & S. Wurm (eds), *Language and society: Anthropological issues*. The Hague: Mouton, 1979.

Argente, J., Castellanos, J., Jorba, M., Molas, J., Murgades, J., Nadal, J. & Sulla, E. A nation without a state, a people without a language. *Polyglot*, 1981, *3(Fiche 1)*.

Arthur, B., Farrar, D. & Bradford, G. Evaluation reactions of college students to dialect differences in the English of Mexican-Americans. *Language and Speech*, 1974, *17*, 255–70.

Asuncion-Lande, N. The social implications of bilingualism: Language use and interpersonal communication in the Philippines. Paper to the Fifth World Congress of Applied Linguistics, Montreal, 1978.

Asuncion-Lande, N. & Pascasio, E. Language maintenance and code switching among Filipino bilingual speakers. In W. Mackey & J. Ornstein (eds), *Sociolinguistic studies in language contact*. The Hague: Mouton, 1979.

Azurmendi, M. Language and the Spanish Basque revival. *Language and Society*, 1981, *4*, 19–22.

Baetens Beardsmore, H. Bilingualism in Belgium. *Journal of Multilingual and Multicultural Development*, 1980, *1*, 145–54.

Baetens Beardsmore, H. Substratum, adstratum and residual bilingualism in Brussels. *Journal of Multilingual and Multicultural Development*, 1983, *4*, 1–14.

Baetens Beardsmore, H. (ed.) Language and television. *International Journal of the Sociology of Language*, 1984, *48*.

Baldauf, R. The language situation in American Samoa: Planners, plans and planning. *Language Planning Newsletter*, 1982, *8(1)*.

Barker, E. *National character and the factors in its formation*. London: Methuen, 1927.

Barnard, F. *Herder's social and political thought*. Oxford: Clarendon Press, 1965.

Barnard, F. (ed.) *J.G. Herder on social and political culture*. Cambridge: Cambridge University Press, 1969.

Barnes, D. The implementation of language planning in China. In J. Cobarrubias & J. Fishman (eds), *Progress in language planning*. Berlin: Mouton, 1983.

Baron, S. *Modern nationalism and religion*. New York: Harper, 1947.

Barth, F. (ed.) *Ethnic groups and boundaries*. Boston: Little, Brown, 1969.

Beckett, J. *A short history of Ireland*. London: Hutchinson, 1981.

Beebe, L. & Giles, H. Speech accommodation theories: A discussion in terms of second-language acquisition. *International Journal of the Sociology of Language*, 1984, *46*, 5–32.

Bell, A. Broadcast news as a language standard. *International Journal of the Sociology of Language*, 1983, *40*, 29–42.

Bell, R. *Sociolinguistics*. London: Batsford, 1976.

Bell, W. & Freeman, W. (eds) *Ethnicity and nation-building*. Beverly Hills: Sage, 1974.

Benn, S. Nationalism. In P. Edwards (ed.), *Encyclopedia of philosophy (Vol. 5)*. New York: Macmillan & Free Press, 1967.

Bentahila, A. Language attitudes among Arabic–French bilinguals in Morocco. Clevedon, Avon: Multilingual Matters, 1983. (a)

Bentahila, A. Motivations for code-switching among Arabic–French bilinguals in Morocco. *Language and Communication*, 1983, *3*, 233–43. (b)

Benton, R. *The legal status of the Maori language: Current reality and future prospects*. Wellington: Maori Research Unit, New Zealand Council for Educational Research, 1979. (a)

Benton, R. *Moves towards bilingual education in New Zealand in the 1970s*. Wellington: Maori Research Unit, New Zealand Council for Educational Research, 1979. (b).

Benton, R. The Philippine bilingual education program – Education for the masses or the preparation of a new elite? *Philippine Journal of Linguistics*, 1980, *11(2)*, 1–14. (a)

Benton, R. Changes in language use in a rural Maori community 1963–78. *Journal of the Polynesian Society*, 1980, *89*, 455–78. (b)

Benton, R. *The New Zealand Council for Educational Research Maori language survey*.

Wellington: Maori Research Unit, New Zealand Council for Educational Research, 1983. (a)

Benton, R. Bilingual education and the survival of the Maori language. Paper to the Fifteenth Pacific Science Congress, Maori Studies Symposium, Dunedin, 1983. (b).

Bergin, O. *Irish spelling.* Dublin: Browne & Nolan, 1911.

Berlin, I. *Vico and Herder: Two studies in the history of ideas.* London: Hogarth, 1976.

Berry, J. Psychological aspects of cultural pluralism: Unity and identity reconsidered. In R. Brislin (ed.), *Topics in culture learning (Vol. II).* Honolulu: East-West Center, 1974.

Berry, J. Native peoples and the larger society. In R. Gardner & R. Kalin (eds), *A Canadian social psychology of ethnic relations.* Toronto: Methuen, 1981. (a)

Berry, J. Multicultural attitudes and education. Paper to the Invitational Symposium on Multiculturalism in Education, Kingston (Ontario), 1981. (b)

Berry, J., Kalin, R. & Taylor, D. *Multiculturalism and ethnic attitudes in Canada.* Ottawa: Supply & Services Canada, 1977.

Berry, J., Mawhinney, T., Wintrob, R. & Sindell, P. James Bay Cree attitudes towards cultural relations and cultural retention. Paper to the Canadian Psychological Association, Toronto, 1981.

Bethell, T. Against bilingual education. *Harpers,* 1979, *258(1545),* 30–3.

Betts, C. *Culture in crisis: The future of the Welsh language.* Upton, Wirral: Ffynnon Press, 1976.

Bhatia, T. English and the vernaculars of India: Contact and change. *Applied Linguistics,* 1982, *3,* 235–45.

Bickerton, D. Can English and Pidgin be kept apart? In C. Kennedy (ed.), *Language planning and language education.* London: Allen & Unwin, 1984.

Bickley, V. English as a language of mediation. *English Around the World,* 1980, *23.*

Billigmeier, R. *A crisis in Swiss pluralism.* The Hague: Mouton, 1979.

Binchy, D. Review of *Gaelic and Scottish education and life* (J. Campbell). *The Bell,* 1945, *10,* 362–6.

Birch, A. *Political integration and disintegration in the British Isles.* London: Allen & Unwin, 1977.

Blanc, H. The Israeli koine as an emergent national standard. In J. Fishman, C. Ferguson & J. Das Gupta (eds), *Language problems of developing nations.* New York: Wiley, 1968.

Blanco, G. The education perspective. In Center for Applied Linguistics (ed.), *Bilingual education: Current perspectives (Vol. 1).* Arlington, Virginia: CAL, 1977.

Bodmer, F. *The loom of language.* London: Allen & Unwin, 1943.

Boelens, K. *Frisian–Dutch primary schools.* The Hague: Ministry of Education, 1976.

Bolinger, D. *Language – The loaded weapon.* London: Longman, 1980.

Bolton, K. & Luke, K. A sociolinguistic profile of Hong Kong. Paper to the Seventh World Congress of Applied Linguistics, Brussels, 1984.

Bourhis, R. Language policies and language attitudes: Le monde de la francophonie. In E. Ryan & H. Giles (eds), *Attitudes towards language variation.* London: Edward Arnold, 1982.

Bourhis, R. *Conflict and language planning in Quebec.* Clevedon, Avon: Multilingual Matters, 1984.

Bourhis, R., Giles, H., Leyens, J. & Tajfel, H. Psycholinguistic distinctiveness: Language divergence in Belgium. In H. Giles & R. St. Clair (eds), *Language and social psychology.* Oxford: Basil Blackwell, 1979.

Bourhis, R., Giles, H. & Rosenthal, D. Notes on the construction of a 'Subjective Vitality Questionnaire' for ethnolinguistic groups. *Journal of Multilingual and Multicultural Development*, 1981, *2*, 145–55.

Bowen, J. The structure of language. In A. Marckwardt (ed.), *Linguistics in school programs*. Chicago: University of Chicago Press, 1970.

Brann, C. A typology of language education in Nigeria. In W. McCormack & S. Wurm (eds), *Language and society: Anthropological issues*. The Hague: Mouton, 1979. (a)

Brann, C. Multilingualism in Nigerian education. In W. Mackey & J. Ornstein (eds), *Sociolinguistic studies in language contact*. The Hague: Mouton, 1979. (b)

Brann, C. The ethnolinguistic giant of Africa. *Language and Society*, 1983, *11*, 23–6.

Brass, P. *Language, religion and politics in North India*. Cambridge: Cambridge University Press, 1974.

Brass, P. Ethnicity and nationality formation. *Ethnicity*, 1976, *3*, 225–41.

Breatnach, D. Bás nó beatha? *Éire-Ireland*, 1969, *4(1)*, 13–38.

Breatnach, R. Revival or survival? An examination of the Irish language policy of the state. *Studies*, 1956, *45*, 129–45.

Brennan, E. & Brennan, J. Accent scaling and language attitudes: Reactions to Mexican American English speech. *Language and Speech*, 1981, *24*, 207–21. (a)

Brennan, E. & Brennan, J. Measurements of accent and attitude toward Mexican-American speech. *Journal of Psycholinguistic Research*, 1981, *10*, 487–501. (b)

Brennan, M. The restoration of Irish. *Studies*, 1964, *53*, 263–77.

Brennan, M. Language, personality and the nation. In B. Ó Cuív (ed.), *A view of the Irish language*. Dublin: Government Stationery Office, 1969.

Brennan, P. Issues of language and law in Papua New Guinea. *Language Planning Newsletter*, 1983, *9(2)*.

Breton, R. *Les ethnies*. Paris: Presses Universitaires de France, 1981.

Breton, R. & Pinard, M. Group formation among immigrants: Criteria and processes. *Canadian Journal of Economics and Political Science*, 1960, *26*, 465–77.

Breton, R., Reitz, J. & Valentine, V. *Cultural boundaries and the cohesion of Canada*. Montreal: Institute for Research on Public Policy, 1980.

Bright, W. *Sociolinguistics*. The Hague: Mouton, 1966.

Brooks, S. *The new Ireland*. Dublin: Maunsel, 1907.

Brown, S. What is a nation? *Studies*, 1912, *1*, 496–510.

Brown, T. *Ireland: A social and cultural history, 1922–79*. Glasgow: Collins/Fontana, 1981.

Bullivant, B. Multiculturalism – No. *Education News*, 1980 *17*, 17–20. (a)

Bullivant, B. Searching for an ideology of pluralism: Some results of a cross-national survey. *Ethnic and Racial Studies*, 1980, *3*, 465–74. (b)

Bullivant, B. *The pluralist dilemma in education*. Sydney: Allen & Unwin, 1981. (a)

Bullivant, B. Multiculturalism – Pluralist orthodoxy or ethnic hegemony? *Canadian Ethnic Studies*, 1981, *13(2)*, 1–22. (b)

Bullivant, B. Power and control in the multi-ethnic school: Towards a conceptual model. *Ethnic and Racial Studies*, 1982, *5*, 53–70. (a)

Bullivant, B. Pluralist debate and educational policy – Australian style. *Journal of Multilingual and Multicultural Development*, 1982, *3*, 129–47. (b)

Bullivant, B. Ethnolinguistic minorities and multicultural policy in Australia. In J. Edwards (ed.), *Linguistic minorities, policies and pluralism*. London: Academic Press, 1984. (a)

Bullivant, B. *Pluralism: Cultural maintenance and evolution*. Clevedon, Avon: Multilingual Matters, 1984. (b)

204	*References*

Burnet, J. The policy of multiculturalism within a bilingual framework: An interpretation. In A. Wolfgang (ed.), *Education of immigrant students: Issues and answers.* Toronto: Ontario Institute for Studies in Education, 1975.

Burnet, J. Myths and multiculturalism. *Canadian Journal of Education,* 1979, *4(4),* 43–58.

Burns, D. Bilingual education in the Andes of Peru. In J. Fishman, C. Ferguson & J. Das Gupta (eds), *Language problems of developing nations.* New York: Wiley, 1968.

Byrne, D. *The attraction paradigm.* New York: Academic Press, 1971.

Byrne, E. Where the Irish language still lives. *Ireland–American Review,* 1938, *1,* 50–5.

Cahill, E. Irish in the early middle ages. *Irish Ecclesiastical Record,* 1935, *46,* 363–76. (a)

Cahill, E. The Irish national tradition. *Irish Ecclesiastical Record,* 1935, *46,* 2–10. (b)

Cahill, E. Irish in the Danish and pre-Norman period. *Irish Ecclesiastical Record,* 1936, *47,* 337–54.

Carranza, M. Attitudinal research on Hispanic language varieties. In E. Ryan & H. Giles (eds), *Attitudes towards language variation.* London: Edward Arnold, 1982.

Carranza, M. & Ryan, E. Evaluation reactions of bilingual Anglo and Mexican American adolescents toward speakers of English and Spanish. *International Journal of the Sociology of Language,* 1975, *6,* 83–104.

Carroll, J. International comparisons of foreign language learning in the IEA project. In J. Alatis (ed.), *Georgetown University Round Table on languages and linguistics.* Washington DC: Georgetown University Press, 1978.

Cashel, A. Language and thought: Their bearing on nationality. *Irish Monthly,* 1917, *45,* 397–403.

Castonguay, C. The anglicization of Canada, 1971–81. Paper to the Seventh World Congress of Applied Linguistics, Brussels, 1984.

Center for Applied Linguistics (ed.) *Bilingual education: Current perspectives* (5 vols). Arlington, Virginia: CAL, 1977–8.

Central Statistical Board of the USSR. *Peoples of the USSR: Facts and figures 1922–82.* Moscow: Novosti, 1982.

Chadwick, N. *The Celts.* Harmondsworth, Middlesex: Penguin, 1970.

Charpentier, J. L'aspect en pidgin Bichelamar. Paper to the Seventh World Congress of Applied Linguistics, Brussels, 1984.

Chazan, B. Models of ethnic education: The case of Jewish education in Great Britain. *British Journal of Educational Studies,* 1978, *26,* 54–72.

Cheng, R. Language unification in Taiwan: Present and future. In W. McCormack & S. Wurm (eds), *Language and society: Anthropological issues.* The Hague: Mouton, 1979.

Citizens for Better Broadcasting. *Aspects of RTÉ television broadcasting.* Dublin: Conradh na Gaeilge, 1976.

Clammer, J. The institutionalization of ethnicity: The culture of ethnicity in Singapore. *Ethnic and Racial Studies,* 1982, *5,* 127–39.

Clark, R. Euzkadi: Basque nationalism in Spain since the civil war. In C. Foster (ed.), *Nations without a state: Ethnic minorities in Western Europe.* New York: Praeger, 1980.

Clément, R. Ethnicity, contact and communicative competence in a second language. In H. Giles, P. Robinson & P. Smith (eds), *Language: Social psychological perspectives.* Oxford: Pergamon, 1980.

Cobarrubias, J. Language planning: The state of the art. In J. Cobarrubias & J. Fishman (eds), *Progress in language planning.* Berlin: Mouton, 1983. (a)

Cobarrubias, J. Ethical issues in status planning. In J. Cobarrubias & J. Fishman (eds), *Progress in language planning.* Berlin: Mouton, 1983. (b)

Cobarrubias, J. & Fishman, J. (eds) *Progress in Language planning*. Berlin: Mouton, 1983.

Cole, M. & Scribner, S. *Culture and thought*. New York: Wiley, 1974.

Comber, T. The revival. *Múinteoir Náisiúnta*, 1960, *5(7)*, 23, 24, 27.

Combs, M. & Jernudd, B. Kumision I Fino' Chamorro (Guam). *Language Planning Newsletter*, 1981, *7(3/4)*.

Comeau, J. The Nova Scotia Acadians and the Nova Scotia government. Paper to the St Mary's University Conference on Ethnic Identity in Atlantic Canada, Halifax, 1981.

Comhaire, J. Haitian creole – A problem in the sociology of language and of linguistic research. Paper to the Seventh World Congress of Applied Linguistics, Brussels, 1984.

Commission on the Restoration of the Irish Language. *Summary, in English, of final report*. Dublin: Government Stationery Office, 1963.

Committee on Irish Language Attitudes Research. *Report*. Dublin: Government Stationery Office, 1975.

Comrie, B. *The languages of the Soviet Union*. Cambridge: Cambridge University Press, 1981.

Connor, W. Ethnonationalism in the first world: The present in historical perspective. In M. Esman (ed.), *Ethnic conflict in the Western world*. Ithaca, New York: Cornell University Press, 1977.

Connor, W. A nation is a nation, is a state, is an ethnic group, is a... *Ethnic and Racial Studies*, 1978, *1*, 377–400.

Connor, W. Review of *Ethnic chauvinism* (O. Patterson). *Ethnic and Racial Studies*, 1980, *3*, 355–9.

Cooper, R. The spread of Amharic in Ethiopia. In J. Fishman (ed.), *Advances in the study of societal multilingualism*. Berlin: Mouton, 1978. (a).

Cooper, R. Research methodology in bilingual education. In J. Alatis (ed.), *Georgetown University Round Table on languages and linguistics*. Washington DC: Georgetown University Press, 1978. (b)

Cooper, R. (ed.) Sociolinguistic perspectives on Israeli Hebrew. *International Journal of the Sociology of Language*, 1983, *41*.

Cooper, R. & Carpenter, S. Linguistic diversity in the Ethiopian market. In J. Fishman (ed.), *Advances in the sociology of language*. The Hague: Mouton, 1972.

Cooper, R. & Fishman, J. The study of language attitudes. *International Journal of the Sociology of Language*, 1974, *3*, 5–19.

Corcoran, T. *State policy in Irish education AD 1536 to 1816*. Dublin: Fallon, 1916.

Corcoran, T. How the Irish language can be revived. *Irish Monthly*, 1923, *51*, 26–30. (a)

Corcoran, T. The native speaker as teacher. *Irish Monthly*, 1923, *51*, 187–90. (b)

Corcoran, T. How English may be taught without anglicising. *Irish Monthly*, 1923, *51*, 269–73. (c)

Corcoran, T. The Irish language in the Irish schools. *Studies*, 1925, *14*, 377–88.

Corcoran, T. *Education systems in Ireland from the close of the middle age*. Dublin: University College, 1928.

Corcoran, T. The home within the school. *Irish Monthly*, 1934, *62*, 35–9.

Corcoran, T. Education in Éire. *Yearbook of Education*, 1939, 282–94.

Corkery, D. *The fortunes of the Irish language*. Cork: Mercier, 1968.

Corvalán, G. Review of *Paraguay: Nación bilingüe* (F. Hensey). *Language Problems and Language Planning*, 1983, *7*, 81–4.

Cottle, B. *The plight of English*. Newton Abbot: David & Charles, 1975.

Covington, A. Black people and Black English. In D. Harrison & T. Trabasso (eds), *Black English*. Hillsdale, New Jersey: Erlbaum, 1976.

Cowan, M., *Humanist without portfolio: An anthology of the writings of Wilhelm von Humboldt.* Detroit: Wayne State University Press, 1963.

Craft, M. *Education for diversity: The challenge of cultural pluralism.* Nottingham: University of Nottingham, 1982.

Creissels, D. *Les langues d'URSS. Paris: Institut d'Etudes Slaves, 1979.*

Cummins, J. Biliteracy, language proficiency and educational programs. In J. Edwards (ed.), *The social psychology of reading.* Silver Spring, Maryland: Institute of Modern Languages, 1981.

Cummins, J. Linguistic minorities and multicultural policy in Canada. In J. Edwards (ed.), *Linguistic minorities, policies and pluralism.* London: Academic Press, 1984.

Cummins, J. & Swain, M. Analysis-by-rhetoric: Reading the text or the reader's own projections? A reply to Edelsky *et al. Applied Linguistics,* 1983, *4,* 23–41.

Cutts, E. The background of Macaulay's Minute. *American Historical Review,* 1953, *58,* 824–53.

Dalby, D. Fighting off the English invasion. *Times Higher Education Supplement,* 25 February 1983.

Das Gupta, J. Ethnicity, language demands and national development in India. In N. Glazer & D. Moynihan (eds), *Ethnicity: Theory and experience.* Cambridge, Massachusetts: Harvard University Press, 1975.

Dashefsky, A. (ed.) *Ethnic identity in society.* Chicago: Rand McNally, 1976.

Davies, A. When political constraints and professional advice in ELT conflict. Paper to the Seventh World Congress of Applied Linguistics, Brussels, 1984.

de Fréine, S. The dominance of the English language in the nineteenth century. In D. Ó Muirithe (ed.), *The English language in Ireland.* Cork: Mercier, 1977.

de Fréine, S. *The great silence.* Cork: Mercier, 1978.

Dench, G. *Maltese in London: A case study of erosion of ethnic consciousness.* London: Routledge & Kegan Paul, 1975.

Denison, N. Language death or language suicide? *International Journal of the Sociology of Language,* 1977, *12,* 13–22.

de Terra, D. The linguagenesis of society: The implementation of the national language plan in West Malaysia. In B. Bain (ed.), *The sociogenesis of language and human conduct.* New York: Plenum, 1983.

Deutsch, K. The trend of European nationalism – The language aspect. In J. Fishman (ed.), *Readings in the sociology of language.* The Hague: Mouton, 1968.

de Valdés, M. Bilingual education program for Spanish-speaking children in the United States. *Canadian Modern Language Review,* 1979, *35,* 407–14.

DeVos, G. & Romanucci-Ross, L. (eds), *Ethnic identity.* Palo Alto, California: Mayfield, 1975.

Dharmadasa, K. Nativism, diglossia and the Sinhalese identity in the language problem in Sri Lanka. *International Journal of the Sociology of Language,* 1977, *13,* 21–31.

Dhillon, P. An historical view of small group interests and the implications for language planning and policy. Paper to the Seventh World Congress of Applied Linguistics, Brussels, 1984.

Dilger, B. The education of minorities. *Comparative Education,* 1984, *20,* 155–64.

Dillon, M. Comment. *University Review,* 1958, *2(2),* 22–7

Dinnerstein, L., Nichols, R. & Reimers, D. *Natives and strangers.* New York: Oxford University Press, 1979.

Di Pietro, R. Culture and ethnicity in the bilingual classroom. In J. Alatis (ed.), *Georgetown University Round Table on languages and linguistics.* Washington DC: Georgetown University Press, 1978.

Dodson, C. & Jones, R. A Welsh-medium TV channel for Wales: Development, controversies, problems, implications. *International Journal of the Sociology of Language*, 1984, *48*, 11–32.

Donahue, T. Toward a broadened context for modern bilingual education. *Journal of Multilingual and Multicultural Development*, 1982, *3*, 77–87.

Donaldson, B. *Dutch: A linguistic history of Holland and Belgium*. Leiden: Martinus Nijhoff, 1983.

Dorian, N. Grammatical change in a dying dialect. *Language*, 1973, *49*, 413–38.

Dorian, N. The problem of the semi-speaker in language death. *International Journal of the Sociology of Language*, 1977, *12*, 23–32.

Dorian, N. The dying dialect and the role of the school: East Sutherland Gaelic and Pennsylvania Dutch. In J. Alatis (ed.), *Georgetown University Round Table on languages and linguistics*. Washington DC: Georgetown University Press, 1978.

Dorian, N. Review of *Welsh and the other dying languages in Europe* (M. Adler). *Language in Society*, 1979, *8*, 69–71.

Dorian, N. *Language death: The life cycle of a Scottish Gaelic dialect*. Philadelphia: University of Pennsylvania Press, 1981.

Dorian, N. Language loss and maintenance in language contact situations. In R. Lambert & B. Freed (eds), *The loss of language skills*. Rowley, Massachusetts: Newbury House, 1982.

Dorotich, D. Ethnic diversity and national unity in Yugoslav education: The socialist autonomous province of Vojvodina. *Compare*, 1978, *8*, 81–91.

Douglas, W. Review of *Attitudes toward English usage* (E. Finegan), *American tongue in cheek* (J. Quinn) and *Paradigms lost* (J. Simon). *College English*, 1982, *44*, 72–83.

Drake, G. *The role of prescriptivism in American linguistics, 1820–1970*. Amsterdam: Benjamins, 1977.

Drake, G. Ethnicity, values and language policy in the United States. In H. Giles & B. Saint-Jacques (eds), *Language and ethnic relations*. New York: Pergamon, 1979.

Drake, G. Problems of language planning in the United States. In J. Edwards (ed.), *Linguistic minorities, policies and pluralism*. London: Academic Press, 1984.

Dressler, W. On the phonology of language death. *Papers of the Chicago Linguistic Society*, 1972, *8*, 448–57.

Dressler, W. & Wodak-Leodolter, R. Language preservation and language death in Brittany. *Linguistics*, 1977, *191*, 33–44.

Driedger, L. (ed.) *The Canadian ethnic mosaic*. Toronto: McClelland & Stewart, 1978.

Driedger, L. Ethnic and minority relations. In R. Hagedorn (ed.), *Sociology*. Toronto: Holt, Rinehart & Winston, 1980.

Durkacz, V. Gaelic education in the nineteenth century. *Scottish Educational Studies*, 1977, *9(1)*, 18–28.

Durkacz, V. *The decline of the Celtic languages*. Edinburgh: John Donald, 1983.

Durkheim, E. *Sociology and philosophy*. New York: Free Press, 1953.

Du Toit, B. (ed.) *Ethnicity in modern Africa*. Boulder, Colorado: Westview, 1978.

Eastman, C. *Language planning*. San Francisco: Chandler & Sharp, 1983.

Eastman, C. Language, ethnic identity and change. In J. Edwards (ed.), *Linguistic minorities, policies and pluralism*. London: Academic Press, 1984.

Eastman, C. & Reese, T. Associated language: How language and ethnic identity are related. *General Linguistics*, 1981, *21*, 109–16.

Edelsky, C., Hudelson, S., Flores, B., Barkin, F., Altwerger, B. & Jilbert, K. Semilingualism and language deficit. *Applied Linguistics*, 1983, *4*, 1–22.

Edwards, A. *Language in culture and class.* London: Heinemann, 1976.

Edwards, J. Current issues in bilingual education. *Ethnicity,* 1976, *3,* 70–81.

Edwards, J. Ethnic identity and bilingual education. In H. Giles (ed.), *Language, ethnicity and intergroup relations.* London: Academic Press, 1977. (a)

Edwards, J. Review of *Report* (Committee on Irish Language Attitudes Research). *Language Problems and Language Planning,* 1977, *1,* 54–9. (b)

Edwards, J. Review of *The Cornish language and its literature* (P. Ellis), *The lion's tongue* (K. MacKinnon) and *Culture in crisis: The future of the Welsh language* (C. Betts). *Language Problems and Language Planning,* 1977, *1,* 97–102. (c)

Edwards, J. The speech of disadvantaged Dublin children. *Language Problems and Language Planning,* 1977, *1,* 65–72. (d)

Edwards, J. Reading, language and disadvantage. In V. Greaney (ed.), *Studies in reading.* Dublin: Educational Company, 1977. (e)

Edwards, J. Education, psychology and eclecticism. In D. Mulcahey (ed.), *Proceedings of the Second Annual Conference of the Educational Studies Association.* Cork: University College, 1978.

Edwards, J. Review of *After Babel: Aspects of language and translation* (G. Steiner). *Language Problems and Language Planning,* 1979, *3,* 51–4. (a)

Edwards, J. *Language and disadvantage.* London: Edward Arnold, 1979. (b)

Edwards, J. Judgements and confidence in reactions to disadvantaged speech. In H. Giles & R. St. Clair (eds), *Language and social psychology.* Oxford: Basil Blackwell, 1979. (c)

Edwards, J. Bilingual education: Facts and values. *Canadian Modern Language Review,* 1980, *37,* 123–7. (a)

Edwards, J. Critics and criticisms of bilingual education. *Modern Language Journal,* 1980, *64,* 409–15. (b)

Edwards, J. The context of bilingual education. *Journal of Multilingual and Multicultural Development,* 1981, *2,* 25–44. (a)

Edwards, J. The social and political context of bilingual education. Paper to the Invitational Symposium on Multiculturalism in Education, Kingston (Ontario), 1981. (b)

Edwards, J. Psychological and linguistic aspects of minority education. In J. Megarry, S. Nisbet & E. Hoyle (eds), *World yearbook of education 1981: Education of minorities.* London: Kogan Page, 1981. (c)

Edwards, J. Language attitudes and their implications among English speakers. In E. Ryan & H. Giles (eds), *Attitudes towards language variation.* London: Edward Arnold, 1982. (a)

Edwards, J. Bilingual education revisited: A reply to Donahue. *Journal of Multilingual and Multicultural Development,* 1982, *3,* 89–101. (b)

Edwards, J. Attitudes towards Gaelic and English among Gaelic speakers in Cape Breton Island, Nova Scotia. Paper to the Sixth Congress of the International Association of Cross-Cultural Psychology, Aberdeen, 1982. (c)

Edwards, J. Review of *Bilingual education: Current Perspectives* (Center for Applied Linguistics). *Language Problems and Language Planning,* 1983, *7,* 72–7. (a)

Edwards, J. Review essay *The language trap* (J. Honey). *Journal of Language and Social Psychology,* 1983, *2,* 67–76. (b)

Edwards, J. *The Irish language: An annotated bibliography of sociolinguistic publications, 1772–1982.* New York: Garland, 1983. (c)

Edwards, J. Review of *The language of children reared in poverty* (L. Feagans & D. Farran). *Journal of Language and Social Psychology,* 1983, *2,* 80–3. (d)

Edwards, J. Language, disadvantage and minority education. In G. Verma & C. Bagley (eds), *Race relations and cultural differences*. London: Croom Helm, 1983. (e)

Edwards, J. Language, diversity and identity. In J. Edwards (ed.), *Linguistic minorities, policies and pluralism*. London: Academic Press, 1984. (a)

Edwards, J. Irish and English in Ireland. In P. Trudgill (ed.), *Language in the British Isles*. Cambridge: Cambridge University Press, 1984. (b)

Edwards, J. Introduction. In J. Edwards (ed.), *Linguistic minorities, policies and pluralism*. London: Academic Press, 1984. (c)

Edwards, J. Irish: Planning and preservation. *Journal of Multilingual and Multicultural Development*, in press. (a)

Edwards, J. Review of *The decline of the Celtic languages* (V. Durkacz) and *The languages of Britain* (G. Price). *Journal of Language and Social Psychology*, in press. (b)

Edwards, J. Review of *Progress in language planning* (J. Cobarrubias & J. Fishman) and *Language planning* (C. Eastman). *Journal of Language and Social Psychology*, in press. (c)

Edwards, J. Language and educational disadvantage: The persistence of linguistic 'deficit' theory. In K. Durkin (ed.), *Language development during the school years*. London: Croom Helm, in press. (d)

Edwards, J. & Chisholm, J. Language and group identity in Nova Scotia. In preparation.

Edwards, J. & Giles, H. Applications of the social psychology of language: Sociolinguistics and education. In P. Trudgill (ed.), *Applied sociolinguistics*. London: Academic Press, 1984.

Edwards, J. & McKinnon, M. Perceptions of disadvantage: A Canadian study in a rural context. In preparation.

Edwards, J. & Shearn, C. Language and identity in Belgium. In preparation.

Edwards, O. Ireland. In O. Edwards, G. Evans, I. Rhys & H. MacDiarmid (eds), *Celtic nationalism*. London: Routledge & Kegan Paul, 1968.

Edwards, V. *The West Indian language issue in British schools*. London: Routledge & Kegan Paul, 1979.

Edwards, V. Language policy in multicultural Britain. In J. Edwards (ed.), *Linguistic minorities, policies and pluralism*. London: Academic Press, 1984.

Ellis, P. *The Cornish language and its literature*. London: Routledge & Kegan Paul, 1974.

Ellis, P. & Mac A'Ghobhainn, S. *The problem of language revival*. Inverness: Club Leabhar, 1971.

Engelbrecht, G. & Ortiz, L. Guaraní literacy in Paraguay. *International Journal of the Sociology of Language*, 1983, 42, 53–67.

Epstein, N. Bilingual and bicultural education: The role of the scholar. In J. Alatis (ed.), *Georgetown University Round Table on languages and linguistics*. Washington DC: Georgetown University Press, 1978. (a)

Epstein, N. *Language, ethnicity and the schools*. Washington DC: Institute for Educational Leadership, 1978. (b)

Ernest Dichter International Institute for Motivational Research. *A motivational research study for the greater use of the Irish language*. Croton-on-Hudson, New York: EDIIMR, 1968.

Escobar, A. Review of *Variaciones sociolingüísticas del castellano en el Perú* (F. Hensey). *Language Problems and Language Planning*, 1983, 7, 87–92.

Esman, M. (ed.) *Ethnic conflict in the Western world*. Ithaca, New York: Cornell University Press, 1977.

Evans, D. The story of Cornish. *Studies*, 1969, 58, 293–308.

Falc'hun, F. *Les origines de la langue bretonne*. Brest: Faculté des Lettres et Sciences Sociales, 1977.

Feagans, L. & Farran, D. (eds) *The language of children reared in poverty.* London: Academic Press, 1982.

Feather, N. National sentiment in a newly independent nation. *Journal of Personality and Social Psychology,* 1981, *40,* 1017–28. (a)

Feather, N. Culture contact and national sentiment. *Australian Journal of Psychology,* 1981, *33,* 149–56. (b)

Feitsma, A. Why and how do the Frisian language and identity continue? In E. Haugen, J. McClure & D. Thomson (eds), *Minority languages today.* Edinburgh: Edinburgh University Press, 1981.

Fellman, J. *The revival of a classical tongue: Eliezer Ben-Yehuda and the modern Hebrew language.* The Hague: Mouton, 1973. (a)

Fellman, J. Concerning the 'revival' of the Hebrew language. *Anthropological Linguistics,* 1973, *15,* 250–7. (b)

Fellman, J. On the revival of the Hebrew language. *Language Sciences,* 1976, *43,* 17.

Fellman, J. The Academy of Ethiopian Languages. *Language Planning Newsletter,* 1983, *9(3).*

Fennell, D. The last days of the Gaeltacht/Why the Gaeltacht wasn't saved. *Irish Times,* 3 and 4 June 1980.

Fennell, D. Can a shrinking linguistic minority be saved? In E. Haugen, J. McClure & D. Thomson (eds), *Minority languages today.* Edinburgh: Edinburgh University Press, 1981.

Ferguson, C. The role of Arabic in Ethiopia: A sociolinguistic perspective. In J. Alatis (ed.), *Georgetown University Round Table on languages and linguistics.* Washington DC: Georgetown University Press, 1970.

Ferguson, C. Language planning and language change. In J. Cobarrubias & J. Fishman (eds), *Progress in language planning.* Berlin: Mouton, 1983.

Ferguson, C. & Dil, A. Universals of language planning in national development. In W. McCormack & S. Wurm (eds), *Language and society: Anthropological issues.* The Hague: Mouton, 1979.

Fichte, J. *Addresses to the German nation.* New York: Harper & Row, 1968 (original, 1922).

Field, T. Language survival in a European context: The future of Occitan. *Language Problems and Language Planning,* 1981, *5,* 251–63.

Figueroa, P. Minority pupil progress. In M. Craft (ed.), *Education and cultural pluralism.* London: Falmer, 1984.

Fischer, J. The speech community of Ponape, Caroline Islands. *Language Sciences,* 1979, *1,* 85–93.

Fishman, J. Language maintenance and language shift as fields of inquiry. *Linguistics,* 1964, *9,* 32–70.

Fishman, J. *Language loyalty in the United States.* The Hague: Mouton, 1966.

Fishman, J. (ed.) *Readings in the sociology of language.* The Hague: Mouton, 1968.

Fishman, J. Preface. In J. Fishman (ed.), *Advances in the sociology of language (Vol. 1).* The Hague: Mouton, 1971. (a)

Fishman, J. The impact of nationalism on language planning. In J. Rubin & B. Jernudd (eds), *Can language be planned?* Honolulu: East-West Center Press, 1971. (b)

Fishman, J. *Language and nationalism.* Rowley, Massachusetts: Newbury House, 1972.

Fishman, J. (ed.) Israel. *International Journal of the Sociology of Language,* 1974, *1.* (a)

Fishman, J. (ed.) *Advances in language planning.* The Hague: Mouton, 1974. (b)

Fishman, J. The sociology of language in Israel. *Language Sciences,* 1976, *40,* 28–31. (a)

Fishman, J. *Bilingual education: An international sociological perspective.* Rowley, Massachusetts: Newbury House, 1976. (b)

Fishman, J. A gathering of vultures, the 'legion of decency' and bilingual education in the USA. *NABE Journal,* 1976, *2(2),* 13-16. (c)

Fishman, J. The social science perspective. In Center for Applied Linguistics (ed.), *Bilingual education: Current perspectives (Vol. 1).* Arlington, Virginia: CAL, 1977. (a)

Fishman, J. Language and ethnicity. In H. Giles (ed.), *Language, ethnicity and intergroup relations.* London: Academic Press, 1977. (b)

Fishman, J. Comments (on the *New York Times* article on 'bilingual danger'). *TESOL Quarterly,* 1977, *11,* 109-11. (c)

Fishman, J. (ed.) Sociology of Yiddish. *International Journal of the Sociology of Language,* 1980, *24.* (a)

Fishman, J. Minority language maintenance and the ethnic mother-tongue school. *Modern Language Journal,* 1980, *64,* 167-72. (b)

Fishman, J. Language maintenance. In S. Thernstrom, A. Orlov & O. Handlin (eds), *Harvard encyclopedia of American ethnic groups.* Cambridge, Massachusetts: Harvard University Press, 1980. (c)

Fishman, J. Bilingualism and biculturism as individual and as societal phenomena. *Journal of Multilingual and Multicultural Development,* 1980, *1,* 3-15. (d)

Fishman, J. (ed.) The sociology of Jewish languages. *International Journal of the Sociology of Language,* 1981, *30.*

Fishman, J. Progress in language planning: A few concluding sentiments. In J. Cobarrubias & J. Fishman (eds), *Progress in language planning.* Berlin: Mouton, 1983. (a)

Fishman, J. The rise and fall of the 'ethnic revival' in the USA. *Journal of Intercultural Studies,* 1983, *4(3),* 5-46. (b)

Fishman, J. Studies of language as an aspect of ethnicity and nationalism. (A bibliographic introduction.) *Sociolinguistics Newsletter,* 1984, *14(2),* 1-6.

Fishman, J., Ferguson, C. & Das Gupta, J. (eds) *Language problems of developing nations.* New York: Wiley, 1968.

Fishman, J. & Fishman, D. Yiddish in Israel: A case study of efforts to revise a monocentric language policy. In J. Fishman (ed.), *Advances in the study of societal multilingualism.* The Hague: Mouton, 1978.

Flather, P. & Wilby, P. 'Do not publish' row on school race research. *The Sunday Times,* 8 April 1984.

Fleming, J. Multiculturalism. *Canadian Ethnic Studies Association Bulletin,* 1982, *9(3),* 9.

Flugel, J. Esperanto and the international language movement. *International Journal of Psychoanalysis,* 1925, *6.*

Forster, P. *The Esperanto movement.* Berlin: Mouton, 1982.

Foster, C. (ed.) *Nations without a state: Ethnic minorities in Western Europe.* New York: Praeger, 1980.

Francis, E. The nature of the ethnic group. *American Journal of Sociology,* 1947, *52,* 393-400.

Francis, E. *Interethnic relations.* New York: Elsevier, 1976.

Fraser, B. Some 'unexpected' reactions to various American-English dialects. In R. Shuy & R. Fasold (eds), *Language attitudes.* Washington DC: Georgetown University Press, 1973.

Fullerton, R. The place of Irish in Ireland's education. *Irish Educational Review,* 1912, *5,* 456-66.

Furnivall, J. *Netherlands India: A study of plural economy.* Cambridge: Cambridge University Press, 1939 (reprinted, 1967).

Gaarder, A. Organization of the bilingual school. *Journal of Social Issues,* 1967, *23(2),* 110–20.

Gaarder, A. The first 76 bilingual education projects. In J. Alatis (ed.), *Georgetown University Round Table on languages and linguistics.* Washington DC: Georgetown University Press, 1970.

Gaarder, A. Review of *Bilingual education: Theories and issues* (C. Paulston). *Modern Language Journal,* 1981, *65,* 205–6.

Gaelic League. *You may revive the Gaelic language.* Dublin: Gaelic League, 1937.

Gair, J. Sinhala and English: The effects of a language act. *Language Problems and Language Planning,* 1983, *7,* 43–59.

Gans, H. Symbolic ethnicity: The future of ethnic groups and cultures in America. *Ethnic and Racial Studies,* 1979, *2,* 1–20.

Gardner, R. Social psychological aspects of second-language acquisition. In H. Giles & R. St. Clair (eds), *Language and social psychology.* Oxford: Basil Blackwell, 1979.

Gardner, R. Language attitudes and language learning. In E. Ryan & H. Giles (eds), *Attitudes towards language variation.* London: Edward Arnold, 1982.

Gardner, R. & Lambert, W. *Attitudes and motivation in second-language learning.* Rowley, Massachusetts: Newbury House, 1972.

Garvin, P. & Mathiot, M. The urbanization of the Guaraní language: A problem in language and culture. In J. Fishman (ed.), *Readings in the sociology of language.* The Hague: Mouton, 1968.

Geertz, C. Distinguished lecture: Anti anti-relativism. *American Anthropologist,* 1984, *86,* 263–78.

Gellner, E. *Thought and change.* London: Weidenfeld & Nicolson, 1964.

Gellner, E. The new idealism: Cause and meaning in the social sciences. In I. Lakatos & A. Musgrave (eds), *Problems in the philosophy of science.* Amsterdam: North-Holland, 1968.

Gellner, E. *Nations and nationalism.* Oxford: Basil Blackwell, 1983.

Genesee, F. Bilingualism and biliteracy: A study of cross-cultural contact in a bilingual community. In J. Edwards (ed.), *The social psychology of reading.* Silver Spring, Maryland: Institute of Modern Languages, 1981. (a)

Genesee, F. Cognitive and social consequences of bilingualism. In R. Gardner & R. Kalin (eds), *A Canadian social psychology of ethnic relations.* Toronto: Methuen, 1981. (b)

Genesee, F. Bilingual education of majority-language children: The immersion experiments in review. *Applied Psycholinguistics,* 1983, *4,* 1–46.

George, K. The problems involved in reviving Cornish. Paper to the Conference on The Celtic World Today, London, 1984.

Ghosh, R. Implementation of the three-language formula in India: Some issues in multilingualism and language education. Paper to the Seventh World Congress of Applied Linguistics, Brussels, 1984.

Ghrib-Maamouri, E. The introduction of Arabic as a medium of instruction in Tunisia. Paper to the Seventh World Congress of Applied Linguistics, Brussels, 1984.

Gibbons, J. The issue of the language of instruction in the lower forms of Hong Kong secondary schools. *Journal of Multilingual and Multicultural Development,* 1982, *3,* 117–28.

Gibbons, J. Attitudes towards languages and code-mixing in Hong Kong. *Journal of*

Multilingual and Multicultural Development, 1983, *4*, 129–48.

Giglioli, P. Introduction. In P. Giglioli (ed.), *Language and social context*. Harmondsworth, Middlesex: Penguin, 1973.

Giles, H. Evaluative reactions to accents. *Educational Review*, 1970, *22*, 211–27.

Giles, H. Patterns of evaluation in reactions to RP, South Welsh and Somerset accented speech. *British Journal of Social and Clinical Psychology*, 1971, *10*, 280–1.

Giles, H. Communicative effectiveness as a function of accented speech. *Speech Monographs*, 1973, *40*, 330–1.

Giles, H. Sociolinguistics and social psychology: An introductory essay. In H. Giles & R. St. Clair (eds), *Language and social psychology*. Oxford: Basil Blackwell, 1979. (a)

Giles, H. Ethnicity markers in speech. In K. Scherer & H. Giles (eds), *Social markers in speech*. Cambridge: Cambridge University Press, 1979. (b)

Giles, H., Bourhis, R. & Davies, A. Prestige speech styles: The imposed norm and inherent value hypotheses. In W. McCormack & S. Wurm (eds), *Language and society: Anthropological issues*. The Hague: Mouton, 1979.

Giles, H., Bourhis, R. & Taylor, D. Towards a theory of language in ethnic group relations. In H. Giles (ed.), *Language, ethnicity and intergroup relations*. London: Academic Press, 1977.

Giles, H., Bourhis, R., Trudgill, P. & Lewis, A. The imposed norm hypothesis: A validation. *Quarterly Journal of Speech*, 1974, *60*, 405–10.

Giles, H. & Byrne, J. An intergroup approach to second-language acquisition. *Journal of Multilingual and Multicultural Development*, 1982, *3*, 17–40.

Giles, H. & Edwards, J. (eds) Language attitudes in multilingual settings. *Journal of Multilingual and Multicultural Development*, 1983, *4(2/3)*.

Giles, H., Hewstone, M. & Ball, P. Language attitudes in multilingual settings: Prologue with priorities. *Journal of Multilingual and Multicultural Development*, 1983, *4*, 81–100.

Giles, H. & Johnson, P. The role of language in ethnic-group relations. In J. Turner & H. Giles (eds), *Intergroup behaviour*. Oxford: Basil Blackwell, 1981.

Giles, H. & Powesland, P. *Speech style and social evaluation*. London: Academic Press, 1975.

Giles, H. & Smith, P. Accommodation theory: Optimal levels of convergence. In H. Giles & R. St. Clair (eds), *Language and social psychology*. Oxford: Basil Blackwell, 1979.

Giles, H., Smith, P. & Robinson, P. Social psychological perspectives on language: Prologue. In H. Giles, P. Robinson & P. Smith (eds), *Language: Social psychological perspectives*. Oxford: Pergamon, 1980.

Glazer, N. Toward a sociology of small ethnic groups. A discourse and discussion. *Canadian Ethnic Studies*, 1980, *12(2)*, 1–16.

Glazer, N. *Beyond the melting pot* twenty years after. *Journal of American Ethnic History*, 1981, *1*, 43–55.

Glazer, N. Introduction. In N. Glazer & K. Young (eds), *Ethnic pluralism and public policy*. London: Heinemann, 1983.

Glazer, N. & Moynihan, D. *Beyond the melting pot*. Cambridge, Massachusetts: MIT Press, 1963.

Gleason, P. Confusion compounded: The melting pot in the 1960s and 1970s. *Ethnicity*, 1979, *6*, 10–20.

Gleason, P. American identity and Americanization. In S. Thernstrom, A. Orlov &

O. Handlin (eds), *Harvard encyclopedia of American ethnic groups*. Cambridge, Massachusetts: Harvard University Press, 1980.

Gleason, P. Pluralism and assimilation: A conceptual history. In J. Edwards (ed.), *Linguistic minorities, policies and pluralism*. London: Academic Press, 1984.

Gleitman, L. & Gleitman, H. *Phrase and paraphrase*. New York: Norton, 1970.

Glock, N. Extending the use of Saramaccan in Suriname. *Journal of Multilingual and Multicultural Development*, 1983, *4*, 349–60.

Gonzalez, A. Pilipino in the year 2000. In B. Sibayan & A. Gonzalez (eds), *Language planning and the building of a national language*. Manila: Linguistic Society of the Philippines, 1977.

Gonzalez, A. *Language and nationalism: The Philippine experience thus far*. Manila: Ateneo de Manila University Press, 1980.

Gonzalez, A. Language policy and language-in-education policy in the Philippines. In R. Kaplan, A. d'Anglejan, J. Cowan, B. Kachru & G. Tucker (eds), *Annual review of applied linguistics 1981*. Rowley, Massachusetts: Newbury House, 1982.

González, J. Letter. *Harpers*, 1979, *258(1547)*, 6.

Goodman, E. World state and world language. In J. Fishman (ed.), *Readings in the sociology of language*. The Hague: Mouton, 1968.

Gordon, J. *The French language and national identity*. The Hague: Mouton, 1978.

Gordon, M. *Assimilation in American life*. New York: Oxford University Press, 1964.

Gordon, M. *Human nature, class and ethnicity*. New York: Oxford University Press, 1978.

Gordon, M. Models of pluralism: The new American dilemma. *Annals of the American Academy of Political and Social Science*, 1981, *454*, 178–88.

Gorter, D. Some recent developments in official language planning in Friesland. In E. Haugen, J. McClure & D. Thomson (eds), *Minority languages today*. Edinburgh: Edinburgh University Press, 1981.

Goyvaerts, D., Semikenke, M. & Naeyaert, D. Language and education policy in the multilingual city of Bukavu. *Journal of Multilingual and Multicultural Development*, 1983, *4*, 47–62.

Grafton, A. Wilhelm von Humboldt. *American Scholar*, 1981, *50*, 371–81.

Grant, N. The education of linguistic minorities in the USSR. In J. Megarry, S. Nisbet & E. Hoyle (eds), *World yearbook of education 1981: Education of minorities*. London: Kogan Page, 1981.

Gray, T. Reaganomics and education. *Linguistic Reporter*, 1982, *24(6)*. (a)

Gray, T. And debate goes on:... *Linguistic Reporter*, 1982, *24(7)*. (b)

Gray, T. Bilingual program? What's that? *Linguistic Reporter*, 1982, *24(9)*. (c)

Great Britain: Department of Education and Science. *A language for life* (The Bullock Report). London: HMSO, 1975.

Greeley, A. *Why can't they be like us?* New York: Dutton, 1971.

Greeley, A. *Ethnicity in the United States*. New York: Wiley, 1974.

Greeley, A. After Ellis Island. *Harpers*, 1978, *257(1542)*, 27–30.

Greeley, A. The persistence of diversity. *Antioch Review*, 1981, *39*, 141–55.

Greene, D. The Atlantic group: Neo-Celtic and Faroese. In E. Haugen, J. McClure & D. Thomson (eds), *Minority languages today*. Edinburgh: Edinburgh University Press, 1981.

Greenland, J. Minority group interests within nation-building policies in Africa. In J. Megarry, S. Nisbet & E. Hoyle (eds), *World yearbook of education 1981: Education of minorities*. London: Kogan Page, 1981.

Greenwood, D. Continuity in change: Spanish Basque ethnicity as a historical process.

In M. Esman (ed.), *Ethnic conflict in the Western world*. Ithaca, New York: Cornell University Press, 1977.

Gregor, D. *Celtic: A comparative study*. New York: Oleander, 1980.

Grigulevich, I. & Kozlov, S. *Ethnocultural processes and national problems in the modern world*. Moscow: Progress, 1981.

Grosjean, F. *Life with two languages: An introduction to bilingualism*. Cambridge, Massachusetts: Harvard University Press, 1982.

Guitarte, G. & Torres-Quintero, R. Linguistic correctness and the role of the academies in Latin America. In J. Fishman (ed.), *Advances in language planning*. The Hague: Mouton, 1974.

Gullick, C. Language and sentiment in Malta. *New Community*, 1974, *3*, 92–103.

Gumperz, J. (ed.) *Language and social identity*. Cambridge: Cambridge University Press, 1982. (a)

Gumperz, J. *Discourse stategies*. Cambridge: Cambridge University Press, 1982. (b)

Haarmann, H. *Soziologie der Kleinen Sprachen Europas*. Hamburg: Helmut Buske Verlag, 1973.

Haarmann, H. *Soziologie und Politik der Sprachen Europas*. Munich: Deutschen Taschenbuch, 1975.

Haarmann, J. *Quantitative Aspekte des Multilingualismus: Studien zur Gruppenmehrsprachigkeit ethnischer Minderheiten in der Sowjetunion*. Hamburg: Helmut Buske Verlag, 1979.

Hall, R. Pidgins and creoles as standard languages. In J. Pride & J. Holmes (eds), *Sociolinguistics*. Harmondsworth, Middlesex: Penguin, 1972.

Hall, R. *External history of the Romance languages*. New York: Elsevier, 1974.

Halliday, M. The users and uses of language. In J. Fishman (ed.), *Readings in the sociology of language*. The Hague: Mouton, 1968.

Halls, W. Belgium: A case study in educational regionalism. *Comparative Education*, 1983, *19*, 169–77.

Hamers, J. The language question in Belgium. *Language and Society*, 1981, 5, 17–20.

Hamp, E. Problems of multilingualism in small linguistic communities. In J. Alatis (ed.), *Georgetown University Round Table on languages and linguistics*. Washington DC: Georgetown University Press, 1978.

Hansen, M. The third generation in America. *Commentary*, 1952, *14*, 492–500.

Harries, L. Swahili in modern East Africa. In J. Fishman, C. Ferguson & J. Das Gupta (eds), *Language problems of developing nations*. New York: Wiley, 1968.

Harries, L. The nationalization of Swahili in Kenya. *Language in Society*, 1976, 5, 153–64.

Harris, J. *Spoken Irish in primary schools*. Dublin: Linguistics Institute, 1984.

Harris, T. (ed.) Sociology of Judezmo: The language of the eastern Sephardim. *International Journal of the Sociology of Language*, 1982, 37.

Harrison, G. Mandarin and the mandarins: Language policy and the media in Singapore. *Journal of Multilingual and Multicultural Development*, 1980, *1*, 175–80.

Harrison, M. The revival of Irish. *Secondary Teacher*, 1976, *6(1)*, 34–5.

Haugen, E. Dialect, language, nation. *American Anthropologist*, 1966, 68, 922–35. (a)

Haugen, E. *Language conflict and language planning: The case of modern Norwegian*. Cambridge, Massachusetts: Harvard University Press, 1966. (b)

Haugen, E. *The ecology of language*. Stanford: Stanford University Press, 1972.

Haugen, E. Bilingualism in retrospect: A personal view. In J. Alatis (ed.), *Georgetown University Round Table on languages and linguistics*. Washington DC: Georgetown University Press, 1978.

Haugen, E. The implementation of corpus planning: Theory and practice. In J. Cobarrubias & J. Fishman (eds), *Progress in language planning*. Berlin: Mouton, 1983.

Haugen, E., McClure, J. & Thomson, D. (eds) *Minority languages today*. Edinburgh: Edinburgh University Press, 1981.

Hauptfleisch, T. *Language loyalty in South Africa: Vol. 1: Blingual policy in South Africa: Opinions of White adults in urban areas*. Pretoria: South African Human Sciences Research Council, 1977.

Hauptfleisch, T. (ed.) *Literacy in South Africa*. Pretoria: South African Human Sciences Research Council, 1978.

Hayakawa, S. Pay for your own tongue. *Maclean's*, 1980, *93(29)*, 12.

Heath, S. A national language academy? Debate in the new nation. *International Journal of the Sociology of Language*, 1977, *11*, 9–43.

Hechter, M. *Internal colonialism: The Celtic fringe in British national development, 1530–1966*. London: Routledge & Kegan Paul, 1975.

Heine, B. *Sprache, Gesellschaft und Kommunikation in Afrika*. Munich: Weltforum, 1979.

Hélias, P. *Le cheval d'orgueil: Mémoires d'un breton du pays bigouden*. Paris: Plon, 1975.

Henk, M., Tomasi, S. & Baroni, G. *Pieces of a dream*. New York: Center for Migration Studies, 1972.

Héraud, G. *Peuples et langues d'Europe*. Paris: Presses d'Europe, 1968.

Héraud, G. *L'Europe des ethnies*. Paris: Presses d'Europe, 1974.

Héraud, G. Le statut des langues dans les différents états et en particulier en Europe. *Annales de la Faculté de Droit de l'Université de Toulon et du Var*, 1979–82, *5*, 81–106.

Herman, S. Explorations in the social psychology of language choice. *Human Relations*, 1961, *14*, 149–64.

Hernández-Chávez, E. Language maintenance, bilingual education, and philosophies of bilingualism in the United States. In J. Alatis (ed.), *Georgetown University Round Table on languages and linguistics*. Washington DC: Georgetown University Press, 1978.

Hertz, F. *Nationality in history and politics*. New York: Oxford University Press, 1944.

Hertzler, J. Toward a sociology of language. *Social Forces*, 1953, *32*, 109–19.

Hertzler, J. *The sociology of language*. New York: Random House, 1965.

Higham, J. *Send these to me*. New York: Atheneum, 1975.

Higham, J. Current trends in the study of ethnicity in the United States. *Journal of American Ethnic History*, 1982, 2, 5–15.

Hill, J. & Coombs, D. The vernacular remodelling of national and international languages. *Applied Linguistics*, 1982, *3*, 224–34.

Hinton, P. Where have the new ethnicists gone wrong? *Australian and New Zealand Journal of Sociology*, 1981, *17*, 14–19.

Hobsbawm, E. & Ranger, T. (eds) *The invention of tradition*. Cambridge: Cambridge University Press, 1983.

Hoffmann, F. *Sprachen in Luxemburg*. Luxemburg: Institut Grand-Ducal, 1979.

Hoffmann, F. Triglossia in Luxemburg. In E. Haugen, J. McClure & D. Thomson (eds), *Minority languages today*. Edinburgh: Edinburgh University Press, 1981.

Homans, G. *Social behaviour*. New York: Harcourt, Brace & World, 1961.

Honey, J. *The language trap*. Kenton, Middlesex: National Council for Educational Standards, 1983.

Hulbert, J. *Dictionaries: British and American*. London: André Deutsch, 1968.

Husband, C. & Saifullah Khan, V. The viability of ethnolinguistic vitality: Some creative doubts. *Journal of Multilingual and Multicultural Development*, 1982, *3*, 193–205.

Hyde, D. A plea for the Irish language. *Dublin University Review*, 1886, 2, 666-76.
Hyde, D. The necessity for de-anglicising Ireland. In C. Duffy, G. Sigerson & D. Hyde (eds), *The revival of Irish literature*. London: T. Fisher Unwin, 1894.
Hymes, D. Speech and language: On the origins and foundations of inequality among speakers. In E. Haugen & M. Bloomfield (eds), *Language as a human problem*. New York: Norton, 1974.
Ireland. *The restoration of the Irish language*. Dublin: Government Stationery Office, 1965.
Ireland. *White paper on the restoration of the Irish language: Progress report for the period ended 31 March, 1966*. Dublin: Government Stationery Office, 1966.
Ireland. *White paper on the restoration of the Irish language: Progress report for the period ended 31 March, 1968*. Dublin: Government Stationery Office, 1969.
Ireland. *White paper on educational development*. Dublin: Government Stationery Office, 1980.
Irish National Teachers' Organization. *Report of committee of inquiry into the use of Irish as a teaching medium to children whose home language is English*. Dublin: INTO, 1942.
Irish National Teachers' Organization. *A plan for education*. Dublin: INTO, 1947.
Irwin, R. Judgements of vocal quality, speech fluency, and confidence of southern Black and White students. *Language and Speech*, 1977, 20, 261-6.
Isaacs, H. The new pluralists. *Commentary*, 1972, 53(3), 75-9.
Isajiw, W. Definitions of ethnicity. In J. Goldstein & R. Bienvenue (eds), *Ethnicity and ethnic relations in Canada*. Toronto: Butterworth, 1980.
Issawi, C. The struggle for linguistic hegemony, 1780-1980. *American Scholar*, 1981, 50, 382-7.
Jaakkola, M. Diglossia and bilingualism among two minorities in Sweden. *International Journal of the Sociology of Language*, 1976, 10, 67-84.
Jacob, H. *A planned auxiliary language*. London: Dobson, 1947.
Jakob, N. Sprachplanung in einer komplexen Diglossiesituation dargestellt am Beispiel Luxemburg. *Language Problems and Language Planning*, 1981, 5, 153-74.
Jakobson, R. The beginning of national self-determination in Europe. In J. Fishman (ed.), *Readings in the sociology of language*. The Hague: Mouton, 1968.
James, A. & Jeffcoate, R. (eds) *The school in the multicultural society*. London: Harper & Row, 1981.
Jaspars, J. & Warnaen, S. Intergroup relations, ethnic identity and self-evaluation in Indonesia. In H. Tajfel (ed.), *Social identity and intergroup relations*. Cambridge: Cambridge University Press, 1982.
Jeffcoate, R. Ideologies and multicultural education. In M. Craft (ed.), *Education and cultural pluralism*. London: Falmer, 1984.
Jespersen, O. *Language: Its nature, development and origin*. London: Allen & Unwin, 1922.
Jespersen, O. *An international language*. London: Allen & Unwin, 1928.
Jespersen, O. *Mankind, nation and individual*. London: Allen & Unwin, 1946.
Johnson, P. *Enemies of society*. London: Weidenfeld & Nicolson, 1977.
Johnson, P., Giles, H. & Bourhis, R. The viability of ethnolinguistic vitality: A reply. *Journal of Multilingual and Multicultural Development*, 1983, 4, 255-69.
Jones, B. Welsh: Linguistic conservation and shifting bilingualism. In E. Haugen, J. McClure & D. Thomson (eds), *Minority languages today*. Edinburgh: Edinburgh University Press, 1981.
Jones, H. *Wales/Ireland: A TV contrast*. Dublin: Conradh na Gaeilge, 1974.

Kachru, B. English in south Asia. In J. Fishman (ed.), *Advances in the study of societal multilingualism*. The Hague: Mouton, 1978.

Kahane, H. & Kahane, R. Decline and survival of western prestige languages. *Language*, 1979, *55*, 183–98.

Kallen, H. Democracy versus the melting pot. *The Nation*, 18 and 25 February 1915.

Kallen, H. *Culture and democracy in the United States*. New York: Boni & Liveright, 1924.

Kallen, H. *Cultural pluralism and the American idea*. Philadelphia: University of Pennsylvania press, 1956.

Kanuri, J. Situation and problems of national language in Kenya. Paper to the Seventh World Congress of Applied Linguistics, Brussels, 1984.

Kaplan, R. The language situation in New Zealand. *Linguistic Reporter*, 1981, *23(9)*.

Kaplan, R. The language situation in the Philippines. *Linguistic Reporter*, 1982, *24(5)*.

Kaplan, R. & Tse, J. The language situation in Taiwan. *Linguistic Reporter*, 1982, *25(2)*.

Kavanagh, P. The bones of the dead. *The Bell*, 1948, *15(4)*, 62–4.

Kearney, R. Language and the rise of Tamil separatism in Sri Lanka. Unpublished paper, 1976.

Kedourie, E. *Nationalism*. London: Hutchinson, 1961.

Kellog, F. The structure of Romanian nationalism. *Canadian Review of Studies in Nationalism*, 1984, *11*, 21–50.

Kenner, H. The word police. *Harpers*, 1982, *264(1585)*, 68–71.

Keskitalo, A. The status of the Sámi language. In E. Haugen, J. McClure & D. Thomson (eds), *Minority languages today*. Edinburgh: Edinburgh University Press, 1981.

Khleif, B. Ethnic awakening in the first world: The case of Wales. In G. Williams (ed.), *Social and cultural change in contemporary Wales*. London: Routledge & Kegan Paul, 1978.

Khleif, B. *Language, ethnicity and education in Wales*. Berlin: Mouton, 1980.

Khubchandani, L. Language ideology and language development. *International Journal of the Sociology of Language*, 1977, *13*, 33–51.

Khubchandani, L. Distribution of contact languages in India: A study of the 1961 bilingualism returns. In J. Fishman (ed.), *Advances in the study of societal multilingualism*. The Hague: Mouton, 1978.

Khubchandani, L. Language planning processes for pluralistic societies: A critical review of the Indian scene. *Language Problems and Language Planning*, 1979, *2*, 141–61.

Khubchandani, L. *Plural languages, plural cultures*. Honolulu: University of Hawaii Press, 1983.

Khubchandani, L. Sociolinguistics in India: The decade past, the decade to come. *International Journal of the Sociology of Language*, 1984, *45*, 47–64.

Kiberd, D. Synge and the Irish language. London: Macmillan, 1979.

Kiberd, D. The perils of nostalgia: A critique of the revival. In P. Connolly (ed.), *Literature and the changing Ireland*. Gerrard's Cross, Buckinghamshire: Colin Smythe, 1980.

Kiberd, D. Editorial: The Irish language. *The Crane Bag*, 1981, *5(2)*, 4–6.

King, C. Devil's advocates needed: A mini-editorial. *Modern Language Journal*, 1979, *63*, 291.

Kirp, D. Elusive equality: Race, ethnicity, and education in the American experience. In N. Glazer & K. Young (eds), *Ethnic pluralism and public policy*. London: Heinemann, 1983.

Kjolseth, R. Bilingual education in the United States: For assimilation or pluralism?

In B. Spolsky (ed.), *The language education of minority children*. Rowley, Massachusetts: Newbury House, 1972.

Kloss, H. Umriss eines Forschungsprogrammes zum Thema 'Sprachentod'. *International Journal of the Sociology of Language*, 1984, *45*, 65–76.

Koefoed, G., Seuren, P. & Wekker, H. Sranan after independence: A case study of recent superstrate influence. Paper to the Seventh World Congress of Applied Linguistics, Brussels, 1984.

Kohn, H. *The idea of nationalism: A study in its origins and background*. New York: Macmillan, 1961.

Kohn, H. *Prelude to nation-states: The French and German experience, 1789–1815.* Princeton, New Jersey: Van Nostrand, 1967.

Kolack, S. Lowell, an immigrant city: The old and the new. In R. Bryce-Laporte (ed.), *Sourcebook on the new immigration*. New Brunswick, New Jersey: Transaction, 1980.

Kopan, A. Melting pot: Myth or reality? In E. Epps (ed.), *Cultural pluralism*. Berkeley: McCutchan, 1974.

Korhonen, O. Linguistic and cultural diversity among the Saamis and the development of Standard Saamish. *International Journal of the Sociology of Language*, 1976, *10*, 51–66.

Kravetz, N. Education of ethnic and national minorities in the USSR: A report on current developments. *Comparative Education*, 1980, *16*, 13–23.

Kreindler, I. The changing status of Russian in the Soviet Union. *International Journal of the Sociology of Language*, 1982, *33*, 7–39.

Krejčí, J. & Velímský, V. *Ethnic and political nations in Europe*. London: Croom Helm, 1981.

Krishnamurti, B. Problems of language standardization in India. In W. McCormack & S. Wurm (eds), *Language and society: Anthropological issues*. The Hague: Mouton, 1979.

Krug, M. *The melting of the ethnics*. Bloomington, Indiana: Phil Delta Kappa Educational Foundation, 1976.

Kumanëv, V. Universal literacy of the formerly backward peoples of the Soviet Union: A factor of their social self-awareness. In W. McCormack & S. Wurm (eds), *Language and society: Anthropological issues*. The Hague: Mouton, 1979.

Kuo, E. Language planning in Singapore. *Language Planning Newsletter*, 1980, *6(2)*.

Kuo, E. Mass media and language planning: Singapore's 'Speak Mandarin' campaign. *Journal of Communication*, 1984, *34(2)*, 24–35.

Labov, W. *The social stratification of English in New York City*. Washington DC: Center for Applied Linguistics, 1966.

Labov, W. *Sociolinguistic patterns*. Philadelphia: University of Pennsylvania Press, 1972.

Labov, W. *Language in the inner city*. Philadelphia: University of Pennsylvania Press, 1976.

Laitin, D. *Politics, language and thought: The Somali experience*. Chicago: University of Chicago Press, 1977.

Lambert, R. & Curtis, J. Opposition to multiculturalism among Quebecois and English-Canadians. *Canadian Review of Sociology and Anthropology*, 1983, *20*, 193–207.

Lambert, R. & Freed, B. (eds) *The loss of language skills*. Rowley, Massachusetts: Newbury House, 1982.

Lambert, W. A social psychology of bilingualism. *Journal of Social Issues*, 1967, *23(2)*, 91–109.

Lambert, W., Hodgson, R., Gardner, R. & Fillenbaum, S. Evaluational reactions to

spoken languages. *Journal of Abnormal and Social Psychology*, 1960, *60*, 44–51.
Langacker, R. An initial look at language. In R. Abrahams & R. Troike (eds), *Language and cultural diversity in American education*. Englewood Cliffs, New Jersey: Prentice-Hall, 1972.
Lanham, L. & MacDonald, C. *The standard in South African English and its social history*. Heidelberg: Gross, 1979.
Lastra de Suárez, Y. Bilingualism in Mexico. In J. Alatis (ed.), *Georgetown University Round Table on languages and linguistics*. Washington DC: Georgetown University Press, 1978.
Laurén, C. Bilingual Finland. *Language and Society*, 1980, *3*, 7–10.
Lee, J. *The modernisation of Irish society 1848–1918*. Dublin: Gill & Macmillan, 1973.
Lehmann, W. (ed.) *Language and linguistics in the People's Republic of China*. Austin: University of Texas Press, 1975.
Lemaire, H. Franco-American efforts on behalf of the French language in New England. In J. Fishman (ed.), *Language loyalty in the United States*. The Hague: Mouton, 1966.
Lenin, V. *Critical remarks on the national question*. Moscow: Progress, 1951.
Lenneberg, E. *Biological foundations of language*. New York: Wiley, 1967.
LePage, R. *The national language question*. London: Oxford University Press, 1964.
LePage, R. Retrospect and prognosis in Malaysia and Singapore. *International Journal of the Sociology of Language*, 1984, *45*, 113–26.
Lewis, E. Migration and language in the USSR. *International Migration Review*, 1971, *5*, 147–79.
Lewis, E. Bilingualism and blingual education: The ancient world to the Renaissance. In J. Fishman (ed.), *Bilingual education: An international sociological perspective*. Rowley, Massachusetts: Newbury House, 1976.
Lewis, E. The morality of bilingual education. In J. Alatis (ed.), *Georgetown University Round Table on languages and linguistics*. Washington DC: Georgetown University Press, 1978.
Lewis, E. *Bilingualism and bilingual education: A comparative study*. Albuquerque: University of New Mexico Press, 1980.
Lewis, E. Implementation of language planning in the Soviet Union. In J. Cobarrubias & J. Fishman (eds), *Progress in language planning*. Berlin: Mouton, 1983.
Lieberman, E. Esperanto and trans-national identity: The case of Dr Zamenhof. *International Journal of the Sociology of Language*, 1979, *20*, 89–107.
Liebkind, K. The Swedish-speaking Finns: A case study of ethnolinguistic identity. In H. Tajfel (ed.), *Social identity and intergroup relations*. Cambridge: Cambridge University Press, 1982.
Light, T. Bilingualism and standard language in the People's Republic of China. In J. Alatis (ed.), *Georgetown University Round Table on languages and linguistics*. Washington DC: Georgetown University Press, 1980.
Lindstrom, L. Say what? Language and political boundaries on Tanna (Vanuatu). *Anthropological Linguistics*, 1983, *25*, 387–403.
Linguistic Minorities Project. *Linguistic minorities in England*. London: Institute of Education, 1983.
Lipkin, J. & Lawson, R. Perspectives on multiculturalism in North America: Minority education in Toronto and Montreal. *Compare*, 1978, *3*, 31–44.
Little, A. *Educational policies for multi-racial areas*. London: Goldsmith's College, 1978.
Llamzon, T. A requiem for Pilipino. In B. Sibayan & A. Gonzalez (eds), *Language*

planning and the building of a national language. Manila: Linguistic Society of the Philippines, 1977.

Llobera, J. The idea of *Volksgeist* in the formation of Catalan nationalist ideology. *Ethnic and Racial Studies,* 1983, 6, 332–50.

Lorwin, V. Linguistic pluralism and political tension in modern Belgium. In J. Fishman (ed.), *Advances in the sociology of language.* The Hague: Mouton, 1972.

Lowth, R. *A short introduction to English grammar.* Menston, Yorkshire: Scholar Press, 1967 (facsimile reprint of 1762 edition).

Lowy, E., Fishman J., Gertner, M., Gottesman, I. & Milán, W. Ethnic activists view the ethnic revival and its language consequences: An interview study of three American ethnolinguistic minorities. *Journal of Multilingual and Multicultural Development,* 1983, 4, 237–54.

Lupul, M. Multiculturalism and educational policies in Canada. *Compare,* 1978, 8, 45–9.

Luzares, C. Languages-in-education in the Philippines. In R. Kaplan, A. d'Anglejan, J. Cowan, B. Kachru & G. Tucker (eds), *Annual review of applied linguistics 1981.* Rowley, Massachuseets: Newbury House, 1982.

Lynch, J. (ed.) *Teaching in the multicultural school.* London: Ward Lock, 1981.

Lynch, J. *The multicultural curriculum.* London: Batsford, 1983.

Lyons, F. *Ireland since the famine.* London: Weidenfeld & Nicolson, 1971.

Mackey, W. A typology of bilingual education. *Foreign Language Annals,* 1970, 3, 596–608.

Mackey, W. The importation of bilingual education models. In J. Alatis (ed.), *Georgetown University Round Table on languages and linguistics.* Washington DC: Georgetown University Press, 1978.

Mackey, W. Safeguarding language in schools. *Language and Society,* 1981, 4, 10–14.

Mackey, W. Bilingual education and its social implications. In J. Edwards (ed.), *Linguistic minorities, policies and pluralism.* London: Academic Press, 1984.

MacKinnon, K. *The lion's tongue.* Inverness: Club Leabhar, 1974.

MacKinnon, K. *Language, education and social processes in a Gaelic community.* London: Routledge & Kegan Paul, 1977.

MacKinnon, K. Development of Gaelic in the Scottish communities, 1971 to 1981. Paper to the Conference on The Celtic World Today, London, 1984.

Mac Lochlainn, A. The racism of Thomas Davis: Root and branch. *Journal of Irish Literature,* 1976, 5(2), 112–22.

Mac Lochlainn, A. Gael and peasant: A case of mistaken identity? In D. Casey & R. Rhodes (eds), *Views of the Irish peasantry 1800–1916.* Hamden, Connecticut: Archon, 1977.

Macnamara, J. *Bilingualism and primary education: A study of Irish experience.* Edinburgh: Edinburgh University Press, 1966.

Macnamara, J. Successes and failures in the movement for the restoration of Irish. In J. Rubin & B. Jernudd (eds), *Can language be planned?* Honolulu: East-West Center Press, 1971.

Macnamara, J. Attitudes and learning a second language. In R. Shuy & R. Fasold (eds), *Language attitudes.* Washington DC: Georgetown University Press, 1973.

Macnamara, J. & Edwards, J. *Attitudes to learning French in the English-speaking schools of Quebec.* Quebec: Quebec Official Publisher, 1973.

Magocsi, P. The language question as a factor in the national movement. In A. Markovits & F. Sysyn (eds), *Nationbuilding and the politics of nationalism: Essays on Austrian Galicia.* Cambridge, Massachusetts: Harvard University Press, 1982.

Malone, C. English literature in Ireland: A comment on school courses. *Catholic Bulletin*, 1935, *25*, 199–204.

Mann, A. *The one and the many: Reflections on the American identity.* Chicago: University of Chicago Press, 1979.

Mansour, G. The dynamics of multilingualism: The case of Senegal. *Journal of Multilingual and Multicultural Development*, 1980, *1*, 273–93.

Martin, H. & Pelletier, C. *Vocabulaire de la téléphonie.* Québec: Gouvernement du Québec, 1984.

Martin-Jones, M. & Romaine, S. Semilingualism: A half-baked theory of communicative competence. Paper to the Fourth Nordic Symposium on Bilingualism, Uppsala, 1984.

Marx, K. & Engels, F. *Ireland and the Irish question.* London: Lawrence Wishart, 1978.

Mascarenhas, A. The news in many tongues by satellite and bicycle. *The Sunday Times*, 3 April 1983.

Matthews, R. Bilingualism in a Swiss canton: Language choice in Ticino. In W. Mackey & J. Ornstein (eds), *Sociolinguistic studies in language contact.* The Hague: Mouton, 1979.

Maurud, O. Reciprocal comprehension of neighbour languages in Scandinavia. *Scandinavian Journal of Educational Research*, 1976, *20(2)*, 49–72.

McDavid, R. The sociology of language. In A. Marckwardt (ed.), *Linguistics in school programs.* Chicago: University of Chicago Press, 1970.

McEachran, F. *The life and philosophy of Johann Gottfried Herder.* Oxford: Clarendon Press, 1939.

McQuown, N. *Language, culture and education.* Stanford: Stanford University Press, 1982.

Mead, G. *Philosophy of the present.* Chicago: Open Court, 1959 (original, 1934).

Medhurst, K. Basques and Basque nationalism. In C. Williams (ed.), *National separatism.* Cardiff: University of Wales Press, 1982.

Milán, W. Contemporary models of standardized New World Spanish: Origin, development and use. In J. Cobarrubias & J. Fishman (eds), *Progress in language planning.* Berlin: Mouton, 1983.

Mill, J.S. *Considerations on representative government.* London: Dent, 1968 (original, 1861).

Miller, J. The politics of Philippine national language policy. *Language Problems and Language Planning*, 1981, *5*, 137–52.

Mkilifi, M. Triglossia and Swahili–English bilingualism in Tanzania. In J. Fishman (ed.), *Advances in the study of societal multilingualism.* The Hague: Mouton, 1978.

Modiano, N. Bilingual education for children of linguistic minorities. *América Indígena*, 1968, *28*, 405–14.

Moodley, K. Review of *Education and anthropology: Other cultures and the teacher* (F. Musgrove). *Canadian Journal of Education*, 1984, *9*, 347–50.

Moore, D. Multiculturalism: Myth or reality? Paper to the Biennial Conference of the Canadian Ethnic Studies Association, Vancouver, 1979.

Morgan, P. From a death to a view: The hunt for the Welsh past in the romantic period. In E. Hobsbawm & T. Ranger (eds), *The invention of tradition.* Cambridge: Cambridge University Press, 1983.

Morris, C. *Signs, language and behavior.* Englewood Cliffs, New Jersey: Prentice-Hall, 1946.

Morrison, J. & Zabusky, C. *American mosaic.* New York: Meridian, 1980.

Murphy, C. The crisis in Irish. *Irish Times*, 25–8 May 1981.

Murray, K. *Caught in the web of words.* New Haven, Connecticut: Yale University Press, 1977.

Musgrove, F. *Education and anthropology: Other cultures and the teacher.* Chichester: Wiley, 1982.

Nahir, M. The five aspects of language planning: A classification. *Language Problems and Language Planning*, 1977, *1*, 107–23.

Nahir, M. Sociocultural factors in the revival of Hebrew. *Language Problems and Language Planning*, 1983, *7*, 263–84.

Nahir, M. Language planning and language acquisition: The 'great leap' in the Hebrew revival. Paper to the Seventh World Congress of Applied Linguistics, Brussels, 1984.

Nairn, T. *The break-up of Britain: Crisis and neo-nationalism.* London: Verso, 1981.

Ndoma, U. National language policy in education in Zaire. *Language Problems and Language Planning*, 1984, *8*, 172–84.

Neustupný, J. Towards a paradigm for language planning. *Language Planning Newsletter*, 1983, *9(4)*.

Newman, E. *Strictly speaking: Will America be the death of English?* Indianapolis: Bobbs-Merrill, 1974.

Newman, E. *A civil tongue.* Indianapolis: Bobbs-Merrill, 1976.

Nieves-Squires, S. Anthropology. In Center for Applied Linguistics (ed.), *Bilingual education: Current perspectives (Vol. 1).* Arlington, Virginia: CAL, 1977.

Ní Ghallchóir, C. Diglossic bilingualism: Domain usage and its implications for Irish and English in one community. *Northern Ireland Speech and Language Forum*, 1981, *7*, 48–56.

Nokes, D. The man behind the caricature. *Times Higher Education Supplement*, 29 June 1984.

Novak, M. *The rise of the unmeltable ethnics.* New York: Macmillan, 1971.

Novak, M. Pluralism: A humanistic perspective. In S. Thernstrom, A. Orlov & O. Handlin (eds), *Harvard encyclopedia of American ethnic groups.* Cambridge, Massachusetts: Harvard University Press, 1980.

Nurullah, S. & Naik, J. *A history of education in India.* Bombay: Macmillan, 1951.

O'Brien, C. On the rights of minorities. *Commentary*, 1973, *55(6)*, 46–50.

O'Brien, T. Economic support for minority languages. In A. Alcock, B. Taylor & J. Welton (eds), *The future of cultural minorities.* London: Macmillan, 1979.

O'Bryan, K., Reitz, J. & Kuplowska, O. *Non-official languages: A study in Canadian multiculturalism.* Ottawa: Supply & Services Canada, 1976.

Ó Caollaí, M. *Open broadcasting: An alternative.* Dublin: Conradh na Gaeilge, 1976.

Ó Catháin, S. The future of the Irish language. *Studies*, 1973, *62*, 303–22.

Ó Conaire, B. Flann O'Brien, 'An béal bocht' and other Irish matters. *Irish University Review*, 1973, *3*, 121–40.

O'Connell, T. *History of the Irish National Teachers Organization, 1868–1968.* Dublin: INTO, 1968.

Ó Danachair, C. The Gaeltacht. In B. Ó Cuív (ed.), *A view of the Irish language.* Dublin: Government Stationery Office, 1969.

O'Donnell, F. *The ruin of education in Ireland.* London: Nutt, 1903.

O'Faolain, S. Gaelic: The truth. *The Bell*, 1943, *5*, 335–40.

O'Faolain, S. The death of nationalism. *The Bell*, 1951, *17(2)*, 44–53.

Ó Gadhra, N. Broadcasting in Ireland: Problem or opportunity? *Irish Broadcasting Review*, 1978, *1*, 33–4.

Ó Gadhra, N. Language report: Developments in 1980. *Éire–Ireland*, 1981, *16(1)*, 109–18.

O'Hickey, M. *The true national idea*. Dublin: Gaelic League, 1898.

Olson, P. & Burns, G. Politics, class and happenstance: French immersion in a Canadian context. *Interchange*, 1983, *14(1)*, 1–16.

O'Rahilly, T. *Irish dialects past and present*. Dublin: Institute for Advanced Studies, 1972 (original, 1932).

O'Reilly, J. What religion has lost by the decay of the Irish language. *New Ireland Review*, 1898, *8*, 362–74.

Ó Riagáin, P. & Ó Gliasáin, M. *The Irish language in the Republic of Ireland 1983: Preliminary report of a national survey*. Dublin: Linguistics Institute, 1984.

Ornstein, J. Review of *Bilingual schooling in the United States* (T. Andersson & M. Boyer). *Modern Language Journal*, 1979, *63*, 132.

Ornstein-Galicia, J. Review of *Language, culture and education* (N. McQuown). *Journal of Language and Social Psychology*, 1982, *1*, 163–6.

Orridge, A. Varieties of nationalism. In L. Tivey (ed.), *The nation-state: The formation of modern politics*. Oxford: Martin Robertson, 1981.

Orwell, G. *Collected essays*. London: Secker & Warburg, 1961.

Ó Sé, L. The Irish language revival: Achilles heel. *Éire–Ireland*, 1966, *1(1)*, 26–49.

Otheguy, R. & Otto, R. The myth of static maintenance in bilingual education. *Modern Language Journal*, 1980, *64*, 350–6.

Paden, J. Language problems of national integration in Nigeria: The special position of Hausa. In J. Fishman, C. Ferguson & J. Das Gupta (eds), *Language problems of developing nations*. New York: Wiley, 1968.

Palmer, H. (ed.) *Immigration and the rise of multiculturalism*. Toronto: Copp Clark, 1975.

Pandit, P. Perspectives on sociolinguistics in India. In W. McCormack & S. Wurm (eds), *Language and society: Anthropological issues*. The Hague: Mouton, 1979.

Park, R. Social assimilation. In *Encyclopedia of the social sciences*. New York: Macmillan, 1930.

Park, R. & Burgess, E. *Introduction to the science of sociology*. Chicago: University of Chicago Press, 1969 (original, 1921).

Parker, L. & Heath, S. Current perspectives. In Center for Applied Linguistics (ed.), *Bilingual education: Current perspectives (Vol. 5)*. Arlington, Virginia: CAL, 1978.

Parrillo, V. *Strangers to these shores*. Boston: Houghton Mifflin, 1980.

Pascasio, E. (ed.) *The Filipino bilingual: Studies on Philippine bilingualism and bilingual education*. Quezon City: Manila University Press, 1977.

Pascasio, E. & Hidalgo, A. How role-relationships, domains and speech situations affect language use among bilinguals. In W. McCormack & S. Wurm (eds), *Language and society: Anthropological issues*. The Hague: Mouton, 1979.

Pattanayak, D. *Multilingualism and mother-tongue education*. Delhi: Oxford University Press, 1981.

Patterson, O. *Ethnic chauvinism: The reactionary impulse*. New York: Stein & Day, 1977.

Paulston, C. Nationalism, ethnicity and language: A bibliography. *Sociolinguistics Newsletter*, 1984, *14(2)*, 7–9.

Paulston, C. & Paulston, R. Language and ethnic boundaries. *Language Sciences*, 1980, *2*, 69–101.

Pearse, P. *The murder machine and other essays*. Cork: Mercier, 1976 (original, 1912).

Petersen, W. On the subnations of western Europe. In N. Glazer & D. Moynihan (eds), *Ethnicity: Theory and experience*. Cambridge, Massachusetts: Harvard University Press, 1975.

Petyt, K. Romania, a multilingual nation. *International Journal of the Sociology of Language*, 1975, *4*, 75–101.

Petyt, K. *The study of dialect*. London: André Deutsch, 1980.

Pietersen, L. Language ideology, national ideology, bilingualism: The Frisian case. In A. Verdoodt & R. Kjolseth (eds), *Language in sociology*. Louvain: Editions Peeters, 1976.

Pietersen, L. Issues and trends in Frisian bilingualism. In J. Fishman (ed.), *Advances in the study of societal multilingualism*. The Hague: Mouton, 1978.

Pipes, R. Reflections on the nationality problem in the Soviet Union. In N. Glazer & D. Moynihan (eds), *Ethnicity: Theory and experience*. Cambridge, Massachusetts: Harvard University Press, 1975.

Pi-Sunyer, O. Dimensions of Catalan nationalism. In C. Foster (ed.), *Nations without a state: Ethnic minorities in Western Europe*. New York: Praeger, 1980.

Platt, J. The sub-varieties of Singapore English: Their sociolectal and functional status. In W. Crewe (ed.), *The English language in Singapore*. Singapore: Eastern University Press, 1977.

Platt, J. The lingue franche of Singapore: An investigation into strategies of inter-ethnic communication. In H. Giles, P. Robinson & P. Smith (eds), *Language: Social psychological perspectives*. Oxford: Pergamon, 1980.

Platt, J. The Chinese community in Malaysia: Language policies and relationships. In J. Megarry, S. Nisbet & E. Hoyle (eds), *World yearbook of education 1981: Education of minorities*. London: Kogan Page, 1981.

Platt, J. & Lian, H. A case of language indigenisation: Some features of colloquial Singapore English. *Journal of Multilingual and Multicultural Development*, 1982, *3*, 267–76.

Platt, J. & Weber, H. *English in Singapore and Malaysia: Status, features, functions*. Kuala Lumpur: Oxford University Press, 1980.

Podhoretz, N. The idea of a common culture. *Commentary*, 1972, *53(6)*, 4–6.

Polomé, E. The choice of official languages in the Democratic Republic of the Congo. In J. Fishman, C. Ferguson & J. Das Gupta (eds), *Language problems of developing nations*. New York: Wiley, 1968.

Porter, J. Canada: Dilemmas and contradictions of a multi-ethnic society. In J. Goldstein & R. Bievenue (eds), *Ethnicity and ethnic relations in Canada*. Toronto: Butterworth, 1980 (originally published, 1972).

Porter, J. Ethnic pluralism in Canadian perspective. In N. Glazer & D. Moynihan (eds), *Ethnicity: Theory and experience*. Cambridge, Massachusetts: Harvard University Press, 1975.

Postman, N. Bilingualism: A symposium. *The Nation*, 17 March 1979.

Potter, S. *Language in the modern world*. London: André Deutsch, 1975.

Price, G. *The present position of minority languages in Western Europe: A selective bibliography*. Cardiff: University of Wales Press, 1969.

Price, G. The present position and viability of minority languages. In A. Alcock, B. Taylor & J. Welton (eds), *The future of cultural minorities*. London: Macmillan, 1979.

Price, G. *The languages of Britain*. London: Edward Arnold, 1984. (a)

Price, G. Linguistic censuses and minority languages. Paper to the Seventh World Congress of Applied Linguistics, Brussels, 1984. (b)

Quirk, R. *The use of English*. London: Longman, 1962.

Quirk, R. *Style and communication in the English language*. London: Edward Arnold, 1982.

Radovanović, M. Linguistic theory and sociolinguistics in Yugoslavia. *International Journal of the Sociology of Language*, 1983, *44*, 55–69.

226

References

Ravitch, D. On the history of minority group education in the United States. *Teachers College Record*, 1976, *78*, 213–28.

Ravitch, D. Forgetting the questions: The problem of educational reform. *American Scholar*, 1981, *50*, 329–40.

Raybould, W. Welsh as a living language. Paper to the Conference on The Celtic World Today, London, 1984.

Reece, J. Internal colonialism: The case of Brittany. *Ethnic and Racial Studies*, 1979, *2*, 275–92.

Rees, J. Some contemporary problems and sociolinguistic developments affecting the Catalan language. *Polyglot*, 1981, *3(Fiche 1)*.

Reitz, J. Language and ethnic community survival. In J. Goldstein & R. Bienvenue (eds), *Ethnicity and ethnic relations in Canada*. Toronto: Butterworth, 1980.

Renan, E. Qu'est ce qu'une nation? In H. Psichari (ed.), *Oeuvres complètes de Ernest Renan*. Paris: Calmann-Lévy, 1947 (original, 1882).

Reuter, M. The status of Swedish in Finland in theory and practice. In E. Haugen, J. McClure & D. Thomson (eds), *Minority languages today*. Edinburgh: Edinburgh University Press, 1981.

Richardson, M. An evaluation of certain aspects of the academic achievement of elementary pupils in a bilingual program. Unpublished Ed.D. thesis, University of Miami, 1968.

Ridler, N. Language economics: The Canadian experience. Paper to the Seventh World Congress of Applied Linguistics, Brussels, 1984.

Riesman, D. *Individualism reconsidered*. New York: Free Press, 1965.

Riley, G. Language loyalty and ethnocentrism in the Guamanian speech community. *Anthropological Linguistics*, 1975, *17*, 286–92.

Riley, G. Language loyalty and ethnocentrism in the Guamanian speech community: Seven years later. *Anthropological Linguistics*, 1980, *22*, 329–33.

Rist, R. Student social class and teacher expectations: The self-fulfilling prophecy in ghetto education. *Harvard Educational Review*, 1970, *40*, 411–51.

Robinson, I. *The survival of English*. Cambridge: Cambridge University Press, 1973.

Rodriguez, R. Aria: A memoir of a bilingual childhood. *American Scholar*, 1980, *50*, 25–42. (a)

Rodriguez, R. An education in language. In L. Michaels & C. Ricks (eds), *The state of the language*. Berkeley: University of California Press, 1980. (b)

Rodriguez, R. *Hunger of memory*. New York: Bantam, 1983.

Roeming, R. Bilingualism and the national interest. In J. Alatis (ed.), *Georgetown University Round Table on languages and linguistics*. Washington DC: Georgetown University Press, 1970.

Roeming, R. Bilingualism and the national interest. *Modern Language Journal*, 1971, *55*, 73–81.

Rogers, K. Selected recent studies in linguistic nationalism in the Romance languages. *Canadian Review of Studies in Nationalism*, 1981, *8*, 267–83.

Rokkan, S. & Urwin, D. *Economy, territory, identity*. London: Sage, 1983.

Ros i Garcia, M. & Strubell i Trueta, M. (eds) Catalan sociolinguistics. *International Journal of the Sociology of Language*, 1984, *47*.

Royal Institute of International Affairs. *Nationalism*. London: Frank Cass, 1963 (original, 1939).

Royce, A. *Ethnic identity*. Bloomington, Indiana: Indiana University Press, 1982.

Rubin, J. Language education in Paraguay. In J. Fishman, C. Ferguson & J. Das Gupta (eds), *Language problems of developing nations.* New York: Wiley, 1968. (a)

Rubin, J. *National bilingualism in Paraguay.* The Hague: Mouton, 1968. (b)

Rubin, J. Bilingual usage in Paraguay. In J. Fishman (ed.), *Readings in the sociology of language.* The Hague: Mouton, 1968. (c)

Rubin, J. Language problems and educational systems in Indonesia. In B. Sibayan & A. Gonzalez (eds), *Language planning and the building of a national language.* Manila: Linguistic Society of the Philippines, 1977.

Rubin, J. Toward bilingual education for Paraguay. In J. Alatis (ed.), *Georgetown University Round Table on languages and linguistics.* Washington DC: Georgetown University Press, 1978.

Rumilly, R. *Histoire des Franco-Américaines.* Montréal: L'Union Saint-Jean-Baptiste d'Amérique, 1958.

Rundle, S. *Language as a social and political force in Europe.* London: Faber & Faber, 1946.

Rustow, D. Nation. In D. Sills (ed.), *International encyclopedia of the social sciences (Vol. II).* New York: Collier-Macmillan, 1968.

Ryan, A. More country matters. *The Sunday Times,* 4 March 1984.

Ryan, E. Why do low-prestige varieties persist? In H. Giles & R. St. Clair (eds), *Language and social psychology.* Oxford: Basil Blackwell, 1979.

Ryan, E. & Carranza, M. Evaluative reactions of adolescents toward speakers of Standard English and Mexican American accented English. *Journal of Personality and Social Psychology,* 1975, *31,* 855–63.

Ryan, E. & Carranza, M. Ingroup and outgroup reactions to Mexican American language varieties. In H. Giles (ed.), *Language, ethnicity and intergroup relations.* London: Academic Press, 1977.

Ryan, E., Carranza, M. & Moffie, R. Reactions towards varying degrees of accentedness in the speech of Spanish–English bilinguals. *Language and Speech,* 1977, *20,* 267–73.

Ryan, E., Giles, H. & Sebastian, R. An integrative perspective for the study of attitudes toward language variation. In E. Ryan & H. Giles (eds), *Attitudes towards language variation.* London: Edward Arnold, 1982.

Ryan, E., Hewstone, M. & Giles, H. Language and intergroup attitudes. In J. Eiser (ed.), *Attitudinal judgement.* New York: Springer, 1984.

Ryan, F. On language and political ideals. *Dana,* 1905, *1,* 273–89.

Saifullah Khan, V. The 'mother-tongue' of linguistic minorities in multicultural England. *Journal of Multilingual and Multicultural Development,* 1980, *1,* 71–88.

Sala, R. Language, culture and national identity: Some reflections on Catalan *normalització. Polyglot,* 1981, *3(Fiche 1).*

Samarin, W. Lingua francas of the world. In J. Fishman (ed.), *Readings in the sociology of language.* The Hague, Mouton, 1968.

Samuda, R., Berry, J. & Laferrière, M. (eds) *Multiculturalism in Canada: Social and educational perspectives.* Toronto: Allyn & Bacon, 1984.

Sapir, E. *Language: An introduction to the study of speech.* New York: Harcourt Brace, 1921.

Sarnoff, I. Social attitudes and the resolution of motivational conflict. In M. Jahoda & N. Warren (eds), *Attitudes.* Harmondsworth, Middlesex: Penguin, 1970.

Saulson, S. *Institutionalized language planning: Documents and analysis of the revival of Hebrew.* The Hague: Mouton, 1979.

Saville-Troike, M. *The ethnography of communication.* Oxford: Basil Blackwell, 1982.

Schermerhorn, R. *Comparative ethnic relations.* New York: Random House, 1970.

Schermerhorn, R. *Ethnic plurality in India.* Tucson: University of Arizona Press, 1978.

Schiller, H. *New modes of cultural domination.* Dublin: Conradh na Gaeilge, 1978.

Schlieben-Lange, B. The language situation in southern France. *International Journal of the Sociology of Language,* 1977, *12,* 101–8.

Schlossman, S. Is there an American tradition of bilingual education? German in the public elementary schools, 1840–1919. *American Journal of Education,* 1983, *91,* 139–86. (a)

Schlossman, S. Self-evident remedy? George I. Sanchez, segregation, and enduring dilemmas in bilingual education. *Teachers College Record,* 1983, *84,* 871–907. (b)

Schrag, P. *The decline of the WASP.* New York: Simon & Schuster, 1971.

Schuring, G. *A multilingual society: English and Afrikaans amongst Blacks in the RSA.* Pretoria: South African Human Sciences Research Council, 1979.

Scotton, C. Language in East Africa: Linguistic patterns and political ideologies. In J. Fishman (ed.), *Advances in the study of societal multilingualism.* The Hague: Mouton, 1978.

Scotton, C. The linguistic situation and language policy in eastern Africa. In R. Kaplan, A. d'Anglejan, J. Cowan, B. Kachru & G. Tucker (eds), *Annual review of applied linguistics 1981.* Rowley, Massachusetts: Newbury House, 1982.

Secord, P. & Backman, C. *Social psychology.* New York: McGraw-Hill, 1964.

Seelye, H. Sociology and education. In Center for Applied Linguistics (ed.), *Bilingual education: Current perspectives (Vol. 1).* Arlington, Virginia: CAL, 1977.

Seton-Watson, H. *Nations and states.* London: Methuen, 1977.

Seton-Watson, H. *Language and national consciousness.* London: British Academy, 1981.

Seton-Watson, H. The history of nations. *Times Higher Education Supplement,* 27 August 1982.

Shafer, B. *Nationalism: Myth and reality.* New York: Harcourt Brace, 1955.

Shafer, S. Australian approaches to multicultural education. *Journal of Multilingual and Multicultural Development,* 1983, *4,* 415–35.

Sharp, H. *Selections from educational records, Part 1: 1781–1839.* Calcutta: Superintendent, Government Printing, 1920.

Shibutani, T. & Kwan, K. *Ethnic stratification.* New York: Macmillan, 1965.

Shorish, M. Planning by decree: The Soviet language policy in central Asia. *Language Problems and Language Planning,* 1984, *8,* 35–49.

Shuy, R. Bilingualism and language variety. In J. Alatis (ed.), *Georgetown University Round Table on languages and linguistics.* Washington DC: Georgetown University Press, 1978. (a).

Shuy, R. Toward a cross-disciplinary view. In Center for Applied Linguistics (ed.), *Bilingual education: Current perspectives (Vol. 5).* Arlington, Virginia: CAL, 1978. (b)

Sibayan, B. Some Philippine sociolinguistic concerns: 1967–92. *International Journal of the Sociology of Language,* 1984, *45,* 127–37. (a)

Sibayan, B. Survey of language use and attitudes towards language in the Philippines. In C. Kennedy (ed.), *Language planning and language education.* London: Allen & Unwin, 1984. (b)

Sidel, R. Review of *Education and anthropology: Other cultures and the teacher* (F. Musgrove). *Contemporary Sociology,* 1983, *12,* 676–7.

Siguan, M. Education and bilingualism in Catalonia. *Journal of Multilingual and Multicultural Development,* 1980, *1,* 231–42.

Skutnabb-Kangas, T. Children of guest workers and immigrants: Linguistic and

References 229

educational issues. In J. Edwards (ed.), *Linguistic minorities, policies and pluralism.* London: Academic Press, 1984.

Smith, A. Theories of nationalism. London: Duckworth, 1971.

Smith, A. Towards a theory of ethnic separatism. *Ethnic and Racial Studies,* 1979, 2, 21–37. (a)

Smith, A. *Nationalism in the twentieth century.* Oxford: Martin Robertson, 1979. (b)

Smith, A. *The ethnic revival.* Cambridge: Cambridge University Press, 1981.

Smith, A. Nationalism, ethnic separatism and the intelligentsia. In C. Williams (ed.), *National separatism.* Cardiff: University of Wales Press, 1982.

Smolicz, J. Personal cultural systems in a plural society. *Media Asia,* 1979, 6(1), 43–52. (a)

Smolicz, J. *Culture and education in a plural society.* Canberra: Curriculum Development Centre, 1979. (b)

Smolicz, J. Multiculturalism – Yes. *Education News,* 1980, 17, 12–16.

Smolicz, J. Cultural pluralism and educational policy: In search of stable multiculturalism. *Australian Journal of Education,* 1981, 25, 121–45. (a)

Smolicz, J. Core values and cultural identity. *Ethnic and Racial Studies,* 1981, 4, 75–90. (b)

Smolicz, J. Modification and maintenance: Language among school-children of Italian background in South Australia. *Journal of Multilingual and Multicultural Development,* 1983, 4, 313–37.

Smolicz, J. & Harris, R. Ethnic languages in Australia. *International Journal of the Sociology of Language,* 1977, 14, 89–108.

Smolicz, J. & Lean, R. Parental attitudes to cultural and linguistic pluralism in Australia: a humanistic sociological approach. *Australian Journal of Education,* 1979, 23, 227–49.

Smolicz, J. & Lean, R. Parental and student attitudes to the teaching of ethnic languages in Australia. *ITL: Review of Applied Linguistics,* 1980, 49/50, 91–116.

Snyder, L. (ed.) *The dynamics of nationalism.* Princeton, New Jersey: Van Nostrand, 1964.

Solomonick, A. The concept of 'people's language'. Paper to the Seventh World Congress of Applied Linguistics, Brussels, 1984.

Sonntag, S. Language planning and policy in Nepal. *ITL: Review of Applied Linguistics,* 1980, 48, 71–92.

Southall, J. *Wales and her language.* Newport: Southall, 1892.

Southall, J. *The Welsh language census of 1891.* Newport: Southall, 1895.

Southall, J. *The Welsh language census of 1901.* Newport: Southall, 1904.

Sowell, T. Ethnicity in a changing America. *Daedalus,* 1978. 107(1), 213–37.

Spolsky, B. Bilingual education in the United States. In J. Alatis (ed.), *Georgetown University Round Table on languages and linguistics.* Washington DC: Georgetown University Press, 1978.

Stein, H. & Hill, R. *The ethnic imperative.* University Park, Pennsylvania: Pennsylvania State University Press, 1977.

Steinberg, S. *The ethnic myth.* New York: Atheneum, 1981.

Steiner, G. *Language and silence.* London: Faber, 1967.

Steiner, G. *Extraterritorial.* London: Faber, 1972.

Steiner, G. *After Babel: Aspects of language and translation.* London: Oxford University Press, 1975.

Steiner, G. *On difficulty.* Oxford: Oxford University Press, 1978.

Stephens, J. The Breton language in the past fifteen years. Paper to the Conference on The Celtic World Today, London, 1984.

Stephens, M. (ed.) *The Welsh language today.* Llandysul: Gomer, 1973.

Stephens, M. *Linguistic minorities in Western Europe.* Llandysul: Gomer, 1976.

Stern, H. Immersion schools and language learning. *Language and Society,* 1981, *5,* 3–6.

Stevens, P. Ambivalence, modernisation and language attitudes: French and Arabic in Tunisia. *Journal of Multilingual and Multicultural Development,* 1983, *4,* 101–14.

Stone, M. *The education of the Black child in Britain: The myth of multiracial education.* London: Fontana, 1981.

Straka, M. (ed.) *Handbuch der Europäischer Volksgruppen.* Stuttgart: Braumüller, 1970.

Street, R. & Giles, H. Speech accommodation theory: A social cognitive approach to language and speech behavior. In M. Roloff & C. Berger (eds), *Social cognition and communication.* Beverly Hills: Sage, 1982.

Streib, C. The restoration of the Irish language: Behavioral and symbolic aspects. *Ethnicity,* 1974, *1,* 73–89.

Strubell i Trueta, M. Catalan sociolinguistics: A brief review of research. *International Journal of the Sociology of Language,* 1982, *38,* 70–84.

Štrukelj, I. The dynamics of societal bilingualism: Bilingual education in Slovenia. *Compare,* 1978, *8,* 93–100.

Stuewe, P. The mark of the exile. *Books in Canada,* 1981, *10(8),* 4–5.

Suresh, J. Minority languages and mother-tongue education in India: Problems and solutions. Paper to the Seventh World Congress of Applied Linguistics, Brussels, 1984.

Suseendirarajah, S. Religion and language in Jaffna society. *Anthropological Linguistics,* 1980, *22,* 345–62.

Swanson, M. Bilingual education as a profession. In J. Alatis (ed.), *Georgetown University Round Table on languages and linguistics.* Washington DC: Georgetown University Press, 1978.

Swing, E. Education for separatism: The Belgian experience. In B. Hartford, A. Valdman & C. Foster (eds), *Issues in international bilingual education.* New York: Plenum, 1982.

Swing, E. Flemings and Puerto Ricans: Two applications of a conflict paradigm in bilingual education. *International Journal of the Sociology of Language,* 1983, *44,* 27–42.

Tabouret-Keller, A. Introduction: Regional languages in France. *International Journal of the Sociology of Language,* 1981, *29,* 5–14.

Tajfel, H. Social identity and intergroup behaviour. *Social Science Information,* 1974, *13,* 65–93.

Tajfel, H. (ed.) *Differentiation between social groups: Studies in the social psychology of intergroup behaviour.* London: Academic Press, 1978.

Tajfel, H. *Human groups and social categories.* Cambridge: Cambridge University Press, 1981.

Taylor, A. Language policy in Papua New Guinea. *Linguistic Reporter,* 1981, *24(1).*

Teitelbaum, H. & Hiller, R. The legal perspective. In Center for Applied Linguistics (ed.), *Bilingual education: Current perspectives (Vol. 3).* Arlington, Virginia: CAL, 1977.

Thakerar, J., Giles, H. & Cheshire, J. Psychological and linguistic parameters of speech accommodation theory. In C. Fraser & K. Scherer (eds), *Advances in the social psychology of language.* Cambridge: Cambridge University Press, 1982.

Theodorson, G. & Theodorson, A. *A modern dictionary of sociology.* New York: Crowell, 1969.

Thernstrom, A. Language: Issues and legislation. In S. Thernstrom, A. Orlov &

O. Handlin (eds), *Harvard encyclopedia of American ethnic groups.* Cambridge, Massachusetts: Harvard University Press, 1980.

Thomas, A. Change and decay in language. In D. Crystal (ed.), *Linguistic controversies.* London: Edward Arnold, 1982.

Thomas, B. (ed.) *The Welsh economy: Studies in expansion.* Cardiff: University of Wales Press, 1962.

Tierney, M. The revival of the Irish language. *Studies,* 1927, *16,* 1–10.

Timm, L. Modernization and language shift: The case of Brittany. *Anthropological Linguistics,* 1973, *15,* 281–98.

Timm, L. Bilingualism, diglossia and language shift in Brittany. *International Journal of the Sociology of Language,* 1980, *25,* 29–41.

Timm, L. Language treatment in Brittany. *Language Planning Newsletter,* 1982, *8(3).*

Tivey, L. (ed.) *The nation-state: The formation of modern politics.* Oxford: Martin Robertson, 1981.

Todd, L. Language options for education in a multilingual society: Cameroon. In C. Kennedy (ed.), *Language planning and language education.* London: Allen & Unwin, 1984.

Tollefson, J. The language planning process and language rights in Yugoslavia. *Language Problems and Language Planning,* 1980, *4,* 141–56.

Tollefson, J. *The language situation and language policy in Slovenia.* Washington DC: University Press of America, 1981. (a)

Tollefson, J. Centralized and decentralized language planning. *Language Problems and Language Planning,* 1981, *5,* 175–88. (b)

Tomlinson, S. Home, school and community. In M. Craft (ed.), *Education and cultural pluralism.* London: Falmer, 1984.

Tonkin, H. *Esperanto and international language problems: A research bibliography.* Washington DC: Esperantic Studies Foundation, 1977.

Topping, D. Language planning issues in Vanuatu. *Language Planning Newsletter,* 1982, *8(2).*

Toynbee, A. *A study of history.* London: Oxford University Press, 1956 (two-volume abridgement by D. Somervell).

Treffgarne, C. Language policies in west and east Africa. In J. Megarry, S. Nisbet & E. Hoyle (eds), *World yearbook of education 1981: Education of minorities.* London: Kogan Page, 1981.

Troike, R. & Pérez, E. At the crossroads. In Center for Applied Linguistics (ed.), *Bilingual education: Current perspectives (Vol. 5).* Arlington, Virginia: CAL, 1978.

Trudgill, P. *Sociolinguistics.* Harmondsworth, Middlesex: Penguin, 1974. (a)

Trudgill, P. *The social differentiation of English in Norwich.* London: Cambridge University Press, 1974. (b)

Trudgill, P. *Accent, dialect and the school.* London: Edward Arnold, 1975. (a)

Trudgill, P. Sex, covert prestige and linguistic change in the urban British English of Norwich. In B. Thorne & N. Henley (eds), *Language and sex.* Rowley, Massachusetts: Newbury House, 1975. (b)

Trudgill, P. *On dialect.* Oxford: Basil Blackwell, 1983.

Tse, J. Language policy in the Republic of China. In R. Kaplan, A. d'Anglejan, J. Cowan, B. Kachru & G. Tucker (eds), *Annual review of applied linguistics 1981.* Rowley, Massachusetts: Newbury House, 1982.

Tsow, M. Ethnic minority community languages: A statement. *Journal of Multilingual and Multicultural Development,* 1983, *4,* 361–84.

Tucker, G. & Crandall, J. Language policy and the delivery of social services in the United States. Paper to the Seventh World Congress of Applied Linguistics, Brussels, 1984.

Tucker, G. & Lambert, W. White and Negro listeners' reactions to various American-English dialects. *Social Forces*, 1969, *47*, 463–8.

Tudjman, F. *Nationalism in contemporary Europe*. Boulder, Colorado: East European Monographs, 1981.

UNESCO. *The use of vernacular languages in education*. Paris: UNESCO, 1953.

United States Commission on Civil Rights. *A better chance to learn: Bilingual-bicultural education*. Washington DC: United States Government Printing Office, 1975.

Ussher, A. *The face and mind of Ireland*. London: Gollancz, 1949.

Valdman, A. Language standardization in a diglossia situation: Haiti. In J. Fishman, C. Ferguson & J. Das Gupta (eds), *Language problems of developing nations*. New York: Wiley, 1968.

Vallee, F. The sociology of John Porter: Ethnicity as anachronism. *Canadian Review of Sociology and Anthropology*, 1981, *18*, 639–50.

Vallins, G. *Spelling*. London: André Deutsch, 1954.

Van den Berghe, P. *Race and racism*. New York: Wiley, 1967.

Van den Berghe, P. Language and 'nationalism' in South Africa. In J. Fishman, C. Ferguson & J. Das Gupta (eds), *Language problems of developing nations*. New York: Wiley, 1968.

Van der Plank, P. The assimilation and non-assimilation of European linguistic minorities. In J. Fishman (ed.), *Advances in the study of societal multilingualism*. The Hague: Mouton, 1978.

Van Eerde, J. Facets of the Breton problem. *Language Problems and Language Planning*, 1979, *3*, 1–8.

Van Wyk, E. Language contact and bilingualism. In L. Lanham & K. Prinsloo (eds), *Language and communication studies in South Africa*. Cape Town: Oxford University Press, 1978.

Vázquez, J. Federal, state and local policies as they affect programmatic activities: A closer look at comprehensive planning. In J. Alatis (ed.), *Georgetown University Round Table on languages and linguistics*. Washington DC: Georgetown University Press, 1978.

Venezky, R. Non-standard language and reading: Ten years later. In J. Edwards (ed.), *The social psychology of reading*. Silver Spring, Maryland: Institute of Modern Languages, 1981.

Verdoodt, A. Social and linguistic structures of Burundi, a typical 'unimodal' country. In W. McCormack & S. Wurm (eds), *Language and society: Anthropological isues*. The Hague: Mouton, 1979.

Verstegan, R. *A restitution of decayed intelligence*. Antwerp: Burney, 1605.

von Humboldt, W. *Linguistic variability and intellectual development*. Coral Gables: University of Miami Press, 1971.

Vossler, K. *The spirit of language in civilization*. London: Routledge, 1932.

Walker, A. Some factors concerning the decline of the North Frisian tongue. In P. Nelde (ed.), *Languages in contact and conflict*. Wiesbaden: Franz Steiner, 1980. (a)

Walker, A. North Frisia and linguistics. *Nottingham Linguistic Circular*, 1980, *9(1)*, 18–42. (b)

Walker, A. Applied sociology of language: Vernacular languages and education. In P. Trudgill (ed.), *Applied sociolinguistics*. London: Academic Press, 1984.

Wall, M. The decline of the Irish language. In B. Ó Cuív (ed.), *A view of the Irish language*. Dublin: Government Stationery Office, 1969.

Walzer, M. Pluralism: A political perspective. In S. Thernstrom, A. Orlov & O. Handlin (eds), *Harvard encyclopedia of American ethnic groups*. Cambridge, Massachusetts: Harvard University Press, 1980.

Waterman, J. *A history of the German language*. Seattle: University of Washington Press, 1966.

Watson, J. Education and pluralism in South-East Asia, with special reference to peninsular Malaysia. *Comparative Education*, 1980, *16*, 139–58. (a)

Watson, J. Cultural pluralism, nation-building and educational policies in peninsular Malaysia. *Journal of Multilingual and Multicultural Development*, 1980, *1*, 155–74. (b)

Weber, M. *Economy and society*. New York: Bedminster, 1968.

Webster, N. *Grammatical institutes, Part 1*. Hartford: Hudson & Goodwin, 1783.

Webster, N. *Dissertations on the English language*. Boston: Thomas, 1789.

Weichselbaum, P. National integration and bilingual education policy in Peru. Paper to the North-eastern Anthropological Association, Quebec, 1978.

Weinfeld, M. Myth and reality in the Canadian mosaic: Ethnic identification in Toronto. *Working Papers in Migration and Ethnicity (McGill University)*, 1978, *3*.

Weinreich, U. *Languages in contact*. The Hague: Mouton, 1974.

Weinstein, B. Francophonie: A language-based movement in world politics. *International Organization*, 1976, *30*, 485–506.

Weinstein, B. *The civic tongue*. New York: Longman, 1983.

Whiteley, W. Ideal and reality in national language policy: A case study from Tanzania. In J. Fishman, C. Ferguson & J. Das Gupta (eds), *Language problems of developing nations*. New York: Wiley, 1968.

Wilby, P. The classroom melting pot. *Sunday Times*, 17 June 1984.

Wilkinson, A. Spoken English. *Educational Review*, 1965, *17(supplement)*.

Willemyns, R. The treaty of linguistic union in the Dutch language area. *Language Planning Newsletter*, 1984, *10(3)*.

Williams, C. Cultural nationalism in Wales. *Canadian Review of Studies in Nationalism*, 1976, *4*, 15–37.

Williams, C. Ethnic separatism in western Europe. *Tijdschrift voor Economic en Sociale Geografie*, 1980, *71*, 142–58.

Williams, C. (ed) *National separatism*. Cardiff: University of Wales Press, 1982.

Williams, C. More than tongue can tell: Linguistic factors in ethnic separatism. In J. Edwards (ed.), *Linguistic minorities, policies and pluralism*. London: Academic Press, 1984.

Williams, G(lanmor). *Religion, language and nationality in Wales*. Cardiff: University of Wales Press, 1979.

Williams, G. Language group allegiance and ethnic interaction. In H. Giles & B. Saint-Jacques (eds), *Language and ethnic relations*. New York: Pergamon, 1979.

Williams, G. Review of *Implications of the ethnic revival in modern, industralized society* (E. Allardt). *Journal of Multilingual and Multicultural Development*, 1980, *1*, 363–70.

Williams, G. Review of *Variance and invariance in language form and context* (J. Fishman). *Journal of Multilingual and Multicultural Development*, 1981, *2*, 219–25.

Williams, J. *Bilingualism: A bibliography of 1,000 references with special reference to Wales*. Cardiff: University of Wales Press, 1971.

Williamson, R. & Van Eerde, J. 'Subcultural' factors in the survival of secondary languages: A cross-national sample. *International Journal of the Sociology of Language,* 1980, *25,* 59–83.

Williamson, S. Bibliography: Language skills attrition project/Summary chart of findings from previous research on language loss. In R. Lambert & B. Freed (eds), *The loss of language skills.* Rowley, Massachusetts: Newbury House, 1982.

Wilson, W. *The declining significance of race.* Chicago: University of Chicago Press, 1978.

Withers, C. A case study in historical geolinguistics: The decline of Gaelic in northern Scotland, 1698–1901. *Discussion Papers in Geolinguistics,* 1982, *7.*

Wixman, R. *The peoples of Russia and the USSR.* London: Macmillan, 1984.

Wolff, H. Intelligibility and inter-ethnic attitudes. *Anthropological Linguistics,* 1959, *1,* 34–41.

Wood, R. A review essay on 21 Scandinavian language books. *Language Problems and Language Planning,* 1978, *2,* 35–50.

Wood, R. Scotland: The unfinished quest for linguistic identity. *Word,* 1979, *30,* 186–202.

Wood, R. Selected recent studies in linguistic nationalism in the Germanic languages. *Canadian Review of Studies in Nationalism,* 1981, *8,* 55–84.

Wurm, S. Papua New Guinea nationhood: The problem of a national language. In J. Fishman, C. Ferguson & J. Das Gupta (eds), *Language problems of developing nations.* New York: Wiley, 1968.

Wurm, S. New Guinea Pidgin: Today and tomorrow. In B. Sibayan & A. Gonzalez (eds), *Language planning and the building of a national language.* Manila: Linguistic Society of the Philippines, 1977.

Wurm, S. Towards language planning in Papua New Guinea. *Language Planning Newsletter,* 1978, *4(3).*

Wurm, S. *New Guinea and neighboring areas: A sociolinguistic laboratory.* The Hague: Mouton, 1979.

Wyld, H. *The best English.* Oxford: Clarendon, 1934.

Yabes, L. History of Pilipino as the common national language. In B. Sibayan & A. Gonzalez (eds), *Language planning and the building of a national language.* Manila: Linguistic Society of the Philippines, 1977.

Yancey, W., Ericksen, E. & Juliani, R. Emergent ethnicity: A review and reformulation. *American Sociological Review,* 1976, *41,* 391–403.

Young, J. Education in a multicultural society: What sort of education? What sort of society? *Canadian Journal of Education,* 1979, *4(3),* 5–20.

Zima, P. Hausa in West Africa: Remarks on contemporary role and function. In J. Fishman, C. Ferguson & J. Das Gupta (eds), *Language problems of developing nations.* New York: Wiley, 1968.

Zolberg, A. Splitting the difference: Federalization without federalism in Belgium. In M. Esman (ed.), *Ethnic conflict in the Western world.* Ithaca, New York: Cornell University Press, 1977.

Zolf, L. Mulling over multiculturalism. *Macleans's,* 1980, *93(15),* 6.

Index of Languages

Index of Names

Abramson, H., 195
Acton, J., 14, 37–9, 193
Adams, G., 53
Adams, J., 32
Adler, M., 76
Agheyisi, R., 146
Agnew, J., 69, 74
Aitchison, J., 49, 52
Akenson, D., 55, 57
Akere, F., 172
Alatis, J., 127, 196
Alba, R., 107
Albó, X., 176
Alcock, A., 76
Alisjahbana, S., 177
Allardt, E., 76, 77, 99
Allworth, E., 180
Altehenger-Smith, S., 179
Alter, R., 106, 195
Altoma, S., 29
Amayo, A., 172
Andersen, R., 194
Anderson, A., 77
Anderson, B., 13, 15, 29, 31, 40, 193
Anderson, C., 96
Andersson, T., 120, 122
Andreski, S., 191
Andrews, L., 193
Andrzejewski, B., 173
Appel, R., 188
Apte, M., 177
Argente, J., 189
Arndt, E., 192
Arthur, B., 148
Asuncion-Lande, N., 183
Azurmendi, M., 188

Backman, C., 139
Bacon, F., 35

Baetens Beardsmore, H., 184
Baldauf, R., 183
Barker, E., 5, 13
Barnard, F., 23, 24
Barnes, D., 176
Baron, S., 5, 15, 191
Barth, F., 7, 73, 97
Beckett, J., 54
Beebe, L., 154
Bell, A., 34
Bell, C., 113
Bell, R., 91
Bell, W., 78
Benn, S., 37
Bentahila, A., 90, 172
Bentinck, W., 31
Benton, R., 181, 183
Ben-Yehuda, E., 87, 88
Bergin, O., 58
Berlin, I., 24
Berry, J., 105, 143, 195
Bethell, T., 124
Betts, C., 50, 66
Bhatia, T., 177
Bickerton, D., 182
Bickley, V., 135
Billigmeier, R., 189
Binchy, D., 51, 54
Birch, A., 69, 73, 74, 101, 195
Blanco, G., 123, 124, 127
Blount, C. (Lord Mountjoy), 54
Bodmer, F., 35
Boelens, K., 186, 188
Bolinger, D., 34
Bolton, K., 176
Bopp, F., 48, 49
Bourhis, R., 27, 77, 153, 154, 157, 184, 196, 198

Bowen, J., 192
Boyer, M., 120, 122
Brann, C., 172
Brass, P., 177, 191
Breatnach, D., 194
Breatnach, R., 63
Brennan, E., 149
Brennan, J., 149
Brennan, M., 61, 62
Brennan, P., 182
Breton, R., 8, 77, 119
Bright, W., 4
Brooks, S., 51
Brown, S., 62
Brown, T., 2, 41, 58
Bullivant, B., 78, 109, 116, 119, 130, 136, 195, 197, 198
Burgess, E., 104
Burnet, J., 108, 109
Burns, D., 176
Burns, G., 197
Byrne, D., 151
Byrne, E., 58
Byrne, J., 153, 154, 198

Cahill, E., 53, 62
Cardenas, J., 126
Carpenter, S., 172
Carranza, M., 77, 148, 149, 198
Carroll, J., 146
Cashel, A., 62
Castonguay, C., 196
Chadwick, N., 67
Chamlin, M., 107
Charles V (French king), 192
Charles V (German king), 192
Charpentier, J., 184

Index of Names

Index of Subjects

Académie Française, 27, 28, 32
academies (general), 23, 27–30, 32, 162, 192
accommodation: group, 105 *et passim*;
  linguistic, 151, 152
amalgamation, 104, 106
anglo-conformity, 103, 104
'artificial' languages, *see* constructed
  languages
assimilation, 103–10, 165 *et passim*
'associated' language, 111
attitudes, 139–50, 167
attractiveness (personality dimension),
  148–50
Australia, 32, 136
autonomism, 105

Belgium, 84, 184
bilingual education, 2, 111, 120–8, 135–8,
  166, 196–8; maintenance/transition,
  126–8, 137, 138
bilingualism, 69, 71, 72, 79, 80, 83, 84, 96,
  108, 109, 150, 196, 197 *et passim*
Bolivia, 80
Bord na Gaeilge, 59
Brittany, 67, 68
broadcasting, 33, 34, 60, 70–2, 194
Burundi, 78, 181

Cameroon, 79, 171
Canada, 15, 42, 43, 67, 68, 108–10, 136,
  143, 195–7
Canadian Consultative Council on
  Multiculturalism, 108
Catalonia, 84, 94, 188, 189
Celtic-Cornish Society, 66
cercles celtiques, 67, 68
Cheshaght Ghailckagh, *see* Gaelic League,
  Manx
China, 20, 81, 176

Comhairle na Gaeilge, 58
Committee on Irish Language Attitudes
  Research, 60–3, 142, 143, 194
competence (personality dimension), 148–50
Conradh na Gaeilge, *see* Gaelic League, Irish
constructed languages, 35–7, 193
convergence (linguistic), 152
Cornwall, 66, 67, 78, 86, 87
covert prestige, 149
Cowethas Kelto-Kernuak, *see* Celtic-Cornish
  Society
creole, 35
cultural pluralism, *see* pluralism
Cymdeithas yr Iaith Gymraeg, *see* Welsh
  Language Society

Denmark, 13
dialect, 19–22; mutual intelligibility, 18, 20,
  21; nonstandard/standard, 21, 22, 132–5
dictionaries, 28–31, 33, 162, 192, 193
diffusion (development model), 73, 74
divergence (linguistic), 152

Ecuador, 29, 80
economics, 91–6, 163, 164, 170, 194
education, 31, 54–7, 60–3, 118–38, 166
England, 13, 30–4, 136, 141, 147–9
Ethiopia, 29, 171, 172
ethnic: boundaries, 7–10, 15, 77, 97, 161,
  169; conflict (theory), 104, 105; persistence, 100, 101, 164, 165 *et passim*;
  revival, 41, 99–117 *et passim*; separatism,
  105, 106, 110
Ethnic Heritage Studies Act (USA), 145
ethnicity, 1, 2, 5, 10–14 *et passim*;
  anachronistic/regressive, 106, 116;
  symbolic, 9, 10, 110–13
ethnolinguistic vitality, 150, 153–8, 167, 168

relativism: cultural, 43–6, 113–17, 120, 165;
    linguistic, 25, 114, 115, 192
religion, 6, 54, 56, 62, 66, 70, 74, 75, 81,
    82, 87, 93, 194
Romania, 84, 188
Romans, 35
romanticism, 12–14, 24–6, 39 *et passim*
Royal Institute of International Affairs
    (GB), 92, 93
Royal Society, 30

Samoa, 82, 183
Scotland, 68, 69
Scottish National Party, 69, 110
segregation, 105, 106
Senegal, 173
separatism, *see* ethnic separatism
Sianel Pedwar Cymru, 70
Singapore, 81, 178, 179
sociolinguistics, 3–5
sociology of language, 4, 5
solidarity, 148–50
Somalia, 78, 79, 173
Sons of Cornwall, 66
South Africa, 32, 79, 80, 173
Spain, 29, 50, 67, 84, 94, 188
Sri Lanka, 82, 179

Suriname, 80, 176
Sweden, 29, 83, 189
Switzerland, 84, 189
symbolic ethnicity, *see* ethnicity, symbolic

Taiwan, 81, 179, 180
Tanzania, 30, 79, 173, 174
television, *see* broadcasting
three-language formula (India), 177
transition, *see* bilingual education
Tunisia, 78, 174

Údarás na Gaeltachta, 58
United States, 9, 15, 30–3, 41, 42, 51, 68,
    99, 104, 105, 111, 120–8, 135–8, 140–5
USSR, 29, 82, 83, 180

Vanatu, 82, 183, 184
vitality, *see* ethnolinguistic vitality

Wales, 68–71, 194
Welsh Language Society, 70
Whorfianism, *see* relativism

Yugoslavia, 84, 190

Zaire, 79, 174